POSITIVE PSYCHOLOGY IN SPORT AND PHYSICAL ACTIVITY

Positive psychology (PP) is a fast-developing area of research that emphasizes personal growth and the positive qualities of life. This is the first book to apply the principles and practice of PP to sport and physical activity.

In attempting to help people enjoy sport, sport psychology has paradoxically often focused on topics such as anxiety, stress and burnout. By contrast, this reader-friendly introduction to PP shows how it can improve sporting performance while also enhancing physical and mental well-being. Demonstrating the practical relevance of PP for all those who participate in sport and physical activity at any level, it covers a variety of topics, including:

- passion, enjoyment and flow
- positive pedagogy and appreciative inquiry for sports leaders, coaches and teachers
- gratitude, mindfulness, optimism and hope
- positive psychology coaching for sports leaders and practitioners
- character strengths, growth mindset and resilience.

With expert contributors from around the globe, real-life case studies, practical strategies and suggestions for future research in every chapter, this book is inspirational reading for all students, coaches, researchers and practitioners with an interest in sport and exercise psychology, mental health and well-being.

Abbe Brady is Programme Director for Sports Coaching at St Mary's University, London, UK. Through her applied work as a registered Sport and Exercise Psychologist as well as her research, Abbe has developed an interest in well-being and positive psychology applications within sport and business. She has led symposia and workshops introducing positive psychology to students and practitioners in sport, and she presents on a range of PP-related themes at national and international conferences.

Bridget Grenville-Cleave is a lecturer in Applied Positive Psychology at Anglia Ruskin University, Cambridge, UK. She runs well-being, resilience and engagement training programmes in business, health and education sectors and is passionate about community development using applied positive psychology. Bridget has written five psychology books, including *Positive Psychology: A Toolkit for Happiness, Purpose and Well-being* (2012). She is also an international speaker on positive psychology and a founding member of the International Positive Psychology Association.

POSITIVE PSYCHOLOGY IN SPORT AND PHYSICAL ACTIVITY

An Introduction

Edited by
Abbe Brady and
Bridget Grenville-Cleave

Routledge
Taylor & Francis Group

LONDON AND NEW YORK

First published 2018
by Routledge
2 Park Square, Milton Park, Abingdon, Oxon OX14 4RN

and by Routledge
711 Third Avenue, New York, NY 10017

Routledge is an imprint of the Taylor & Francis Group, an informa business

British Library Cataloguing-in-Publication Data
A catalogue record for this book is available from the British Library

Library of Congress Cataloging-in-Publication Data
A catalog record for this book has been requested

ISBN: 978-1-138-23559-5 (hbk)
ISBN: 978-1-138-23560-1 (pbk)
ISBN: 978-1-315-30439-7 (ebk)

Typeset in Bembo
by Apex CoVantage, LLC

To my mum Gloria – always with me; Helen for being there – and for Dad, Catherine, Mark, Christopher and Hannah with love [Abbe]
To Neil and Hugo, a constant source of positive emotion, insight and inspiration [Bridget]

CONTENTS

FIGURES

TABLES

CONTRIBUTORS

Rudy Alleyne, University of the West Indies, Barbados

Arabella Ashfield, British Cycling, UK

Scott Bradley, University of Northampton, UK

Kathryn H. Britton, Theano Coaching LLC and Silicon Valley Change Executive Coaching, USA

Lung Hung Chen, National Taiwan Sport University, Taiwan

Tanya Chichekian, Université du Québec à Montréal, Canada

Samuel Giles, Loughborough University and The English Institute of Sport, UK

Henrik Gustafsson, Karlstads University, Sweden

Stephanie J. Hanrahan, University of Queensland, Australia

Joanna Harrison, The English Institute of Sport, UK

Dan Jolley, League Football Education (LFE), UK

Hanna Kampman, University of East London, UK

Emma Kavanagh, Bournemouth University, UK

Jay Kimiecik, Miami University, USA

Richard L. Light, University of Canterbury, New Zealand

Tim Lomas, University of East London, UK

Carolina Lundqvist, Linköping University, Sweden

Graham Mallen, Manor School Sports College, UK

Liam McCarthy, St Mary's University, UK

Paul McCarthy, Glasgow Caledonian University, UK

Chris McCready, Manchester United Football Club and Liverpool John Moore's University, UK

Deanna Morrison, Miami University, USA

Robert J. Vallerand, Université du Québec à Montréal, Canada and Australian Catholic University

Robin S. Vealey, Miami University, USA

Piers Worth, Buckinghamshire New University, UK

Emily Wright, Miami University, USA

John M. Yeager, Culver Academies and Yeager Leadership Group LLC, USA

FOREWORD

Since its inception almost 20 years ago, the growth of positive psychology (PP) has been phenomenal in terms of theoretical developments, research, publications and practical applications. PP developed initially to rebalance psychology's preoccupation with pathology, and it is framed as the science and application of knowledge about human strengths and virtues and of positive subjective experience, individual traits and institutions. Whilst not yet prominent within sport and exercise psychology or sport and physical activity more broadly, based on its impact in business, education and health, it has much potential to extend existing knowledge and practice. This book is a first in the area, and it brings together experts from around the world who through new or existing work have recognized the potential to extend our understanding of sport and physical activity through the lenses of PP.

This book introduces PP in a frank and grounded manner, and as well as covering the scope and value of PP, it also addresses key criticisms levelled at the field. The editors have constructed a text which captures many of the contemporary insights and applications of PP in sport and physical activity, and they promote its value for complementing and extending sport and exercise psychology, supporting holistic practice and gaining greater insight into people's experiences of sport and physical activity. As well as providing a grounding in key topics such as well-being, gratitude, hope and optimism, character strengths, passion, and enjoyment and flow, the second half of the book is devoted to integrated real-world applications of PP in a range of contexts, many of which receive attention for the first time. A wide range of settings, populations and practices are considered such as professional football academies, secondary schools, coach development, disadvantaged youth and Olympic and Paralympic performance lifestyle support as well as the practice of sport and exercise psychology.

As a collection of key topics and applied case studies capturing the latest ideas from expert academics and practitioners, many of whom are at the forefront of researching and applying PP in sport and physical activity, this book provides a valuable introduction to PP and the fullest account to date of its application in sport and physical activity. Chapters are rich with new theories and novel ideas, the latest research insights and user-friendly activities, many of which are new to sport and physical activity and will help extend our thinking and practices. This book is a refreshing addition to existing literature, and it offers an up-to-date account of this rapidly developing area. It will particularly appeal to those who are keen to extend theory and practice to critically embrace new knowledge about positive qualities, characteristics and communities and how this knowledge may inform practice.

It has been a pleasure to contribute the foreword to this book, and I am confident it will be a great resource for both academics and practitioners in a variety of contexts.

Dr. Brian Hemmings, CPsychol, AFBPsS, FBASES
Consultant in Private Practice and Research
Fellow in Sport Psychology
St. Mary's University, Twickenham, UK

ACKNOWLEDGEMENTS

All our contributors for agreeing to be part of this wonderful project and persevering during the editing process, often with very tight deadlines, as well as making it such a positive experience for everyone involved.

Jim Clough for his meticulous editing and improvements.

Ilona Boniwell for enabling us to embark on this journey into positive psychology all those years ago. Many fabulous things have happened since we met in 2006.

Cecily Davey, Simon Whitmore and the team at Routledge for all their support, expert advice and encouragement throughout.

AN INTRODUCTION TO POSITIVE PSYCHOLOGY IN SPORT AND PHYSICAL ACTIVITY

Abbe Brady and Bridget Grenville-Cleave

Purpose of the book

The aim of positive psychology (PP) is to acknowledge the importance of understanding qualities associated with what makes life most worth living and to use this to balance psychology's preoccupation with pathology. Since its emergence from 1998 as a formal movement, PP has developed a new knowledge landscape about positive subjective experience, positive individual characteristics and positive communities. This knowledge has facilitated alternative questions and approaches in applied work in a range of settings such as education, business, health and government policy. Based on our first-hand experiences through many different roles in these fields, we the editors and authors believe that sport and physical activity too can benefit from the application of PP. Paradoxically, in attempting to promote health and well-being and help people enjoy sport/physical activity, realise their potential and achieve peak performances, sport and exercise psychology has frequently focused on topics such as anxiety, stress, burnout, emotional problems, dropout, choking and overtraining. Why do we know relatively little about enjoyment, excitement, friendship and meaning in sport? It is proposed that engagement with PP can enhance knowledge and practice in sport and physical activity and extend the sub-discipline of sport and exercise psychology and related fields. This book is designed to be a reader-friendly introduction to core topics and contemporary issues in PP which we propose will add value to the study, research and practice of sport and physical activity.

Who is the book for?

This book is designed for anyone who is open to learning and keen to understand more about how sport and physical activity can contribute to health, well-being, optimal functioning and performance across a range of settings. It aims to provide higher-education students and practitioners already working in related fields with new ideas and insights from PP. We hope readers will be inspired to embrace some of the many themes within this text and use the ideas to make a meaningful and sustainable impact on their own or others' sport and physical activity experiences.

What will readers gain that is valuable?

This book is the first of its kind to introduce the new and exciting field of PP when applied to sport and physical activity. In its short history, PP has already made a dramatic and unique contribution to many disciplines and fields of practice, and this book shows how sport and physical activity may also benefit from its ideas and application. Readers will gain an overview of contemporary themes and issues within PP and how these can be effectively applied across many diverse contexts and with participants in sport and physical activity. Using the latest theory and research findings, each chapter presents key concepts and issues, practical examples and suggestions for applied activities, so that readers are able to appreciate the real-world significance and practical value of the topics. The uniqueness of each chapter's format reflects the particular style and approach of its author(s) which we hope readers will find refreshing.

Structure of the book

This book is arranged in four parts. The opening part provides an introduction to the emergence and scope of PP, including an overview of contemporary issues. It reflects on similarities and differences between sport and exercise psychology and PP, and makes the case for the value of PP to enhance the former. This is followed by an accessible overview of the multidimensional core concept of well-being, as well as a review of the contemporary findings about the value of well-being and strategies to enhance it.

The second part introduces eight chapters, each addressing a key topic in PP, namely: passion, character strengths, optimism, mindfulness, enjoyment, gratitude, relationships, and resilience and mindsets. Each chapter provides an introduction to the main theories, research findings and applied practices, and reviews how, if at all, the topic has been applied in sport and physical activity settings. The chapters introduce a range of ways in which the topic could be of value in real-world settings and provide suggestions for research topics and activities within applied practice.

The third part of the text shifts its focus to emerging applications of PP across a range of foci and settings in sport and physical activity, including: positive pedagogy for teachers and coaches and PP coaching for leaders in sport and physical activity; positive reflective practice for coaches and coach developers; as well as PP applied to sport and exercise psychology, career transitions in professional football; and using physical activity and games to support health and well-being in deprived youth. Each chapter provides practical examples and ideas about how to understand

and use PP. The final part of the book addresses the concluding thoughts of the editors by highlighting key insights from across the chapters. Future directions are proposed, with guidance and implications for practitioners and considerations for research.

Although the styles of chapters vary across sections, they include most or all of the following:

- questions to encourage reflection and engagement with the topic;
- case studies, stories, narratives and/or data to support ideas;
- activities for those interested in applying PP ideas in sport and physical activity;
- suggestions for future research.

PART 1

Why a text on positive psychology in sport and physical activity?

1

INTRODUCING POSITIVE PSYCHOLOGY AND ITS VALUE FOR SPORT AND PHYSICAL ACTIVITY

Abbe Brady and Bridget Grenville-Cleave

A brief history of positive psychology

Positive psychology (PP) originates from the University of Pennsylvania, USA. It was founded in the late 1990s by psychology professors Martin Seligman, whose academic interests shifted from learned helplessness to learned optimism, and Mihaly Csikszentmihalyi, a world expert in creativity and flow. One of the main reasons often stated for the creation of this new branch of psychology is the view that traditional psychology had focused too heavily on pathology – in other words, understanding human problems such as depression, anxiety and post-traumatic stress disorder. It was argued that traditional psychology devoted very little attention to the study of wellness and the 'positive' aspects of life, such as resilience, character strengths and well-being, with the same academic rigour. As an example, consider the psychology of coach-athlete relationships. A conventional social psychology approach may focus on aspects of power (use and abuse), communication preferences, conflict management, commitment and compatibility. Applying a PP lens we might instead look at the contribution that each individual's character strengths make to the relationship, the effect of over- and underplayed strengths, harmony, inspiration, creativity, co-operation, celebration, passion, trust, honesty, forgiveness, shared meaning and the role of playfulness and humor in these relationships.

This imbalance between negative and positive foci in psychology has been illustrated by comparing the total number of academic papers published about 'negative' psychology topics with the total number published about 'positive' psychology topics. During the three decades spanning 1972 – 2006, in the PsycARTICLES database more than 113,000 articles were published about depression. In the same period, fewer than 23,000 were published about well-being and fewer than 1,600 about subjective well-being. Even if we accept the argument that disease merits greater professional attention than wellness, it is clear that an opportunity exists to increase our scientific understanding of wellness.

Since 1998 many researchers and practitioners have been inspired to work in this field, writing research articles and books on the subject, publishing new academic journals dedicated to the science of happiness and establishing several professional associations. Across the world, universities have introduced PP undergraduate modules and postgraduate degrees starting with the University of Pennsylvania MAPP, the MSc in Applied Positive Psychology at the University of East London and the Graduate Certificate in Applied Positive Psychology at the University of Sydney.

PP is not just making its mark in academia, however. Following the pioneering example set by the Kingdom of Bhutan in the 1970s, the national and local governments of many countries have concluded that conventional objective and largely economic measures such as gross domestic product are insufficient on their own to measure society's progress. As a result, they are adopting the view that PP considerations, particularly the emphasis on subjective well-being and how people think and feel about their lives, can help create more meaningful and effective public policy.

The landscape of positive psychology

Although the PP movement is well into its second decade, it would be fair to say that there is no unifying theory. Many scholars seem content to accept relatively loose definitions of PP, for example, "the scientific study of what goes right in life, from birth to death and at all the stops in between" (Peterson, 2006, p. 4), "the scientific study of ordinary human strengths and virtues" (Sheldon & King, 2001, p. 216) and "(the) science of positive subjective experience, positive individual traits, and positive institutions" (Seligman & Csikszentmihalyi, 2000, p. 5). Importantly, these scholars do not claim to have invented happiness and well-being, nor to be the first to study them. Numerous different definitions and theories of well-being, happiness and flourishing exist, some of which are discussed in Chapter 2.

PP incorporates a multitude of topics, some of which are undoubtedly new to scientific study (e.g. forgiveness and awe) and others which are not (e.g. motivation and emotional intelligence). PP is probably most usefully described as an 'umbrella' term which brings together into one collective body many individual, sometimes isolated, sometimes novel and often familiar, strands of research and theory related to well-being. Notwithstanding the recent emergence of 'Second Wave Positive Psychology' or 'Positive Psychology 2.0' which we discuss further in this chapter, there is every reason to believe that PP will continue to exist as a separate field of scientific inquiry until such time as conventional psychology naturally gives as much attention to the study of what is good in life as it does to what is problematic.

Park and Peterson (2003) suggest that positive institutions facilitate the development of positive traits at the individual level, which, in turn, lead to positive subjective experiences and states. In contrast to this top-down view of human happiness, Barbara Fredrickson whose major contribution to PP has been the broaden-and-build theory of positive emotions (2001), suggests that a bottom–up approach is equally valid. She argues that our everyday subjective experience of positive emotions leads to a broadening of our natural ways of thinking and behaving, as well as to the development of additional personal resources, such as problem-solving ability and creativity, over time. In other words, our long-term happiness and ability to flourish and succeed are built on our short-term positive subjective experience. These contrasting approaches demonstrate how far PP still has to travel before we reach a common shared understanding of human flourishing – what it is, its origins and its outcomes.

To illustrate the wealth of topics commonly included under the positive psychology umbrella, the mindmap of PP topics and applications in Figure 1.1 provides a useful starting point.

To illustrate the scope of PP it can be helpful initially to consider two contrasting views of human happiness, hedonia and eudaimonia, which have their roots in Greek philosophy. Simply put, hedonic well-being concerns the form of happiness

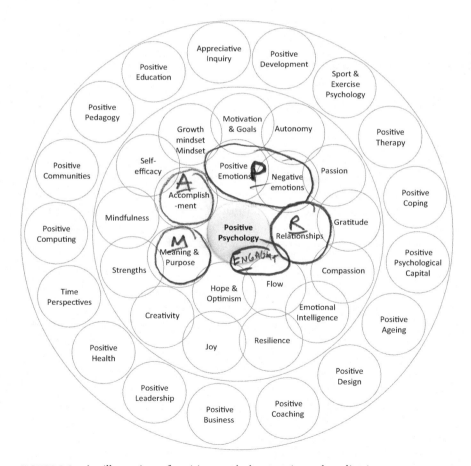

FIGURE 1.1   An illustration of positive psychology topics and applications

experienced from feeling pleasure in the moment. Eudaimonic well-being is a broad term often used to refer to the happiness gained from having meaning and purpose in our lives, doing things which facilitate personal growth and enable us to fulfill our potential, and feeling that we are in some way connected to the wider world or have a higher calling.

Some scholars have proposed other forms of well-being, including 'prudential' happiness (Haybron, 2000), 'chaironic' happiness (Wong, 2009) and 'halcyonic' happiness (Gruman & Bors, 2012), which are worthy of separate consideration. Do people the world over experience happiness in the same way or is it culture-specific (Lo & Gilmour, 2004)? What is the role of socio-economic factors in well-being (however defined)? Does PP only apply to residents of countries which are 'WEIRD' (western, educated, industrialised, rich, democratic), and so on.

Contemporary issues in positive psychology

Since its inception, the exponential growth of PP has produced a vast new landscape of enquiry. Understandably, the field has attracted some criticism. What is presented next are some of the more important criticisms, which are useful for both students and practitioners to consider.

1. It's nothing more than positive thinking

One of the major criticisms consistently levelled at PP is that it takes a 'Pollyanna' approach to life, promoting the Norman Vincent Peale (1953) notion that *if you think positively everything will be all right*. In doing so, some critics argue that PP ignores or negates the value of commonplace 'negative' emotions such as anger, sadness and fear. Of course, what this particular interpretation also suggests is that mainstream psychology is negative and that PP is somehow a replacement for it. Seligman (2003), however, has made clear that PP is not a substitute for conventional psychology, rather it is a supplement to it.

Seligman has also distanced PP from Peale's positive thinking approach by emphasising the fact that the latter is an armchair activity whereas the former is a science, based on a programme of rigorous empirical research. Whilst it is the case that some motivational speakers and trainers have become extremely successful by promoting the power of positive thinking, we cannot ignore the fact that the evidence base underpinning cognitive behavioral therapy, for example, does show that our ways of thinking about the world, how we feel and how we behave are interconnected (Hofmann, Asnaani, Vonk, Sawyer, & Fang, 2012). However, to state that PP is positive thinking is incorrect.

Despite the advantages associated with optimism and positive construal, there are times when positive thinking could lead to disaster and problem-focused thinking is in fact preferable. Thinking that you can wing your final exams, that the red brake warning light on your dashboard is simply faulty, or that despite your lack of exercise over the last year you can begin a new fitness regime with a 10k run, are clearly not helpful uses of positive thinking, and may actually lead to difficulty, failure or worse. Seligman himself is keen to ensure that practitioners foster *realistic optimism* rather than blind optimism or optimism at any cost, which could do more harm than good. Positive psychology also acknowledges the importance that defensive pessimism and negative thinking play in high performance and well-being (Norem & Cantor, 1986; Norem & Chang, 2002). However, not content with these rebuttals and defences, some PP researchers have launched what is now referred to as 'Second Wave Positive Psychology' or 'PP 2.0', in which they also lambaste their 'first wave' colleagues with similar criticisms and present a 'new' phase of positive psychology study and practice to counteract them. This may seem somewhat unnecessary to those researchers and practitioners who have always taken a more holistic and nuanced approach; however, if it finally lays the ghosts of positive thinking to rest, perhaps that is a good thing. In conclusion we hope that even a brief glance at the mindmap in Figure 1.1 convinces readers that PP has a much broader and deeper reach than positive thinking.

2. *Problems with definition, description and prescription*

A second major criticism concerns the discomfort that many scholars feel at defining what is meant by 'positive' (and 'negative') and the suggestion that PP prescribes what you should (and shouldn't) do to be happy and live a good life (Held, 2002). Even basic terminology, such as 'happiness', defies universally agreed definition (cf. Bok, 2010). "The nature of happiness has not been defined in a uniform way. Happiness can mean pleasure, life satisfaction, positive emotions, a meaningful life or a feeling of contentment, among other concepts" (Diener, Scollon & Lucas, 2009, p. 6). Terms such as 'engagement' and 'resilience' fare no better. Students and practitioners alike must therefore tread carefully.

Furthermore, notwithstanding the aforementioned point about the perceived need for a 'Second Wave', as PP matures and its evidence base grows, the importance of context (McNulty & Fincham, 2012) and culture are gaining ground. Constructs such as eudaimonic well-being have certain moral overtones: in this case, that we should all lead good lives and make a positive contribution to the world. Despite his own work in the field of learned optimism, resilience and strengths, as well as his best-selling books (*Authentic Happiness*, 2003; *Flourish*, 2011), Seligman's Positive Psychology Center at the University of Pennsylvania maintains that as a science, PP should describe but not prescribe.

Seligman says they seek to describe - positive vs prescribe - normative

3. *It's not new*

Early critics (e.g. Cowen & Kilmer, 2002; Lazarus, 2003) argued that PP completely ignored its roots in humanistic psychology, primary prevention and wellness enhancement, stress and coping theory and is masquerading as a new science even though many of its topics (e.g. motivation, emotional intelligence and optimism) pre-date it by decades. Whilst this may be the case (the late Chris Peterson being one of the few early positive psychologists to acknowledge this point), a devil's advocate may be tempted to ask, 'So what?' As long as PP researchers do not claim

PP is sort of like CBT in that it pulled together a set of tools that already existed

New Areas

others' work as their own and do not bring the discipline into disrepute, it could be said that this is simply academic bad manners or alternatively, marketing spin. The annexing by PP of topics already in existence is a criticism noted by Brown (in press). However, it is the case that there are many areas of scientific study within positive psychology that *are* new, such as gratitude, forgiveness, awe, inspiration, hope, curiosity and humor. Positive psychologists argue that these merit just as much research time and attention as the more established topics.

4. Positive psychology makes unhappy people unhappier

Clinical psychologist Barbara Held (2002), one of the most vocal early critics of PP, suggested that even the focus on subjective well-being may be enough to reduce happiness in some people. "In my own experience," she wrote, "I have repeatedly noticed that some people seem to feel guilty, defective, or both when they can't feel good. They sometimes apologize for not being able to smile in the face of adversity, as if they were committing an act of treason by feeling and acting unhappy" (Held, 2002, p. 984). She argues that PP, with its claim that happiness is within the individual's control, means that some victims of unfortunate circumstances or other sufferers feel they are to blame for their own misery. This is an important point because it highlights the fact that until recently through the work of Felicia Huppert and colleagues (Huppert, Roffey, King, Grenville Cleave, & deVries, 2017), positive psychologists have not devoted any time to exploring the wider social, cultural and economic issues which contribute to the increase in psychological illnesses (perhaps because they are not viewed as directly psychology-related). Additionally, the implicit cultural mandate that unhappiness is not acceptable ensures that, rather than helping people feel better, PP could make them feel worse. In their haste to bring positive psychology's findings to a wider audience, some practitioners are unaware of ignore or gloss over the facts, although researchers are well aware of the problem (e.g. Peterson, 2006). Others have suggested that until positive psychologists and practitioners are regulated in the same way as other psychologists, nothing will change (Lomas & Ivtzan, 2016).

An additional factor associated with the rapid development and increased output of the field has been a publication bias favoring research findings that show positive associations between constructs. The concern is that these positive associations may be enthusiastically interpreted as causal when they are correlational. To address this there is a need for more longitudinal and causal research designs in PP to establish a sound evidence base, more rigorous peer review as well as the acceptance and promotion of more qualitative and mixed research methodologies.

5. Well-being cannot be measured objectively

Last but not least, some argue that it is not possible to measure human happiness in a scientifically meaningful or objective way and therefore positive psychology cannot be considered a science (White, 2014; Haybron, 2008). Currently, numerous definitions of well-being–related constructs exist each with different scales and measurement methods. However, over the past decade and a half research in the field by eminent scholars such as Ed Diener in the USA, Felicia Huppert in the UK and Ruut Veenhoven in the Netherlands has increased our understanding of happiness, its components and correlates. Diener and Suh (1997) provide a thorough review of the science involved in measuring well-being, and argue that objective and subjective measures must be used in concert; neither is sufficient on its own:

> A thorough understanding of subjective well-being requires knowledge of how objective conditions influence people's evaluations of their lives. Similarly, a complete understanding of objective indicators and how to select them requires that we understand people's values, and have knowledge about how objective indicators influence people's experience of well-being.
>
> *(Diener & Suh, 1997, p. 214)*

Whilst a superficial glance at PP's portrayal in the popular media may leave readers thinking that it is no more than 'happiology', a more in-depth review of the extensive peer-reviewed research reveals its rigor, complexity, richness and variety. Positive psychology researchers seek to acknowledge and address criticisms in order to support the appropriate development of the field.

The similarities and differences between positive psychology and sport and exercise psychology

Quite understandably a person might ask, 'Is there a need for PP when sport and exercise psychology (SEP) exists?' To address this question, it is important to establish that although there may be some overlap in the respective foci of these domains of psychology, they can be very different. So the purpose of this section is to highlight briefly some of the ways SEP and PP are similar to and different from each other.

A key characteristic of PP is that it intentionally addresses a gap in mainstream psychology by examining what is desirable in people and what makes life worth living. When referring to the emergence of PP, eminent sport psychologist Dan Gould (2002) identified how SEP and PP were alike because in comparison to mainstream psychology, the focus of SEP has been more aligned with positive concepts in predominantly non-clinical populations. In many respects we can agree with Gould because SEP has examined topics and areas beyond pathology and problems experienced by those involved in sport and exercise. However, an overview of the foci and developments in SEP highlights how some of its most frequently published and researched topics reflect the agenda set by mainstream and sub-disciplines of psychology working with clinical populations. Although SEP has a mission to

TABLE 1.1 Frequency of citation of deficit and abundance concepts in sport psychology articles in the SPORTDiscus, socINDEX, psycARTICLES and psycINFO databases during three time periods between 1980 and 2005

	Concept (as noted in article title)	Frequency of citation		
		1980–85	1990–95	2000–05
Abundance-focused concepts	Confidence	10	14	24
	Satisfaction	5	6	19
	Flow	3	5	17
	Self-esteem	9	8	10
	Enjoyment	7	6	5
	Well-being	0	3	9
	Mental toughness	0	0	8
	Fun	0	1	3
	Pride	0	0	1
	Happiness	1	0	0
	Hardiness	0	1	1
Deficit-focused concepts	Anxiety	68	71	66
	Stress	36	82	71
	Injury	4	24	31
	Mood	2	25	30
	Aggression	15	6	15
	Eating disorder	0	2	11
	Fear	18	5	8
	Depression	7	7	8
	Burnout	4	11	5
	Pain	3	3	6
	Violence	8	4	5

Source: Brady (2009)

help people enjoy the activity, realise their goals and potential and achieve peak experience/performance, analysis of published literature in sport (Table 1.1) reflects how sport psychology had frequently focused on topics such as anxiety, stress, burnout, emotional problems, dropout, choking and overtraining (Jackson, 2000; Brady, 2009). This incongruity between the aims of SEP and domains of research and published literature in sport psychology is especially stark given SEP's focus on mainly non-clinical populations. These lacunae form a major justification for the value of engaging with PP in sport and physical activity.

Instead of studying the full range of human characteristics and experiences, historically sport psychology has followed the directive of mainstream psychology which has been preoccupied with an approach characterised by strategies to reduce or reframe negative experiences and behaviors rather than to increase or optimise the positive experiences and behaviors. These objectives can be considered as deficit and abundance notions, respectively.

Informed by contemporary PP, abundance-focused sport and exercise psychologists might consider concepts such as:

• Friendship	• Passion	• Enjoyment	• Optimism
• Courage	• Competence	• Gratitude	• Humility
• Character strengths	• Kindness	• Empathy	• Forgiveness
• Trust	• Honesty	• Wisdom	• Co-operation
• Love	• Spirituality	• Inspiration	• Creativity
• Faith	• Well-being	• Quality of Life	• Interpersonal Skill
• Aesthetic Sensibility	• Future Mindedness	• Peak Experience	• Personal Growth
• Excitement	• Compassion	• Hope	• Humor

These topics lend themselves to consideration from an abundance perspective in SEP because, with some leeway for cultural and historical variation, many are considered to be important in human lived experience and are intuitively resonant with our most valued experiences in sport and physical activity.

As well as reflecting the agenda of mainstream psychology regarding topics and applications, another explanation for the pathology-oriented focus of many key topics in sport psychology seen in Table 1.1 is presented by Andersen (2006), who stated that sports practitioners and researchers devote much of their time and energy to trying to repair the damage and manage challenges associated with involvement in competitive sport, which may be even more apparent in high-performance settings. Another justification for introducing PP into sport and physical activity relates to the potential for the performance bias and instrumental emphases of SEP rather than other outcomes associated with alternative experiences or conceptions in sport or physical activity, such as enjoyment, friendship, identity, meaning, spirituality and health. Topics in PP directly address these subjects and so may offer alternative insights through which to enrich the scope of SEP.

A criticism sometimes levelled at sport and exercise sciences including SEP research is that the athlete, coach or exerciser can become dehumanised as s/he is reduced to a performance/intervention variable where his/her subjective experience, well-being and humanness are neglected in favor of more tangible objective indices such as performance achievements, target behaviors or bodily responses. Engaging with topics in PP offers us the opportunity to acknowledge and examine a fuller range of human experience and meanings associated with sport and physical activity. In so doing we move closer to understanding and valuing our humanness which contributes to our capacity to understand and achieve holistic practice.

Well-being is a core concept in PP and with advances in measurement, contemporary research has shown how well-being is positively related and causally linked to factors contributing to health, productivity and performance in domains such as medicine, education and business (Huppert & So, 2013; Lyubomirsky, King, & Diener, 2005). The scale of such findings has helped to challenge some ideas about how desirable outcomes might best be achieved, with considerable potential to support new insights and inform practices in SEP as well as other sport- and physical activity–related disciplines.

The applicability of positive psychology across diverse contexts in sport and physical activity

A key aim of this book is to show how PP may be usefully applied to a range of situations in sport and physical activity. An important task therefore is to highlight the diversity in contexts, activities and possible meanings associated with the concept of sport and physical activity. Because the term *sport* can be used to represent so many different activities, it can be hard to capture it within a single statement. The following definition captures some of its breadth:

> Sport means all forms of physical activity which, through casual or organised participation, aim at expressing or improving physical fitness and mental well-being, forming social relationships, obtaining results in competition at all levels.
> *(Council of Europe, 2001)*

Though helpful because it alludes to a wide range of activities and some core motives associated with involvement in sport, except for the personal and social aspects, this functional description does not emphasise the cultural, political, commercial, vocational or contextual aspects of sport, nor its dynamic nature. For example, sport and physical activity may be experienced in many varied ways such as one or more of the following: active or passive leisure; alone or with others; a health intervention; a pursuit for achievement and realising one's potential; to experience teamwork, excitement or catharsis; a family commitment; a volunteer activity; and as a full- or part-time occupation. Distinct sub-cultures, lifestyles and identities develop around and through engagement in different sport and physical activities. Regardless of the amount or nature of engagement, sport and/or physical activity can become a highly meaningful and valued activity in people's lives. PP can make a significant contribution to sport by helping us understand more about these varied experiences and outcomes that can be derived (or diminished) through involvement in particular sport and physical activities.

Modern-day sport and physical activity have undergone considerable change and growth linked to government and commercial interests. Governments have increasingly recognised the many ways sport and physical activity may address challenges relating to areas such as population health and productivity; community engagement and active citizenship; social enterprise, tourism and business generation; national identity, pride; and international status and relations. The commercial development of sport and physical activity exists across many contexts, though it is probably most apparent in the global commodification of particular brands, lifestyle activities, professional sports and major events such as the Olympics and Paralympics.

As a consequence of increased media and commercial involvement, some of the most valuable brands and recognised people worldwide are those associated with sport (Forbes, 2015). One aspect of the changing landscape of sport and physical activity has been the increased professionalization of its organisations and practices via the evolution of specialist knowledge and skills, which in turn have created new roles, occupations and academic sub-disciplines. This book is an example of the increasing specialization in the study and practice of sport and physical activity by introducing new concepts and findings from PP.

Sport and physical activity are considered microcosms of society (Coakley, 2001), and for this reason they have enduring appeal for studying human experience and provide unique contexts for enquiry into contemporary issues. Issues may include varied forms of exclusion and inequality; participant welfare and safety; sedentary lifestyles and attrition; doping, corruption and spiralling costs (and rewards); the pervasiveness of a 'win at all costs' ethos; and declining time for physical education and sport in school curricula. We know that attitudes and beliefs formed early in life about not enjoying sport and physical activity or not being 'the sporty type' are enduring and may reduce or delay the chances of engaging in sport and/or physical activity in later life (Russell & Limle, 2013), with potential consequences for mental and physical health.

Although sport is attributed with varied benefits and is used to address a wide range of individual and social goals and issues, sports policy researcher Fred Coalter (2007) suggests that the evidence base for some of the claims about the benefits is weak. This relates in part to methodological problems, and Coalter proposes that there is a need to adopt a different approach to research and evaluation to improve understanding and knowledge about the impacts and benefits of sport- and physical activity–related initiatives. We propose that PP can provide new ideas to assist in understanding some of the many individual and collective benefits of sport and physical activity and the mechanisms by which certain desirable outcomes occur.

As noted earlier, PP provides a broader vocabulary of concepts associated with what is good at individual and collective levels, and we propose that it will add to how we can understand what makes sport and physical activity such a powerful factor. PP may also be valuable in helping us understand or address problems in or associated with sport and physical activity because some of the major contributions of contemporary PP have been in offering new insight to personal and social issues such as depression (Sin & Lyubomirsky, 2009), physical illness (Mutrie & Faulkner, 2004), obesity (Hendricks, Dhurandhar, Fontaine, & Hendricks, 2015) and drug abuse (Jafari, Ahmadi, Mohammadzadeh, & Najafi, 2012; Krentzman, 2013).

Linked to increasing specialization in the field, we now recognise a more differentiated landscape where distinctions are made between sport, exercise and physical activity. Whilst overlapping in some respects, these domains are considered to generate and require specialist knowledge and understanding. To highlight the applicability of PP across varied domains, each chapter in Part 2 intentionally draws upon a range of examples to help the reader appreciate the multiple applications of the topic. The chapters in Part 3 show how PP has been and can be fruitfully applied to distinct settings and contexts in sport, exercise and physical activity, and in Part 4 we provide some examples of how particular PP topics could be used in a range of sport- and physical activity–related contexts.

The aim of this opening chapter was to provide an introduction to PP: what it is (and what it is not), where it has come from, its main themes and some of the key contemporary issues. We also outlined how it is similar to and different from SEP and, most importantly, considered how and why it has practical relevance whether one is a student of sport and physical activity, coach, athlete, parent, teacher or prac-titioner in sports science or medicine.

References

Andersen, M. B. (2006). *Challenges for sport psychology*. Keynote speech at the British Associa-tion of Sport and Exercise Sciences (BASES) Annual Conference, University of Wolver-hampton (September).

Bok, S. (2010). *Exploring Happiness: From Aristotle to Brain Science*. New Haven, CT: Yale University Press.

Boniwell, I. (2012). *Positive Psychology in a Nutshell* (3rd ed.). Maidenhead: Open University Press.

Brady, A. (2009). *Research publication trends associated with deficit and abundance concepts in sport psychology*. Oral presentation as part of the symposium 'Enriching sport psychology: Engag-ing with positive psychology' presented by A. Brady, A. Ashfield, J. Allan, J. McKenna, & E. Duncan. *BASES Annual Conference*. Leeds Metropolitan University, Leeds, Sept.

Brown, N. J. L. (in press). An introduction to criticality for students of positive psychology. In N. J. L. Brown, T. Lomas, & F. J. Eiroa-Orosa (Eds.), *The Routledge International Handbook of Critical Positive Psychology* (Chapter 12). London: Routledge.

Coakley, J.J. (2001). *Sport and society: Issues and controversies* (7th ed.). St. Louis, MO: Mosby.

Coalter, F. (2007). *A Wider Social Role for Sport: Who's Keeping Score?* Oxon: Routledge.

Council of Europe (2001). *Committee of Ministers on the revised European Sports Charter*. (16 May, 2001) Retrieved from https://search.coe.int/cm/Pages/result_details.aspx?ObjectID=09000016804c9dbb [Accessed 15 September, 2014].

Cowen, E., & Kilmer, R. (2002). Positive psychology: Some plusses and some open issues. *Journal of Community Psychology*, 30(4), 449–460.

Diener, E., Scollon, C. N., & Lucas, R. E. (2009). The evolving concept of subjective well-being: The multifaceted nature of happiness. In E. Diener (Ed.), *Assessing Well-Being: The Collected Work of Ed Diener*. Dordrecht: Springer.

Diener, E., & Suh, E. (1997). Measuring quality of life: Economic, social and subjective indi-cators. *Social Indicators Research*, 40, 189–216.

Forbes. (2015). The world's highest paid celebrities. Retrieved July 27 2015, from www.forbes.com/celebrities/#tab:overall_page:10

Fredrickson, B. L. (2001). The role of positive emotions in positive psychology: The broaden-and-build theory of positive emotions. *American Psychologist*, 56(3), 218–226.

Gould, D. (2002). Sport psychology in the new millennium: The psychology of excellence and beyond. *Journal of Applied Sport Psychology*, 14, 137–139.

Gruman, J. A., & Bors, D. A. (2012). *Do nothing: Be happy: Halcyonic well-being*. Paper presented at the inaugural meeting of the Canadian Positive Psychology Association, Toronto, July 20.

Haybron, D. (2008). *The Pursuit of Unhappiness: The Elusive Psychology of Well-Being*. Oxford: Oxford University Press.

Haybron, D. M. (2000). Two philosophical problems in the study of happiness. *The Journal of Happiness Studies*, 1, 207–225.

Held, B. (2002). The tyranny of the positive attitude in America: Observation and specula-tion. *Journal of Clinical Psychology*, 58, 965–992.

Hendricks, A. N., Dhurandhar, E. J., Fontaine, K. R., & Hendricks, P. S. (2015). Hope think-ing and past trauma mediate the relationships of body mass index with perceived mental health treatment need and mental health treatment use. *Clinical Obesity*, 5(1), 31–37.

Hofmann, S. G., Asnaani, A., Vonk, I. J. J., Sawyer, A. T., & Fang, A. (2012). The efficacy of cognitive behavioral therapy: A review of meta-analyses. *Cognitive Therapy and Research*, 36(5), 427–440.

Huppert, F.A., & So, T.T. (2013). Flourishing across Europe: Application of a new conceptual framework for defining well-being. *Social Indicators Research*, 110(3), 837–861.

Huppert, F., Roffey S. King, V., Grenville Cleave, B., & deVries, M. (2017). *How Can Positive Psychology Contribute to Universal Well-Being?* An Invitation to Conversation and Action. Culture & Global Issues Panel session at 5th World Congress on Positive Psychology, Montreal, Canada, July.

Jafari, E., Ahmadi, M., Mohammadzadeh, A., & Najafi, M. (2012). The effectiveness of lifestyle training in relapse prevention and resiliency enhancement for people with substance dependency. *International Journal of High Risk Behaviors and Addiction*, 1(1), 34–38.

Krentzman, A. (2013). Review of the application of positive psychology to substance use, addiction, and recovery research. *Psychology of Addictive Behaviors*, 27(1), 151–165.

Jackson, S. A. (2000). Joy, fun, and flow state in sport. In Hanin, Y. (Ed.), *Emotions in Sport* (pp. 135–155). Champaign: IL, Human Kinetics.

Lazarus, R. S. (2003). Does the positive psychology movement have legs? *Psychological Inquiry*, 14(2), 93–109.

Lo, L., & Gilmour, R. (2004). Culture and conceptions of happiness: Individual oriented and social oriented SWB. *Journal of Happiness Studies*, 5, 269–291.

Lomas, T & Ivtzan, I. (2016). Second Wave Positive Psychology: exploring the positive - negative dialectics of wellbeing. *Journal of Happiness Studies,* 17(4), 1753–1768.

Lyubomirsky, S., King, L., & Diener, E. (2005). The benefits of frequent positive affect: Does happiness lead to success? *Psychological Bulletin*, 131(6), 803–855.

McNulty, J., & Fincham, F. (2012). Beyond positive psychology? Toward a contextual view of psychological processes and well-being. *American Psychologist*, 67(2), 101–110.

Mutrie, N., & Faulkner, G. (2004). Physical activity: Positive psychology in motion. In P. Linley & S. Joseph (Eds.), *Positive Psychology in Practice* (pp. 146–164). Hoboken, NJ: Wiley.

Norem, J., & Cantor, N. (1986). Defensive pessimism: Harnessing anxiety as motivation. *Journal of Personality and Social Psychology*, 51(6), 1208–1217.

Norem, J., & Chang, E. C. (2002). The positive psychology of negative thinking. *Journal of Clinical Psychology*, 58, 993–1001.

Park, N., & Peterson, C. (2003). Early intervention from the perspective of positive psychology. *Prevention and Treatment*, 6(1), 2–8.

Peale, N.V. (1953). *The Power of Positive Thinking*. New York: Prentice Hall Inc.

Peterson, C. (2006). *A Primer in Positive Psychology*. New York: Oxford University Press.

Russell, W. D., & Limle, A. N. (2013). The relationship between youth sport specialization and involvement in sport and physical activity in young adulthood. *Journal of Sport Behavior*, 36(1), 82–98.

Seligman, M. (2003). *Authentic Happiness*. London: Nicholas Brealey Publishing.

Seligman, M.E.P. (2011). *Flourish: A Visionary New Understanding of Happiness and Well-being*. New York: Free Press.

Seligman, M., & Csikszentmihalyi, M. (2000). Positive psychology: An introduction. *American Psychologist*, 55, 5–14.

Sheldon, K. M., & King, L. (2001). Why positive psychology is necessary. *American Psychologist*, 56(3), 216–217.

Sin, N. L., & Lyubomirsky, S. (2009). Enhancing well-being and alleviating depressive symptoms with positive psychology interventions: A practice-friendly meta-analysis. *Journal of Clinical Psychology: In Session*, 65, 467–487.

White, M. D. (2014). *The problems with measuring and using happiness for policy purposes*. Mercatus Working Paper, George Mason University. Retrieved from www.mercatus.org/system/files/White-Happiness.pdf.

Wong, P. (2009). Positive existential psychology. In S. Lopez (Ed.), *Encyclopedia of Positive Psychology* (pp. 345–351). Oxford: Blackwell.

2

THE COMPONENTS OF WELL-BEING

Bridget Grenville-Cleave and Abbe Brady

Well-being has become an important social indicator and outcome in domains as diverse as education, business and health, yet there is a lack of consensus around its definition, both in theoretical and practical terms. For scientists, academics and practitioners, this suggests that the field is not as robust as it could and should be; unsurprisingly, critics of positive psychology (PP) emphasise this weakness (e.g. Brown, Lomas & Eiroa-Orosa, in press). From a psychological perspective, it is worth noting that some researchers in mainstream psychology and sport and exercise psychology take a mitigative approach; even if they do not conceptualise well-being as a lack of something unwanted, they measure it by the absence of depression or anxiety (e.g. Miller & Hoffman, 2009; Woods, Breslin, & Hassan, 2017). The question to be considered, therefore, is whether the absence of ill-being automatically presumes the presence of well-being. As in PP (e.g. Keyes & Lopez, 2002; Hefferon & Boniwell, 2011), emerging sport and physical activity literature now also acknowledges the idea that ill- and well-being are separate constructs and that the absence of ill-being does not automatically confer well-being (Adie & Bartholomew, 2010; Brady, 2016) as represented in Figure 2.1. Other researchers take a constructive approach, conceptualising well-being as the presence of something valued, for example, measuring it in terms of resilience, hope or self-esteem (e.g. Amorose, Anderson-Butcher, & Cooper, 2009; Williams, Collingwood, Coles, & Schmeer, 2015).

Though rarely credited, understanding well-being as a positive state came to public attention through the work of the World Health Organization (WHO) which in 1948 published a definition of health as 'a state of complete physical, mental and social well-being, and not merely the absence of disease or infirmity' (WHO, 2014). This remains the most widely cited reference to health, and we propose that it has been instrumental in supporting modern-day conceptions of well-being as distinct asset-oriented phenomena.

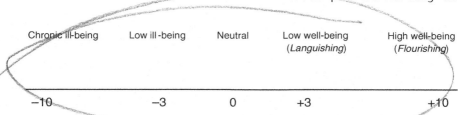

Chronic ill-being	Low ill-being	Neutral	Low well-being (*Languishing*)	High well-being (*Flourishing*)
−10	−3	0	+3	+10

FIGURE 2.1 A simplified continuum distinguishing between ill-being and well-being

Table 2.1 summarizes some of the ways in which well-being has been conceptualised in psychology. Rather than suggesting a preference or making a recommendation, the table illustrates the range of approaches, and thus the options that are open to researchers and practitioners in sport and physical activity. It also suggests that well-being is more than the absence of the characteristics of disorder. Readers are encouraged to explore these concepts in more depth in relation to their application in sport and physical activity settings, as well as to expand their knowledge and add to the table by studying other scholars' and practitioners' work. Scores of new measures of well-being have been created in the past two decades; even if the majority has been psychometrically validated, from a practitioner perspective it is essential to consider the definitions of well-being when making decisions about application, evaluation and measurement. Agreement about the essence of well-being is most evident in Huppert, Baylis and Keverne's (2004) description as 'a positive and sustainable state that allows individuals, groups or nations to thrive and flourish' (pp. 13 – 31).

Notwithstanding the lack of consensus about the conceptualisation of well-being, in contemporary PP and in sport and physical activity literatures there are two main theoretical positions on well-being: hedonic and eudaimonic. It could be said that there is more agreement amongst academics and practitioners about the nature of hedonic well-being, which focuses on 'feeling good' broadly construed. Many researchers adopt Diener, Emmons, Larsen, and Griffin's (1985) use of the term *subjective well-being* (SWB) to refer to the presence of positive emotion and the relative absence of negative emotion combined with satisfaction with life – in other words the experience of pleasure/displeasure, plus one's judgment about the good/bad aspects of one's life. Thus SWB combines both affect and cognition. Since the mid-1980s the hedonic approach has dominated the field of well-being research and has been characterised by research linked to SWB. Key tenets of SWB theory include that people are the best judges of their own well-being and that cognitive and affective dimensions of SWB may not necessarily tally; for example, one may have high life satisfaction but low positive emotions in the moment (Diener & Suh, 1997). Newman, Tay, and Diener (2014) present a bottom-up conceptual framework that highlights the key pathways between leisure and SWB (Figure 2.2). The framework shows how domain-specific SWB contributes to global SWB, and it highlights a number of psychological mechanisms through which domain SWB is experienced.

TABLE 2.1 Component domains of well-being and common indicators

Well-Being Domain	Indicator
Subjective well-being (SWB) (Diener, Emmons, Larsen, & Griffin, 1985; Diener & Suh, 1997)	Satisfaction with life Positive and negative affect
Eudaimonic well-being (EWB) (Ryan & Deci, 2001)	Meaning Self-realization The degree to which one is fully functioning
Psychological well-being (PWB) (Ryff, 1989)	Autonomy Environmental mastery Personal growth Positive relations with others Purpose in life Self-acceptance
Emotional well-being (Schalock & Verdugo, 2002)	Contentment Self-concept/identity Lack of stress
Physical well-being (Schalock & Verdugo, 2002)	Physical health Activities of daily living Leisure
Material well-being (Schalock & Verdugo, 2002; Cummins, 1996)	Financial status/standard of living Employment Housing
Developmental well-being (Schalock & Verdugo, 2002; Cummins, 1996)	Education Personal competence Performance/achievement in life
Social well-being (Keyes, 1998; Cummins, 1996)	Social coherence Social integration/part of a community Social acceptance Social contribution Social actualization
Rights/civic well-being (Schalock & Verdugo, 2002)	Human Legal
Safety/security (Cummins, 1996)	Personal safety Future security

Many of these align closely with constructs associated with eudaimonic accounts of psychological well-being.

A significant development in recent hedonic research focuses on the positive affect component. Evidence from the rapidly expanding body of neuroscientific and biopsychosocial research highlights how positive emotions and cognitions confer much more to our physical, cognitive and social development, health and resilience, than previously realised (Davidson & Schuyler, 2015; Dockray & Steptoe, 2010).

Fredrickson's (1998, 2001) broaden–and–build theory of positive emotions provides an explanation of the purpose and consequences of positive affect. The central

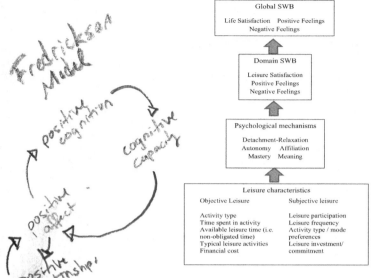

Fredrickson Model
positive cognition
cognitive capacity
positive affect
positive relationship

FIGURE 2.2   Conceptual model linking domain specific- and global- subjective well-being in the context of leisure (adapted from Newman et al., 2014)

proposition is that positive emotions have distinct developmental significance at the time of experiencing the positive affect as well as supporting the development of resources in the future. Positive emotions encourage environmental engagement, play and exploration through which knowledge, skills and connection with others are acquired, and these physical, intellectual, social and psychological resources facilitate adaptive responses and resilience in challenging or uncertain situations (Fredrickson, 1998, 2001). Positive emotions also influence our thinking, our decisions and our connections with others (Isen, 2001) and so they can have considerable implications for how we experience various situations and circumstances. Whereas negative affect causes a narrowing of or tunnel vision impact on cognition, positive affect broadens attentional and cognitive capacity and thought-action repertoires which lead to greater cognitive efficiency and flexibility, innovation and creativity (Isen, 2001; Fredrickson, 2001). Across many situations, positive affect has been demonstrated to enhance memory, problem-solving, decision-making, creativity, and flexible and efficient cognitive activity and in terms of interpersonal behaviour, it promotes helping, generosity and interpersonal understanding (Isen, 2001; Fredrickson, 1998, 2001). A central proposition in Fredrickson's theory is the cyclical processes of reciprocity that occur as positive affect elicits positive cognition and increased cognitive capacity which, in turn, elicits positive affect and may increase positive interpersonal or social exchanges that are likely to further enhance positive affect (Fredrickson & Joiner, 2002).

Fredrickson and Levenson (1998) proposed that positive emotions also serve to undo the lingering effects of negative emotions via various biological and cognitive processes. An example of the undoing effect was demonstrated in a study in which those who had experienced induced mild joy or contentment following a highly anxious condition also experienced a faster cardiovascular recovery (i.e. heart rate, peripheral vasoconstriction and blood pressure) from anxiety compared with those who had a neutral or negative emotion state inducement following a highly anxious condition. In later work Fredrickson and colleagues also demonstrated that positive emotions support the capacity to bounce back from negative emotional experiences (Tugade & Fredrickson, 2004) and predict the development of ego resilience (Cohn, Fredrickson, Brown, Mikels, & Conway, 2009). These findings have considerable implications for how we might approach and support participants in challenging learning and problem-solving situations in sport and physical activity.

In a landmark paper, Lyubomirsky, King, and Diener (2005) provided evidence that in addition to being an outcome of desirable life events, positive affect was causally associated with desirable life events and behaviours paralleling success. The research team conducted a series of large-scale meta-analyses across a range of 225 papers involving cross-sectional, longitudinal and experimental designs involving a total of 275,000 participants. Findings provided compelling evidence that positive affect fosters a range of desirable behaviours, skills and resources linked with success, including sociability and activity, altruism, liking of self and others, strong bodies and immune system, and effective conflict resolution skills.

Lyubomirsky et al. (2005) describe how the ongoing success of happy people may stem from their frequent positive moods, which increase the probability of them approaching and working on new goals and the possession of skills and resources that they have cultivated during previous periods of positive mood and endeavour. Happy people may possess characteristics which may facilitate their adaptability and resilience when experiencing difficult times. The authors describe the concepts of 'costs' and 'trade-offs' because not all positive affect is adaptive or desirable. For example, a cost may relate to how, in some cognitive tasks and achievement situations, very high positive affect may not facilitate optimal performance. A trade-off is when people are prepared intentionally or otherwise to forego positive affect to achieve other goals which are linked to the situation and cultural norms. This concept may have considerable salience in competitive sport and challenging physical activity.

Eudaimonic well-being covers a wide range of concepts, including meaning and purpose, personal growth, authenticity, personal expressiveness (Waterman, 1993) and, reflecting the ancient Greek origins of the word 'daimon', achieving one's true nature and potential. However, there seems to be less agreement over the nature and scope of eudaimonic well-being, a term coined by Ryan and Deci (2001) to refer to 'the degree to which one is fully functioning' (p. 141). Importantly, eudaimonic theories suggest that some valued outcomes, whilst pleasurable, may not actually result in (higher) well-being when achieved (e.g. catching the bus home from work instead of walking home). Additionally, some valued outcomes, which would result in (higher) well-being when achieved, may actually be unpleasant in the moment or require the deferral of gratification (e.g. training hard and foregoing social events to improve training and recovery quality). Supporters of the eudaimonic approach therefore argue that there is more to well-being than subjective happiness and feeling good in the present.

A distinct area of well-being research that has emerged is that associated with self-determination theory (SDT, Ryan & Deci, 2001) and one of its sub-theories, basic psychological needs theory (BPNT). The three basic psychological needs are autonomy, competence and relatedness, and their fulfilment is essential to well-being. Considerable research using a range of designs including longitudinal studies demonstrates very clearly how behaviours and environments that support the fulfilment of the basic needs are associated with enhanced well-being (e.g. Amorose, Anderson-Butcher, & Cooper, 2009; Adie, Duda, & Ntoumanis, 2012). Evidence exists to support the suggestion that greater well-being may be experienced based on either an additive effect or a balanced satisfaction of the three basic needs (Mack, Wilson, Oster, Kowalski, Crocker, & Sylvester, 2011).

Ryff (1989) has investigated psychological well-being (PWB), presenting a multidimensional approach to well-being measurement, which taps into six distinct aspects of human actualization: autonomy, personal growth, self-acceptance, life purpose, mastery and positive relatedness. According to Ryff and Singer (1998), greater PWB is associated with better immunological functioning and physical health. Heralding recent PP research on the importance to high well-being of relationships and active social lives as well as acknowledging positive relatedness in Ryff's earlier PWB model, Keyes' (1995) proposed a five-dimensional model of social well-being which is explained later.

Though PWB has only relatively recently received attention in the sport and PA literatures, it resonates highly with many important features of our experiences in sport and PA. If explored and understood, PWB holds much promise for capturing the essence of why sport and physical activity is so meaningful and engaging. Using Ryff's PWB scale Edwards and Edwards (2011) found that whilst they had different PWB profiles, sports participants from running, gym, hockey, surfing and soccer all had significantly higher aggregate PWB compared with those who did not participate in sport or exercise. Understanding when and why particular sports may contribute to PWB is worthy of further exploration. In a mixed-methods study Ferguson, Kowalski, Mack, Wilson, and Crocker (2012) examined women's health-related physical activity (HEPA) and PWB. Using Ryff's scale they found HEPA level (frequency, intensity, duration) was unexpectedly not significantly related to PWB, but the quality of the HEPA experience was significantly related to PWB, and follow-up interviews identified PWB was achieved in HEPA through offering goal-setting and striving opportunities, providing bonding experiences, promoting self-reflection and developing a physical/able body. Ferguson et al. (2012) recommended that rather than HEPA quantity, HEPA quality should be carefully considered to facilitate well-being in this population. PWB has considerable potential to illuminate meaningful experiences in sport and physical activity; Table 2.2 introduces a valuable way of gaining more insight about what PWB may look like when optimal and when impaired.

Because people evaluate their personal well-being in relation to their experiences in society, Keyes (1998) proposed the concept of social well-being (SocWB)

TABLE 2.2 Characterising the six dimensions of psychological well-being (PWB) when impaired and optimal

Impaired	PWB Dimension	Optimal
Has difficulty in managing everyday activities; feels unable to change or improve the situation; is unaware of surrounding opportunities; lacks a sense of control over external events	Environmental mastery	A sense of mastery and competence in managing the environment; controls external activities; makes effective use of surrounding opportunities; is able to create or choose contexts suitable to personal needs and values
A sense of stagnation; lacks a sense of improvement or development over time; feels bored and uninterested in life; is unable to develop new attitudes or behaviours	Personal growth	A feeling of ongoing development; sees self as growing and expanding; is open to new experiences and learning; has a sense of realizing own potential; recognises improvement in self and behaviour over time
Lacks a sense of meaning or direction in life; has few goals and does not see purpose in past life; has no outlooks or beliefs that give life meaning	Purpose in life	Has aims and goals in life and a sense of directedness; feels there is meaning to present and past life; holds beliefs that give life purpose
Overly concerned with expectations and evaluation of others; relies on judgement of others to make important decisions; conforms to social pressures to act or think in particular ways	Autonomy	Self-determining and independent; able to resist social pressures; regulates behaviour from within; evaluates self by personal standards
Feels dissatisfied with self; disappointed with life so far; troubled about certain personal qualities; wishes to be different	Self-acceptance	Has a positive attitude toward self; accepts their good and bad qualities; feels positive about their past life
Few close, trusting relationships; finds it difficult to be open; isolated and frustrated in interpersonal relationships; unwilling to make compromises to sustain important ties with others	Positive relations with others	Warm and trusting relationships with others; concerned about the welfare and well-being of others; capable of strong empathy, affection and intimacy; understands the give and take of relationships

Source: Adapted from Ruini and Fava (2004)

and demonstrated its theoretical distinctiveness from PWB. SocWB represents the extent to which individuals perceive they are functioning well and flourishing in their social lives. Keyes (ibid) identified five dimensions which reflect social and public criteria, including: *social acceptance* (feel positively toward, acknowledge and accept others), *social actualization* (care about and think the world is developing positively), *social contribution* (feel one's contribution to society is positive and valued by one's community), *social coherence* (perception that the social world is intelligible, logical and predictable), and *social integration* (sense of social belonging, support and similarity to others). SocWB has been incorporated into large-scale population surveys and is also present in some integrated models of well-being. Given that the nature of engagement in many sport and physical activities may often require inter-action with others, examining participants' social well-being may provide many salient insights about important features of the experience. Despite its potential value in sport and physical activity, relatively few studies have examined social well-being explicitly. Social well-being emerged as a key domain in a systematic review examining the impact of sport and physical activity on the well-being of combat veterans (Caddick & Smith, 2014); examples of emerging themes included social support via working together, offering practical and emotional support, the impor-tance of relationships for connection and camaraderie through having shared expe-riences of trauma and a military background, and providing support and inspiration. Considerable potential exists to explore the social dimensions of well-being across many different settings in sport and physical activity, because other people and our relations with them can play such an important role in our experiences.

Hedonic well-being is often symbolised by the image of a treadmill, illustrating the finding that positive emotions are relatively short-lived (Fredrickson, 2001), and thus hedonic well-being does not last and needs frequent 'topping up'. In contrast, eudaimonic well-being is often symbolised by the image of a staircase, representing the idea of personal development and growth. Although some positive psychologists (e.g. Kashdan, Biswas-Diener, & King, 2008) have been critical of drawing a distinc-tion between hedonic and eudaimonic approaches, stating there is empirical evi-dence of overlaps, nevertheless we argue that it is a useful starting point: well-being is not a straightforward construct, meaning different things to different people, as well as incorporating both how one feels and how one functions.

Though eudaimonic and hedonic traditions of well-being research have long been in opposition, recent developments in well-being theory have included integrated models of well-being (Table 2.3) in recognition of the distinct but closely related nature of both hedonic and eudaimonic traditions (see Keyes & Lopez, 2002; Lun-dqvist, 2011; Page & Vella-Brodrick, 2009; Seligman, 2011). An experience which combines feeling good (high hedonic well-being) and functioning well (high eudai-monic well-being) is when the state of flourishing is most likely to be achieved. To be high in either type of well-being but not both does not confer optimal benefits (Keyes & Annas, 2009); and according to Dolan (2014) there needs to be a balance.

Examining the integrated models of well-being, one is struck by the diversity of components that comprise each model, and this reflects the conceptual variance in the field which may provide both concern and reassurance. There may be concern

TABLE 2.3 Integrated theoretical and applied models of well-being

Well-Being Domain	Indicator
Well-being (Seligman, 2011)	Positive emotion Engagement ⓅＥＲＭＡ Relationships Meaning Accomplishment
Flourishing (Huppert & So, 2013)	Competence Emotional stability Engagement Meaning Optimism Positive emotion Positive relationships Resilience Self-esteem Vitality
Positive mental health (Jahoda, 1958)	Attitudes toward self Self-actualization Integration Autonomy Perception of reality Environmental mastery
Five ways to well-being (NEF, 2008)	Connect Be active Take notice Keep learning Give
Social happiness* (Thin, 2012)	Anticipation (hope, ambition, expectations) Experience (good feelings) Interpretation (appreciation, meaning) Outcomes (pride in achievement, unplanned successes) Unpleasantness (e.g. disappointment, boredom, trauma)

* For an in-depth exploration as to why 'happiness' is a preferable term to 'well-being' see Thin (2012, pp. 32–43).

because it appears that there is little consensus about well-being which may undermine its significance as a theoretical concept; the lack of a single unifying theory has been a criticism of the area (Ryff, 1989; Brown et al., in press). The extent to which these models of well-being correspond with lay conceptions of well-being is an empirical question that Hone, Jarden, Schofield, and Duncan (2014) state should and could be answered. Conversely, the variety of approaches may reflect the diverse and equally meaningful ways to conceive well-being and offer a rich range of options for those wishing to engage with the topic linked to particular interests. For example, of note, only one of the models acknowledges the role of physical activity in well-being (Five Ways to Well-being, NEF, 2008), a model which has been widely adopted by health organisations throughout the UK.

In the following section we discuss two of these integrated models, before considering an integrated model proposed specifically for sport and physical activity. Seligman (2011) revised his earlier theory of authentic happiness, in the form of the PERMA model, adding to the original three dimensions of positive emotions (P), engagement (E) and meaning (M) (2003) two new dimensions of relationships (R) and accomplishment (A), both of which are highly relevant in sport and exercise settings. According to Seligman, these five components, which are 'the best approximation of what humans pursue for their own sake' (2011, p. 97), together define well-being. Though few studies have empirically examined PERMA, Kern, Waters, Adler, and White (2015) tested the PERMA model as an organizing framework for measuring adolescent student well-being. They found strong support for all but one of the five dimensions (meaning), and concluded that future research should further elicit how meaning evolves over adolescence. Analyses showed that the distinct dimensions of PERMA correlated differently with key concepts such as life satisfaction, hope, gratitude, school engagement, growth mindset, physical vitality and physical activity which supported a multidimensional approach to understanding adolescent well-being. Kern and colleagues (Kern, Benson, Steinberg, & Steinberg, 2016) subsequently presented the EPOCH (engagement, perseverance, optimism, connectedness, and happiness) measure of adolescent well-being as a multidimensional measure of well-being for use in educational settings, proposing that assessing student well-being across multiple domains provides schools with the opportunity to more systematically understand and promote well-being.

Huppert and So's (2013) model of flourishing reflects the finding that well-being is not merely the absence of ill-being, but its opposite. Initially listing all the symptoms of common mental disorders such as anxiety and depression in the *Diagnostic and Statistical Manual of Mental Disorders* (American Psychiatric Association, 1994) and the *International Classification of Diseases* (World Health Organization, 1992), the researchers then defined their opposites. The model of flourishing draws upon hedonic and eudaimonic dimensions of well-being and proposes 10 components, including: positive emotions, engagement, positive relationships, meaning, competence, emotional stability, vitality, optimism, resilience and self-esteem.

Using data from 43,000 European Social Survey participants, Huppert and So (ibid) found that even when countries had similar life satisfaction scores overall, they showed remarkable differences in their national profiles. This suggests that policy-makers wishing to increase well-being need to be aware of and attend to the features that are specific to their different demographic (or national) groups.

There is scope to consider using some or all of the concepts from Huppert and So's model of flourishing in sport and physical activity. Qualitative research examining flourishing among athletes found that it is viewed as an individualised notion of optimal well-being (Ashfield, McKenna, & Backhouse, 2012). Practitioners in sport- and physical activity–allied professions have only recently begun to consider what optimal well-being may look like, and to better support participants there is a need to develop insight and advance theory in this area.

With this in mind an integrated model of well-being has been designed specifically for sport and physical activity by Lundqvist (2011) which represents a significant conceptual development (Figure 2.3). The model includes components of subjective and eudaimonic well-being and, as well as the global account taken from existing generic models of well-being, it also presents a sport-contextualized

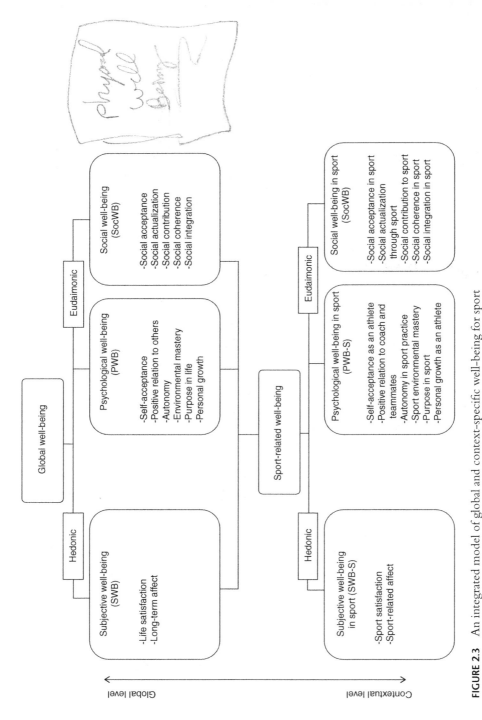

FIGURE 2.3 An integrated model of global and context-specific well-being for sport

Source: Lundqvist (2011), used with permission

version of each well-being component. Lundqvist's (2011) sport-specific domains of well-being are direct translations of SWB, PWB and SocWB as noted here:

- subjective well-being in sport (SWB-S) refers to *sport-related affect and sport satisfaction);*
- psychological well-being in sport (PWB-S) *refers to positive relationships with coach and teammates, self-acceptance as an athlete, sport environmental mastery, purpose in sport, autonomy in sport practice, and personal growth as an athlete;*
- social well-being in sport (SocWB-S) *refers to social acceptance in sport, social contribution to sport, social coherence in sport, social integration in sport and social actualization through sport.*

● physical well-being in sport

This is an important development for facilitating understanding and supporting engagement with well-being in sport and exercise psychology; following developments in other areas of psychology (e.g. employee well-being, Page & Vella Brodrick, 2009), it invites us to make connections between what might otherwise be separate components of well-being and different levels of well-being (global and situation-specific). Importantly, Lundqvist suggests that qualitative accounts should be pursued in athlete well-being to add to the depth of understanding and also to inform the design of specific measures of athlete well-being. Lundqvist and Sandin (2014) used the model to explore elite orienteers' experiences of well-being. Key findings emphasised the interactive effects among the different types of well-being, and the need to acknowledge the holistic view of both sport and non–sport–related factors influencing well-being. Additionally they found that global well-being was seen as underpinning sport-related well-being and also as a protective factor when facing setback setbacks in sport (Lundqvist & Sandin, 2014). MacDougall, O'Halloran, Sherry, and Shields (2016) extended Lundqvist's (2011) model of well-being in sport by adding a physical well-being dimension at both the global and sport-specific levels. Future research in sport may not only provide support for this new dimension, but also highlight other salient dimensions according to the particular setting (e.g. prisons, academies, schools, exercise referral class) and population (e.g. youth, officials, injured, health-related groups, support staff, volunteers).

References

Adie, J. W., & Bartholomew, K. J. (2010). The well- and ill-being of participants in competitive sport settings: A review of motivational determinants. In C. Mohiyeddini (Ed.), *Advances in the Psychology of Sports and Exercise* (pp. 109–140). Hauppauge, NY: Nova Science Publishers.

Adie, J. W., Duda, J. L., & Ntoumanis, N. (2012). Perceived coach-autonomy support, basic need satisfaction and the well- and ill-being of elite youth soccer players: A longitudinal investigation. *Psychology of Sport and Exercise*, 13(1), 51–59.

American Psychiatric Association (1994). *Diagnostic and Statistical Manual of Mental Disorders, 4th Edn. Revised. DSM-IV.* Washington, DC: American Psychiatric Association.

Amorose, A. J., Anderson-Butcher, D., & Cooper, J. (2009). Predicting changes in athletes' well being from changes in need satisfaction over the course of a competitive season. *Research Quarterly for Exercise and Sport*, 80, 386–392.

Ashfield, A., McKenna, J., & Backhouse, S. (2012). The athlete's experience of flourishing. *QMIP Bulletin*, 14, 4–13.

Brady, A. (2016). Athlete well-being: A case study. In S. Cotterill, N. Weston, & G. Breslin (Eds.), *Sport and Exercise Psychology: Practitioner Case Studies* (pp. 315–331). Oxford: Wiley-Blackwell.

Brown, N. J. L., Lomas, T., & Eiroa-Orosa, F. J. (Eds.). (in press). *The Routledge International Handbook of Critical Positive Psychology*. London: Routledge.

Caddick, N., & Smith, B. (2014). The impact of sport and physical activity on the well-being of combat veterans: A systematic review. *Psychology of Sport and Exercise*, 15(1), 9–18.

Cohn, M. A., Fredrickson, B. L., Brown, S. L., Mikels, J. A., & Conway, A. M. (2009). Happiness unpacked: Positive emotions increase life satisfaction by building resilience. *Emotion* (Washington, DC), 9(3), 361–368. doi:10.1037/a0015952.

Cummins, R. A. (1996). The domains of life satisfaction: An attempt to order chaos. *Social Indicators Research*, 38(3), 303–328.

Davidson, R. J., & Schuyler, B. S. (2015). Neuroscience of happiness. In J. F. Helliwell, R. Layard, & J. Sachs (Eds.), *World Happiness Report 2015* (pp. 88–105). New York: Sustainable Development Solutions Network.

Diener, E., Emmons, R., Larsen, R., & Griffin, S. (1985). The satisfaction with life scale. *Journal of Personality Assessment*, 49(1), 71–75.

Diener, E., & Suh, E. (1997). Measuring quality of life: Economic, social, and subjective indicators. *Social Indicators Research*, 40(1), 189–216.

Dockray, S., & Steptoe, A. (2010). Positive affect and psychobiological processes. *Neuroscience and Biobehavioral Reviews*, 35, 69–75.

Edwards, S. D., & Edwards, D. J. (2011). A report on psychological well-being and physical self-perception in five sports groups. *African Journal for Physical, Health Education, Recreation and Dance* (AJPHERD), 17(1), 9–21.

Ferguson, L. J., Kowalski, K. C., Mack, D. E., Wilson, P. M., & Crocker, P. R. E. (2012). Women's health-enhancing physical activity and eudaimonic well being. *Research Quarterly for Exercise and Sport*, 83(3), 451–463.

Fredrickson, B. L. (2001). The role of positive emotions in positive psychology The broaden-and-build theory of positive emotions. *American Psychologist*, 56(3), 218–226.

Fredrickson, B. L., & Joiner, T. (2002). Positive emotions trigger upward spirals toward emotional well-being. *Psychological Science*, 13(2), 172–175.

Fredrickson, B. L., & Levenson, R. W. (1998). Positive emotions speed recovery from the cardiovascular sequelae of negative emotions. *Cognition and Emotion*, 12, 191–220.

Hefferon, K., & Boniwell, I. (2011). *Positive Psychology: Theory, Research and Applications*. Maidenhead: Open University Press.

Hone, L. C., Jarden, A., Schofield, G., & Duncan, S. (2014). Measuring flourishing: The impact of operational definitions on the prevalence of high levels of wellbeing. *International Journal of Wellbeing*, 4(1), 62–90.

Huppert, F. A., Baylis, N., & Keverne, E. B. (2004). Introduction: Why do we need a science of well-being? *Philosophical Transactions of the Royal Society, Biological Sciences*, 259, 1331–1332.

Huppert, F. A., & So, T. T. (2013). Flourishing across Europe: Application of a new conceptual framework for defining well-being. *Social Indicators Research*, 110(3), 837–861.

Isen, A. M. (2001). An influence of positive affect on decision making in complex situations: Theoretical issues with practical implications. *Journal of Consumer Psychology*, 11(2), 75–85.

Jahoda, M. (1958). *Current Concepts of Positive Mental Health*. New York: Basic Books.

Kashdan, T. B., Biswas-Diener, R., & King, L. A. (2008). Reconsidering happiness: The costs of distinguishing between hedonics and eudaimonia. *Journal of Positive Psychology*, 3, 219–233.

Kern, M. L., Benson, L., Steinberg, E., & Steinberg, L. (2016). The EPOCH measure of adolescent well-being. *Psychological Assessment*, 28(5), 586–597.

Kern, M. L., Waters, L. E., Adler, A., & White, M. A. (2015). A multidimensional approach to measuring well-being in students: Application of the PERMA framework. *Journal of Positive Psychology*, 10(3), 262–271.

Keyes, C. L. M. (1998). Social well-being. *Social Psychology Quarterly*, 61(2), 121–140.

Keyes, C. L. M., & Annas, J. (2009). Feeling good and functioning well: Distinctive concepts in ancient philosophy and contemporary science. *The Journal of Positive Psychology*, 4(3), 197–201.

Keyes, C. L. M., & Lopez, S. (2002). Toward a science of mental health: Positive directions in diagnosis and intervention. In C. R. Snyder & S. J. Lopez (Eds.), *Handbook of Positive Psychology* (pp. 45–62). New York: Oxford University Press.

Lundqvist, C. (2011). Well-being in competitive sports – the feel-good factor? A review of conceptual consideration of well-being. *International Review of Sport and Exercise Psychology*, 4, 109–127.

Lundqvist, C., & Sandin, F. (2014). Well-Being in elite sport: Dimensions of hedonic and eudaimonic well-being among elite orienteers. *The Sport Psychologist*, 28, 245–254.

Lyubomirsky, S., King, L., & Diener, E. (2005). The benefits of frequent positive affect: Does happiness lead to success? *Psychological Bulletin*, 131(6), 803–855.

MacDougall, H., O'Halloran, P., Sherry, E., & Shields, N. (2016). Needs and strengths of Australian Para athletes: Identifying the subjective, psychological, social, and physical health and well-being. *The Sport Psychologist*, 30, 1–12.

Mack, D. E., Wilson, P. M., Oster, K. G., Kowalski, K. C., Crocker, P. R. E., & Sylvester, B. D. (2011). Well-being in volleyball players: Examining the contributions of independent 15 and balanced psychological need satisfaction. *Psychology of Sport and Exercise*, 12, 16 533–539. doi:10.1016/j.pscyhsport.2011.05.006.

Miller, K. E., & Hoffman, J. H. (2009). Mental well-being and sport-related identities in college students. *Sociology of Sport Journal*, 26(2), 335–356.

New Economics Foundation (NEF). (2008). *Measuring well-being in policy: Issues and applications*. A paper prepared for the Project and available through www.foresight.gov.uk

Newman, D. B., Tay, L., & Diener, E. (2014). Leisure and subjective well-being: A model of psychological mechanisms as mediating factors. *Journal of Happiness Studies*, 15, 555–578.

Page, K. M., & Vella-Brodrick, D. A. (2009). The 'what', 'why' and 'how' of employee well-being: A new model. *Social Indicators Research*, 90, 441–458.

Ruini, C., & Fava, G. A. (2004). Clinical applications of well-being therapy. In Linley P. A. and Joseph S. (Eds), *Positive psychology in practice* (pp. 371–387). Hoboken, NJ: Wiley.

Ryan, R., & Deci, E. (2001). On happiness and human potentials: A Review of research on hedonic and eudaimonic well-being. *Annual Review of Psychology*, 52, 141–166.

Ryff, C. D. (1989). Happiness is everything, or is it? Explorations on the meaning of psychological well-being. *Journal of Personality and Social Psychology*, 57(6), 1069–1081.

Ryff, C. D., & Keyes, C. L. M. (1995). The structure of psychological well-being revisited. *Journal of Personality and Social Psychology*, 69(7), 19–27.

Ryff, C. D., & Singer, B. (1998). The contours of positive human health. *Psychological Inquiry*, 9, 1–28.

Schalock, R. L., & Verdugo, M. A. (2002). *Handbook on Quality of Life for Human Service Professionals*. Washington, DC: American Association on Mental Retardation.

Seligman, M. E. P. (2003). *Authentic Happiness*. London: Nicholas Brealey Publishing.

Seligman, M. E. P. (2011). *Flourish: A New Understanding of Happiness and Well-Being and How to Achieve Them*. London: Nicholas Brealey Publishing.

Thin, N. (2012). *Social Happiness: Theory into Policy and Practice*. Bristol: Policy Press.

Tugade, M. M., & Fredrickson, B. L. (2004). Resilient individuals use positive emotions to bounce back from negative emotional experiences. *Journal of Personality and Social Psychology*, 86, 320–333.

Waterman, A. S. (1993). Two conceptions of happiness: Contrasts of personal expressiveness (eudaimonia) and hedonic enjoyment. *Journal of Personality and Social Psychology*, 64, 678–691.

Williams, D., Collingwood, L., Coles, J., & Schmeer, S. (2015). Evaluating a rugby sport intervention programme for young offenders. *Journal of Criminal Psychology*, 5(1), 51–64.

Woods, D., Breslin, G., & Hassan, D. (2017). A systematic review of the impact of sport-based interventions on the psychological well-being of people in prison. *Mental Health and Physical Activity*, 12, 50–61.

World Health Organization (WHO). (1992). *ICD-10 Classification of Mental and Behavioural Disorders: Diagnostic Criteria for Research*. Geneva: World Health Organization.

World Health Organization (WHO). (2014). *Basic Documents* (48th ed.). Geneva: World Health Organization.

3

CONTEMPORARY FINDINGS ABOUT THE VALUE OF WELL-BEING AND POSITIVE PSYCHOLOGY IN SPORT AND PHYSICAL ACTIVITY SETTINGS

Abbe Brady and Bridget Grenville-Cleave

This chapter provides an overview of contemporary findings associated with well-being in a range of sport and physical activity domains. The chapter is organized in two sections, the first of which focuses on the value of engagement in physical activity for a range of physical and mental health and well-being–related outcomes. Here we also consider relatively new topics, including green and blue exercise and parasocial relationships. The second section addresses ideas about well-being and performance relationships, with particular reference to competitive achievement domains in sport. We review how the role of well-being in sport performance is evolving in light of contemporary evidence from positive psychology (PP) and sport and exercise psychology (SEP), and we touch on a number of emerging research foci such as athlete well-being, coach well-being and emotional contagion.

Physical activity, health and well-being

Recent epidemiological research shows that the health-protecting effects of well-being are independent from the effects of reducing ill-being (Dockray & Steptoe, 2010). For example, the biological correlates and benefits of positive affect are separate from the systems and symptoms alleviated by the absence of ill-being, which further supports the theoretical distinction between well-being and ill-being (ibid). Davidson and Schuyler (2015) reviewed recent developments in affective and social neuroscience and illustrate how well-being–related research has evolved in four main areas: sustained positive emotion, recovery from negative emotion, pro-social behaviors and generosity, and attentional-affect factors. Whilst related to self-reported well-being (e.g. positive affect and life satisfaction), patterns of brain function associated with both positive emotions and negative emotions are also related to systemic biological measures associated with physical health, which provide new insights about mechanisms linking psychological well-being and physical health (ibid).

The health benefits associated with sport and physical exercise are generally well accepted (Scully, Kremer, Meade, Graham, & Dudgeon,1998; Mutrie & Faulkner, 2004). Arguably the most well-known research concerning the benefits of physical activity quoted by proponents of positive psychology is Babyak et al.'s (2000) study of the impact of a four-month course of SSRI medication and physical exercise on 156 adults diagnosed with major depressive disorder. Participants were randomly assigned to one of three groups: 1) aerobic exercise, 2) medication only or 3) a combination of exercise and medication. Although participants in all three groups exhibited significant improvement after four months, researchers found that after 10 months those in the exercise-only group were more likely to be partially or fully recovered and were less likely to have relapsed compared with participants in the medication-only or medication plus exercise groups. Remarkably, Babyak et al. found that each 50-minute increment in exercise per week was associated with a 50% decrease in the odds of being classified as depressed. They concluded that even a modest program of physical exercise (e.g. three times per week with 30 minutes at 70% of maximum heart rate reserve each time) is an effective treatment for major depression for people who want to participate in physical activity, and that the benefits are likely to last for those people who take up physical exercise on a regular basis.

Regarding the general population, the benefits for physical and mental health and well-being of regularly engaging in sport and physical activity are well documented. In children and young people, for example, research suggests that regular participation reduces physical health issues such as overweight, obesity and type 2 diabetes (Hills, Andersen, & Byrne, 2011; Monasta et al., 2010) as well as alleviating mental health issues such as depression and anxiety (Brown, Pearson, Braithwaite, Brown, & Biddle, 2013; Biddle & Asare, 2011; McMahon et al., 2017; Norris, Carroll, & Cochrane, 1992). Regular participation in sport and physical exercise can also significantly enhance self-esteem and self-concept in children and adolescents (Ahn & Fedewa, 2011; Babic et al., 2014; Liu, Wu, & Ming, 2015). In adults, regular participation in sport and physical activity enhances psychological well-being (Hills & Argyle, 1998), reduces the risks of depression (Babyak et al., 2000) and anxiety (Anderson & Shivakumar, 2015), reduces feelings of distress (Cairney, Faulkner, Veldhuizen, & Wade, 2009) and increases quality of sleep (Reid et al., 2010). With older adults, the benefits of participation include reducing the risks of mortality (Moore et al., 2012), cognitive impairment (Fox, 1999) and dementia (Potter, Ellar, Rees, & Thorogood, 2011).

Physical activity and inactivity

Bouchard and Shephard (1994) describe physical activity as any body movement produced by the skeletal muscles resulting in a substantial increase over resting energy expenditure. Physical activity includes play, walking and cycling, sport and recreational activities, doing household chores and gardening.

Physical inactivity has been described by Bull et al. (2004) as doing no or very little physical activity at work, at home, for transport or during discretionary time, and not reaching physical activity guidelines deemed necessary to benefit health.

TABLE 3.1 National comparisons of the estimated relative risk (as a percentage) for CHD, type 2 diabetes, breast cancer, colon cancer, and all–cause mortality associated with physical inactivity (adapted from Lee, Shiroma, Lobelo, Puskan, Blair & Katzmarzyk, 2012)

	CHD	Type 2 diabetes	Breast cancer	Colon cancer	All–cause mortality
UK	10.5	13.0	17.9	18.7	16.9
Germany	4.6	5.7	7.4	8.3	7.5
India	2.6	3.2	4.8	4.6	4.2
China	5.1	6.4	8.4	9.2	8.3
USA	6.7	8.3	12.4	12.0	10.8

According to WHO (2010), physical inactivity is the fourth-leading cause of global mortality in middle and high income countries, and many of the main causes of ill health and non communicable disease in today's society (e.g. heart disease, cancer and type 2 diabetes) could be prevented if more inactive people were to become active. Requested new Figure be used and will need to replace worldwide and UK with National comparisons of the contribution of physical inactivity to ill health and disease are shown in Table 3.1. The economic burden of physical inactivity on health care is significant and Oldridge (2008) suggests that in developed countries this accounts for between 1.5% and 3% of the total direct costs to health care. Scarborough et al. (2011) argued that the direct cost to the UK's National Health Service (NHS) a decade ago (2006 – 2007) was £0.9bn p.a. Indirect costs (e.g. costs to employers, unemployment or health-related benefits, provision of medical aids) associated with physical inactivity are, of course, much larger. When considered in conjunction with the mental and physical health benefits associated with physical activity outlined previously, the case for change in terms of encouraging higher levels of public participation in all forms of sport and physical activity is not just compelling; in our view it is indisputable.

The Five Ways to Well-being

The New Economics Foundation (NEF), one of the UK's leading think tanks promoting social, economic and environmental justice, was commissioned by the UK Government Office for Science to identify a set of practical, evidence-based strategies to improve well-being, reflecting both hedonic and eudaimonic aspects. To make an appropriate selection of strategies from the broad array on offer in PP literature, NEF identified several key considerations:

1 they must be evidence-based;
2 they must have universal impact;
3 they must be appropriate for the individual (rather than groups or society generally);
4 they must provide variety.

The resultant short list of five is shown in Table 2.3 (p.28). Of particular relevance, because they are largely absent from other accounts of well-being in sport and physical activity settings, are 1) be active and 2) give:

Be active – This does not mean having to participate in organized sport; it could refer to simply walking the dog, walking in nature or gardening. Although the mind-body connection has been formally made in positive psychology (Hefferon, 2013), most models of well-being persist in focusing solely on psychological attributes. The Five Ways to Well-being embraces a holistic approach by including physical, social and psychological domains of well-being, which goes some way toward explaining its popularity in the UK's National Health Service.

Give – Being intrinsically motivated to do good for others increases our well-being not just because we feel good as a result but because giving helps develop social relationships. Giving could be viewed as a route to well-being via well-doing. The evidence for giving, whether through doing random acts of kindness (Lyubomirsky et al., 2005), expressing our gratitude (Emmons & Shelton, 2002) or volunteering (Schwartz & Sendor, 1999), is clear. This is particularly relevant in sport and physical activity environments which rely on the enormous contribution made by individuals and groups who regularly volunteer. In England every month on average 5.6 million people volunteer in sport and physical activity, and the benefits to volunteers' well-being are actively promoted (Sport England, 2016).

Green and blue exercise

Participating in organized sport outdoors (e.g. football, hockey), as well as being active in more informal ways whilst outdoors (e.g. hiking, gardening) are both good for well-being. According to Barton, Bragg, Wood, and Pretty (2016), people who can easily access natural settings, such as parks, gardens and green spaces, are three times more likely to engage in physical activity, suffer less mental distress and enjoy higher well-being. Whilst both physical activity and being outdoors in nature are independently beneficial for well-being, there is growing evidence from the field of 'green exercise' (Pretty, Peacock, Sellens, & Griffin, 2005) to suggest that, when combined, the effects are magnified. Although the opportunities for green activities may be greater, the term 'blue exercise' has been coined to describe the types of physical activity (e.g. wild swimming, sailing and canoeing) which can take place in or near outdoor water such as rivers, lakes and the coast (Depledge & Bird, 2009; White et al., 2016). Evidence suggests that being in green or blue nature has restorative power, reducing stress levels, with the impact of combined blue/green environments being greater than either on its own (White et al., 2010). Whilst accessing blue environments may be more difficult (e.g. health and safety reasons; access to equipment) for teachers, coaches and policy-makers, it makes sense to ensure that sport and physical activity includes a green outdoor element where possible.

Parasocial relationships

Based on the concept of parasocial interaction identified by Horton and Wohl (1956) in relation to mass media users, parasocial relationships refer to the one-sided relationship that some individuals develop with media celebrities such as actors, athletes/teams and TV/radio presenters as well as with fictional characters, such that the individual feels as if the relationship is mutual. Much of the psychology literature to date has focused on the extreme presentation of parasocial relationships ('celebrity worship'), for example, Maltby, McCutcheon, Ashe, and Houran (2001), and the negative impact on well-being, for example, on body image (Maltby, Giles, Barber, & McCutcheon, 2005). There has been some acknowledgement of the desirable effects that can be offered by such relationships, for example, the provision of social support and thus shielding against loneliness (Lakey & Orehek, 2011; Lakey, Cooper, Cronin, & Whitaker, 2014), boosting self-esteem (Derrick, Gabriel, & Tippin, 2008) and psychological health (Wann, 2006). Although celebrity sports people are very often seen as role models, it is intriguing that little research appears to have been carried out in PP on the ways in which parasocial relationships may be used in an intentional manner by athletes and teams for the benefit of their fans' health and well-being. The explosion of mass communication from TV into online platforms has fuelled considerable research and inquiry into the abusive aspects and consequences of technology-mediated relationships (e.g. cyber-bullying and trolling). The absence of inquiry about the potential benefits of such mediated relationships provides fertile ground for PP research.

Sport performance and well-being

A key development in well-being research with considerable implications for understanding the relationship between sport performance and well-being is that well-being contributes to performance success and is not merely an outcome of successful performance, that is, there is a two-way relationship between well-being and success. Growing evidence from a wide range of disciplines and contexts (e.g. neuroscience, education, health, work settings and many sub-disciplines of psychology) has illuminated a range of ways that well-being is directly or indirectly related to performance success (Davidson & Schuyler, 2015; Fredrickson, 2001; Isen, 2001; Lyubomirsky et al., 2005). Findings provide compelling evidence that positive affect fosters a range of desirable behaviors, skills and resources linked with success, including: sociability and activity, altruism, liking of self and others, strong bodies and immune systems, and effective conflict resolution skills (ibid). Lyubomirsky et al. (2005) conclude that physical activity may be the critical mediator in the relationship between well-being and culturally valued success.

According to Jacobs Bao and Lyubomirsky (2013), the mechanism underlying well-being and performance relationships is positive emotion. As described in Chapter 2, Fredrickson's (2001) broaden-and-build theory suggests that experiencing frequent positive emotions develops people's 'thought–action repertoires' (e.g. they think and behave in new ways), with the result that they develop additional psychological, physical, social and intellectual resources which generate qualities and behaviors associated with success. For example, positive emotions are associated with supporting creativity, adaptivity and resilience when facing setbacks (Fredrickson, 2001).

Research findings about the role of positive emotions in performance have made a particularly significant contribution, and they are all the more notable because they have until recently received relatively little empirical attention in sport and physical activity. As scholars have noted, where emotions have received attention in sport and exercise psychology the focus has been mainly on negatively valenced emotions such as anxiety and its effects on performance (Jackson, 2000; McCarthy, 2011; Woodman et al., 2009).

It is important to qualify that research is not stating that high positively valenced emotions and low negatively valenced emotions are always necessary for performance success. There are situations in the midst of particular types of performance when positive affect (or negative affect) or awareness of an emotional state will not be ideal or appropriate, and may impair processes that support performance. For example, in accounts of experiences of flow states which are linked to optimal experience and optimal performance, performers describe being totally absorbed in the activity in the present rather than being aware of particular emotions (Csikszentmihalyi, 1990; Seifert & Hedderson, 2010).

Although positive emotions and experiences such as enjoyment, excitement, fun and flow are often associated with peak experiences in sport and physical activity, they remain dwarfed by output in anxiety and stress (Brady, 2009; Jackson, 2000). Compared with our understanding of relationships between anxiety and performance, we have comparatively little empirical knowledge about the direct or indirect relationships between positive emotions and sports performance. This is an area ripe for exploration particularly because increasing insight supports the positive and causal relationship between positive emotions and psychological constructs and successful development and performance achievement in sport and physical activity.

In his review of positive emotions and sports performance, McCarthy (2011) identified two theories in SEP which may contribute toward an understanding of the role of positive emotion in sport performance; these are Individual Zones of Optimal Functioning (IZOF) (Hanin, 1997) and the Theory of Challenge and Threat States in Athletes (TCTSA) (Jones, Meijen, McCarthy, & Sheffield, 2009). Through IZOF Hanin (1997) acknowledged the multidimensionality of emotions and the potential for positive and negative emotions to have both desirable and undesirable influences on performance. In his text entitled 'Emotions in sport', Hanin (1997, 2000) was one of a handful of early advocates calling for the need to acknowledge the role of positively and negatively valenced emotions. Hanin proposed that IZOF could be used for several performance-related reasons: to monitor emotions generating personal profiles of optimal/dysfunctional performance; to gain insights about emotional profiles relating to injury prediction; and to identify the optimal training and recovery loads and the threat of overtraining or burnout. Hanin (2000) also called for the need to understand the interplay of emotions and performance-related processes to move away from existing uni-dimensional analyses of pre-performance states and crude performance outcomes; this remains a challenge for researchers.

Through developments aligned with PP and other disciplines, increasing evidence exists to show positive emotions and well-being are likely to play a much more significant role in successful sports performance than previously recognized. Whilst necessary for performance in sport, it might not be as obvious to see the impact of positive emotions because they may manifest themselves indirectly rather than directly (McCarthy, 2011) and compared with negative emotions, we have not yet developed the tools or models required to aid sport- and physical activity–specific inquiry. As McCarthy (2011, p. 63) concluded, 'positive emotions might be the catalysts of excellence in sport and deserve space on our workbenches if we are to raise the level of competitive performance among sport performers'.

Emotional contagion in sport

An additional perspective on the influence of positive emotions on performance is the finding that our emotions are influenced by those around us and may even be contagious. Totterdell (2000) examined collective mood in cricketers and found significant associations between collective and individual happy moods and subjective performances. Mood linkage was particularly prevalent for positive emotions, in collective activities and also among older players and those highly committed to the team. Ilies, Wagner, and Morgeson (2007) expanded on Totterdell's research and found that affective states among team members were related (even after controlling for team performance), and individual differences in susceptibility to emotional contagion and collectivistic tendencies moderated the relationship. An examination of well-being and ill-being contagion among coach and athlete dyads showed that there was evidence of contagion from authority figures to those under their instruction but not vice versa (Stebbings, Taylor & Spray, 2016). As well as human-human emotional contagion, human-animal contagion effects exist; one such study demonstrated how the heart rates of horses responded to emotion induction and heart rate changes of those leading or riding them (Keeling, Jonare, & Lanneborn, 2009).

Athlete well-being

In a review of research examining athlete well-being, Lundqvist (2011) found most studies adopted a quantitative perspective, often lacked a definition or strong theoretical framework for well-being and findings provided only general insights into well-being. Lundqvist found a diverse range of constructs were used to represent well-being (or the absence of ill-being), for example, symptoms of depression, burnout, emotional/physical exhaustion, stability of self-concept, subjective vitality, self-esteem, positive and negative affect, life satisfaction, intrinsic interest in sport and sport satisfaction. As a result of the review, Lundqvist (ibid) proposed an integrated and more holistic model of well-being to guide future inquiry in the sport domain which includes social, subjective and psychological well-being at a global and a context-specific level (see Chapter 2 for details). Gaining an insight to personal accounts of context-related well-being in different sport and physical activity settings may illuminate distinct and shared aspects of well-being which may, in turn, serve to provide not only greater understanding about well-being and its dynamics in the specific setting (including relationships with health and performance), but also findings may be used to inform future practices within that context.

In high-performance sport settings, attempting to achieve success may encourage conforming to particular cultural practices which may paradoxically compromise well-being and induce ill-being (Beamish & Ritchie, 2006; Miller & Kerr, 2002; Theberge, 2008) such as practices to make weight, training or competing when injured or ill and exclusive investment in an athletic identity. In a large population of elite youth athletes, those who attached far greater importance to their role as an athlete than their aims in life beyond sport were much more likely to take health risks (Schnell, Mayer, Diehl, Zipfel, & Theil, 2014). Hence, a particular challenge facing many elite athletes within a demanding performance-focused environment is the need to protect and stimulate their well-being (Lundqvist & Sandin, 2014). Using the integrated model of well-being, global well-being was proposed by elite orienteers to underpin sport-specific well-being and also confer a protective factor when facing obstacles in sport (ibid). This finding supports the value of adopting a holistic view of athlete well-being by understanding how life outside of sport may also influence the relationship between well-being and performance in sport.

Although sport and physical activity is promoted as beneficial for health, experiencing injury is a risk associated with participation. Injuries may be associated with considerable stress and discomfort and in serious cases, they may impose long-term or permanent effects. In a study of injury risk in female youth soccer players, Watson, Brickson, Brooks, and Dunn (2017) found that in-season injury was predicted independently by decreased affective well-being and higher acute training load and also, acute training load had an immediate and negative impact on well-being. Watson et al. (ibid) recommended that monitoring well-being and training load may inform interventions to promote athlete health. In relation to injury, rehabilitation and recovery evidence showed that low levels of negative affect and rehabilitation adherence was positively related to returning to play (Ivarsson, Tranaeus, Johnson, & Stenling, 2017). Lu and Hsu (2013) found that injured athletes' level of hopeful belief about rehabilitation and social support predicted their subjective well-being. Compared with injured athletes high in hope, those with low hope perceived social support was associated with higher subjective well-being (ibid).

Responding to the need to supplement the monitoring of athlete training responses with monitoring positive emotions as well as negative emotions, Lundqvist and Kentta (2010) developed the Emotional Recovery Questionnaire (EmRecQ). As well as monitoring training loads and recovery, positive emotions and other indices of well-being could be monitored during rehabilitation from injury because, as Lundqvist and Kentta (ibid) remark about training, it may be problematic to rely on the absence of negative emotions since positive emotions serve different functions during the recovery process.

Coach well-being

Stebbings et al. (2016) found that coaches' pre-session well- and ill-being influenced their coaching interpersonal style (autonomy supportive or controlling) which affected athletes' well-being. Also, coaches' perceptions of their own interpersonal style during the session were associated with their own post-session well- and ill-being. An adaptive autonomy supportive coaching style, characterized by fostering volition, explanations about the purpose of tasks, involvement in decision-making and acknowledgement of feelings, was positively related to the coaches' and athletes' well-being. A controlling environment characterized by coercive, punitive and critical leader behaviors, is associated with reduced well-being, depression, low self-esteem and burnout in longitudinal research (ibid). Controlling and autonomy-supportive interpersonal behaviors of coaches were predicted by different correlates of well- and ill-being, respectively (Stebbings, Taylor, & Spray, 2015). Job security, opportunities for professional development and lower work–life conflict were associated with autonomy supportive and psychological need satisfaction and, in turn, psychological well-being (Stebbings, Taylor, Spray, & Ntoumanis, 2012). By contrast, higher work – life conflict and fewer opportunities for development were linked to a maladaptive process of thwarted psychological needs, psychological ill-being and controlling behaviors.

Coaching is recognized as being very demanding, and over the course of a season coach burnout increased and coach well-being decreased. Bentzen, Lemyre, and Kenttä (2016) proposed this outcome was triggered by a change in perceived environment which reduced autonomous motivation. In recognition of the high stress associated with multiple sources of performance-related demands, Longshore and Sachs (2015) examined the effect of daily mindfulness training over six weeks on coaches and found that trained coaches reported less anxiety and greater emotional stability along with benefits for their coaching, athletes and the coaches' personal lives.

When one reviews our understanding of well-being in sport and physical activity, what is clear is that there remains much to do if we are to develop an evidence base and harness the consequences of well-being found in other disciplines and domains of practice. This prospect is exciting and heralds the potential for many new insights.

References

Ahn, S., & Fedewa, A. L. (2011). A meta-analysis of the relationship between children's physical activity and mental health. *Journal of Pediatric Psychology*, 36(4), 385–397.

Anderson, E., & Shivakumar, G. (2015). Effects of exercise and physical activity on anxiety. In F. B. Schuch, N. Rocha, & E. L. Cadore (Eds.). *Progress in physical activity and exercise and affective and anxiety disorders: Translational studies, perspectives and future directions* (pp. 46–49). Frontiers in Psychiatry Frontiers Media, SA (online). doi: 10.3389/978-2-88919-471-1.

Babic, M. J., Morgan, P. J., Plotnikoff, R. C., Lonsdale, C., White, R. L., & Lubans, D. R. (2014). Physical activity and physical self-concept in youth: Systematic review and meta-analysis. *Sports Medicine*, 44(11), 1589–1601.

Babyak, M., Blumenthal, J. A., Herman, S., Khatri, P., Doraiswamy, M., Moore, K., Craighead, W.E, Baldewicz, T.T, & Krishnan, K. R. (2000). Exercise treatment for major depression: Maintenance of therapeutic benefit at 10 months. *Psychosomatic Medicine*, 62(5), 633–638.

Barton, J., Bragg., R., Wood, C., & Pretty, J. (Eds.). (2016). *Green Exercise: Linking Nature, Health and Well-Being*. Oxford: Routledge.

Beamish, R. & Ritchie, I. (2006). *Fastest, Highest, Strongest: A Critique of High Performance Sport.* Abingdon, Oxon: Routledge.

Bentzen, M., Lemyre, P-N., & Kenttä, G. (2016). Changes in motivation and burnout indices in high-performance coaches over the course of a competitive season. *Journal of Applied Sport Psychology*, 28(1), 28–48. doi:10.1080/10413200.2015.1053160.

Biddle, S. J., & Asare, M. (2011). Physical activity and mental health in children and adolescents: A review of reviews. *British Journal of Sports Medicine*, 45(11), 886–895.

Bouchard, C., & Shephard, R. J. (1994). Physical activity, fitness, and health: The model and key concepts. In C. Bouchard, R. J. Shephard, & T. Stephens (Eds.), *Physical Activity, Fitness and Health: International Proceedings and Consensus Statement* (pp. 77–88). Champaign, IL: Human Kinetics.

Brady, A. (2009). *Research publication trends associated with deficit and abundance concepts in sport psychology*. Oral presentation as part of the symposium 'Enriching sport psychology: Engaging with positive psychology' presented by A. Brady, A. Ashfield, J. Allan, J. McKenna, & E. Duncan. *BASES Annual Conference*. Leeds Metropolitan University, Leeds, September.

Brown, H. E., Pearson, N., Braithwaite, R. E., Brown, W. J., & Biddle, S. J. (2013). Physical activity interventions and depression in children and adolescents. *Sports Medicine*, 43(3), 195–206.

Bull, F. C., Armstrong, T. P., Dixon, T., Ham, S., Neiman, A., & Pratt, M. (2004). Physical inactivity. In M. Ezzati, A. D. Lopez, A. Rodgers, & C. J. L. Murray (Eds.), *Comparative Quantification of Health Risks: Global and Regional Burden of Disease Attributable to Selected Major Risk Factors* (Vol. 1, pp. 729–881). Switzerland: WHO Press.

Cairney, J., Faulkner, G., Veldhuizen, S., & Wade, T. J. (2009). Changes over time in physical activity and psychological distress among older adults. *The Canadian Journal of Psychiatry*, 54(3), 160–169.

Csikszentmihalyi, M. (1990). *Flow: The Psychology of Optimal Performance*. New York: Cambridge University Press.

Davidson, R. J., & Schuyler, B. S. (2015). Neuroscience of happiness. In J. F. Helliwell, R. Layard, & J. Sachs (Eds.), *World Happiness Report 2015* (pp. 88–105). New York: Sustainable Development Solutions Network.

Depledge, M. H., & Bird, W. J. (2009). The Blue Gym: Health and wellbeing from our coasts. *Marine Pollution Bulletin*, 58(7), 947–948.

Derrick, J. L., Gabriel, S., & Tippin, B. (2008). Parasocial relationships and self-discrepancies: Faux relationships have benefits for low self-esteem individuals. *Personal Relationships*, 15(2), 261–280.

Dockray, S. & Steptoe, A. (2010). Positive affect and psychobiological processes. *Neuroscience and Biobehavioral Reviews*, 35, 69–75. Doi:10.1016/j.neubiorev.2010.01.006.

Emmons, R. A., & Shelton, C. M. (2002). Gratitude and the science of positive psychology. *Handbook of Positive Psychology*, 18, 459–471.

Fox, K. R. (1999). The influence of physical activity on mental well-being. *Public Health Nutrition*, 2(3a), 411–418.

Fredrickson, B. L. (2001). The role of positive emotions in positive psychology: The broaden-and-build theory of positive emotions. *American Psychologist*, 56(3), 218–226.

Hanin, Y.L. (1997). Emotions and athletic performance: Individual zones of optimal functioning model. *European Yearbook of Sport Psychology*, 1, 29–72.

Hanin, Y. L. (Ed.), (2000). *Emotions in sport*. Champaign: lL; Human Kinetics.

Hefferon, K. (2013). *Positive Psychology and the Body: The Somatopsychic Side to Flourishing.* Maidenhead, UK: McGraw-Hill Education.

Hills, A. P., Andersen, L. B., & Byrne, N. M. (2011). Physical activity and obesity in children. *British Journal of Sports Medicine*, 45(11), 866–870.

Hills, P., & Argyle, M. (1998). Positive moods derived from leisure and their relationship to happiness and personality. *Personality and Individual Differences*, 25(3), 523–535.

Horton, D., & Wohl, R. (1956). Mass communication and para-social interaction: Observations on intimacy at a distance. *Psychiatry*, 19(3), 215–229.

Ilies, R., Wagner, D. T., & Morgeson, F. P. (2007). Explaining affective linkages in teams: Individual differences in susceptibility to contagion and individualism-collectivism. *Journal of Applied Psychology*, 92(4), 1140–1148. doi:10.1037/0021-9010.92.4.1140.

Isen, A. M. (2001). An influence of positive affect on decision making in complex situations: Theoretical issues with practical implications. *Journal of Consumer Psychology* 11(2), 75–85.

Ivarsson, A., Tranaeus, U., Johnson, U., & Stenling, A. (2017). Negative psychological responses of injury and rehabilitation adherence effects on return to play in competitive athletes: A systematic review and meta-analysis. *Open Access Journal of Sports Medicine*, 9, 8:27–32. doi:10.2147/OAJSM.S112688.

Jackson, S. A. (2000). Joy, fun and flow state in sport. In Y. L. Hanin (Ed.), *Emotions in Sport* (pp. 135–155). Champaign, IL: Human Kinetics.

Jacobs Bao, K., & Lyubomirsky, S. (2013). Making it last: Combating adaptation in romantic relationships. *Journal of Positive Psychology*, 8, 196–206.

Jones, M., Meijen, C., McCarthy, P. J., & Sheffield, D. (2009). A theory of challenge and threat states in athletes. *International Review of Sport and Exercise Psychology*, 2, 161–180.

Keeling, L. J., Jonare, L., & Lanneborn, L. (2009). Investigating horse – human interactions: The effect of a nervous human. *The Veterinary Journal*, 181, 70–71.

Lakey, B., Cooper, C., Cronin, A., & Whitaker, T. (2014). Symbolic providers help people regulate affect relationally: Implications for perceived support. *Personal Relationships*, 21(3), 404–419.

Lakey, B., & Orehek, E. (2011). Relational regulation theory: A new approach to explain the link between perceived social support and mental health. *Psychological Review*, 118(3), 482.

Lee, I., Shiroma, E. J., Lobelo, F., Puska, P., Blair, S. N., & Katzmarzyk, P. T. (2012). Impact of physical inactivity on the world's major non-communicable diseases: an analysis of burden of disease and life expectancy. *Lancet*, 380, 219–229.

Lu, F. J. H. & Hsu, Y. (2013). Injured athletes' rehabilitation beliefs and subjective well-being: The contribution of hope and social support. *Journal of Athletic Training*, 48(1), 92–98. doi: 10.4085/1062-6050-48.1.03.

Liu, M., Wu, L., & Ming, Q. (2015). How does physical activity intervention improve self-esteem and self-concept in children and adolescents? Evidence from a meta-analysis. *PLOS ONE*, 10(8), e0134804.

Longshore, K., & Sachs, M. (2015). Mindfulness training for coaches: A mixed-method exploratory study. *Journal of Clinical Sport Psychology*, 9(2), 116–137.

Lundqvist, C. (2011). Well-being in competitive sports- the feel-good factor? A review of conceptual considerations of well-being. *International Review of Sport and Exercise Psychology*, 4(2), 109–127.

Lundqvist, C., & Kentta, G. (2010). Positive emotions are not simply the absence of the negative ones: Development and validation of the Emotional Recovery Questionnaire (EmRecQ). *The Sport Psychologist*, 24(4), 468–488.

Lundqvist, C., & Sandin, F. (2014). Well-being in elite sport: Dimensions of hedonic and eudaimonic well-being among elite orienteers. *The Sport Psychologist*, 28(3), 245–254.

Lyubomirsky, S., King, L., & Diener, E. (2005). The benefits of frequent positive affect: Does happiness lead to success? *Psychological Bulletin*, 131(6), 803–855.

Maltby, J., Giles, D. C., Barber, L., & McCutcheon, L. E. (2005). Intense-personal celebrity worship and body image: Evidence of a link among female adolescents. *British Journal of Health Psychology*, 10(1), 17–32.

Maltby, J., McCutcheon, L. E., Ashe, D. D., & Houran, J. (2001). The self-reported psychological well-being of celebrity worshippers. *North American Journal of Psychology*, 3(3), 441–451.

McCarthy, P. J. (2011). Positive emotion in sport performance: Current status and future directions. *International Review of Sport and Exercise Psychology*, 4(1), 50–69[1].

McMahon, E. M., Corcoran, P., O'Regan, G., Keeley, H., Cannon, M., Carli, V., . . . Balazs, J. (2017). Physical activity in European adolescents and associations with anxiety, depression and well-being. *European Child & Adolescent Psychiatry*, 26(1), 111–122.

Miller, P. S., & Kerr, G. (2002). Conceptualising excellence: Past, present and future. *Journal of Applied Sport Psychology*, 14, 140–153.

Monasta, L., Batty, G. D., Cattaneo, A., Lutje, V., Ronfani, L., van Lenthe, F. J., et al. (2010). Early-life determinants of overweight and obesity: A review of systematic reviews. *Obesity Reviews*, 11(10), 695–708.

Moore, S. C., Patel, A. V., Matthews, C. E., Berrington de Gonzalez, A., Park, Y., Katki, H. A., et al. (2012). Leisure time physical activity of moderate to vigorous intensity and mortality: A large pooled cohort analysis. *PLOS Medicine*, 9(11), e1001335.

Mutrie, N. & Faulkner, G. (2004). Physical activity: positive psychology in motion. In P. A. Linley & S. Joseph (Eds.), *Positive Psychology in Practice* (pp.146–164). New Jersey: John Wiley And Sons.

Norris, R., Carroll, D., & Cochrane, R. (1992). The effects of physical activity and exercise training on psychological stress and well-being in an adolescent population. *Journal of Psychosomatic Research*, 36(1), 55–65.

Oldridge, N. B. (2008). Economic burden of physical inactivity: Healthcare costs associated with cardiovascular disease. *European Journal of Preventive Cardiology*, 15(2), 130–139.

Potter, R., Ellard, D., Rees, K. & Thorogoog, M. (2011). A systematic review of the effects of physical activity on physical functioning, quality of life and depression in older people with dementia. *International Journal of Geriatric Psychiatry*, 26(10), 1000–1011. doi: 10.1002/gps.2641.

Pretty, J., Peacock, J., Sellens, M., & Griffin, M. (2005). The mental and physical health outcomes of green exercise. *International Journal of Environmental Health Research*, 15(5), 319–337.

Reid, K. J., Baron, K. G., Lu, B., Naylor, E., Wolfe, L., & Zee, P. C. (2010). Aerobic exercise improves self-reported sleep and quality of life in older adults with insomnia. *Sleep Medicine*, 11(9), 934–940.

Scarborough, P., Bhatnagar, P., Wickramasinghe, K. K., Allender, S., Foster, C., & Rayner, M. (2011). The economic burden of ill health due to diet, physical inactivity, smoking, alcohol and obesity in the UK: An update to 2006–2007 NHS costs. *Journal of Public Health*, 33(4), 527–535.

Schnell, A., Mayer, J., Diehl, K., Zipfel, S., & Thiel, A. (2014). Giving everything for athletic success! Sports-specific risk acceptance of elite adolescent athletes. *Psychology of Sport and Exercise*, 15, 165–172. doi:10.1016/j.psychsport.2013.10.012.

Schwartz, C. E., & Sendor, R. M. (1999). Helping others helps oneself: Response shift effects in peer support. *Social Science & Medicine*, 48(11), 1563–1575.

Scully, D., Kremer, J., Meade, M. M., Graham, R., & Dudgeon, K. (1998). Physical exercise and psychological well being: A critical review. *British Journal of Sports Medicine*, 32(2), 111–120.

Seifert, T., & Hedderson, C. (2010). Intrinsic motivation and flow in skateboarding: An ethnographic study. *Journal of Happiness Studies*, 11, 277–292. doi:10.1007/s10902-009-9140-y.

Sport England. (2016). *Volunteering in an Active Nation: Strategy 2017–2021*. London: Sport England. Retrieved February 20, 2017, from www.sportengland.org/media/11323/volunteering-in-an-active-nation-final.pdf.

Stebbings, J, Taylor, I. M., & Spray, C. M. (2015). The relationship between psychological well- and ill-being, and perceived autonomy supportive and controlling interpersonal styles: A longitudinal study of sport coaches. *Psychology of Sport and Exercise*, 19, 42–19.

Stebbings, J., Taylor, I. M., & Spray, C. M. (2016). Interpersonal mechanisms explaining the transfer of well- and ill-being in coach-athlete dyads. *Journal of Sport and Exercise Psychology*, 38(3), 292–304.

Stebbings, J., Taylor, I. M., Spray, C. M., & Ntoumanis, N. (2012). Antecedents of perceived coach interpersonal behaviors: The coaching environment and coach psychological well- and ill-being. *Journal of Sports and Exercise Psychology*, 34, 481–502. doi:10.1123/jsep.34.4.481.

Theberge, N. (2008). "Just a normal part of what I do": Elite athletes accounts of the relationship between health and sport. *Sociology of Sport Journal*, 25, 206–222.

Totterdell, P. (2000). Catching moods and hitting runs: Mood linkage and subjective performance in professional sport teams. *Journal of Applied Psychology*, 85, 848–859.

Wann, D. L. (2006). Understanding the positive social psychological benefits of sport team identification: The team identification-social psychological health model. *Group Dynamics: Theory, Research, and Practice*, 10(4), 272.

Watson, A., Brickson, S., Brooks, A., & Dunn, W. (2017). Subjective well-being and training load predict in-season injury and illness risk in female youth soccer players. *British Journal of Sports Medicine*, 51, 194–199.

White, M. P., Bell, S., Elliott, L. R., Jenkin, R., Wheeler, B. W., & Depledge, M. H. (2016). The health benefits of blue exercise in the UK. In J. Barton, R. Bragg, C. Wood, & J. Pretty (Eds.), *Green Exercise: Linking Nature, Health & Well-Being* (pp. 69–78). Oxford: Routledge.

White, M. P., Smith, A., Humphryes, K., Pahl, S., Snelling, D., & Depledge, M. (2010). Blue space: The importance of water for preference, affect, and restorativeness ratings of natural and built scenes. *Journal of Environmental Psychology*, 30, 482–493.

Woodman, T., Davis, P. A., Hardy, L., Callow, N., Glasscock, I., & Yuill-Proctor, J, (2009). Emotions and sport performance: An exploration of happiness, hope, and anger. *Journal of Sport & Exercise Psychology*, 31, 169–188.

World Health Organization. (2010). *Global Recommendations on Physical Activity for Health*. Geneva, Switzerland: WHO Press.

PART 2

Key topics in positive psychology and their value in sport and physical activity

4

POSITIVE PSYCHOLOGY MEETS EDUCATION IN THE CONTEXT OF PASSION FOR SPORTS

Implications for sports-study programs

Tanya Chichekian and Robert J. Vallerand

Positive psychology (PP) refers to the scientific study (and scientifically informed applications) of the factors that allow individuals, organizations, and communities to thrive (IPPA website, 2016; Jarden, 2012) and feel like life is worth living for (Vallerand, 2008). Over the past decade, much research has shown that passion represents an important factor to consider within the PP perspective. Indeed, being passionate for an enjoyable and meaningful activity has been found to affect people's lives in a positive and significant way. Evidence also reveals that a significant percentage of people are passionate for sport and exercise (Vallerand et al., 2003, Study 1), implying that passion also matters for a positive psychology of sport and exercise. Further, a large portion of those individuals who engage in sport do so within the framework of sports-study programs. Thus, a better understanding of the passion concept should also have important implications for this population.

In light of the foregoing, the goal of this chapter is to show how passion matters for a positive psychology of sport and exercise and to derive implications for individuals involved in sports-study programs. We first present the passion concept and introduce the main theoretical passion framework – the Dualistic Model of Passion (Vallerand, 2008, 2010, 2015). Second, we briefly review empirical evidence on the role of passion in a number of outcomes typically studied in PP (e.g., positive emotions, flow, psychological well-being, relationships, and expert performance). We then show that several studies on passion have been conducted in sport and exercise psychology. Finally, we conclude by underscoring crucial implications for sports-study programs, including suggestions of avenues for future research.

The concept of passion

Most people who engage in sport and exercise are not simply motivated, they are passionate toward the activity they engage in (Vallerand et al., 2003, Study 1). We define passion as a strong inclination toward a personally meaningful and highly valued activity that one loves, invests substantial time and energy in, and finds self-defining (Vallerand et al., 2003; Vallerand & Houlfort, 2003; Vallerand, 2008). As such, passion may serve to channel positive emotional experiences through self-regulation, enthusiasm, and task engagement, leading to a balanced, purposeful life. At the same time, passion may also be manifested as a compulsive and rigid behavior resulting in maladaptive outcomes and limited self-growth. Thus, two distinct types of passion are at play (Vallerand, 2016): Harmonious Passion (HP), in which people choose to engage in an activity without any contingencies attached to it, and Obsessive Passion (OP), in which the activity becomes part of us because of its extrinsic benefits (e.g., being popular, boost in self-esteem).

Harmonious passion (HP)

The Dualistic Model of Passion (DMP) posits that individuals displaying HP willingly pursue and fully partake in an activity with an openness that is conducive to positive experiences (Hodgins & Knee, 2002). With this type of passion, the activity does not occupy an overpowering space in the person's identity, and creates little or no conflict with other aspects of the person's life. Given that one can decide when to and when not to engage in the activity, people with HP are committed to the task at hand and are expected to experience positive outcomes both during task engagement (e.g., positive affect, concentration, flow, etc.) as well as after task engagement (general positive affect, satisfaction, etc.). Thus, when confronted with the possibility of playing basketball or studying for tomorrow's exam, a student-athlete with an HP for basketball should be able to say "No, I'll take a rain check" to playing basketball with his friends the night before preparing for an important physics test for which he has not studied. Furthermore, when other circumstances prevent them from engaging in their passionate activity, people with an HP should display a flexible, adaptive perspective on the situation and focus their energy on other tasks that require their attention (such as school matters), without suffering or ruminating about the missed sport opportunity. They may even decide to eventually terminate the relationship with the activity if they judge it has become a permanent negative factor in their life. Thus, with HP, behavioral engagement in the passionate activity can be seen as flexible.

Obsessive passion (OP) — Not able to resist + feel bad when you do

Individuals who typically display an uncontrollable urge to partake in an enjoyable activity tend to find themselves with an OP where certain contingencies are attached to the activity such as feelings of social acceptance or self-esteem (Crocker & Park, 2004; Mageau, Carpentier, & Vallerand, 2011). For example, if that same student was to have a predominant OP for playing basketball, he may not have been able to resist joining in the basketball scrimmage with his friends. During the scrimmage, he might feel upset with himself for playing ball instead of preparing for tomorrow's exam and risk experiencing conflicting feelings and other negative affect. He might, therefore, have difficulties focusing on the task at hand (playing basketball) and may not experience as much flow and positive affect as he could during and after activity engagement. On the other hand, if he managed to refuse the invitation to play basketball, our student might still feel upset with himself and have difficulties focusing on preparing for an exam because of ruminations about the lost opportunity to play basketball. In such cases, individuals with a predominant OP come to display a rigid persistence toward the activity – they often cannot help but to engage in the passionate activity and risk developing a dependence on the activity. Although such persistence may very well lead to high performance in an activity, it may also lead individuals to experience conflict with other elements of their life (such as school activities), as well as to frustration and rumination about the activity when prevented from engaging in it because of a lack of flexibility in persistence.

Although both types of passion have been found to relate to an activity one identifies with, OP has been found to also relate to measures of conflict with other life activities when compared with HP (Marsh et al., 2013; Vallerand et al., 2003; Vallerand, Ntoumanis et al., 2008). Overall, the role of passion in PP can allow us to uncover some of the processes underlying performance as well as adaptive and maladaptive outcomes, especially how passion toward an activity contributes to psychological well-being, optimal functioning, physical health, and life satisfaction.

Passion and adaptive outcomes

Based on the DMP, it would be expected that HP leads to adaptive outcomes often studied in positive psychology, whereas OP should not, or at least less so. This is so because with HP integrative self-processes are at play, leading the person to fully partake in the passion activity with an openness that is conducive to mindful involvement or self-awareness. The situation is different when OP is at play because ego-invested processes are involved (Hodgins & Knee, 2002), thereby leading individuals to adopt a defensive orientation that only permits a partial investment in the activity, and thus to experience less than adaptive, and at times maladaptive, outcomes.

Over the past 10 years or so a number of studies have been conducted on the role of passion in optimal functioning (for reviews see Curran, Hill, Appleton, Vallerand, & Standage, 2015; Vallerand, 2010, 2015). Such research has been typically conducted in field settings with a variety of real-life participants such as athletes, musicians, actors, dancers, painters, teachers, nurses, administrators, video gamers, and others. In most studies, participants are asked to complete the Passion Scale with respect to their favorite activity (e.g., tennis), and scales assessing optimal functioning (e.g., flow, well-being, positive affect, performance, creativity, etc.) are completed using a variety of methodological designs (e.g., cross-sectional, longitudinal, diary study).

The results of these studies yield remarkably similar findings and can be summarized as follows. First, HP leads to higher levels of optimal functioning both at the intrapersonal (e.g., concentration, flow, psychological well-being, positive affect, vitality and energy, health, engagement, motivation) and interpersonal (e.g., relationships) levels than OP. Second, OP positively predicts maladaptive outcomes (e.g., general negative affect, anxiety, life conflict, rumination, burnout), whereas HP is either unrelated or even negatively associated with these negative outcomes. In other words, HP for a given activity may protect one against negative outcomes and ill-being. Third, non-passionate people (the 15 to 20% of the population that do not experience passion for any activity in life) display lower levels of adaptive outcomes (especially psychological well-being; see Philippe, Vallerand, Andrianarisoa, & Brunel, 2009) than those who display HP, but do not differ from those with an obsessive passion. Where non-passionate and OP differ, however, is that while non-passionate individuals display a moderate level of well-being, those with OP for an activity are on a yo-yo pattern in which their well-being goes up and down as a function of their performance on the activity that they are passionate about (see Lafrenière, St-Louis, Vallerand, & Donahue, 2012; Mageau et al., 2011). Finally, it should be underscored that the adaptive outcomes engendered by HP are experienced on a recurrent basis because people engage in the activity that they are passionate about regularly and on average eight hours per week. Thus, contrary to the often reported "treadmill effect" in which gains are not sustained, the positive effects resulting from HP are indeed sustainable (see Vallerand, 2010, 2012a, 2015).

Passion and adaptive outcomes in sport and exercise

Of importance is the fact that a number of studies have been conducted in sport and exercise to look at the role of passion in adaptive outcomes (see Vallerand, 2012b; Vallerand & Miquelon, 2007). Such research has looked at a variety of outcomes and with a variety of sports participants: athletes (e.g., Vallerand, Rousseau, Grouzet, Dumais, & Grenier, 2006), coaches (e.g., Lafrenière et al., 2008), referees (e.g., Philippe, Vallerand, & Lavigne, 2009), and sport fans (e.g., Schellenberg, Bailis, & Crocker, 2013; Vallerand, Mageau et al., 2008). In this chapter we provide selected examples of research on certain outcomes known to be important in PP and conducted in sport and exercise settings, such as flow, positive emotions, psychological well-being, relationships, and expert performance.

Flow (Csikszentmihalyi, 1978) is an important construct in PP. It refers to a desirable state that people experience when they feel completely immersed in the activity (e.g., "I have a feeling of total control"). Based on the DMP, it would be expected that HP facilitates the experience of flow, whereas OP should not, or with certain limits. Research provides strong support for this hypothesis in sport and exercise. For instance, in a study with international soccer referees, HP was found to facilitate the experience of flow, whereas OP did not (Philippe, Vallerand, Andrianarisoa, & Brunel, 2009, Study 1). Other sport studies found the same findings (see Vallerand, 2012b for a review in sport and physical activity).

Although research in PP has shown that positive emotions represent a key state that facilitates a number of adaptive outcomes (Fredrickson, 2013; Lyubomirsky et al., 2005), limited studies have looked at the determinants of positive emotions (see Vallerand, 2015). Research has shown that HP leads to the experience of positive emotions both during activity engagement and after it, which is not the case with OP; OP typically leads to negative affect both during and after activity engagement (see the meta-analysis of Curran et al., 2015). This finding has been obtained with high-level athletes (Vallerand et al., 2006), coaches (e.g., Lafrenière et al., 2008), referees (e.g., Philippe et al., 2009), and sports fans (e.g., Vallerand et al., 2008).

Engaging in a meaningful and enjoyable activity that provides us with opportunities for self-improvement and actualization should facilitate one's psychological well-being to the extent that one's passion for the activity is harmonious in nature (Philippe et al., 2009). Research with young adults and teenagers using different measures of psychological well-being has shown that HP facilitates psychological well-being in athletes (e.g., Vallerand et al., 2006, 2008, Study 2), whereas OP is either negatively related (e.g., Bonneville-Roussy, Lavigne, & Vallerand, 2011) or unrelated (Vallerand et al., 2008, Study 2) to well-being.

If passion affects psychological well-being, then what are the processes mediating such effects? We think that the answer lies in the repeated experience of situational (or state) positive affect during the course of engagement of the passionate activity. The work of Barbara Fredrickson (e.g., Fredrickson, 2001; Fredrickson & Joiner, 2002) reveals that positive emotions open the mind to various positive functions, including having access to adaptive cognitive and self-repertoires that allow one to thrive and to adapt positively to various situations. As discussed previously, research on passion (e.g., Mageau et al., 2005; Vallerand et al., 2003, Study 1) has shown that HP positively contributes to the experience of positive affect during activity engagement. Because passionate individuals engage on average for about eight hours per week in their passionate activity, this means that harmonious passion can lead people to experience eight hours of cumulative positive affect per week on top of what may be experienced in other life domains. Such cumulative experience of positive affect may facilitate psychological well-being over time (Fredrickson, 2001), thereby leading to sustainable psychological well-being (see Vallerand, 2012a).

A study by Rousseau and Vallerand (2008) provided support for this hypothesis with passion toward physical activity. At Time 1, older individuals completed the Passion Scale with respect to physical activity, as well as measures of psychological well-being. At Time 2, immediately following an exercise bout, they completed situational measures of positive and negative affect. Finally, at Time 3, they completed measures of psychological well-being again. Results from a path analysis revealed that HP positively predicted positive affect, which led to increases in psychological well-being from Time 1 to Time 3. On the other hand, OP was unrelated to positive affect, but predicted negative affect and a decrease in well-being. Overall, these findings provide strong support for the role of situational positive affect experienced during task engagement as a mediator of the effect of HP on psychological well-being. Research in other settings has replicated these findings as well (see Houlfort, Vallerand, Laframboise, Fernet, & Koestner, 2015).

Relationships represent another important outcome heavily studied in positive psychology. Passion for a given activity can affect people's relationships in at least two ways. First, because passion affects the way people engage in the passionate activity, it can also indirectly influence the quality of relationships that take place within the purview of the activity. The DMP posits that having an HP for a given activity should facilitate having positive relationships with others while engaging in the passionate activity. Further, such positive effects should be mediated by the experience of positive affect. This is so because positive affect facilitates smiling, positive sharing of the activity, connection, and openness toward others that are conducive to positive relationships (see Waugh & Fredrickson, 2006). Conversely, because it is typically unrelated to positive affect and even related to negative affect, obsessive passion should not be positively related to quality of relationships and may even be detrimental to quality relationships.

Results from several studies, including some conducted in sports and exercise, have provided support for these hypotheses (e.g., Jowett, Lafrenière, & Vallerand, 2013; Lafrenière et al., 2008; Philippe, Vallerand et al., 2010). With HP, athletes report better friendships (new and existing relationships) with other athletes than with OP, and such effects are indeed mediated by positive emotions. The same findings were obtained when the quality of relationships was assessed by the athletes themselves or by informants who observed athletes interacting with other athletes, such as their coaches. Thus, the same processes operate for the development and maintenance of relationships. Finally, these findings were found to take place not only among athletes, but also within the quality of relationships between athletes and coaches, from the perspectives of both (e.g., Jowett et al., 2013; Lafrenière et al., 2008).

A second type of effect that passion has on relationships deals with the impact that one's passion for an activity (e.g., being a soccer fan) has on the quality of relationships (e.g., one's romantic relationship) that one has outside of the passionate activity. For instance, in a study with English soccer fans (Vallerand et al., 2008, Study 3), it was found that having an OP for being a soccer fan predicted conflict between soccer and the quality of the couple relationship. Conflict, in turn, negatively predicted satisfaction with the romantic relationship. Such was not the case with HP that was unrelated to conflict.

Research in the area of expert performance reveals that to reach international levels in most domains (sport, music, arts, etc.), one must put in an exorbitant amount of hours of practice over a 10-year period (Ericsson & Charness, 1994; Starkes & Ericsson, 2003). One important type of practice is called *deliberate practice*. Deliberate practice entails engaging in the activity with clear goals of improving on certain task components (Ericsson & Charness, 1994). For instance, an athlete may work hard on a new basketball technique for hours until it is successfully mastered. Passion represents the major reason why the athlete will persist engaging in deliberate practice although it is not easy or even fun to do so. Indeed, if one is to engage in the activity for long hours over several years and sometimes a lifetime, one must love the activity dearly and have the desire to persist in the activity, especially when times are tough. Thus, the two types of passion (both HP and OP) should lead to engagement in deliberate practice that, in turn, should lead to improved performance.

The aforementioned model was tested in a study with basketball players (Vallerand et al., 2008, Study 1). Male and female student-athletes (basketball players) completed scales assessing their passion for basketball as well as deliberate practice (based on Ericsson & Charness, 1994). Coaches independently rated the athletes' performances. Results from a path analysis revealed that both types of passion led to engagement in deliberate practice in basketball that, in turn, led to objective performance. These findings were replicated in a five-month prospective design with water polo and synchronized swimming athletes (Vallerand, Mageau et al., 2008, Study 2). Of additional interest, mastery goals (seeking mastery of the activity; Elliot, 1997) mediated the impact of HP (and slightly less OP) on deliberate practice, whereas performance avoidance goals negatively mediated the OP-performance relationship. Finally, HP was also positively and significantly related to life satisfaction, whereas OP was unrelated to it. It thus appears that both types of passion positively contribute to deliberate practice and thus, indirectly, to performance. However, with HP, there is a bonus effect because one may reach high levels of performance while being happy at the same time. One need not choose between the performance and happiness if HP is involved. These are the two roads to performance: the harmonious and the obsessive (see Vallerand, 2015).

In sum, the previous cursory review reveals that passion matters greatly with respect to important outcomes in sports, exercise, and in positive psychology more generally. Further, HP leads to more adaptive outcomes than OP. Such research has important implications for athletes involved in sport-study programs.

Implications for student-athletes

Sport and physical activity are one of the favorite types of passionate activities that people engage in. For instance, in one of the earlier studies about passion (Vallerand et al., 2003), 60% of college students indicated that they had a passion for some form of individual or a team sport or physical activity. Further, some individuals eventually join an intensive Sports Excellence program offered in parallel to a high school curriculum (see examples of "Sports-Etudes" in Quebec, or Sport1study programs in Canada and North America). In fact, in North America alone, thousands of teenagers and young adults are enrolled in such settings (Fredricks, Alfeld, & Eccles, 2010). In light of our discussion, passion for sport and physical activity may have a number of important implications for the lives of student-athletes. We mention a few here and suggest some research directions.

A first obvious implication is the role that athletes' passion for their sport may have in sports outcomes. As mentioned previously, athletes who display an HP partake in sports with mindfulness (St-Louis, Verner-Filion, Bergeron, & Vallerand, 2016) and an openness that is conducive to positive experiences (Hodgins & Knee, 2002), and are able to fully focus on the task at hand and experience positive

58 Tanya Chichekian and Robert J. Vallerand

outcomes during task engagement (e.g., positive affect, flow, etc.). This is typically not the same picture with OP in which less than adaptive outcomes are experienced. We have seen that there are two roads to excellence: the harmonious and the obsessive roads. Research has shown that the harmonious road leads to expert performance and a life well lived, filled with happiness. On the other hand, the obsessive road may lead to success that comes with a cost: a loss of happiness and a less successful life outside of sport. Research on the development and consequences of adopting the two roads of excellence in sports-study programs is necessary to yield fruitful applications.

A second implication for sports-study programs is that passion for sports can also affect outcomes outside of sport into athletes' educational realm. HP typically leads to adaptive outcomes after task engagement that, for instance, include the absence of conflict between sports and school-related activities and lingering positive affect (see Vallerand et al., 2003, Study 1). Thus, when prevented from engaging in sports, athletes with an HP should be able to adapt well to the situation and focus their attention and energy on other tasks that need to be done (e.g., preparing for an exam the next day). Because with HP, the athlete is flexible and can decide when and when not to engage in sports, he will not be confronted between two choices as he will readily tell his coach or peers that he'll take a rain check and proceed to be fully immersed in the preparation of the exam without thinking about the missed opportunity to practice. These kinds of behavioral engagements in sports can be manifested differently in class and present a different set of challenges (e.g., bringing locker room conversations to class) that teachers should learn how to channel rather than counter, both in terms of maintaining a productive learning environment and experiencing self-growth as a student. Conversely, athletes with an OP toward their sport can find themselves in a position of experiencing an uncontrollable urge to partake in their sport and risk having conflicts that may have some adverse outcomes in their studies.

Clearly, the foregoing suggests that research on the role of athletes' passion for their sports in educational outcomes represents an important avenue. Another outcome that merits attention pertains to friendships that athletes may develop both in sports and outside of it. Student-athletes usually form a well-defined cohort because they all enroll in the same classes, practice in similar athletic settings, and travel together to competitions, but they also have to adjust to demanding sport participation, as well as new teammates and coaches. These experiences play a significant role in student-athletes' interpersonal relationships such that their development of passion for sports may vary as a function of how social factors influence coping strategies (Schellenberg, Gaudreau, & Crocker, 2013) and behavior in school as well as the quality of relationships involving "teacher-student" or "coach-athlete" (e.g., Lafrenière et al., 2008). Style of competition varies to a certain extent from task- (e.g., one's fitness level) to other-oriented (e.g., volleyball tournament) such that task-oriented competition correlates with a lower number of conflicts in friendships, friendlier competition, and longer-lasting relationships (Masden, Leung, Shore, Schneider, and Udvari, 2015). Student-athletes' friendships also appear to be different in notable nuances from what is known about adolescent friendships generally. These relationships provide a rich context in which to study how student-athletes respond to negative conflicts with a good friend because teachers are often concerned about harmony and collaboration in the classrooms (Strahan, L'Esperance, & Van Hoose, 2009). In one study Chichekian and Shore (2017) investigated perspective-taking (the extent to which one is flexible to resolve a conflict and reinforce or protect the relationship). Student-athletes reported having a greater number of friends and valued their friendships differently compared with non-athletes; they were flexible in their approach to conflict resolution and attributed more weight to modifying one's viewpoint during a disagreement with a friend as opposed to maintaining their own position. In a similar vein, student-athletes with an HP develop new friendships while maintaining existing ones of high quality within the purview of the passionate activity (e.g., Lafrenière et al., 2008; Philippe et al., 2010, Study 2). On the other hand, OP hindered the quality of such relationships. Of importance, such effects can take place in the classroom and may vary as a function of the type of passion. Research on these issues within the dual perspective of sport and school would appear important.

We have discussed so far the role of passion in sport and classroom outcomes. However, it is important to briefly address the determinants of passion. A first issue is that we know very little about how passion may be transmitted from teachers to students or coaches to athletes (see Vallerand, 2015). We know that coaches who have an HP toward coaching provide more autonomy support toward their athletes that, in turn, fosters HP in athletes for their sport (e.g., Jowett et al., 2013; Lafrenière et al., 2008). Conversely, coaches with a predominant OP for coaching display higher levels of controlling behavior toward their athletes that, in turn, foster OP in athletes for their sport. Being a student-athlete, however, adds an extra layer of complexity to this dynamic, because an athlete may develop a passion toward school in addition to the already existing passion for sports. Both types of passion are important. Passion for sports may lead teenagers to remain involved in a healthy, active lifestyle for life while finding a passion for something in school that may encourage students to succeed in school and to eventually discover a satisfying career and lead a meaningful, balanced life. Research is just starting to assess the impact of passion toward two activities on psychological well-being and outcomes (Schellenberg & Bailis, 2015). The simultaneous development among student-athletes of passion toward both school and sports represents an important area of future research.

A second issue regarding the determinants of passion is how passion for sports and school, once developed, go up and down as a function of various social factors (see Vallerand, 2010, 2012b, 2015). One important factor studied in the work domain is the perception of the demands that one faces at work and the available resources to face such demands (Trépanier, Fernet, Austin, Forest, & Vallerand, 2014). Research has shown that experiencing high demands in the absence of sufficient resources leads to OP for one's work and, in turn, negative outcomes such as burnout. Student-athletes may feel overwhelmed in both their sports and studies if the demands are too high in one or both areas, and may come to experience burnout (see Curran et al., 2013). Thus, research is needed to determine how best to facilitate a more integrated sport-school environment in striving for excellence that is conducive to the development and maintenance of HP in each life domain and, consequently, to optimal functioning.

Conclusion

The purpose of this chapter was to introduce the concept of passion, show its relevance to the field of sports and physical activity by presenting the Dualistic Model of Passion (Vallerand, 2016), and explore its implication in sports-study programs. The research reviewed in this chapter leads to two major conclusions: support for the existence of two types of passion and its potential effect on educational and sport outcomes. We have provided evidence to show the extent to which obsessive and harmonious passion could entail control over an activity and how it could coexist with other activities of one's life. We have also introduced how passion can lead to important effects for both teachers and students on a variety of outcomes that include psychological well-being, physical health, meaningful relationships, and high levels of performance.

Specifically, in sports-study programs, teachers and coaches should keep in mind the important role that they play in helping student-athletes navigate through a period of self-growth, including the guidance they offer students in pursuing their passion. Helping students find some connection with their identity and to experience the joy of mastering a challenging subject in the classroom or a new and complex skill in their sports is essential to a lifelong pursuit of knowledge and self-discovery conducive to the development of passion. Fostering such a connection can be done through the transmission of coaches' or teachers' own passion for a given subject or sport, but fostering environments in which students find their own passion is also important because it develops a sense of identity. Sports-study programs are such ideal environments. Student-athletes' passion for sports flourishes beyond the classroom and, reciprocally, can act as a motivational drive to keep them connected with their school (Fredricks, Alfeld, & Eccles, 2010).

Given that passion represents the psychological force that drives individuals to excel in a given area such as sports and school, further research is warranted to investigate if and how school settings in which passion is encouraged both inside and outside the classroom act as preventive outlets from school disengagement and dropout. Additional research is also needed to shed light on the very processes that link passion with different levels of adaptive outcomes that will be experienced in student-athletes as they progress in such programs.

In sum, we believe that the present views about passion for sports in the context of education can contribute to our understanding of the psychological processes through which social dynamics influence student-athletes' future intentions to persist in a passionate activity; however, future research is needed to shed light on the intricacies through which passion for sports operate in the prediction of high performance both in physical activity and educational outcomes.

References

Bonneville-Roussy, A., Lavigne, G. L., & Vallerand, R. J. (2011). When passion leads to excellence: The case of musicians. *Psychology of Music*, 39, 123–138.

Chichekian, T., & Shore, B. M. (2017). Hold firm: Gifted learners value standing one's ground in disagreements with a friend. *Journal for the Education of the Gifted*, 40(2), 152–167. doi: 10.1177/0162353217701020.

Crocker, J., & Park, L. E. (2004). The costly pursuit of self-esteem. *Psychological Bulletin*, 130(3), 392–414.

Csikszentmihalyi, M. (1978). Attention and the holistic approach to behavior. In K. S. Pope & J. L. Singer (Eds.), *The Stream of Consciousness* (pp. 335–358). New York: Plenum.

Curran, T., Appleton, P. R., Hill, A. P., & Hall, H. K., (2013). The mediating role of psychological need satisfaction in relationships between types of passion for sport and athlete burnout. *Journal of Sport Sciences*, 31, 597–606.

Curran, T., Hill, A. P., Appleton, P. R., Vallerand, R. J., & Standage, M. (2015). The psychology of passion: A meta-analytical review of a decade of research on intrapersonal outcomes. *Motivation and Emotion*, 39, 631–655.

Elliot, A. J. (1997). Integrating the "classic" and "contemporary" approaches to achievement motivation: A hierarchical model of approach and avoidance achievement motivation. In M. L. Maehr & P. R. Pintrich (Eds.), *Advances in Motivation and Achievement* (Vol. 10, pp. 143–179). Greenwich, CT: JAI Press.

Ericsson, K. A., & Charness, N. (1994). Expert performance: Its structure and acquisition. *American Psychologist*, 49, 725–747.

Fredricks, J. A., Alfeld, C., & Eccles, J. (2010). Developing and fostering passion in academic and non academic domains. *Gifted Child Quarterly*, 54(1), 18–30.

Fredrickson, B. L. (2001). The role of positive emotions in positive psychology: The broaden-and-build theory of positive emotions. *The American Psychologist*, 56(3), 218–226.

Fredrickson, B. L. (2013). Positive emotions broaden and build. In P. Devine & A. Plant (Eds.), *Advances in Experimental Social Psychology* (Vo. 47, pp. 1–54). San Diego, CA: Academic Press.

Fredrickson, B. L., & Joiner, T. (2002). Positive emotions. In C. R. Snyder & S. J. Lopez (Eds.), *Handbook of Positive Psychology* (pp. 120–134). New York: Oxford University Press.

Hodgins, H. S., & Knee, R. (2002). The integrating self and conscious experience. In E. L. Deci & R. M. Ryan (Eds.), *Handbook on Self-Determination Research: Theoretical and Applied Issues* (pp. 87–100). Rochester, NY: University of Rochester Press.

Houlfort, N., Vallerand, R. J., Laframboise, A., Fernet, C., & Koestner, R. (2015). The role of passion for work and need satisfaction in post-retirement psychological adjustment. *Journal of Vocational Behavior*, 88, 84–94.

IPPA. (2016, March 15). IPPA aims on homepage. Retrieved from http://www.ippanet work.org.

Jarden, A. (2012). Positive psychologists on positive psychology: Robert Vallerand. *International Journal of Wellbeing*, 2(2), 125–130.

Jowett, S., Lafrenière, M-A. K., & Vallerand, R. J. (2013). Passion for activities and relationship quality: A dyadic approach. *Journal of Social and Personal Relationship*, 30, 734–749.

Lafrenière, M-A. K., Jowett, S., Vallerand, R. J., Donahue, E. G., & Lorimer, R. (2008). Passion in sport: On the quality of the coach-player relationship. *Journal of Sport and Exercise Psychology*, 30, 541–560.

Lafrenière, M-A. K., St-Louis, A. C., Vallerand, R. J., & Donahue, E. G. (2012). On the relation between performance and life satisfaction: The moderating role of passion. *Self and Identity*, 11, 516–530.

Lyubomirsky, S., King, L., & Diener, E. (2005). The benefits of frequent positive affect: Does happiness lead to success? *Psychological Bulletin*, 131, 803–855.

Mageau, G. A., Vallerand, R. J., Rousseau, F. L., Ratelle, C. F., & Provencher, P. J. (2005). Passion and gambling: Investigating the divergent affective and cognitive consequences of gambling. *Journal of Applied Social Psychology*, 35, 100–118.

Mageau, G., Carpentier, J., & Vallerand, R. J. (2011). The role of self-esteem: Contingencies in the distinction between Obsessive and Harmonious Passion. *European Journal of Social Psychology*, 6, 720–729.

Marsh, H. W., Vallerand, R. J., Lafreniere, M. A. K., Parker, P., Morin, A. J. S., Carbonneau, N., . . . Paquet, Y. (2013). Passion: Does one scale fit all? Construct validity of two-factor passion scale and psychometric invariance over different activities and languages. *Psychological Assessment*, 25(3), 796–809.

Masden, C. A., Leung, O. N., Shore, B. M., Schneider, B. H., & Udvari, S. J. (2015). Social-perspective coordination in gifted adolescent friendships. *High Ability Studies*, 26, 3–38.

Philippe, F., Vallerand, R. J., Andrianarisoa, J., & Brunel, P. (2009). Passion in referees: Examining affective and cognitive experiences in sport situations. *Journal of Sport & Exercise Psychology*, 31, 1–21.

Philippe, F. L., Vallerand, R. J., Houlfort, N., Lavigne, G. L., & Donahue, E. G. (2010). Passion for an activity and quality of interpersonal relationships: The mediating role of emotions. *Journal of Personality and Social Psychology*, 98, 917–932.

Philippe, F. L., Vallerand, R. J., & Lavigne, G. (2009). Passion does make a difference in people's lives: A look at well-being in passionate and non-passionate individuals. *Applied Psychology: Health and Well-Being*, 1, 3–22.

Rousseau, F. L., & Vallerand, R. J. (2008). An examination of the relationship between passion and subjective well-being in older adults. *International Journal of Aging and Human Development*, 66, 195–211.

Schellenberg, B. J., & Bailis, D. S. (2015). Can passion be polyamorous? The impact of having multiple passions on subjective well-being and momentary emotions. *Journal of Happiness Studies*, 16(6), 1365–1381.

Schellenberg, B. J., Bailis, D. S., & Crocker, P. R. (2013). Passionate hockey fans: Appraisals of, coping with, and attention paid to the 2012–2013 National Hockey League lockout. *Psychology of Sport and Exercise*, 14(6), 842–846.

Schellenberg, B. J., Gaudreau, P., & Crocker, P. R. (2013). Passion and coping: Relationships with changes in burnout and goal attainment in collegiate volleyball players. *Journal of Sport and Exercise Psychology*, 35(3), 270–280.

Starkes, J. L., & Ericsson, K. A. (Eds.). (2003). *Expert Performance in Sports: Advances in Research on Sport Expertise*. Champaign, IL: Human Kinetics.

St-Louis, A., Verner-Filion, J., Bergeron, C., & Vallerand, R. J. (2016). Passion and mindfulness: Accessing adaptive self-processes. *The Journal of Positive Psychology,* 1-10.

Strahan, D., L'Esperance, M., & Van Hoose, J. (2009). *Promoting Harmony: Young Adolescent Development and Classroom Practices.* Westerville, OH: National Middle School Association.

Trépanier, S.-G., Fernet, C., Austin, S., Forest, J., & Vallerand, R. J. (2014). Linking job demands and resources to burnout and work engagement: Does passion underlie these differential relationships? *Motivation and Emotion*, 38(3), 353–366.

Vallerand, R. J. (2008). On the psychology of passion: In search of what makes people's lives most worth living. *Canadian Psychology*, 49, 1–13.

Vallerand, R. J. (2010). On passion for life activities: The dualistic model of passion. In M.P. Zanna (Ed.), *Advances in Experimental Social Psychology* (Vol. 42, pp. 97–193). New York: Academic Press.

Vallerand, R. J. (2012a). The role of passion in sustainable psychological well-being. *Psychological Well-Being: Theory, Research, and Practice*, 2, 1–21.

Vallerand, R. J. (2012b). Passion for sport and exercise: The dualistic model of passion. In G. Roberts & D. Treasure (Eds.), *Advances in Motivation in Sport and Exercise* (Vol. 3, pp. 160–206). Champaign, IL: Human Kinetics.

Vallerand, R. J. (2015). *The Psychology of Passion: A Dualistic Model*. New York: Oxford University Press.

Vallerand, R. J. (2016). The dualistic model of passion: Theory, research, and implications for the field of education. In J. C. K. Wang, L. W. Chia, & R. M. Ryan (Eds.), *Building Autonomous Leaders: Research and Practical Perspectives Using Self-Determination Theory*. New York: Springer.

Vallerand, R. J., Blanchard, C. M., Mageau, G. A., Koestner, R., Ratelle, C. F. . . . Léonard, M. (2003). Les passions de l'âme: On obsessive and harmonious passion. *Journal of Personality and Social Psychology*, 85, 756–767.

Vallerand, R. J., & Houlfort, N. (2003). Passion at work: Toward a new conceptualization. In S. W. Gilliland, D. D. Steiner, & D. P. Skarlicki (Eds.), *Emerging Perspectives on Values in Organizations* (pp. 175–204). Greenwich, CT: Information Age Publishing.

Vallerand, R. J., Mageau, G. A., Elliot, A., Dumais, A., Demers, M-A., & Rousseau, F. L. (2008). Passion and performance attainment in sport. *Psychology of Sport & Exercise*, 9, 373–392.

Vallerand, R. J., & Miquelon, P. (2007). Passion for sport in athletes. In D. Lavallée & S. Jowett (Eds.), *Social Psychology in Sport* (pp. 249–262). Champaign, IL: Human Kinetics.

Vallerand, R. J., Ntoumanis, N., Philippe, F. L., Lavigne, G. L., Carbonneau, N., Bonneville, A., . . . Maliha, G. (2008). On passion and sports fans: A look at football. *Journal of Sports Sciences*, 26, 1279–1293.

Vallerand, R. J., Rousseau, F. L., Grouzet, F. M. E., Dumais, A., & Grenier, S. (2006). Passion in sport: A look at determinants and affective experiences. *Journal of Sport & Exercise Psychology*, 28, 454–478.

Waugh, C. E., & Fredrickson, B. L. (2006). Nice to know you: Positive emotions, self-other overlap, and complex understanding in the formation of new relationships. *Journal of Positive Psychology*, 1, 93–106.

5

CHARACTER STRENGTHS IN SPORT AND PHYSICAL ACTIVITY

Scott Bradley and Piers Worth

We were drawn to positive psychology (PP) and, in particular, strengths-use as a result of a growing frustration with the insufficiency inherent within psychology literature on 'fixing' mental deficiencies and weaknesses. Whilst traditional talking-therapy techniques (e.g. Rational-Emotive Behaviour Therapy) are effective in fixing distorted thinking and behaviour patterns, clients may often emerge with an understanding of managing weakness rather than an enhanced understanding of their qualities. Since working more closely with strength-based approaches, we have found that developing a better understanding of the positive qualities associated with one's character, or those that may evolve over time, can be transformational, emancipatory and valuable knowledge, which contribute in part to sporting performance and excellence.

Character is so interwoven into the fabric of what we consider sporting excellence to be that it is often identified as a 'must have' amongst those seeking to realize and demonstrate potential. To illustrate this assertion in the context of sport:

> It's about making sure the players you bring in are strong of character and can do the tasks we ask them to do when we haven't got the ball. For me it's not just about their ability on the ball . . . the character of the person shines through.
>
> *(Steve Walsh, Head of Recruitment for 2016 Premier League Champions Leicester City – BBC Radio 5 interview)*

Steve Walsh's comments clearly indicate that an individual's character is perceived to be as valuable to team outcomes as technical skill(s) in a high-performance context. Yet he also makes a more profound, and telling, statement in relation to the illuminating quality and transformative nature of character (strength). In describing character as something that 'shines through', he positions it as a positive quality that we attend and react to; thus it is 'energizing' to the individual (and the observer); and is, perhaps, a fundamental part of the individual more readily associated with personal growth tendencies, rather than merely the demonstration of survival and coping behaviour. We believe that it is just as important for athletes, coaches and parents to learn, and teach, how to thrive in life by developing and using our character strengths (CS) to achieve positive human functioning as it is to impart knowledge and teach technical skills associated with overcoming pressure and adversity (Ryff & Singer, 2003).

The purpose of this chapter is to: 1) introduce the concepts of character strength and optimal functioning; 2) explain the evolution of the strengths approach, identify how strengths are defined and explore their raison-d'etre; 3) present an overview of strength models; 4) explore character strengths research in sport, exercise and physical activity (PA); and 5) discuss applied strengths development approaches and suggest recommendations for applied practitioners in sport and exercise contexts. The intention is that the chapter offers introductory views and experience as well as pointing toward a more nuanced understanding of strengths, which may evolve over time.

Character strength and optimal functioning

However one chooses to define character, it is undeniably associated with positive outcomes such as moral behaviour, displays of grit and achievement (Seligman, 2011). Considering that the presence of character is often associated with success, and its absence with failure, developing an enhanced understanding of the psychosocial processes and qualities associated with character development and being the best we can be is a natural focus and goal for those involved in sport, exercise and PA.

According to Niemiec (2013), there are a number of important principles for understanding the best in people, which are based in the science of character:

Best in People Principles.

- CS are at the heart of being our 'best self'. CS and conceptions of 'best self' vary subjectively, socially and contextually.
- CS are interactive, interdependent and transactional in nature. It is likely that a number of dynamic processes influence how strengths interact with and influence one another.
- To be our 'best self' CS must be utilized optimally (i.e. in accordance with Aristotle's golden mean – the right combination of strengths, expressed to the right extent and in the right situation).

The principles outlined by Niemiec (2013) clearly identify that CS are intra-individually stable, and thus similar to personality traits, but that they are also highly contextual. It is important to note, therefore, that CS may develop through different processes in different contexts – strengths which work in one context may not work in another – thus influencing our language for strengths (Figure 5.1).

What are your 'strengths'? Linley (2008) suggests that two-thirds of us cannot say, or even have a language for this characteristic of ourselves. In a sporting context this may be different. Consider what your strengths are across sport, exercise and physical settings.

FIGURE 5.1 Activity: Identifying strengths

Optimal functioning, which is the predominant focus of PP, consists of a broad range of topic areas, for example: character strengths, meaning and engagement, flourishing, positive emotions and well-being (Seligman & Csikszentmihalyi, 2000). Essentially, optimal functioning is concerned with individuals' capacity to be the best they can be as well as their ability, and opportunity, to realize their true potential (Seligman, 2011). Given that character, and more specifically CS, is inextricably linked with conceptions of 'us at our best', psychological well-being and optimal functioning (Maslow, 1970; Seligman, 2011), it is essential that we seek to better understand the relationship between CS and optimal functioning in sport, exercise and PA settings.

Strengths – background, definitions and rationale

Background

In 1998 Martin Seligman and colleagues began a scientific exploration into what is right, rather than what is wrong with us. In doing so he identified three dimensions of happiness: the pleasant life (i.e. focus on positive emotions, and thoughts, surrounding past, present and future experiences), the meaningful life (i.e. developing CS and virtues in pursuit of outcomes which transcend the self) and the good life (i.e. using our strengths to attain virtues and lead an authentic life). Since then the psychology of strengths has attracted interest from researchers and applied practitioners across education, business, sport, coaching, PA and health settings.

Definitions

So, what are strengths? According to Linley and Harrington (2006), a strength is defined as:

> A capacity for feeling, thinking and behaving in a way that allows optimal functioning in the pursuit of valued outcomes.
>
> *(p. 86)*

Therefore, at a subjective level, how we think, feel and behave (in relation to our character strengths), influences, and is influenced by, a multitude of psychosocial

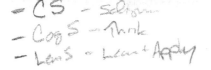

factors which is likely to create a fairly unique set of strengths for each and every one of us. When utilized the individual is capable of "delivering a high level of performance and experiencing a sense of energy" (p. 67). The interpretation of strengths clearly positions them as enabling, generative, authentic to the user and an important component of optimal functioning.

Strengths rationale – where they come from and why they matter

Linley (2008) proposes that strengths evolve (Figure 5.2) through a series of stages (presented as distinct, but deemed to be overlapping):

- evolution (universally adaptive qualities),
- nature (heritable qualities from our parents),
- nurture (socialization experiences),
- chance (random and unpredictable occurrences),
- adaptiveness (experiential learning).

It is certainly interesting to know where strengths might have come from, but it is equally pressing to consider their importance. Why do strengths matter? Character strengths are considered the foundation of human goodness and flourishing (Peterson & Seligman, 2004) and show consistent positive relationships with life satisfaction and well-being (Park, Peterson, & Seligman, 2004). From a well-being perspective, strengths-use represents an important predictor of both the affective and cognitive evaluation of one's life (subjective well-being – SWB), as well as eudaimonic conceptions of growth and self-actualization (psychological well-being – PWB). Interestingly, the CS of hope, zest, gratitude, curiosity and love are consistently shown to be more positively associated with life satisfaction (Park, Peterson, & Seligman, 2004) and SWB than strengths of the head (e.g. judgment). People who use their CS more have also been identified as having more

---

Consider how your own positive qualities have developed. Refer to the stages within Linley's (2008) Origins of Strengths framework and reflect upon the role of each stage in shaping your strengths as you see them.

In discussion with a partner, compare how your strengths, and theirs, have developed. What are the similarities and/or differences? Inner influences? Social influences? According to Linley (2008), it is likely that we will share many patterns of strengths, but that we display them differently based on our own unique experience(s).

What are the implications for sport psychologists and coaches of expanding our vocabulary in this way, and working with these insights?

FIGURE 5.2   Activity: Exploring the evolution of strengths

confidence, energy and vitality – SWB (Govindji & Linley, 2007), as well as being more effective in achieving personal growth – PWB (Sheldon, Kasser, Smith, & Share, 2002). In our experience it is certainly the case that strengths-use is not only associated with increases in clearly advantageous psychological and subjective states, but also that fully embracing CS into one's life can be transformative for the individual, their well-being and achievements (Linley, Nielsen, Gillett, & Biswas-Diener, 2010).

In the context of PA and sport, Lundqvist and Sandin (2014) identify physical activity as generally facilitating well-being, whereas sport participation (especially at an elite level) presents many more significant challenges (e.g. identity foreclosure, coping with injury and performance-related issues) to athlete well-being. Athlete well-being is likely to be complex and heavily nuanced based on various contextual factors (Brady & Shambrook, 2003), which might differentially affect athlete SWB and PWB. For example, Lundqvist and Sandin (ibid) point toward contextually dynamic influences upon athlete vitality and well-being – the experience of vitality being related to SWB. Whilst in team sports, more generally, Reinboth and Duda (2006) identify basic needs satisfaction and perceived motivational climates as differentially influencing indicators of SWB and PWB. Given that competitiveness, opportunity for social comparison and negative affective experience (e.g. anxiety) might be inherent within many sport and PA contexts, it appears warranted to explore the role of CS in buffering against potentially negatively valenced constructs and facilitating well-being in sport and PA. Such endeavours are important for creating models of well-being in sport and PA, which more accurately account for the complex demands and challenges athletes face as well as the role of CS in facilitating athletes' thriving behaviours.

Strengths models

Before we turn to describe leading models of strengths, we encourage you to identify your own strengths (refer to Figure 5.1). Echoing Linley (2008) we believe that the vocabulary for strengths may be infinite, and gaining a familiarity and confidence with our own descriptions is an important first step in their use. This act of skill development stretches our capacity for perception and insight in ways which we find have a direct influence on relationships generally, as well as sport and PA contexts in particular.

Currently there are three dominant strengths models: StrengthsFinder 2.0™, Values-In-Action (VIA) Strengths Classification, and Strengths Profile (previously R2 and Realise2) (Table 5.1). Those new to the concept of strengths face the question of which model or models are the best fit. It may involve one, or alternatively it may involve a flexible use of several measures. It is our intention that the content presented here might be useful in informing choice regarding how strengths are represented and understood, rather than arguing for one approach over another. We encourage you to look further, via the Internet, for the technical manuals of these questionnaires.

TABLE 5.1 Overview of three leading strengths models and psychometric questionnaires

	Values-In-Action (VIA)	StrengthsFinder™	Strengths Profile (previously R2 and Realise2)
Origin/source	VIA Institute on Character www.viacharacter.org Individuals can take the questionnaire. Free to take and feedback provided on ranking and definition of 24 strengths. Additional cost for detailed report or feedback. 120-item on-line questionnaire (five questions per strength). A 'top five' approach but all 24 strengths are fed-back.	Gallup Organization www.gallupstrengthscenter.com Individuals can take the questionnaire. Cost to take. Additional cost for detailed report or feedback. 180-item-pair questions. Questions are timed/have a time limit. Output focuses on the 'Top 5' Signature Themes of talent.	CAPP & Co Ltd in the United Kingdom https://strengthsprofile.com Individuals can take the questionnaire. Cost to take. Charge varies with the level of feedback provided. 180 questions.
Definition of strengths	'Character Strengths are the positive parts of your personality that impact how you think, feel and behave and are the keys to you being your best self'. (VIA website)	The theory assumes talents are found in thoughts, feelings and behaviours, and that with effort and the development of knowledge and skills, these become strengths. (Hodges & Clifton, 2004)	Strengths Profile defines strengths as 'the things that we are good at and that give us energy when we are using them'. (Technical Manual – quoted with permission) Strengths are assessed according to the three dimensions of **Energy, Performance** and **Use** – with each user receiving their feedback, revealing their 'realized' strengths, 'learned behaviours', 'weaknesses and unrealized strengths'.
Number of strengths	24 strengths clustered within six 'virtues'.	34 talent themes.	60 strengths.
Observations/ commentary	Youth version is available. VIA website offers guidance and resources on strengths development. Concepts are based on detailed research in the main cultures and 'wisdom traditions' of the world likely to indicate these strengths are cross-cultural. Detailed manual available (Peterson & Seligman, 2004). VIA website offers extensive information on research undertaken on the questionnaire in different fields of activity.	Talents and strengths are seen as stable and enduring qualities. A questionnaire for children and youth is available, (10 – 14 years). A book describing 'StrengthsFinder' is available and may contain a code for undertaking the questionnaire. Donald Clifton and Marcus Buckingham have both written books related to StrengthsFinder and their experience to support the general public in relating to strengths use.	The questionnaire originates in the UK. Strengths are clustered in five 'families': Being, Communicating, Motivating, Relating and Thinking. Their definition implies three elements: *performance* – how good we are at doing something, *energy* – how much energy we get from doing it, and *use* – how often we get to do it'. For something to be a strength in this questionnaire, each of these three elements – energy, performance and use – must be present. (Willars, Biswas-Diener, & Linley, 2010)

CS in sport, exercise and physical activity

The purpose of this section is to introduce readers to the concept of strengths in sport, exercise and physical activity; provide empirical background information and prompt further thought and exploration. The key areas of focus are the research on strengths and growth-related constructs in exercise, health and sports injury settings. There is also a further, more pressing, debate to summarize in this section, that of the relationship between 'talent' and 'strengths'.

Talent and strengths

The relationship between talent and strengths is complex and despite much focus on the interplay of talent and strengths (Buckingham & Clifton, 2001; Seligman, 2002), in pursuit of optimal functioning and sporting excellence, the landscape remains somewhat unclear, with the language needed for this relationship still maturing. This is, in part, due to the relative and different 'value' attached to each term across sport, business and education settings, as well as the resultant confusion in terminology. The terms 'talent', 'talents' and 'strengths' have often been used interchangeably (Buckingham & Clifton, 2001), leading to conceptual confusion, whilst a lack of clarity also exists regarding the nature and role of key bio-psychosocial variables influencing the talent-strengths relationship (Seligman, 2002).

We propose that in the context of sport it is likely that natural abilities are the 'what' (e.g. aptitudes, intelligences), whilst 'strengths' (e.g. VIA-CS) represent 'how' abilities may be grown and displayed. In an effort to clarify, terminologically and conceptually, we refer readers to Gagne's (2000) Differentiated Model of Giftedness and Talent (DMGT). The DMGT proposes that our abilities (or 'gifts') are innate and require effortful training, support and guidance over time to create talent. Talent is, thus, not exclusive to those in possession of innate sporting capital, but instead the result of deliberate nurturing of psychosocial variables across key development stages. According to Gagne (2000), talent refers to an outcome of the aforementioned process within a specific talent domain (e.g. sport). However, the manifestation of talent is not always predicted by the preceding identification and development processes, with research identifying 90% of eventual top-25 world-level athletes not 'shining' during early development (Martindale, Collins, & Daubney, 2005). The efficacy of such processes may depend entirely on what one is looking for amongst talent potential. Domain-specific ability, motivation, commitment, mental toughness, creativity and resilience all feature as must-haves, yet currently a paucity exists of research focusing on the impact of CS in realizing talent and optimal functioning in sport settings.

It is our assertion that the world of sport could encourage a broader understanding of strengths and their influence upon talents over the athletic lifespan by those, and for those, who later go on to 'shine'. We believe that strengths-use, in the context of sport and physical activity, not only catalyzes talent development, but also that this strengths-focus both energizes and buffers against negative psychological outcomes experienced whilst engaged in learning culturally valuable behaviours.

Significantly, we assert that learned behaviours – previously positioned as potentially or implicitly constraining strength-based development (e.g. Linley, 2008) – are a fundamental part of how athletes manage to survive under pressure and can evolve over time to become strengths or facilitate the capitalization of unrealized strengths. It is worth recognizing here that sport and PA experiences shape character as much as our character shapes our experience. The notion being that we have many kinds of strengths which emerge longitudinally and unpredictably (some of which may exist initially as learnt behaviours), to influence talent development and shape CS. For example, an athlete may possess the CS of perseverance but lack the skills and learnt behaviours associated with effective communication and time management which allows them to be open to, and effectively use, coach feedback to enhance their training and internalize such behaviours over time. Therefore, understanding which strengths are, as well as those learned behaviours that may develop to become, energizing to the individual is essential for facilitating a process of recovery, renewal and continued strengths-use (Figure 5.3).

Linley (2008) refers to the need for athletes to continuously move outside of their comfort zones in order to build both capacity and capability (often involving the acquisition of systematically learnt behaviours) whilst also allowing for recovery and renewal. The proposition, therefore, is that strengths-use (which in itself is energizing) can create a cycle of recovery and renewal for athletes. Whilst we concur with the main body of Linley's (2008, p. 141) original model, a new stage 'awareness' has been included to represent the need for reflexive understanding of the strengths, and learnt behaviours, which are, more or less, associated with personal energy renewal and recovery across different contexts. The requirement for meta-learning and reflexive skills to be possessed by elite-level athletes further

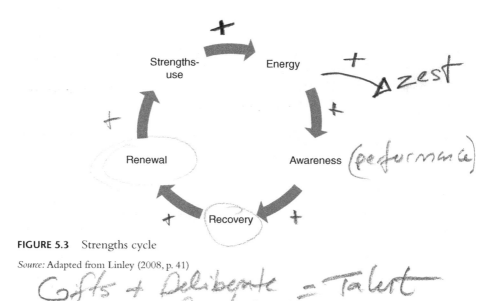

FIGURE 5.3   Strengths cycle

Source: Adapted from Linley (2008, p. 41)

points to the need for the development of self-regulatory abilities and awareness gains to buffer against a wide range of challenging competitive sport demands. Athletes developing such meta-skills may, thus, have more opportunity to experience renewal through understanding how learned behaviours and strengths are productively applied and capitalized upon to optimize the focus of talent development over time.

Therefore, the process of strength and talent development may begin with or include instruction of learned behaviours, but should end with the capitalization of strengths as the primary goal (Subotnik & Jarvin, 2005). Establishing what such a process looks like in sport and PA settings, informed by existing empirically grounded talent and strengths models, would appear a valuable next step in understanding the talent-strengths relationship.

CS, exercise and health

Currently there is an absence of research considering the mediatory influence of CS upon the relationship between important self-constructs and well-being in PA contexts. Given that well-being and achievement in PA, sport and exercise contexts require a positive self-outlook, with self-efficacy also positively related to changes in health-related behaviour (Bandura, 2008) and the ability to sustain such behaviour change (Maddux, 2009), it would appear somewhat remiss to overlook the influential role of CS. It might be that CS-use (e.g. perseverance, self-regulation) positively influences confidence in one's ability to persist and successfully complete tasks despite experiencing increasing physical and psychological costs of fatigue.

According to Peterson, Park, and Seligman (2006), the CS of bravery, kindness and humour support well-being (measured by higher life satisfaction scores) amongst individuals with physical disorders. Given that these strengths are more readily associated with action than, say, wisdom and knowledge-based CS (such as love of learning and open-mindedness), then personal agency beliefs, perceived autonomy, confidence and approach-motivated behaviour might be influential mediators in the relationship between CS and physical health.

A focus on CS-based interventions designed to enhance PA and promote health could be useful in providing a more authentic and energizing experience, whilst simultaneously promoting a 'best-self' conception. Furthering our conceptual understanding of the role of CS in shaping positive health outcomes through research and applied interventions represents a significant challenge and priority area for our discipline.

CS and injury

Injury is typically associated with negative consequences and perceived to be a distressing occurrence within an athlete's life (Evans, Hare, & Mullen, 2006) because of the focus on stressors, barriers to rehabilitation and potential negative outcomes (e.g. performance impairment and sport/career termination). However, not every athlete experiences distress, dysfunction and despair as a result of being injured or engaging in the rehabilitation process. Some researchers have adopted a more balanced view of athletes' sport injury experiences and have suggested that resilience and growth are as likely outcomes as dropout and depression (Wadey & Evans, 2011).

According to Wadey, Evans, Evans, and Mitchell (2011), athletes engaging in more adaptive and growth-related behaviours such as seeking social support, disclosing to others about their injury, adhering to the rehabilitation program, learning about the injury and putting things in perspective are likely to experience more benefits (e.g. increased resilience, enhanced confidence, better coping skills). Gaining a better understanding of an athlete's CS profile or signature strengths might be important in helping professional practitioners and support personnel to structure interventions in order to maximize positive psychological benefits. For example, knowing that an athlete scores highly in wisdom and knowledge strengths might help orient the professional practitioner's intervention toward learning more about the nature of the injury and knowledge of injury prevention.

CS – practical applications and conclusions

The question of how to go about effectively developing and applying CS is not easy to answer, because the literature within the field of applied strength-based psychology is relatively young and still embryonic in its application in sport and PA contexts. A number of general approaches to strength-based practice are discussed, with reference made to applied sport psychology examples where relevant, before presenting our conclusions.

Key to beginning to use CS optimally might be the development of strengths-based language and strength-spotting skills. Similar to other researchers (e.g. Padesky & Mooney, 2012), Linley (2008), advocates developing strengths-based language and using client-generated metaphor in helping create and recall strengths-based practices and qualities. Linley (2008) identifies a number of observable signs of strengths: loss of sense of time, heightened energy and engagement, enhanced learning, task prioritization and being drawn to people or activities associated with strengths-use. Linley also advocates developing skills associated with 'strength-spotting', including observation and listening skills. For example, it is likely that when individuals are capitalizing upon their CS, they use more positively valenced language; they are more expressive and talkative and they speak more energetically, passionately and with a greater sense of purpose. From an applied sport psychology practice perspective, practitioner listening skills are centrally positioned (Katz & Hemmings, 2009) and should, ideally, include strength-spotting alongside more established counselling-based skills.

In sport settings it is feasible that the development of strengths-based language might stimulate athletes to capitalize upon their CS and in so doing overcome obstacles and create opportunities for experiencing 'resonance' (Newburg, Kimiecik, Durand-Bush, & Doell, 2002) – an experiential state characterized by a sense of connection between self and the outer world and persistent pursuit of valued goals over time. It is also likely that environments affording resonance experiences would provide further opportunity for significant others (i.e. coaches) to be influenced and energized by the athlete's own unique talent (Poczwardowski, Barott, & Henschen, 2002). Such transformational-relational benefits could be important within performance sport settings, which are often characterized by intense power-based relationships. If such relational interactions, and created environments, do not take into account the CS of the individual(s) it is possible that this might negatively affect psychological processes associated with energy renewal, subsequent strengths-use and ultimately the realization of potential (Bradley, Morgan & Worth, 2016).

Strength-based development practices (Peterson & Seligman, 2004) often advocate using an 'identify and use' method – represented through an enhanced awareness of one's CS (e.g. through completing a strengths assessment) and encouragement to capitalize upon more frequent strengths-use (typically one's 'Top 5' or 'signature' themes). Whilst such approaches are certainly beneficial to raising awareness of one's CS and becoming familiar with developing a language for strengths, they may provide little opportunity for developing an understanding of how strengths develop, interact with other strengths, or are influenced by environmental and contextual variation. As a result, we believe that the task of understanding strengths development is still maturing, and favour the argument of Biswas-Diener, Kashdan, and Minhas (2011) that practitioners should focus on moving from a 'use it more' approach to developing the meta-skills and self-regulatory abilities to be able to know when, and in what amount(s), to use strengths optimally.

Whilst there are currently few models for strength-based practice in sport settings, we use Niemiec's (2009) Aware-Explore-Apply model as an introduction. Niemiec's (2009) three-step process (Figure 5.4) involves developing an *awareness* of strengths and helping the client build a language for strengths, *exploring* strengths through self-reflexive enquiry and practitioner-guided questioning and *applying* strengths more optimally through action planning, active self-monitoring and experimentation. Throughout the three phases of this model, Niemiec advocates using Linley's (2008) strength-spotting techniques mentioned previously.

In a pioneering piece of applied work conducted with the Sri Lanka Cricket Team, Sandy Gordon employed a strength-based Appreciative Inquiry (AI)–guided intervention (Gordon, 2014). Gordon established core values underpinning process goal pursuit, created a shared reality of 'what works' using AI and open-space technologies, and enhanced player responsibility and social support practices within training in creating strength-based habits associated with Sri Lanka Cricket at its best. Interestingly, a strategic planning technique, allowing players to explore inter-individual perceptions of Strengths, Opportunities, Aspirations and Results (SOAR) amongst team members, was also employed. We would encourage more aspiring, and established, practitioners to look beyond traditional consulting approaches and explore novel approaches from other discipline areas to advance practice. Further

- Aware – proposes that self-directed or therapist-supported awareness of strengths is the first step to change. Allows for a language for strength to be developed and begin attributing strengths to past and current behaviour.
- Explore – facilitates a more reflective and deeper understanding of strengths through self-reflexive enquiry, journal-keeping and joint exploration (e.g. thinking about you at your best, which strengths were evident?).
- Apply – forming an action plan for how to use strengths more in everyday life. Self-monitoring how strengths are used and vary across contexts, emulating role-models/paragons, practicing using strengths in novel and creative ways are some of the practical applications advocated.

Access the model through www.viacharacter.org/resources/ok-now-what-taking-action-with-strength-by-ryan-m-niemiec-psy-d/ and consider the benefits and challenges of using the model as part of an applied sport psychology intervention.

FIGURE 5.4   Aware–Explore–Apply model
Source: Niemiec (2009)

scholarly contributions embracing a strength focus in applied sport contexts (Gordon & Gucciardi, 2011) are also welcomed and applauded.

Conclusion

There is ample reason to believe that sport, exercise and PA settings provide fertile ground for the development of strengths-based approaches and will provide further opportunities for the exploration of strength-based practices. We would encourage any student, coach or athlete to:

- Become familiar with the language of strengths, strengths-spotting in oneself and others
- Where appropriate, measure strengths using available questionnaires
- Explore the 'Strengths Cycle' and the process of 'Aware – Explore – Apply', being reflexively aware of one's experience and contextual influences supporting or constraining strengths development

This area, within sporting practice, is sufficiently new that skill development and research in the aforementioned three areas will represent a significant advance for our discipline.

This is appropriate professional development for any of us. As your experience develops, we encourage you to revisit the other thinking and research summarized within this chapter. We hope that this chapter serves as a useful guide, or starting point, to the journey.

References

Bandura, A. (2008). An agentic perspective on positive psychology. In S. J. Lopez (Ed.), *Positive Psychology: Expecting the Best in People* (Vol. 1). New York: Praeger.

Biswas-Diener, R., Kashdan, T. B., & Minhas, G. (2011). A dynamic approach to psychological strength development and intervention. *Journal of Positive Psychology*, 6(2), 106–118.

Bradley, S., Morgan, P. B., & Worth, P. (2016). Strengths-based approaches and resilience development: A perspective from sports psychology. *AI Practitioner*, 18(2), 1–8.

Brady, A., & Shambrook, C. (2003). Towards an understanding of elite athlete quality of life: A phenomenological study. *Journal of Sports Sciences*, 21, 341–342.

Buckingham, M., & Clifton, D. O. (2001). *Now, Discover Your Strengths: How to Develop Your Talents and Those of the People You Manage.* London: Simon & Schuster.

Evans, L., Hare, R., & Mullen, R. (2006). Imagery use during rehabilitation from injury. *Journal of Imagery Research in Sport and Physical Activity*, 1(1), 1. Retrieved from www.bepress. com/jirspa/vol1/iss1/art1.

Gagne, F. (2000). Understanding the complete choreography of talent development through DMGT – based analysis. In K. A. Heller (Ed.), *International Handbook of Giftedness and Talent* (2nd ed., pp. 67–79). Oxford: Elsevier Science.

Gordon, S. (2014). Roar of the lions: Strength-based consulting with Sri Lanka cricket. In P. C. Terry, L. Zhang, Y. Kim, T. Morris, & S. Hanrahan (Eds.), *Secrets of Asian Sport Psychology.* Retrieved from http://peterterry.wix.com/books.

Gordon, S., & Gucciardi, D. F. (2011). Strengths-based approach to coaching mental toughness. *Journal of Sport Psychology in Action*, 2, 143–155.

Govindji, R., & Linley, P. A. (2007). Strengths use, self-concordance and well-being: Implications for strengths coaching and coaching psychologists. *International Coaching Psychology Review*, 2, 143–153.

Hodges, T. D., & Clifton, D. O. (2004). Strengths-based development in practice. In P. A. Linley & S. Joseph (Eds.), *Positive Psychology in Practice* (pp. 256-268). New Jersey: John Wiley & Sons, Inc.

Katz, J., & Hemmings, B. H. (2009). *Counselling Skills Handbook for the Sport Psychologist.* Leicester, UK: The British Psychological Society.

Linley, P. A. (2008). *Average to A+: Realising Strengths in Yourself and Others.* Coventry, England: CAPP Press.

Linley, P. A., & Harrington, S. (2006). Strengths coaching: A potential-guided approach to coaching psychology. *International Coaching Psychology Review*, 1(1), 37–46.

Linley, P. A., Nielsen, K. M., Gillett, R., & Biswas-Diener, R. (2010). Using signature strengths in pursuit of goals: Effects on goal progress, need satisfaction, and well-being, and implications for coaching psychologists. *International Coaching Psychology Review*, 5(1), 6–15.

Lundqvist, C., & Sandin, F. (2014). Well-being in elite sport: Dimensions of hedonic and eudaimonic well-being among elite orienteers. *The Sport Psychologist*, 28(3), 245–254.

Maddux, J. E. (2009). Self-efficacy: The power of believing you can. In C. R. Snyder & S. J. Lopez (Eds.), *Oxford Handbook of Positive Psychology* (2nd ed., pp. 335–344). New York: Oxford University Press.

Martindale, R. J. J., Collins, D., & Daubney, J. (2005). Talent development: A guide for practice and research within sport. *Quest*, 57, 353–375.

Maslow, A. H. (1970). *Motivation and Personality* (2nd ed.). New York: Harper & Row Publishers.

Newburg, D., Kimiecik, J., Durand-Bush, N., & Doell, K. (2002). The role of resonance in performance excellence and life engagement. *Journal of Applied Sport Psychology*, 14, 249–267.

Niemiec, R. M. (2009). *Ok, Now What? Taking Action.* VIA Institute. Retrieved from www. viacharacter.org/www/AwareExploreApply/tabid/249/language/en-US/Default.aspx.

Niemiec, R. M. (2013). VIA character strengths: Research and practice (The first 10 years). In H. H. Knoop & A. D. Fave (Eds.), *Well-Being and Cultures: Perspectives on Positive Psychology* (pp. 11–30). New York: Springer.

Padesky, C. A., & Mooney, K. A. (2012). Strengths-based cognitive-behavioral therapy: A four-step model to build resilience. *Clinical Psychology and Psychotherapy*, 19, 283–290.

Park, N., Peterson, C., & Seligman, M. E. P. (2004). Strengths of character and well-being. *Journal of Social and Clinical Psychology*, 23, 603–619.

Peterson, C., Park, N., & Seligman, M. E. P. (2006). Greater strengths of character and recovery from illness. *The Journal of Positive Psychology*, 1(1), 17–26.

Peterson, C., Ruch, W., Beerman, U., Park, N., & Seligman, M. E. P. (2007). Strengths of character, orientations to happiness, and life satisfaction. *Journal of Positive Psychology*, 2, 149–156.

Peterson, C., & Seligman, M. E. P. (2004). *Character Strengths and Virtues: A Handbook and Classification.* Washington, DC: American Psychological Association.

Poczwardowski, A., Barott, J. E., & Henschen, K. P. (2002). The athlete and coach: Their relationship and its meaning – Results of an interpretive study. *International Journal of Sport Psychology*, 33, 116–140.

Reinboth, M., & Duda, J. L. (2006). Perceived motivational climate, need satisfaction and indices of well-being in team sports: A longitudinal perspective. *Psychology of Sport and Exercise*, 7(3), 269–286.

Ryff, C. D., & Singer, B. (2003). Flourishing under fire: Resilience as a prototype of challenged thriving. In C. L. M. Keyes & J. Haidt (Eds.), *Positive Psychology and the Life Well-Lived* (pp. 15–36). Washington, DC: APA.

Seligman, M. E. P. (2002). *Authentic Happiness: Using the New Positive Psychology to Realize Your Potential for Lasting Fulfillment.* New York: Free Press.

Seligman, M. E. P. (2011). *Flourish: A New Understanding of Happiness and Well-Being – and How to Achieve Them.* London: Nicholas Brealey Publishing.

Seligman, M. E. P., & Csikszentmihalyi, M. (2000). Positive psychology: An introduction. *American Psychologist*, 55(1), 5–14.

Sheldon, K. M., Kasser, T., Smith, K., & Share, T. (2002). Personal goals and psychological growth: Testing an intervention to enhance goal-attainment and personality integration. *Journal of Personality*, 70, 5–31.

Subotnik, R. F., & Jarvin, L. (2005). Beyond expertise: Conceptions of giftedness as great performance. In R. J. Sternberg & J. E. Davidson (Eds.), *Conceptions of Giftedness* (2nd ed., pp. 343–357). New York: Cambridge University Press.

Wadey, R., & Evans, L. (2011). Working with injured athletes: Research and practice. In S. Hanton & S. D. Mellalieu (Eds.), *Professional Practice in Sport Psychology: A Review* (pp. 107–132). London: Routledge.

Wadey, R., Evans, L., Evans, K., & Mitchell, I. (2011). Perceived benefits following sport injury: A qualitative examination of their antecedents and underlying mechanisms. *Journal of Applied Sport Psychology*, 23(2), 142–158.

Willars, J., Biswas-Diener, R., & Linley, A. (2010). *The Strengths Book.* Coventry: CAPP Press.

6

HOPE AND OPTIMISM IN SPORT

Carolina Lundqvist and Henrik Gustafsson

The future can be exciting to think about because, in contrast to the past, it is an unwritten page with space for hopes and dreams. Dreams or visions about the future offer opportunities to do things better or maybe shift behaviors to obtain improved performance and well-being in sport or life. Competitive sports are commonly associated with myriad ideals related to development and subsequent achievements of personally valued goals. In most cases, progressing toward these valued goals requires significant dedication and a willingness to make great effort. Inherent in competitive sport is also the risk of various adversities, such as injuries, overtraining and performance plateaus. In our own applied work as sport psychologists, where we are supporting primarily high-level elite athletes, we have witnessed many examples in which adversities challenge the athlete's commitment and persistence in the moment. Such situations increase the need for the athlete and the coach to maintain future hope and a positive attitude about the possibility of overcoming the adversity. Successfully coping with experiences of adversity may facilitate personal and athletic growth and provide important lessons for use in future challenging situations.

People differ in how they view their future; subsequently this may also impact the person psychologically and how they behave in various situations. How people perceive the future, in term of its brightness or darkness and their ability to find a route toward significant personal goals, is linked to the scientific constructs of hope and optimism. In this chapter we aim to provide an introduction to the concepts of hope and optimism on a definitional and theoretical level and briefly describe current sport-oriented research together with promising interventions within this field. Throughout the chapter we have a particular focus on how the constructs of hope and optimism may apply to athletes and coaches. Hope and an optimistic thinking pattern have, for example, been linked to characteristics shown in mentally tough athletes (e.g., Coulter, Mallet, & Gucciardi, 2010). Research literature has nevertheless also reported relationships between hope and optimism and positive outcomes in various sport- and non-sport populations, for example, in terms of relationships with well-being, happiness and positive mood states, flourishing, social development, physical activity–related behavior strategies, physical health, sports achievements and improved recovery from illness and injury (e.g., Curry, Snyder, Cook, Ruby, & Rehm, 1997; Everhart, Best, & Flanigan, 2015; Gallagher & Lopez, 2009; Nothwehr, Clark, & Perkins, 2013; Scioli, Scioli-Salter, Sykes, Anderson, & Fedele, 2016). Thus, the reader should keep in mind that issues surrounding hope and optimism may likely be applicable to other populations and contexts than those we explicitly describe in our examples.

Reflection exercise

Before you read any further, take a minute to reflect about various people you meet within and outside your sport context. How do they seem to view their future? Can you identify those who seem to be highly optimistic and hopeful in many situations? Can you also identify those whose future-oriented view is highly pessimistic, with lack of hope? How do these people react and behave when confronting a challenging or stressful situation? Do you notice any differences between those you view as optimistic and hopeful compared with those more prone toward an orientation of pessimism and low hope?

During the reflection exercise you may have recognized that athletes, coaches and other people you meet may differ in views of their future regardless of the true nature of the actual conditions. People prone toward a highly pessimistic and low-hope orientation are likely to perceive that difficulties pile up, that challenges are overwhelming and that they cannot do much to change things or to improve unsatisfactory circumstances for the better. You may have noticed that some people often detect barriers in many situations; they easily give up or hesitate to set goals because they think the goals would be unreachable anyway. On the other hand, other people in the same context maybe appear to have an inner belief that they can make things happen if they engage in an activity highly enough and spend effort to improve the situation. These more optimistic and hopeful people seem prone to see opportunities in most situations, usually set more challenging goals and appear to find routes despite obstacles which lead them toward what they want to achieve. Understanding when and how hope and optimism are variously experienced and how each can be appropriately cultivated in sport and physical activity are crucial objectives if we are to access their many benefits.

Hope, optimism and positive psychology

Definitions of hope and optimism

The terms "hope" and "optimism" in everyday parlance tend to be used interchangeably, and people usually understand the meaning of the constructs at a general level. In the scientific literature, great emphasis has nevertheless been put on definitions and operationalization in order to enable precise assessments of them. The close relationship between hope and optimism has puzzled researchers, and investigation has been undertaken to determine to what extent hope and optimism represent similar or distinct phenomena. For example, researchers have found that hope and optimism relate somewhat differently to measures of well-being, stress, coping, affect, self-efficacy and self-esteem (e.g., Alarcon, Bowling, & Khazon, 2013; Bryant & Cvengros, 2004; Gallagher & Lopez, 2009). Thus, a common opinion in the literature today is that hope and optimism, despite their conceptual closeness, are most useful when considered as two separate constructs. Let us now take a closer look at some conceptual similarities and differences between hope and optimism:

- Hope and optimism both focus on the person's beliefs about how favorable the future will be and the expectations that the person holds of future goal pursuits.
- Optimism refers to the general expectancies a person holds regarding the brightness or darkness of his or her overall future. These general expectancies are in addition hypothesized to affect the person's action tendencies in situations (Carver, Scheier, Miller, & Fulford, 2009). *WILL HAPPEN*
- Hope involves the premise of a person's positive expectations for goal attainment. The construct of hope includes in addition a person's perception that he or she can generate various routes from the present to a desired future (i.e., pathway) and successfully use these routes to reach goals (i.e., agency) (Snyder, Rand, & Sigmon, 2005). *CAN MAKE IT HAPPEN*

As just displayed, the constructs of optimism and hope do differ in that optimism relates to general and more unspecific future expectations than does hope. For example, if you encounter a sports coach or an athlete who holds a general belief that things likely will be fulfilling in sport and life no matter how goals are achieved, it would be appropriate to classify him or her as an optimistic person. On the other hand, if the coach or the athlete seems to have strong belief in his or her capability to achieve valued goals and display volitional action to navigate a way forward toward a personally successful future, it is reasonable to assume that hope is the proper construct to adopt (cf. Alarcon et al., 2013; Bryant & Cvengros, 2004; Gallagher & Lopez, 2009).

Theoretical approaches to hope and optimism

Dispositional optimism

Dispositional optimism is an approach which considers optimism in relation to expectancies to achieve subjectively important goals (Scheier & Carver, 1992). Goals within this approach are viewed as desirable or undesirable states or actions which impact the motivation and behavior of the person. People are in general likely to try to approach goals that they view as highly desirable or pleasing and, on the contrary, they search to avoid things they view as undesirable or aversive (Carver & Scheier, 2005; Carver et al., 2009). According to this perspective, optimism is viewed as a rather stable personality disposition, with a focus on generalized expectancies (i.e., general confidence or doubt) the person holds of future goal pursuit. Optimistic coaches or athletes are, for example, expected to confront situations with higher confidence, persist longer and continue their efforts also when confronting obstacles. Coaches or athletes more inclined toward a pessimistic view are instead expected to react with doubt and hesitate to confront challenging situations (e.g., Carver & Scheier, 2005; Wilson, Hawkins, & Joyner, 2015).

Optimistic explanatory style

The perspective of optimistic explanatory style explains optimism from the view of attributions. Attributions are people's inner and habitual causal explanations as to why good or bad things happen in various situations (Peterson & Steen, 2005, 2009). The explanatory style relates to questions about whether an event/challenge is perceived by the person as uncontrollable or controllable, whether it is global and long-lasting or specific in nature and whether the person perceives it as stable or unstable (Peterson & Seligman, 1984, 1987). According to this perspective, people with a pessimistic or optimistic explanatory style will differ substantially in the causal attributions made when good and bad events happen. A pessimistic explanatory style is characterized by an internal, stable and long-lasting attribution of negative events (e.g., "I lost the game because of my failures as a player; I cannot do anything about my shortcomings, and I will always be a loser"). In contrast, an optimistic explanatory style to negative events is characterized by the opposite – external, unstable and transient (e.g., "I had a lot of bad luck today which resulted in losing the game, but bad luck is temporary and will not last forever"). These optimistic-pessimistic differences in explanatory style are also hypothesized to impact on motivational aspects. For example, they may impact on a person's self-efficacy to strive toward future goals and coping strategies adopted when a person encounters stressful situations (Peterson & Steen, 2005, 2009).

Need both optimism + pessimism

Is high optimism always beneficial?

A substantial amount of studies support beneficial outcomes of optimism, but research also suggests that a healthy proportion of pessimism and self-doubts may be adaptive in some situations (Vancouver, More, & Yoder, 2008). An explanatory style that is too optimistic in the preparation phases of a task poses the risk of a person working less hard and investing less effort in planning the necessary parts of the preparation. Some self-doubts or pessimistic thinking may thus make a person increase efforts in the preparations (e.g., Bandura, 1997; Bandura & Locke, 2003). In a similar manner, in doing easier tasks a highly optimistic person may anticipate that fewer personal resources and actions are needed to reach the goal unless the goal is of high priority and engaging for the person (Carver & Scheier, 1998; Geers, Wellman, & Lassiter, 2009). Others argue that a constant hunt for happiness and positivity may contradictorily lead to a vicious circle based on misconceptions of what it means to be happy. To strive toward happiness without accepting that life imposes both good and bad events and emotions, in combination with a struggle to avoid negative emotions and thoughts, may paradoxically make the person less happy (Harris, 2008). Thus, optimistic explanations and anticipations need to be based in reality to effectively help the person to choose proper goals and to allocate efforts and resources to strive toward them.

Critical thinking question

• Can you identify any situations or events, based on your own experiences or stories described from others, when an overly optimistic orientation poten-tially has been detrimental for preparations or sports performance?

Hope theory

Snyder's (Snyder, 2002; Snyder et al., 1991) Cognitive Theory of Hope is the most used framework to study hope in psychology (cf. Rand & Cheavens, 2009). This theory postulates that hope consists of three interrelated parts: goals, pathways and agency (Snyder et al., 1991). Hope theory considers human actions as goal-directed where goals can be both short or long term, with varying levels of personally per-ceived importance attached to them (Snyder, 2002). Pathways thinking relates to a person's perceived capacity to create feasible ways to a desired goal and to find alternative routes or develop new strategies to their goals if one route is blocked or if obstacles occur. In sport, it could be exemplified by how athletes handle per-formance drawbacks and can find ways to adjust their training to overcome the drawbacks. Agency thinking is the motivational aspect of hope and corresponds to the person's perceived inner drive to pursue their anticipated pathways. People with high hope experience goal-directed mental energy and feelings of "I can do this". Athletes with high hope feel energized to take the challenge and enhance their capacity by following through new training plans to reach their goals (cf. Rodriguez-Hanley & Snyder, 2000; Snyder et al., 2005).

Research on hope and optimism in sport

Many research studies on hope and optimism have been published in main-stream psychology (cf. Carver et al., 2009; Rand & Cheavens, 2009). Nevertheless, researchers in sport psychology have also become interested in the study of hope and optimism and how the constructs may impact sports participants on various competitive levels. In the summary of sport research presented in this section, we do not claim to be comprehensive; instead our intention is to provide examples of areas that have caught researchers' interest within the sport context, including sport

performance, well-being or ill-being and interventions. We also suggest areas for future research.

Sport performance and characteristics of successful athletes and coaches

In the scientific literature, optimism and hope have been linked to successful sport performance and beneficial psychological profiles of athletes. Most research so far is based on correlational designs and is limited since no conclusions can be drawn about causality. To date, the optimism–performance relationship has, however, been supported in some studies (e.g., Gordon, 2008; Seligman, Nolen-Hoeksema, Thornton, & Thornton, 1990; Wilson, Raglin, & Pritchard, 2002). For example, Gordon (2008, Study 1) found that optimistic soccer players performed better (shots on goal, pass completion ratio) than pessimists when losing, but no differences were noted when winning. However, the findings are not clear cut and indicate that pessimism also could be adaptive if failure is attributed to lack of effort instead of lack of ability (Gordon, 2008, Study 2). Moreover, Wilson and colleagues (2002) found that defensive pessimism (i.e., a strategy to consciously set low expectations as a protective mechanism for potential failure and disappointment) was not associated with lower performance (measured as each athlete's performance in terms of percentage of the NCAA qualifying standard for their specific event) than optimism in Collegiate Division 1 track and field athletes. The general opinion, nonetheless, appears to be that optimism is beneficial for athletes.

Based on research in general psychology, optimism is likely to be an important attribute in coaches. Coaches are also performers and have to handle stressful situations and need to be flexible because their job is demanding and ever-changing. Optimism has been found to be related to perceived coaching efficacy (Thelwell, Lane, Weston, & Greenlees, 2008), and coaches who are optimistic appear more likely to focus on athletes' coachability (Solomon, 2015). Thus, highly optimistic coaches may have greater confidence in their abilities and appear to be more positive in their beliefs about their athletes' possibilities. The consequences of optimism in coaches and, for example, how athletes perceive their coaching are interesting areas for future research (cf. Wilson et al., 2015).

The empirical research on hope and performance has shown that high-hope individuals perform better than low-hope individuals, both in academics and sport. For example, high-hope college students had higher semester grade averages (Curry et al., 1997) and higher achievement test scores (Snyder et al., 1997) than their lower-scoring counterparts. Similarly, in a study of female track and field NCAA Division 1 runners, high-hope runners performed significantly better (using a national qualifying mark as a measure of performance) than low-hope athletes, even when controlling for athletic ability and affect (Curry et al., 1997).

The better performance of high-hope individuals has been attributed to higher than average dedication and energy in pursuing goals they find desirable (Rodriguez-Hanley & Snyder, 2000; Snyder et al., 2005). High-hope individuals tend to put forward more effort in pursuit of their goals because they believe a positive outcome will occur. Conversely, because low-hope individuals tend to believe that their efforts will not result in desired outcomes, they typically put forward less energy and drive in pursuit of their goals than their high-hope counterparts (Snyder et al., 1991). For athletes, greater dedication and energy are clearly advantageous in helping them stay focused and motivated over long periods of time, and helping overcome frustrations when goal attainment is thwarted. High-hope individuals tend to set more goals in life than low-hope individuals (Snyder et al., 1991), so when one goal is blocked they can pursue other viable goals. They are also better in creating alternative pathways to reach their goals and thereby less likely to experience total goal blockage. People with high hope also tend to set more challenging goals – referred to as "stretch goals" (Snyder, 2002; Snyder et al., 1991). Even if these goals require high effort, high-hope individuals more often attain their goals than low-hope individuals because the goals are based on their own previous performances (Snyder et al., 1991). An associated explanation for the relationship between hope and performance found in the literature is that high-hope athletes may train harder than their low-hope counterparts. Recent research has indicated that hope seems to be associated with an increased number of training hours (Gustafsson and colleagues, in press).

Hope has also been investigated in relation to cognitive performance. Woodman and colleagues (2009) conducted an experimental study on semi-professional male soccer players where reaction time was assessed as a measure of cognitive performance. The authors of the study found that hope was related to significantly faster reaction times and also appeared to increase athletes' self-reported mental effort on concentrating on the task (Woodman et al., 2009). This implies that increased hope in athletes can be a way for coaches to help athletes improve their concentration and performance.

Research focused on investigating psychological characteristics in successful athletes has directly or indirectly found that hope and optimism might be a valuable asset. Gould, Dieffenbach, and Moffett (2002) interviewed and completed psychological inventories with 10 Olympic champions to explore the athletes' levels of optimism and hope. The results showed that these elite athletes displayed very high levels of hope in terms of both agency and pathway thinking and also displayed high levels of optimism. Later studies have confirmed that international-caliber junior athletes seem to display higher levels of hope than their national, regional or local counterparts (Gustafsson et al., in press).

Optimism and hope have also indirectly been considered as important ingredients in mental toughness, which relates to an umbrella term used for various psychological factors and characteristics (e.g., self-motivation, self-belief, focus, positive and tough attitude, resilience, ability to cope with pressure and an attitude not to give up until the game is over) displayed in highly successful athletes (e.g., Connaughton, Hanton, & Jones, 2010; Coulter et al., 2010). Thus, the findings of studies conducted to date seem to indicate that hope and optimism are valuable characteristics for athletes in their continuous strivings to develop and perform at various competitive sport levels.

Hope, optimism and athlete well-being or ill-being

In line with the majority of research conducted in mainstream psychology, sport psychology studies have in general indirectly or directly supported the notion that optimism and hope are beneficial for athlete well-being (Gustafsson, Skoog, Podlog, Lundqvist, & Wagnsson, 2013; Lu & Hsu, 2013; Lundqvist & Sandin, 2014). Lu and Hsu (2013) performed a study on injured collegiate student–athletes and found that both pathway and agency hope were significantly related to positive affect. In addition, they also found that hope predicted rehabilitation beliefs and that hope agency was associated with higher rehabilitation compliance. Thus, it appears that injured athletes who are hopeful are more likely to follow the rehabilitation plan. Additionally, social support was more related to well-being among low-hope athletes than among high-hope athletes. Thus, the findings suggest that social support, which is often regarded as highly important in times of need, might be most important for athletes low in dispositional hope. Enhancing hope might therefore be an important job among coaches and physiotherapists in sport.

A positive and significant relationship between hope (both agency and pathway) and positive affect was also found when competitive soccer players were investigated (Gustafsson et al., 2013). The study revealed that hope was negatively related to perceived stress and negative affect among these soccer players. Together these findings suggest that hopeful athletes perceive more positive affect together with less stress and negative affect than athletes with lower hope. The role of positive experiences in youth sports has often been put forward as important for personal development and continuation in youth sports (e.g., Cronin & Allen, 2015). Therefore, enhancing hopeful sport environments in youth sports might be beneficial for sport enjoyment and adherence.

Some research has focused on the relationship between optimism, hope and ill-being. Studies have found that both optimism and hope among athletes are negatively related to stress and burnout (Gustafsson, Hassmén, & Podlog, 2010; Gustafsson & Skoog, 2012) and that athletes classified as low in hope seem to score higher on burnout dimensions than medium- and high-hope athletes (Gustafsson et al., 2010). In addition, self-rated stress and positive affect have been indicated to mediate the relationship between hope and burnout among soccer players (Gustafsson et al., 2013). The results from these studies suggest that low–hope athletes might have increased risk of athletic burnout as a consequence of the disturbance of unmet goals and the lack of perceived possibility to find a route to achieve the goals. On the other hand, the ability to preserve hope seems to be related to well-being, decreased levels of stress and as a consequence a decreased risk of burnout.

Interventions on hope and optimism

Intervention research indicates that hope and optimism can be purposefully changed by various methods (Peterson & Steen, 2009). Researchers have explored feasible interventions that might be useful in strengthening these inner capacities among people in an attempt to help them increase well-being and opportunities to flourish in personally significant life contexts. A majority of intervention studies have nevertheless still been conducted on clinical populations (Littman-Ovadia & Nir, 2014). For sport psychology scientists, great opportunities exist to extend research to sport and other physical activity settings.

Optimism interventions

A fundamental argument for much of the intervention research on optimism is the contention that if people can learn helplessness they should also be able to learn optimism (Seligman, 2011). As such, a majority of research on optimism interventions has focused on how habitual thought patterns in terms of explanatory styles (or attributions) can be changed. It is known that techniques adopted from cognitive behavioral therapy (CBT) are effective in teaching people more optimistic interpretation of situations and events (e.g., Laird & Metalsky, 2008; Peterson & Steen, 2009). Jaycox, Reivich, Gillham, and Seligman (1994) developed a program called The Penn Prevention Program (which was later renamed to The Penn Resilience Program) in which they aimed to prevent depressive symptoms among children at risk using principles from CBT and attribution retraining. The program included both a cognitive component (e.g., questioning and re-evaluating negative self-beliefs and beliefs about others, the present situation and the future; training a less pessimistic explanatory style with more accurate attributions) and a social component (e.g., goal-setting, taking a wider perspective on things and gathering information, problem-solving and various coping skills). Children who took part in the program showed decreased depressive symptoms and improved classroom behavior (Gillham, Reivich, Jaycox, & Seligman, 1995; Jaycox et al., 1994). Later studies have confirmed that the program and the methods included seem to be effective at reducing symptoms of depression (cf. Brunwasser, Gillham, & Kim, 2009).

Attribution retraining has also successfully been applied in sport. Rascle, Le Foll, and Higgins (2008) found that oral attribution feedback provided by an external person at a single occasion could induce direct changes in novice golf players' attributions about failure and expectancies as well as behaviors during free-practice. Thus, these results suggest that a coach or a sport psychologist can induce adaptive influences on novice athletes' causal attributions by use of timely feedback. This could, for example, be beneficial when attributions are judged as detrimental to the athlete's performance or pose a risk for loss in the athlete's motivation, increasing the risk of a potential dropout from sport. Parkes and Mallett (2011) implemented CBT techniques (e.g., identifying and testing the accuracy of automatic thoughts and putting them in relation to affect and behavior) in an intervention on rugby players and found qualitative support for the notion that the intervention helped participants to change to a more optimistic explanatory style when facing negative events. One of the participants in the study by Parkes and Mallett (2011) commented on the perceived effects of the intervention as follows: "I dropped a simple pass early in the game ... I looked at it as an opportunity, I would never have done that [seen the opportunity] in the past" (p. 279).

Attributional retraining

Let us take a closer look at how attribution training from a CBT perspective could be implemented (see also, e.g., Laird & Metalsky, 2008) by the sport psychologist or the experienced coach. Overall, the attributional retraining generally follows a number of interrelated phases:

- Assessment and information gathering of the current attributions and thinking distortions (e.g., self-blame or a perception of an excessive personal responsibility) in various situations is recommended. This assessment and analysis act as a tool to individualize the intervention and as a baseline from which progress can be evaluated. The assessment could be obtained by interviewing the athlete and/or by use of self-assessment inventories (e.g., the Sports Attributional Style Scale; Hanrahan & Grove, 1990; Hanrahan, Grove, & Hattie, 1989). Today, however, a general lack of sport-adapted and psychometrically sound measures exist to assess attributional style among athletes and coaches. Researchers within this field should therefore be encouraged to focus on the development of improved sport-adapted assessment tools.
- Goals for the intervention are established together with the athlete. The athlete is also educated about attributional retraining and how thought patterns and images are related to emotions and behavior. In addition, the athlete is trained to identify and analyze maladaptive attributional patterns and question how these cognitive patterns are associated with particular emotions and behavior which, in turn, affect performance.
- Together with the athlete, homework exercises to be conducted between the sessions are chosen in which the athlete starts to practice changing habitual attributions in his or her natural environment. Thus, the athlete practices critically examining evidence (i.e., concrete facts) for and against the attributions and replace distorted attributions with more realistic and adaptive ones. In this phase, it is usually adaptive if the athlete keeps a record of the situations, attributions and associated emotions in combination with the consequences they have for his/her feelings, behavior or performance.
- The records completed by the athlete are discussed and evaluated with the sport psychologist or coach during the following session in order to further stimulate the learning process. The overreaching goal of the training is to educate the athlete to become his or her own sport psychologist in order to be able to analyze, critically challenge and modify distorted attributions automatically on a daily basis and continue the practices independently after the formal intervention has ended.

Brief Optimism Exercise

Would you be willing to challenge yourself during a week to explore whether a brief optimism exercise might have any beneficial effects on you, your life or your

3 positive things for tomorrow

sport participation? Littman-Ovadia and Nir (2014) developed a very brief (five minutes/day) intervention for use with non-clinical participants. In this intervention participants are instructed to think of and write down three positive things they expect to happen during the next day. In addition, participants are instructed to feel the positive feelings associated with one of the things they have written down and maintain this feeling for five minutes. When Littman-Ovadia and Nir (2014) evaluated the effects of the intervention after seven days of practice, they found support for the notion that practicing this brief exercise of optimistic expectations reduced participants' negative states, including pessimism, negative affect and emotional exhaustion.

Hope interventions

Gould et al. (2002) suggested that hope is an especially interesting construct to explore because sport psychology goal-setting research has typically focused on specific goal characteristics. However, the hope model provides a meta or holistic system for analyzing goal-setting with both dispositional and state components, the specific goals one sets, potential pathways for goal attainment, and motivational strategies for dealing with obstacles that block goal achievement (Snyder, 2002). According to Curry and Snyder (2000), hope represents a meta-construct in so far as pathways and agency thinking are considered reciprocal and mutually reinforcing elements related to athletic achievement.

Although research in other areas indicates the benefits and the potential for hope interventions, very few studies have been conducted in the sport realm. In a group of student-athletes Rolo and Gould (2007) investigated the effectiveness of a six-week-long hope intervention. The interventions led to an increased state of hope compared with a control group. However, no differences were found in dispositional hope, academic and athletic domain hope, or perceptions of athletic and academic performance. Furthermore, Curry and Maniar (2003) developed an academic course for student-athletes in which psychological skills training was combined with life skills education. In this 15-week program, dispositional hope, self-esteem and sport confidence significantly improved compared with a control group. These two studies indicate the possibility for hope-enhancing interventions within sport. Noteworthy is that both studies used control groups, but without any randomization which would have increased the possibility to establish causal relationships. Thus, there is a need for randomized-control treatment studies to establish the effectiveness of these kinds of hope-enhancing interventions.

Summary and some future directions

Extensive research evidence exists in general psychology that shows that being optimistic and hopeful is beneficial in many aspects of life. These findings have been somewhat unnoticed in sport research literature, although being optimistic and hopeful is used in colloquial terms among coaches, athletes and other officials in sports. Considering the existing knowledge, it seems that both hope and optimism are highly beneficial characteristics for coaches and athletes involved in various sport settings. Studies conducted in sport have nevertheless foremost focused on athletes and how optimism and hope is associated with better performances and less stress and ill-being. Further research is needed to also investigate *why* hopeful and optimistic athletes perform better. In addition, research on coaches is warranted and is an interesting avenue for future research, including both how they can handle stressful situations as well as how hopeful and optimistic coaches are perceived by their athletes. Finally, more knowledge about intervention approaches, including how to improve hope and optimism by short-term and long-term interventions, and how coaches and sport psychologists can help pessimistic and low-hope athletes, is warranted and would enable better possibilities to transfer theoretical knowledge into the applied sport settings.

References

Alarcon, G. M., Bowling, N. A., & Khazon, S. (2013). Great expectations: A meta-analytic examination of optimism and hope. *Personality and Individual Differences*, 54, 821–827.

Bandura, A. (1997). *Self-Efficacy: The Exercise of Control*. New York: Freeman.

Bandura, A., & Locke, E. (2003). Negative self-efficacy and goal effects revisited. *Journal of Applied Psychology*, 88, 87–89.

Brunwasser, S. M., Gillham, J. E., & Kim, E. S. (2009). A meta-analytic review of the Penn Resiliency Program's effect on depressive symptoms. *Journal of Consulting and Clinical Psychology*, 77, 1042–1054.

Bryant, F. B., & Cvengros, J. A. (2004). Distinguishing hope and optimism: Two sides of a coin, or two separate coins? *Journal of Social and Clinical Psychology*, 23, 273–302.

Carver, C. S., & Scheier, M. F. (1998). *On the Self-Regulation of Behavior*. Cambridge: Cambridge University Press.

Carver, C. S., & Scheier, M. F. (2005). Optimism. In C. R. Synder & S. J. Lopez (Eds.), *Handbook of Positive Psychology* (pp. 231–243). New York: Oxford University Press.

Carver, C. S., Scheier, M. F., Miller, C. J., & Fulford, D. (2009). Optimism. In C. R. Snyder & S. J. Lopez (Eds.), *Oxford Handbook of Positive Psychology* (pp. 303–311). Oxford: Oxford University Press.

Connaughton, D., Hanton, S., & Jones, G. (2010). The development and maintenance of mental toughness in the world's best performers. *The Sport Psychologist*, 24, 168–193.

Coulter, T., Mallett, C. J., & Gucciardi, D. F. (2010). Understanding mental toughness in Australian soccer. Perceptions of players, parents, and coaches. *Journal of Sports Sciences*, 28, 699–716.

Cronin, L. D., & Allen, J. B. (2015). Development experiences and well-being in sport: The importance of the coaching climate. *The Sport Psychologist*, 29, 62–71.

Curry, L. A., & Maniar, S. D. (2003). Academic course combining psychological skills training and life skills education for university students and student-athletes. *Journal of Applied Sport Psychology*, 15, 270–277.

Curry, L. A., & Snyder, C. R. (2000). Hope takes the field: Mind matters in athletic performance. In C. R. Snyder (Ed.), *Handbook of Hope: Theory, Measures and Applications* (pp. 243–259). San Diego, CA: Academic Press.

Curry, L. A., Snyder, C. R., Cook, D. L., Ruby, B. C., & Rehm, M. (1997). Role of hope in academic and sport achievement. *Journal of Personality and Social Psychology*, 73, 1257–1267.

Everhart, J. S., Best, T. M., & Flanigan, D. C. (2015). Psychological predictors of anterior cruciate ligament reconstruction outcomes: A systematic review. *Knee Surgery Sports Traumatology Arthroscopy*, 23, 752–762.

Gallagher, M. W., & Lopez, S. J. (2009). Positive expectancies and mental health: Identifying the unique contributions of hope and optimism. *Journal of Positive Psychology*, 4, 548–556.

Geers, A. L., Wellman, J. A., & Lassiter, G. D. (2009). Dispositional optimism and engagement: The moderating influence of goal prioritization. *Journal of Personality and Social Psychology*, 96, 913–932.

Gillham, J. E., Reivich, K. J., Jaycox, L. H., & Seligman, M. E. P. (1995). Prevention of depressive symptoms in schoolchildren. *Psychological Science*, 6, 343–351.

Gordon, R. A. (2008). Attributional style and athletic performance: Strategic optimism and defensive pessimism. *Psychology of Sport and Exercise*, 9, 336–350.

Gould, D., Dieffenbach, K., & Moffett, A. (2002). Psychological characteristics and their development in Olympic champions. *Journal of Applied Sport Psychology*, 14, 172–204.

Gustafsson, H., Hassmén, P., & Podlog, L. (2010). Exploring the relationship between hope and burnout in competitive sport. *Journal of Sports Sciences*, 28, 1495–1504.

Gustafsson, H., Podlog, L., & Davis, P. (in press). Hope and athletic performance. In M. W. Gallagher & S. J. Lopez (Eds.), *The Oxford Handbook of Hope*. New York: Oxford University Press.

Gustafsson, H., & Skoog, T. (2012). The mediational role of perceived stress in the relation between optimism and burnout in competitive athletes. *Anxiety, Stress & Coping*, 25, 183–199.

Gustafsson, H., Skoog, T., Podlog, L., Lundqvist, C., & Wagnsson, S. (2013). Hope and athlete burnout: Stress and affect as mediators. *Psychology of Sport and Exercise*, 14, 640–649.

Hanrahan, S. J., & Grove, J. R. (1990). Further examination of the psychometric properties of the sport attributional style scale. *Journal of Sport Behavior*, 13, 183–193.

Hanrahan, S. J., Grove, J. R., & Hattie, J. A. (1989). Development of a questionnaire measure of sport related attributional style. *International Journal of Sport Psychology*, 20, 114–134.

Harris, R. (2008). *The Happiness Trap: Stop Struggling, Start Living*. Wollombi: Exisle Publishing, Ltd.

Jaycox, L. H., Reivich, K. J., Gillham, J., & Seligman, M. E. P. (1994). Prevention of depressive symptoms in school children *Behaviour Research and Therapy*, 32, 801–816.

Laird, R. S., & Metalsky, G. I. (2008). Attribution change. In W. T. O'Donohue & J. E. Fischer (Eds.), *Cognitive Behavior Therapy: Applying Empirically Supported Techniques in Your Practice* (2nd ed., pp. 35–39). Hoboken, NJ: Wiley & Sons.

Littman-Ovadia, H., & Nir, D. (2014). Looking forward to tomorrow: The buffering effect of a daily optimism intervention. *The Journal of Positive Psychology*, 9, 122–136.

Lu, F. J. H., & Hsu, Y. (2013). Injured athletes' rehabilitation beliefs and subjective well-being: The contribution of hope and social support. *Journal of Athletic Training*, 48, 92–98.

Lundqvist, C., & Sandin, F. (2014). Well-being in elite sport: Dimensions of hedonic and eudaimonic well-being among elite orienteers at a global and sport specific level. *The Sport Psychologist*, 28, 245–254.

Nothwehr, F., Clark, D. O., & Perkins, A. (2013). Hope and the use of behavioural strategies related to diet and physical activity. *Journal of Human Nutrition and Dietetics*, 26, 159–163.

Parkes, J. F., & Mallett, C. J. (2011). Developing mental toughness: Attributional style retraining in rugby. *The Sport Psychologist*, 25, 269–287.

Peterson, C., & Seligman, M. E. P. (1984). Causal explanations as a risk factor for depression: Theory and evidence. *Psychological Review*, 91, 341–314.

Peterson, C., & Seligman, M. E. P. (1987). Explanatory style and illness. *Journal of Personality*, 55, 237–265.

Peterson, C., & Steen, T. A. (2005). Optimistic explanatory style. In C. R. Snyder & S. J. Lopez (Eds.), *Handbook of Positive Psychology* (pp. 244–256). New York: Oxford University Press.

Peterson, C., & Steen, T. A. (2009). Optimistic explanatory style. In C. R. Snyder & S. J. Lopez (Eds.), *Oxford Handbook of Positive Psychology* (pp. 313–321). Oxford: Oxford University Press.

Rand, K. L., & Cheavens, J. S. (2009). Hope theory. In C. R. Snyder & S. J. Lopez (Eds.), *Oxford Handbook of Positive Psychology* (pp. 323–333). Oxford: Oxford University Press.

Rascle, O., Le Foll, D., & Higgins, N. C. (2008). Attributional retraining alters novice golfers' free practice behavior. *Journal of Applied Sport Psychology*, 20, 157–164.

Rodriguez-Hanley, A., & Snyder, C. R. (2000). The demise of hope: On losing positive thinking. In C. R. Snyder (Ed.), *Handbook of Hope: Theory, Measures and Applications* (pp. 39–54). San Diego, CA: Academic Press.

Rolo, C., & Gould, D. (2007). An intervention for fostering hope, athletic and academic performance in university student-athletes. *International Coaching Psychology Review*, 2, 44–61.

Scheier, M. F., & Carver, C. S. (1992). Effects of optimism on psychological and physical well-being: Theoretical overview and empirical update. *Cognitive Therapy and Research*, 16, 201–228.

Scioli, A., Scioli-Salter, E. R., Sykes, K., Anderson, C., & Fedele, M. (2016). The positive contributions of hope to maintaining and restoring health: An integrative mixed-method approach. *The Journal of Positive Psychology*, 11, 135–148.

Seligman, M. E. P. (2011). *Flourish: A New Understanding of Happiness and Well-Being – and How to Achieve Them*. London: Nicholas Brealey Publishing.

Seligman, M. E. P., Nolen-Hoeksema, S., Thornton, N., & Thornton, K. M. (1990). Explanatory style as a mechanism of disappointing athletic performance. *Psychological Science*, 1, 143–146.

Snyder, C. R. (2002). Hope theory: Rainbows in the mind. *Psychological Inquiry*, 13, 249–275.

Snyder, C. R., Harris, C., Anderson, J. R., Holleran, S. A., Irving, L. M., Sigmon, S. T., . . . Harney, P. (1991). The will and the ways: Development and validation of an individual-differences measure of hope. *Journal of Personality and Social Psychology*, 60, 570–585.

Snyder, C. R., Hoza, B., Pelham, W. E., Rapoff, M., Ware, L., Danovsky, M., . . . Stahl, K. J. (1997). The development and validation of the Children's Hope Scale. *Journal of Pediatric Psychology*, 22, 399–421.

Snyder, C. R., Rand, K. L., & Sigmon, D. R. (2005). Hope theory. In C. R. Snyder & S. J. Lopez (Eds.), *Handbook of Positive Psychology* (pp. 257–276). New York: Oxford University Press.

Solomon, G. B. (2015). The influence of coach optimism on athlete development in intercollegiate sport. *Athletic Insight*, 7, 101–113.

Thelwell, R. C., Lane, A. M., Weston, N. J. V., & Greenlees, I. A. (2008). Examining the relationships between emotional intelligence and coaching efficacy. *International Journal of Sport and Exercise Psychology*, 6, 224–235.

Vancouver, J., More, K., & Yoder, R. (2008). Self-efficacy and resource allocation: Support for a nonmonotonic, discontinuous model. *Journal of Applied Psychology*, 93, 35–47.

Wilson, G. S., Raglin, J. S., & Pritchard, M. E. (2002). Optimism, pessimism, and precompetition anxiety in college athletes. *Personality and Individual Differences*, 32, 893–902.

Wilson, M., Hawkins, B., & Joyner, B. (2015). An investigation of optimism between players and coaches in NCAA men's division I golf. *Journal of Sport Behavior*, 38, 118–140.

Woodman, T., Davis, P. A., Hardy, L., Callow, N., Glasscock, I., & Yuill-Proctor, J. (2009). Emotions and sport performance: An exploration of happiness, hope, and anger. *Journal of Sport & Exercise Psychology*, 31, 169–188.

7

MINDFULNESS IN SPORT AND PHYSICAL EXERCISE

Hanna Kampman and Tim Lomas

The modern age is full of opportunities and information. Today's exerciser and athlete can access new ideas and theories quickly. Furthermore, these findings can be put into practice almost instantaneously. However, often people are untrained to deal with such opportunities, and at times the novelty and sheer volume can render them overwhelming. Such is perhaps true of modern life generally, which is replete with information and distraction. Given this context, athletes and coaches as well as regular exercisers are starting to acknowledge, now more than ever, the benefits of learning skills to ground them in the present moment. A particularly valuable method of attention training that can help athletes and exercisers in this respect is mindfulness.

This chapter begins by exploring what is mindfulness and discussing the importance of mindfulness in sport and exercise. It then provides an introduction to the practice of mindfulness, offering tangible applied examples. The chapter then reviews the current evidence and research around mindfulness in relation to sport and exercise. Finally, we conclude with suggestions for further practice, as well as ideas for researchers to establish stronger evidence for the impact of mindfulness.

What is mindfulness?

> Mindfulness is the awareness that emerges through paying attention on purpose, in the present moment, and nonjudgmentally to the unfolding of experience moment by moment.
>
> —(Kabat-Zinn, 2003, p. 145)

It is useful to think of mindfulness in two main ways: (a) as a quality/state of mind and (b) as a meditation practice that can allow one to cultivate this quality/state.

Its origins lie in Buddhism, a religious philosophy founded by Gautama Siddhartha – better known by his honorific title Buddha, meaning 'enlightened one' – who is believed to have lived around 2,500 years ago in present-day Nepal. One of his foundational teachings is the 'Discourse on the establishment of mindfulness,' which includes instructions for paying close attention to the act of breathing. This teaching masterfully communicates both aspects of mindfulness (a) as a quality/state (of awareness) and (b) as a practice for establishing this state (e.g., paying attenion to the breath). This teaching has influenced contemporary operationalisations of mindfulness, such as the definition provided by Jon Kabat-Zinn, who was pivotal in bringing mindfulness to the West via his pioneering 'Mindfulness-Based Stress Reduction Programme' (Kabat-Zinn, 1982). His definition positions mindfulness both as a quality/state ('. . . the awareness that emerges. . .') and as a practice that helps one to cultivate this state ('. . . through paying attention on purpose. . .').

It is important to differentiate between these two aspects. As a quality/state of mind, mindfulness does not 'belong' to Buddhism. Mindfulness as a quality/state is simply a way of being in this world, involving being non-judgementally aware of one's thoughts, emotions, sensations and so on. Many people who have never meditated may have moments in the day that could be characterised as mindful, moments when they are not mentally lost in a whirlwind of thoughts, but are simply aware of what is happening right now – sights and sounds, how their body is feeling, and so on. Indeed, you the reader may have been graced with moments of this kind of heightened, receptive awareness during particularly good sporting performances or training sessions.

Crucially, this quality/state of mind is not something that simply happens, but can be practised. Like any skill, it takes time and dedication to learn and master. To understand its value further here, the next section elucidates the significance and potential of mindfulness in sport and exercise.

The importance of mindfulness in sport and exercise

Mindfulness has not always been seen as a natural part of sport and exercise. However, it could be argued that mindfulness is a good fit with psychological skills training where the purpose is to develop performance, increase enjoyment and gain greater satisfaction from the activity. Traditionally in sport the focus for mental preparation has been on cognitive-behavioral techniques that improve self-regulation by controlling internal factors (Weinberg & Gould, 2014; Sappington & Longshore, 2015). Often the aim is to avoid or regulate negative internal states to create an optimal environment for peak performance. These practices may be useful but at other times inadequate. Whilst negative internal states may hinder peak performance, controlling them does not guarantee peak performance. Thus, it could be highly beneficial to include skills training focused on developing greater awareness and acceptance as well as controlling negative internal states.

During the past decade, sport and exercise scientists and coaches have started to suggest that it could be valuable to include the practice of mindfulness as part of the athlete's psychological skills training (Baltzell, 2016; Gardner & Moore, 2007; Pineau, Glass, & Kaufman, 2014). Tolerance and acceptance toward feelings, thoughts and emotions could help athletes to stay present and focused on the task at hand (Goodman, Kashdan, Mallard, & Schumann, 2014). The ability to act with awareness within sport and exercise routines, as well as the ability to reduce task-irrelevant thoughts such as worrying, are instrumental skills for an athlete. Studies have shown that mindfulness training can indeed promote these skills and thus provide an advantage in both training and competition settings (Thompson, Kaufman, De Petrillo, Glass, & Arnkoff, 2011).

Research suggests the benefits of mindfulness are manifold. Mindfulness practice can make exercising more enjoyable, and moreover help practitioners to focus, thereby lowering the likelihood of injury (Ivarsson, Johnson, Andersen, Fallby, & Altemyr, 2015; Brani, Hefferon, Lomas, Ivtzan, & Painter, 2014). It has been used in rehabilitation settings to promote commitment to rehabilitation behaviours and to build certainty around returning to sport (Mahoney & Hanrahan, 2011). It has been found to help establish better work-life balance by increasing the ability to stay focused on the moment at hand, whether a sport performance situation or family-orientated activities (Longshore & Sachs, 2015). Finally, research suggests it can positively influence the coach-athlete interactions through improved well-being, reduced stress and lower levels of anxiety (Longshore & Sachs, ibid). Thus, there is robust evidence for the value of mindfulness in a sporting context, and these benefits are just as useful for the regular exerciser. It is then certainly useful to try to implement this practice as part of athletes' training routines, starting with simple practices that enable the cultivation of this skill.

How to practice mindfulness

Mindfulness can be practiced in various ways. Formally speaking, people practice mindfulness through mindfulness meditation. 'Meditation' is an overarching label for a variety of practices that all involve developing one's attention and awareness (Walsh & Shapiro, 2006). *Mindfulness* meditation then specifically means trying to cultivate mindfulness, in contrast to other meditation practices, in which one tries to generate other valuable states of mind.

In line with the conventional image of meditation, you can choose to sit in a quiet place, and to try to be mindful of your breath. The important thing is that you sit with your back relatively straight, enacting a posture which encourages alertness and attentiveness and at the same time feels comfortable (Austin, 1998). Mindfulness can be practiced during any daily activity, from doing the dishes to gardening. Whatever you decide to do, engage with it with awareness and attention, experiencing it moment to moment. You can draw your attention inwards to yourself (e.g. by focusing on the breath) or outwards (by perceiving what is happening around you). Here's how you can try it out:

Take time to notice

1   Look around you. Notice one thing that you can see. What does it look like? What are its colours? Its shape? Is it far away or close by?
2   Now close your eyes. Notice one thing that you can hear. How does it sound? Is it loud? Is it subtle? Is it harmonious – or chaotic?
3   Keep your eyes closed. Now notice one thing that you feel in your body. What do you feel? What does the feeling feel like? Is it strong? Or is it weak?

As this gets easier, develop this exercise by noticing two or three things in each category (e.g. seeing, hearing, feeling). This exercise can be used, for example, at the beginning of a training session if you are feeling unfocused and your mind keeps drifting to other tasks.

When people start practicing mindfulness meditation, it is common that they feel irritated or frustrated when their thoughts wander or their attention escapes. That is a very common experience. Of course, not everyone finds mindfulness meditation suitable for them and indeed, in certain circumstances, people may find mindfulness unhelpful. For instance, while mindfulness has been successfully used to help prevent people from relapsing into depression (Ma & Teasdale, 2004), it is generally not recommended for people who are currently depressed, as they may get drawn further into introspection and rumination (Lustyk, Chawla, Nolan, & Marlatt, 2009). As noted previously, mindfulness can be difficult at first, especially given the mind's tendency to wander off. But with practice it teaches you to accept this habit of the mind, allowing you to acknowledge where the mind goes, and then gently escort it back to the task at hand.

Through practice, we can develop our attention skills, and thus our capacity to be mindful (Chiesa, Calati, & Serretti, 2011). When that happens, our 'meta-cognitive' abilities are enhanced, which, in turn, facilitates well-being (Vago & Silbersweig, 2012). For instance, mindfulness can eventually increase tolerance toward uncomfortable emotional states (e.g. fear) by allowing us to 'decentre' from these qualia (i.e. to 'step back' and view these with greater objectivity and detachment) (Fresco et al., 2007). For example, we might be able to view feelings of anger as 'the anger,' rather than 'my anger,' hence making it easier to let it go. This acceptance toward emotional cues helps to build resilience by increasing the capacity to tolerate discomfort. This is opposite to other, perhaps more traditional Western approaches, which aim to decrease discomfort. Mindfulness practice can increase awareness that life unfolds in moments, and help realise opportunities for growth and transformation (Kabat-Zinn, 2009).

The value of mindfulness practice in sport and exercise

Most people are aware of the benefits of regular exercise. Nevertheless, despite all the advertised benefits, some are left wondering why it is often difficult. A regular exerciser might encounter varying struggles with enjoyment, goal-setting and adherence. Furthermore, too often our bodies are treated as vehicles for something: to have more energy, to bring us health or to look attractive. This can easily lead to forgetting how to enjoy the exercise, and pushing our bodies too hard, beyond what is beneficial. This can then lead to decreased motivation toward the practice.

> You can't stop the waves but you can learn to surf.
>
> *(Kabat-Zinn, ibid, p. 30)*

Similarly, athletes may experience various challenges during their experience in sport. Some athletes may at times struggle with training-related challenges such as motivation, focus, goal-setting and team cohesion. Others may battle with competition-specific issues such as anxiety, arousal regulation, external and internal distractions and uncertainty about the future. Often athletes' careers entail both training and competition-related challenges in varying combinations. This yields a clear need for psychological skills training that provides ways to stay in the present, whilst acting with awareness and acceptance.

How can mindfulness help athletes and exercisers?

An unmindful mind is excellent at reminiscing upon past failings: competitions that were unsuccessful, the one training when performance was under par, or the time when spectators were unforgiving. The mind is asking the unavoidable question: '*Will this happen again?*' Often without any effort this will open up an avenue of opportunities for the mind: the failings that are in the future and the terrifying 'Ifs,' 'Buts' and 'What ifs,' making it hard to keep things in perspective. Furthermore, a stressed mind is less able to think of diverse and creative solutions to problems because stress engenders the 'fight or flight' response (Fredrickson, 2001; Isen, Daubman, & Nowicki, 1987). Hence, it can be very useful for athletes and regular exercisers to pay attention to their inner dialogue, that is, what they are thinking during the competition or training. Often these 'conversations' happen in the background without real awareness. This makes it difficult to address the potentially harmful thought patterns that can influence performance. Thus, the key is to learn how to be aware of these thoughts so that they can be addressed without judgement. This is how you can try it out:

Practice being aware of your inner talk

1 Please take a moment to acknowledge your own inner dialogue.
2 For example, what are you thinking and telling yourself when you are competing?
3 Are you thinking: "I can't swim that fast" or "This audience really hates me"?
4 Is this useful information? Is this relevant for your performance?
5 Acknowledge and be aware of your inner dialogue and if non-productive, gently escort it out.

6   Bring your awareness back to the present moment, for example, by noticing where you are or by following your breath. Let the mind quieten.

You can start trying out this exercise in training settings to get used to it. It is important to acknowledge these inner dialogues without judgement so that you can handle them as momentary states and leave them out of your performance. By being more aware it is possible to focus on the task at hand. This exercise can easily be adapted for an exerciser: just consider the inner dialogue that goes on during your exercise session. For example, what are you thinking at the gym? Are you thinking, "Oh, everyone is watching me; I can't do this"? Follow the previously described steps.

Because of its focus on awareness and acceptance, mindfulness can additionally have an effect on other psychological skills, such as adjustment and the ability to relax. For the same reasons, practicing mindfulness can lower levels of anxiety, sadness and confusion that are sometimes a part of athletes' careers (Keng, Smoski, & Robins, 2011; Peterson, & Pbert, 1992) as well as reduce stress and burnout (Gustafsson, Skoog, Davis, Kenttä, & Haberl, 2015). An enhanced ability to be aware and accept emotions might additionally play a significant role in enhancing team performance. There is already evidence for this in team athletes, because mindfulness practice seems to be linked to building effective team cohesion (Baltzell, Caraballo, Chipman, & Hayden, 2014; Pineau, Glass, Kaufman, & Bernal, 2014). In team settings, experiencing a sense of control can be difficult due to the presence of others. Having more affect tolerance can help to see emotions - both one's own and others' - as information, thus making it easier to accept them. In turn, this may contribute to a more supportive and collaborative environment.

Effortless activity in sport and exercise

Effortless activity in sport and exercise is the outcome of years of practice and experience. It often shows in peak performance and is described as being in *flow* or being *in the zone* (Csikszentmihalyi, 2008; Jackson & Csikszentmihalyi, 1999). Flow is defined as being absorbed by the task at hand, where self-consciousness and sense of time are reduced. The activity itself is so important or engrossing that there is no attention left for anything other than what you are doing (Csikszentmihalyi, 2008; Jackson & Csikszentmihalyi, 1999).

Similarly, when regular exercisers focus on what they are doing, they are more aware of how each movement feels, especially when they are new to the activity. This makes it more likely that they enjoy the activity and less likely that they get injured (Ivarsson, Johnson, Andersen, Fallby, & Altemyr, 2015; Brani, Hefferon, Lomas, Ivtzan, & Painter, 2014). This way the exerciser can additionally be present whilst being physically active, and focus on the journey of practicing rather than the outcome of being fit.

Flow has been studied in sport and is seen as a key component of peak performance (Jackson & Csikszentmihalyi, 1999; Privette, 1983; Privette & Brundrick, 1991; Young & Pain, 1999). Flow is achieved when an athlete works at an optimal level of challenge and ability, thus immersing themselves completely in the activity at hand, which is intrinsically rewarding. Sport and exercise psychologists have been talking about 'staying in the moment whilst competing' for a long time (e.g. Jackson & Csikszentmihalyi, 1999; Orlick, 1990). However, only lately has the practice of mindfulness started to become a more common part of psychological skills training. Furthermore, the value of these skills in both training and competition settings are now better understood understood better. The benefit of early inclusion of mindfulness practice is that these skills can be learned gradually during the athletic career and put into practice both in training and competition.

Furthermore, mindfulness practice has been found to have an effect on the challenge-ability aspect of flow through self-efficacy (Cathcart, McGregor, & Groundwater, 2014; Pineau, Glass, Kaufman, & Bernal, 2014). Self- and team efficacy refer to the belief that the individual or the team has concerning their ability to perform their athletic task successfully. As such, it is an important aspect of peak performance (Bandura, 1994; Weinberg & Gould, 2014). It is further connected to motivation, self-confidence and performance in general (Feltz, 1992; Feltz & Lirgg, 2001; Pineau, Glass, Kaufman, & Bernal, 2014). Because of these various benefits, the potential of mindfulness in sport and exercise has been gradually acknowledged. This has led to the development of mindfulness programmes that are designed specifically to athletes such as:

- Mindful Sport Performance Enhancement (MSPE) (Kaufman, Glass, & Arnkoff, 2009, 2016)
- Mindfulness-Acceptance-Commitment (MAC) (Gardner & Moore, 2004, 2007)
- Mindfulness Meditation Training for Sport (MMTS) (Baltzell & Akhtar, 2014; Baltzell, 2016)
- Mindfulness training for achieving flow (Aherne, Moran, & Lonsdale, 2011)

Mindful Sport Performance Enhancement (MSPE) by Kaufman, Glass, and Arnkoff (2009, 2016) is designed to be adapted to different sports and has had positive results in different sports already. Similarly, the Mindfulness-Acceptance-Commitment (MAC) by Gardner and Moore (2004, 2007) involves sport-focused practices. These results suggest that mindfulness could be a highly beneficial addition to psychological skills training. For an excellent review of these interventions, see *Mindfulness in Sport Performance* (Pineau, Glass, & Kaufman, 2014).

Currently, further empirical evidence is needed to understand how these interventions fit different sports and different individuals. As sport and exercise psychology is moving strongly toward a 'person fit' approach in assigning skills training, it is crucial to understand for whom particular mindfulness interventions are most and least beneficial.

Additionally, some researchers suggest that Langer's conceptualisation of mindfulness (Langer, 1989, 1992; Langer & Moldoveanu, 2000) could have great potential in sport (Pineau, Glass, & Kaufman, 2014). However, because of the lack of empirical evidence in sport settings, it has not been included in this chapter. Nevertheless, future research should investigate its potential in sport and exercise settings. For an excellent systematic comparison of these two different schools of thought in mindfulness (Langer's and Kabat-Zinn's), see *Mind the gap in mindfulness research: A comparative account of the leading schools of thought* (Hart, Ivtzan, & Hart, 2013).

It seems clear that mindfulness is here to stay and has attained the attention of exercisers, athletes, coaches and researchers. Thus, we need now to collect further evidence and understanding about the applications of mindfulness in different sports, how it fits with different individuals as well as gather further understanding about best practices and long-term effects.

The aim of this chapter was to provide an introduction to mindfulness and its applicability to sport and exercise. As we hope we have shown, mindfulness can be a very useful skill to master, whether in coaching, exercising for leisure or practising as an athlete. We also want to emphasize that these skills can be applied to life beyond exercising and sport.

References

Aherne, C., Moran, A. P., & Lonsdale, C. (2011). The effect of mindfulness training on athletes' flow: An initial investigation. *The Sport Psychologist*, 25, 177–189.

Austin, J. H. (1998). *Zen and the Brain: Toward an Understanding of Meditation and Consciousness*. Cambridge, MA: MIT Press.

Baltzell, A. L. (Ed.). (2016). *Mindfulness and Performance*. New York: Cambridge University Press.

Baltzell, A. L., & Akhtar, V. L. V. (2014). Mindfulness Meditation Training for Sport (MMTS) intervention: Impact of MMTS with Division I female athletes. *The Journal of Happiness & Well-Being*, 2(2), 160–173.

Baltzell, A. L., Caraballo, N., Chipman, K., & Hayden, L. (2014). A qualitative study of the Mindfulness Meditation Training for Sport: Division I female soccer players' experience. *Journal of Clinical Sport Psychology*, 8(3), 221–244.

Bandura, A. (1994). *Self-Efficacy*. New York: John Wiley & Sons, Inc.

Brani, O., Hefferon, K., Lomas, T., Ivtzan, I., & Painter, J. (2014). The impact of body awareness on subjective wellbeing: The role of mindfulness. *International Body Psychotherapy Journal*, 13(1), 95–107.

Cathcart, S., McGregor, M., & Groundwater, E. (2014). Mindfulness and flow in elite athletes. *Journal of Clinical Sport Psychology*, 8(2), 119–141.

Chiesa, A., Calati, R., & Serretti, A. (2011). Does mindfulness training improve cognitive abilities? A systematic review of neuropsychological findings. *Clinical Psychology Review*, 31(3), 449–464.

Csikszentmihalyi, M. (2008). *Flow: The Psychology of Optimal Experience*. New York: Harper Perennial Modern Classics edition.

Feltz, D. L. (1992). Understanding motivation in sport: A self-efficacy perspective. In G. S. Roberts (Ed.), *Motivation in Sport and Exercise* (pp. 107–128). Champaign, IL: Human Kinetics.

Feltz, D. L., & Lirgg, C. D. (2001). Self-efficacy beliefs of athletes, teams, and coaches. In R. N. Singer, H. A. Hausenblas, & C. M. Janelle (Eds.), *Handbook of Sport Psychology* (2nd ed., pp. 340–361). New York: Wiley.

Fredrickson, B. L. (2001). The role of positive emotions in positive psychology: The broaden-and-build theory of positive emotions. *The American Psychologist*, 56(3), 218–226.

Fresco, D. M., Moore, M. T., van Dulmen, M. H. M., Segal, Z. V., Ma, S. H., Teasdale, J. D., & Williams, J. M. G. (2007). Initial psychometric properties of the experiences questionnaire: Validation of a self-report measure of decentering. *Behavior Therapy*, 38(3), 234–246.

Gardner, F. L., & Moore, Z. E. (2004). A mindfulness-acceptance-commitment-based approach to athletic performance enhancement: Theoretical considerations. *Behavior Therapy*, 35(4), 707–723.

Gardner, F. L., & Moore, Z. E. (2007). *The Psychology of Enhancing Human Performance: The Mindfulness-Acceptance-Commitment (MAC) Approach*. New York: Springer Publishing Company.

Goodman, F. R., Kashdan, T. B., Mallard, T. T., & Schumann, M. (2014). A brief mindfulness and yoga intervention with an entire NCAA Division I athletic team: An initial investigation. *Psychology of Consciousness: Theory, Research, and Practice*, 1(4), 339–351.

Gustafsson, H., Skoog, T., Davis, P., Kenttä, G., & Haberl, P. (2015). Mindfulness and its relationship with perceived stress, affect, and burnout in elite junior athletes. *Journal of Clinical Sport Psychology*, 9(3), 263–281.

Hart, R., Ivtzan, I., & Hart, D. (2013). Mind the gap in mindfulness research: A comparative account of the leading schools of thought. *Review of General Psychology*, 17(4), 453–466.

Isen, A. M., Daubman, K. A., & Nowicki, G. P. (1987). Positive affect facilitates creative problem solving. *Journal of Personality and Social Psychology*, 52(6), 1122–1131.

Ivarsson, A., Johnson, U., Andersen, M. B., Fallby, J., & Altemyr, M. (2015). It pays to pay attention: A mindfulness-based program for injury prevention with soccer players. *Journal of Applied Sport Psychology*, 27(3), 319–334.

Jackson, S. A., & Csikszentmihalyi, M. (1999). *Flow in Sports*. Champaign, IL: Human Kinetics.

Kabat-Zinn, J. (1982). An outpatient program in behavioral medicine for chronic pain patients based on the practice of mindfulness meditation: Theoretical considerations and preliminary results. *General Hospital Psychiatry*, 4(1), 33–47.

Kabat-Zinn, J. (2003). Mindfulness-based interventions in context: Past, present, and future. *Clinical Psychology: Science and Practice*, 10(2), 144–156.

Kabat-Zinn, J. (2009). *Wherever You Go, There You Are: Mindfulness Meditation in Everyday Life*. London: Hachette.

Kaufman, K. A., Glass, C. R., & Arnkoff, D. B. (2009). Evaluation of Mindful Sport Performance Enhancement (MSPE): A new approach to promote flow in athletes. *Journal of Clinical Sport Psychology*, 25(4), 334–356.

Kaufman, K. A., Glass, C. R., & Pineau, T. R. (2016). Mindful Sport Performance Enhancement (MSPE). Mindfulness and Performance. In A. L. Baltzell (Ed.), *Mindfulness and Performance* (pp. 183–185). New York: Cambridge University Press.

Keng, S. L., Smoski, M. J., & Robins, C. J. (2011). Effects of mindfulness on psychological health: A review of empirical studies. *Clinical Psychology Review*, 31(6), 1041–1056.

Langer, E. J. (1989). *Mindfulness*. Boston, MA: Addison-Wesley/Addison Wesley Longman.

Langer, E. J. (1992). Matters of mind: Mindfulness/mindlessness in perspective. *Consciousness and Cognition*, 1(3), 289–305.

Langer, E. J., & Moldoveanu, M. (2000). Mindfulness research and the future. *Journal of Social Issues*, 56(1), 129–139.

Longshore, K., & Sachs, M. (2015). Mindfulness training for coaches: A mixed-method exploratory study. *Journal of Clinical Sport Psychology*, 9(2), 116–137.

Lustyk, M. K., Chawla, N., Nolan, R., & Marlatt, G. A. (2009). Mindfulness meditation research: Issues of participant screening, safety procedures, and researcher training. *Advances in Mind-Body Medicine*, 24(1), 20–30.

Ma, S. H., & Teasdale, J. D. (2004). Mindfulness-based cognitive therapy for depression: Replication and exploration of differential relapse prevention effects. *Journal of Consulting and Clinical Psychology*, 72(1), 31–40.

Mahoney, J., & Hanrahan, S. J. (2011). A brief educational intervention using acceptance and commitment therapy: Four injured athletes' experiences. *Journal of Clinical Sport Psychology*, 5(3), 252–273.

Orlick, T. (1990). *In Pursuit of Excellence* (2nd ed.). Champaign, IL: Human Kinetics.

Peterson, L. G., & Pbert, L. (1992). Effectiveness of a meditation-based stress reduction program in the treatment of anxiety disorders. *The American Journal of Psychiatry*, 149, 936–943.

Pineau, T. R., Glass, C. R., & Kaufman, K. A. (2014). Mindfulness in sport performance. In A. Ie, C. T. Ngnoumen, & E. J. Langer (Eds.), *The Wiley Blackwell Handbook of Mindfulness*. Chichester, UK: John Wiley & Sons.

Pineau, T. R., Glass, C. R., Kaufman, K. A., & Bernal, D. R. (2014). Self- and team-efficacy beliefs of rowers and their relation to mindfulness and flow. *Journal of Clinical Sport Psychology*, 8(2) 142–158.

Privette, G. (1983). Peak experience, peak performance, and flow: A comparative analysis of positive human experiences. *Journal of Personality and Social Psychology*, 45(6), 1361–1368.

Privette, G., & Brundrick, C. M. (1991). Peak experience, peak performance, and flow: Correspondence of personal descriptions and theoretical constructs. *Journal of Social Behavior and Personality*, 6(5), 169–188.

Sappington, R., & Longshore, K. (2015). Systematically reviewing the efficacy of mindfulness-based interventions for enhanced athletic performance. *Journal of Clinical Sport Psychology*, 9(3), 232–262.

Thompson, R. W., Kaufman, K. A., De Petrillo, L. A., Glass, C. R., & Arnkoff, D. B. (2011). One year follow-up of Mindful Sport Performance Enhancement (MSPE) with archers, golfers, and runners. *Journal of Clinical Sport Psychology*, 5(2), 99–116.

Vago, D. R., & Silbersweig, D. A. (2012). Self-Awareness, self-Regulation, and self-Transcendence (S-ART): A framework for understanding the neurobiological mechanisms of mindfulness. *Frontiers in Human Neuroscience*, 6, 296.

Walsh, R., & Shapiro, S. L. (2006). The meeting of meditative disciplines and western psychology: A mutually enriching dialogue. *American Psychologist*, 61(3), 227–239.

Weinberg, R. S., & Gould, D. (2014). *Foundations of Sport and Exercise Psychology* (6th ed). Champaign, IL: Human Kinetics.

Young, J. A., & Pain, M. D. (1999). The zone: Evidence of a universal phenomenon for athletes across sports. *Athletic Insight: The Online Journal of Sport Psychology*, 1(3), 21–30.

8

RESILIENCE AND GROWTH MINDSET IN SPORT AND PHYSICAL ACTIVITY

Abbe Brady and Rudy Alleyne

[handwritten margin notes: Inherent aspect of sport requires resilience + resourcefulness — loss, injury, culture, etc.]

Introduction

Sport and many physical activities (PA) are renowned for being designed to extend the adaptive efforts and capacities required of participants and engagement in these activities has been recognised as a facilitator of adaptation and resilience in individuals (Hefferon & Boniwell, 2011). However, some situations in sport and PA can be perceived as threatening or harmful (e.g. injury, making a weight, dehumanising culture, defeat, deselection or an unrelenting win at all costs ethos) and may require considerable resiliency and resourcefulness (Kavanagh & Brady, 2014; Sagar, Lavallee, & Spray, 2009; Theberge, 2008). Recent research has shown that experiences of stress and adversity in sport and life have the potential to be rich developmental opportunities if they are carefully managed (Collins & McNamara, 2012; Sarkar, Fletcher, & Brown, 2015). Whether in elite sport, school, the park or the gym, resilience has particular value for understanding how participants may withstand or bounce back or even thrive when facing the inevitable challenges associated with the physical, mental and social demands of their activity as well as in life.

This chapter outlines the key concepts associated with fixed and growth mindsets and the consequences of holding such beliefs for resilience. This chapter frames the discussion using key resilience concepts proposed by Yates, Tyrell, and Masten (2015). Examples are used to illustrate how having a particular mindset across sport and physical activity–related situations can yield quite divergent responses to our experiences of adversity, challenges, failure and success, with stark consequences for resilience and also for learning, motivation and well-being. Considerations for practice are presented to be applicable for a range of contexts in sport and PA. Techniques and interventions to support the development of growth mindset and resilience are offered, and recommendations are presented for future research and practice.

Introduction to the concept of resilience

Psychological resilience is defined in various ways relating in some way to how a person withstands and/or responds to pressure. At a broad level, Masten, Best, and Garmezy (1990, p. 436) define resilience as 'the process of, capacity for or outcome of successful adaptation despite challenging or threatening circumstances', and focusing on a capacity account, Hefferon and Boniwell (2011, p. 115) define resilience as 'the flexibility in response to changing situational demands, and the ability to bounce back from negative emotional experiences'. In the sport literature, Fletcher and Sarkar (2016) distinguish between robust resilience (maintaining well-being and performance) and rebound resilience (regaining well-being and performance).

Resilience is best viewed as a complex process when the person's dynamic adaptive systems (developed within the person, through their relationships and their environment) work effectively to maintain or restore the person's competence and functioning (Masten, 2007). One of the fundamental adaptive systems underlying resilient adaptation relates to mastery-motivational systems (Yates, Egeland, & Sroufe, 2003). Dweck's mindset theory contributes to our understanding of mastery–motivational adaptation and as such it has particular value because it can aid understanding about the important constructs and mechanisms related to resilience. Importantly, when viewed as a process we are invited to recognise, we can develop resilience intentionally through particular activities as well as through reflecting on one's accumulating life experiences.

Particular personal characteristics and skills have been recognised as assets facilitating the resiliency process such as, realistic optimism, conscientiousness, extraversion, empathy, confidence, self-esteem, connecting with others, emotional and arousal regulation, attentional control, accurate causal analysis, problem-solving skills and self-awareness (Jackson & Watkin, 2004; Fletcher & Sarkar, 2016; Yates & Masten, 2004). In stressful situations, positive emotions contribute to the ability to achieve effective emotion regulation (e.g. more rapid recovery of indices of cardiovascular and negative emotional arousal), and positive emotions also help by supporting the finding of constructive meaning from the adversity (Tugade & Fredrickson, 2004). These processes reflect how positive emotions help in the moment by encouraging a broader thinking which contributes to problem-solving and over time, this contributes to the person's personal resources by expanding his or her thought action-repertoire (Fredrickson, 2001). *Thought-Action Repertoire*

Crust and Clough (2011) suggest that the inevitable setbacks and failures that naturally occur in sport and high-investment activities should be the source of growth through reflection, learning and development. Naturally occurring life events and artificially generated challenging times can both offer unique developmental opportunities if they are carefully supported and cultivated for growth (Collins & McNamara, 2012). Fletcher and Sarkar (2016) present a helpful way of identifying environments that may be more or less conducive to cultivating resilience through their 2 × 2 challenge-support matrix (Figure 8.1). A facilitative environment is

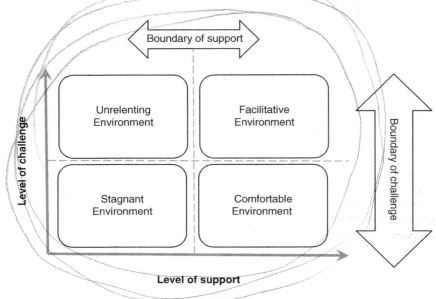

FIGURE 8.1 A challenge-support matrix for describing environments which may influence the development of resilience

Source: Adapted from Fletcher and Sarkar (2016)

characterised by an appropriate amount of support over time for the level of challenge presented, and it is proposed that most resilience is developed in this environment. Importantly, these environments should not be framed by rigid or static boundaries but consciously cultivated and adapted to meet the particular needs of participants in the given context at the time.

Mindsets – contemporary research and key findings

The concept of *mindset* is acknowledged by many leading positive psychologists as making an important contribution toward understanding human achievement behaviors (Biswas-Diener, 2010; Hefferon & Boniwell, 2011). Stanford University Professor Carol Dweck describes a person's mindset as the implicit beliefs about the stability or malleability of personal attributes and behaviors (Dweck, 1999). Implicit beliefs about ability form a crucial element of many other major motivation theories (Li & Lee, 2004). Beliefs about ability and how to achieve success, in turn, can have stark consequences for a person's resilience as well as their aspirations, motivation, the learning strategies they adopt and the enjoyment and satisfaction they experience, both in the short term and long term (Dweck & Leggett, 1988; Dweck, 2006; Yeager & Dweck, 2012). A good example of how beliefs influence our achievements is reflected in how, once the myth of the four-minute mile had been broken, a flurry of other runners also soon achieved that feat.

Research supports the existence of two distinct frameworks of implicit belief viewpoints known as *entity* or *incremental self-theories* (Dweck, 1999). In achievement situations, people are presented as theorists with tacit alignment to one of these positions. Entity theorists (those with a fixed mindset) believe that their ability and attributes are largely innate and relatively stable over time regardless of environment or personal factors. By contrast, incremental theorists (those with a growth mindset) believe that their ability and attributes are relatively malleable and can be developed through both contextual factors such as the environment and feedback, and personal factors such as learning and effort (Dweck, 2006; Jowett & Spray, 2013).

Findings across diverse contexts show repeated distinctions and adaptive or maladaptive consequences associated with fixed and growth mindset beliefs about the malleability or static nature of many personal attributes such as intelligence, personality, parenting, musicality, artistic ability, mathematical or linguistic ability, relationships, sporting ability, social skills and creativity (Dweck, 2017).

Existing research in sport and PA settings have found that a growth mindset predicts or is positively associated with positive affect, higher self-efficacy and enjoyment of physical activity, skill acquisition, performance, task orientation, interest and persistence (Biddle, Wang, Chatzisarantis, & Spray, 2003; Jourden, Bandura, & Banfield, 1991; Kasimatis, Miller, & Marcussen, 1996; Van Yperen & Duda, 1999).

Research in sport settings has found the coexistence of fixed and growth mindsets, as well as different antecedents of acquirable and stable abilities which stemmed from personal factors and also from layers of socio-cultural factors within the sport environment (Jowett & Spray, 2013; Slater, Spray, & Smith, 2012). Olympic hopefuls noted that to be successful an element of talent is preferable; however, all placed more emphasis on the need to work hard through practice and learning to acquire the physical and psychological attributes needed for success (Jowett & Spray, 2013). These aspirant athletes also found ways of reframing setbacks such as injury or deselection, and they held the view that the 'adversity was teaching them the vital skills and attributes needed for their psychological development within the sport' (ibid, p. 152).

Though they recognised the malleable nature of many sport abilities and the capacity to build on talent, Olympic hopefuls also identified the fixed nature of some sport abilities based on physiological factors (e.g. fast twitch fibers in sprinters) (ibid). Research with cricket coaches and players showed how people can hold different mindset-related beliefs about different aspects of the game, with both groups believing that technical and physical attributes were malleable but that psychological and tactical skills were far less amenable to change (Frith & Sykes, 2016). Chase, Galli, Myers, and Machida (2008) examined the mindset beliefs of high school coaches and found that whilst most coaching abilities were viewed as learned rather than innate, game strategy ability was considered more innate than learned. These findings support the coexistence of entity and incremental beliefs and that particular sport/coaching abilities may be viewed as more or less malleable, according to the sport and context. Such findings have implications for how coaches and teachers may approach designing developmental opportunities.

Chase (2010) proposed that coach education and leadership training should focus on helping coaches and leaders develop a growth mindset about their leadership abilities rather than trying to find an elusive formula for leadership. Similarly, Wang and Koh (2006) recommended that for effective physical education (PE) teaching, pre-service training for PE teachers should include information about the importance of PE for promoting autonomy, mastery climate and incremental beliefs. Based on a review of literature and with the aim of facilitating positive motivational, behavioral and affective outcomes for young participants, Vella, Cliff, Okely, Weintraub and Robinson (2014) proposed a model of instructional strategies to promote incremental beliefs in youth sport based on six key areas of theoretical development, that is, focus on effort and persistence, appropriate challenge, value of failure, perceptions of success, promotion of learning and high expectations.

Drawing from basic mindset ideas (Dweck, 1999) and using generalised physical ability as an example, an adolescent exhibiting an entity belief (fixed mindset) about physical ability holds the belief that it is a relatively static ability with little or no propensity for growth and so s/he perceives they have limited control over developing this aspect of the self. This may result in the view that investing effort is futile (if physical ability cannot be changed) and instead s/he might accept that they have a set level of ability. This may impact on motivation and behavior in challenging achievement situations such as a PE lesson or competition (which s/he may not enjoy) as s/he may not try so hard or give up easily and ignore feedback opportunities because trying is pointless. Instead s/he may focus on trying to coast, which may require avoiding challenges, criticism and situations which may expose or threaten perceived physical competence. The limited meaningful engagement in the session and with feedback and information may reduce learning opportunities which may, in turn, affect competency development which may be used to confirm a lack of ability.

By comparison, an adolescent adopting an incremental belief (growth mindset) about physical ability believes it is a malleable attribute which fosters motivation and behavioral tendencies characterised by commitment to goals, persistence in the face of obstacles, pursuing challenges, identifying effort as necessary to the path of mastery, embracing feedback, learning from criticism and finding inspiration from the success of others (Dweck, 2017). The development of a growth mindset fosters a more constructive attitude toward practice, learning and making mistakes which are conducive to developing and maintaining resilience (Jowett & Spray, 2013). When participants are encouraged to view important abilities as those that can be developed over time with effort, appropriate strategies and support, they are more likely to be resilient when they encounter tough challenges in that setting (Yeager & Dweck, 2012).

In an experimental test of mindset theory in sport, Spray, Wang, Biddle, Chatzisarantis, and Warburton (2006) found that whilst incremental beliefs supported mindset theorisation, there seemed to be less evidence for the maladaptive effects of entity beliefs. They proposed in some conditions (e.g. when coexisting high incremental beliefs offset the effect) entity beliefs are not universally maladaptive, and may for some people, in some contexts, lead to adaptive outcomes.

A concern associated with mindset theory is that its ideas are applied too rigidly and so it is important to appreciate the following points:

Mindset Theory Misconceptions

(A) Mindset theory is not stating 'everyone can be anything' because there are many factors that contribute to someone realizing their potential in sport and physical activity; however, without a growth mindset, achieving one's potential is less likely (Frith & Sykes, 2016, p. 51).

(B) Findings from sport research show that people can hold both types of belief and that these can be evoked in different ways by personal or environmental factors (Slater et al., 2012; Jowett & Spray, 2013).

(C) *False growth mindset* is a relatively new phenomenon, and Dweck (2017) relates it to misunderstandings about mindset theory in four key areas:

(1) mindset is wrongly self-ascribed as if it is an enduring trait rather than a process of believing and acting in a manner consistent with a growth mindset;

(2) the assumption that it is all about *effort* and *praising effort* – when actually it is about appreciating the process involving hard work, trying new strategies and seeking input from others. Also problematic is praising effort as a consolation when there is no learning, when it's more important to find out why there was no learning;

Don't praise "hard work" if there was no learning

(3) suggesting that 'anyone can do anything' without also framing this and helping them to gain the skills and resources to progress towards their goal;

(4) labelling someone (especially children) as having a fixed (or a growth) mindset and blaming this for their lack of learning or engagement.

Research from neuroscience about the brain's plasticity has provided evidence for the value of engaging in challenging learning activities for its impact on brain activity and adaptation, and this has been highly effective at supporting engagement with ideas about mindsets through initiatives such as Brainology (Dweck, 2017). The brain's capacity for development can also become a focus for intentional shaping and various activities such as mindfulness and cognitive reframing, and other mental skills have been found to be effective in inducing changes in the brain and enhancing resilience (Davidson & Schuyler, 2015).

There are a number of ways that mindsets may serve to enhance or compromise resilience, and drawing on core constructs central to understanding resilience proposed by Yates et al. (2015) we describe some key ideas as follows:

- Having a growth mindset is likely to be an important *protective factor* supporting resilience if the person believes that s/he can develop resilience. Conversely, believing that resilience is a relatively stable trait not amenable to much meaningful development may be a *vulnerability* moderator of resilience in times of stress if one perceives him/herself to be lacking this trait.

- A growth mindset is closely linked to resilience through the central theme of facilitating *competence* and *adaptivity*. A growth mindset supports adaptivity because it reflects the belief that the person can develop competency and thus it encourages effortful engagement and openness to learning which, in turn, increases exposure to opportunities to participate and gain information about the quality and nature of one's performance.

- *Competence* and *adaptivity* are further achieved via a growth mindset through helping the person see challenges, setbacks and failures as problems to be solved rather than as evidence of incompetence and a signal to give up or withdraw (Molden & Dweck, 2006). Compared to those with a fixed mindset, those with a growth mindset coped more effectively with setbacks and were more likely to attribute failures to flexible factors within their control (e.g. low effort or attention), rather than more global judgements of ability (Hong, Chiu, Dweck, Lin, & Wan, 1999). Similarly, when responding to failure, those with growth mindset orientations were less defensive and were more proactive in using effective strategies (Blackwell, Trzesniewski, & Dweck, 2007).

- Adopting a growth mindset is likely to support the development of particular personal and interpersonal *assets* such as self-awareness, realistic optimism, problem-solving and accurate causal analysis developed through experience and knowledge gained by actively pursuing self-referenced improvement goals for learning. Through reflection the person is likely to have a good sense of themselves, the situation and their progress in relation to goals and attributions at the time.

- In situations that are characterised by uncertainty, criticism or failure, a fixed mindset may become a *risk factor or a source of vulnerability* since, to preserve an image of oneself as talented or competent performers, the person may ignore discrepant or unfavourable feedback or remove him- or herself from situations in which s/he might fail or risk looking incompetent. This may encourage a self-imposed 'comfort zone' (i.e. a stagnant or comfortable personal development environment) through which they trigger a causation of experiencing less challenge and adaptation, thereby gaining less learning-related information, with implications for future goal-setting and perceived ability judgements.

- Linked to the *assets* of self-awareness, realistic optimism and a belief in the value of effort in overcoming challenges, those with a growth mindset are less likely to be thrown off course by setbacks and because they are more likely to reframe the situation by viewing it as offering something developmentally meaningful, see the situation as a challenge and persist (Jowett & Spray, 2013).

- Intentionally viewing a stressful situation as a challenge (as opposed to a threat) may be a helpful *protective strategy* adopted to overcome a particular setback and may also encourage more positive emotions associated with constructively framed goals and attributions about the challenge.

- In achievement situations, a *risk* factor for those with fixed mindsets concerns how goals may relate to proving ability and achieving validation in the present. By comparison, the way those with growth mindsets frame goals may be viewed as an *asset* because they focus on improving abilities for the future and can thus encourage the person to be more patient linked to a meaningful self-referenced development goal (Sevinver, Kluge, & Oettingen, 2014).

Fixed Mindset = risk factor

Beliefs and behaviours associated with a growth mindset	Key concepts in learning and development	Beliefs and behaviours associated with a fixed mindset
With effort, good strategies and help, people can change and develop most qualities and abilities		People's qualities and abilities are largely predetermined, inherited and/or unchangeable once developed
Doing one's best; trying hard Learning and improving Many types of success	Success	Establishing superiority with least effort Being gifted or a natural Success as winning
Sees the bigger picture Is patient; sees progress in steps Uses self-referenced goals	Motivation	Wants immediate results Seeks quick fixes Compares self to others
Relishes challenge Seeks hard but realistic tasks	Challenges	Avoids challenge if risky Seeks easier or unrealistic tasks
Sees effort as investment (effort essential for learning and achievement)	Effort	Not cool to show effort (effort needed by those struggling to achieve)
Persists and finds new ways Engages in problem-solving	Obstacles	Demotivated, lose focus, may feel or act helpless
Views criticism as valuable feedback	Criticism	Ignores, disputes or denigrates criticism
Informative; a wake-up call Stimulates constructive reflection Can be motivating	Failure	Threat to self-esteem and identity Prolonged anger, despair, blame May lead to withdrawal
Draws inspiration and ideas from others' successes	Successes of others	Feels threatened or demoralised by the successes of others
Regains composure and rebounds from setbacks Can maintain robustness during uncertain periods	Resilience	Struggles to retain composure and rebound from setbacks Struggles to maintain robustness during tough times
Actively asks for advice/help Looks to build network, gains insights and learns from others	Support-seeking	Uncomfortable asking for help May remain isolated or hide uncertainty/confusion
More open to experience/new ideas because of beliefs that people can change and find learning and insights from many situations	Openness to experience	Less inclined to be open to experience/new ideas because one's predetermined capacities have dictated what can be learned and how

FIGURE 8.2 Characteristic beliefs and behaviours associated with a fixed or growth mindset linked to key concepts in learning and development in sport and physical activity

Source: Adapted from Brady and Hughes (2013)

Techniques and interventions to support resilience through a growth mindsets

Jackson and Watkin (2004) distinguish between strategies that build enduring protective resources and those that are real-time resilience or 'fast skills' to use during stressful situations. What follows in Table 8.1 are some suggestions for activities to support the development of enduring and also the real time resilience and growth mindset beliefs.

TABLE 8.1 Strategies for promoting growth mindset, adaptation and resilience in sport and physical activity

Strategies

1. Develop self-awareness of mindsets because recognizing it in yourself is an important first step in appreciating that we all have tendencies to adopt different mindset-related behaviors in particular situations. Identifying when and why you tend to be growth or fixed mindset oriented can be very helpful for getting a realistic appreciation about the prevalence of fixed mindset mentalities in us all.
2. Recognizing the coexistence of entity and incremental beliefs about different physical, psychological, technical and tactical aspects of athletic and coaching performance, consider identifying what aspects of performance are viewed as most and least amenable to change. See Frith and Sykes (2016) The Growth Mindset Coaching Kit for a range of great resources to help promote growth mindset potential.
3. Raise self-awareness and provide access to information about; mindsets, resilience as a process that can be developed, brain plasticity and potential to adapt in response to learning challenges and training to develop personal skills to support resilience.
Consider using Dweck's (2006, 2017) Brainology resources and also access the brain scan images showing how learned skills result in changed brain morphology and activity patterns e.g. as demonstrated with musicians and taxi drivers. Maybe engagement with particular sports or physical activities are also associated with particular areas of brain activity and development.
4. Promote engagement in activities that support brain activity associated with resilience e.g. mindfulness and cognitive reframing.
5. Hone the mental skills needed to deal with negative emotions and stressors in the moment through the 3D activity - Distract Distance Dispute
These support resilience by shifting thinking away from the adverse event (distracting), metaphorically stepping back from the immediacy of a stressful situation or event to gain perspective (distancing), and then using a more balanced frame of mind to use reflective self-questioning about the adverse event and finding alternative ways of viewing the situation (disputing).
6. Identify context appropriate activities through which to promote positive emotions to a, buffer / offset the impact of negative stressors, b, to encourage better problem-solving and creativity and c, for problem-setting and the design of activities that offer the right amount and sequence of stretch for adaptation and support.
7. Develop your own bank of evidence, by reflecting on times when you have overcome a difficult period, bounced back from a tough or pressured situation.
8. Acknowledge and praise the efforts of yourself and others to stretch themselves through trying new or more challenging strategies.

9. To develop a growth mindset achievement climate use Vella et al.'s (2014) model of instructional strategies i.e. focus on effort and persistence; appropriate challenge; value of failure; perceptions of success, promote learning and high expectations.
10. Emphasize the importance of self-referenced learning goals rather than outcome goals.
11. Encourage opportunities to reflect on experiences to make learning and progress visible and acknowledged.
12. Encourage participants to share ideas, learn from others, seek social support and also become problem-setters as well as problem-solvers.
13. Practitioners to model desired behaviors including being aware of how language and behaviors will convey beliefs about mindset, adaptation and resilience.
14. Carefully consider the ways in which challenge is cultivated and support is provided (particularly when things seem tough) with a view to creating a suitably flexible facilitative environment.

Notwithstanding the risk of oversimplifying the vast array of rigorous and sometimes complex and contentious evidence bases for mindset research, sometimes it is helpful to have a seemingly simple aide memoire to hand. So as a helpful resource drawn from mindset-based research, Figure 8.2 illustrates some of the distinctions proposed to characterize fixed and growth mindset responses in achievement contexts such as in sport and PA.

Conclusion

Research examining how perceptions of resilience may be constrained or enabled by athletes, exercisers and coaches and trainers with particular mindset orientations may provide valuable insights for context-specific interventions. Similarly, following the example of Dweck and her colleagues, rigorously examining the impact of various mindset interventions on adaptive behaviors and well-being are important avenues for future research in sport and PA. Specific areas ripe for inquiry include examining how coaches'/trainers' beliefs about ability and about resilience affect their own coaching behaviors and well-being and the experience and well-being of their participants. There is potential also to examine the dyadic and collective contagion effect associated with mindset and resilience beliefs between various leader-followers and also in peer groups among practitioners and athletes/exercisers.

What we believe is possible for us to achieve in any particular life domain has considerable influence on how we think, feel and act in the present, how we interpret the past and how we may form ideas about our possible futures. Believing one is capable of developing in a particular activity may encourage greater investment and connectedness with the activity and its community, more openness to learning, more enjoyment and heightened adherence. In addition, in the face of setbacks and adversity, believing in one's abilities may be reflected in greater resilience through focused problem-solving, persistence, effective adaptation and also seeing the adversity as meaningful. Given the potential impact of mindsets to either broaden or constrain a person's beliefs about ability, with consequences for adaptive behavior and the development of resilience, it is imperative that as practitioners in sport and physical activity we consider how to model and facilitate growth mindset behaviors and suitably challenging and supportive environments.

References

Biddle, S. J. H., Wang, C. K. J., Chatzisarantis, N. L. D., & Spray, C. M. (2003). Motivation for physical activity in young people: Entity and incremental beliefs about athletic ability. *Journal of Sport Sciences*, 21, 973–989.

Biswas-Diener, R. (2010). *Practising Positive Psychology Coaching*. Hoboken, NJ: John Wiley & Sons.

Blackwell, L. S., Trzesniewski, K. H., & Dweck, C. S. (2007). Implicit theories of intelligence predict achievement across an adolescent transition: A longitudinal study and an intervention. *Child Development*, 78(1), 246–263.

Brady, A., & Hughes, S. (2013). *Exploring the impact of a best future-self intervention on the well-being of early career sport coaches: The mediating role of mindset*. Presentation at 3rd Biennial Meeting of the British Psychological Society's Division of Sport and Exercise Psychology, Manchester, December.

Chase, M. A. (2010). Should coaches believe in innate ability? The importance of leadership mindset. *Quest*, 62, 296–307.

Chase, M. A., Galli, N., Myers, N., & Machida, M. (2008). *Coaching effectiveness, coaching efficacy and innate abilities: Were you born to be a coach?* Symposium, Presented at the Association of Applied Sport Psychology Annual Conference, St Louis, MO.

Collins, D., & McNamara, A. (2012). The rocky road to the top: Why talent needs trauma. *Sports Medicine*, 1, 42(11), 907–914. doi:10.2165/11635140-000000000-00000.

Crust, L. & Clough, P. (2011). Developing mental toughness: from research to practice. *Journal of Sport Psychology in Action,* 2(1), 21–32.

Davidson, R. J., & Schuyler, B. S. (2015). Neuroscience of happiness. In J. F. Helliwell, R. Layard, & J. Sachs (Eds.), *World Happiness Report 2015* (pp. 88–105). New York: Sustainable Development Solutions Network.

Dweck, C. S. (1999). *Self-theories: Their Role in Motivation, Personality, and Development*. Hove: Psychology Press.

Dweck, C. (2006). *Mindset: The New Psychology of Success*. New York: Random House.

Dweck, C. (2014). *The power of believing that you can improve*. Video on TedTalk. Retrieved January 29, 2015, from www.ted.com/talks/carol_dweck_the_power_of_believing_that_you_can_improve.

Dweck, C. (2016). *What having a "Growth Mindset" actually means*. Harvard Business Review. Retrieved February 14, 2016, from https://hbr.org/2016/01/what-having-a-growth-mindset-actually-means.

Dweck, C. (2017). *Mindset: The New Psychology of Success* (Updated ed.). New York: Random House.

Dweck, C. S., & Leggett, E. L. (1988). A social-cognitive approach to motivation and personality. *Psychological Review*, 95(2), 256.

Fletcher, D., & Sarkar, M. (2016). Mental fortitude training: An evidence-based approach to developing psychological resilience for sustained success. *Journal of Sport Psychology in Action*, 7(3), 135–157.

Fredrickson, B. L. (2001). The role of positive emotions in positive psychology: The broaden-and-build theory of positive emotions. *American Psychologist*, 56(3), 218–226.

Frith, J., & Sykes, R. (2016). *The Growth Mindset Coaching Kit.* Guernsey: Frith Sykes Ltd.

Hefferon, K., & Boniwell, I. (2011). *Positive Psychology: Theory, Research and Applications.* Maidenhead: Open University Press.

Hong, Y., Chiu, C., Dweck, C. S., Lin, D., & Wan, W. (1999). Implicit theories, attributions, and coping: A meaning system approach. *Journal of Personality and Social Psychology, 77,* 588–599. doi:10.1037/0022-3514.77.3.588.

Jackson, R., & Watkin, C. (2004). The resilience inventory: Seven essential skills for overcoming life's obstacles and determining happiness. *Selection & Development Review, 20(6),* 13–17.

Jourden, F., Bandura, A., & Banfield, J. T. (1991). The impact of conceptions of ability on self-regulatory factors and motor skills acquisition. *Journal of Sport and Exercise Psychology, 13,* 213–226.

Jowett, N., & Spray, C. M. (2013). British Olympic Hopefuls: The antecedents and consequences of implicit ability beliefs in elite track and field athletes. *Psychology of Sport and Exercise, 14,* 145–153.

Kasimatis, M., Miller, M., & Marcussen, L. (1996). The effects of implicit theories on exercise motivation. *Journal of Research in Personality, 30,* 510–516.

Kavanagh, E., & Brady, A. (2014). Humanisation is high performance sport. In C. H. Brackenridge & D. Rhind (Eds.), *Athlete Welfare: International Perspectives.* London: Brunel University Press.

Li, W., & Lee, A. (2004). A review of conceptions of ability and related motivational constructs in achievement motivation. *Quest, 56,* 439–461.

Masten, A. (2007). Resilience in developing systems: Progress and promise as the fourth wave rises. *Development and Psychopathology, 19(3),* 921–930. doi:10.1017/S0954579407000442.

Masten, A. S., Best, K. M., & Garmezy, N. (1990). Resilience and development: Contributions from the study of children who overcome adversity. *Development and psychopathology, 2(4),* 425–444.

Molden, D. C., & Dweck, C. S. (2006). Finding "meaning" in psychology: a lay theories approach to self-regulation, social perception, and social development. *American Psychologist, 61(3),* 192–203.

Sagar, S. S., Lavallee, D., & Spray, C. M. (2009). Coping with the effects of fear of failure: A preliminary investigation of young elite athletes. *Journal of Clinical Sports Psychology, 3,* 73–98.

Sarkar, M., & Fletcher, D. (2016). Developing resilience through coaching. In R. Thelwell, C. Harwood, & I. Greenlees (Eds.), *The Psychology of Sports Coaching: Research and Practice* (pp. 235–248). London: Routledge.

Sarkar, M., Fletcher, D., & Brown, D. J. (2015). What doesn't kill me. . .: Adversity-related experiences are vital in the development of superior Olympic performance. *Journal of Science and Medicine in Sport, 18(4),* 475–479.

Sevinver, A. T., Kluge, L., & Oettingen, G. (2014). Implicit theories and motivational focus: Desired future versus present reality. *Motivation and Emotion, 38,* 36–46.

Slater, M. J., Spray, C. M., & Smith, B. M. (2012). "You're only as good as your weakest link": Implicit theories of golf ability. *Psychology of Sport and Exercise, 13(3),* 280–290.

Spray, C. M., Wang, C. K. J., Biddle, S. J. H., Chatzisarantis, N. L. D., & Warburton, V. E. (2006). An experimental test of self-theories of ability in youth sport. *Psychology of Sport and Exercise, 7,* 255–267.

Theberge, N. (2008). Just a normal bad part of what I do: Elite athletes' accounts of the relationship between health and sport. *Sociology of Sport Journal, 25(2),* 206–222.

Tugade, M. M., & Fredrickson, B. L. (2004). Resilient individuals use positive emotions to bounce back from negative emotional experiences. *Journal of Personality and Social Psychology*, 86(2), 320.

Van Yperen, N. W., & Duda, J. (1999). Goal Orientations, beliefs about success, and performance improvement among young elite Dutch soccer players. *Scandinavian Journal of Medicine and Science in Sports*, 9, 358–364.

Vella, S. A., Cliff, D. P., Okely, A. D., Weintraub, D. L., & Robinson, T. N. (2014). Instructional strategies to promote incremental beliefs in youth sport. *Quest*, 66(4), 357–370.

Wang, J. C. K., & Koh, M. T. H. (2006). Sport ability beliefs, achievement goals, self, determination and beliefs about the purposes of physical education among Singaporean pre-service physical education trainees. *Asian Journal of Exercise & Sports Science*, 3(1), 25–34.

Yates, T. M., Egeland, B., & Sroufe, A. (2003). Rethinking resilience. In S. S. Luthar (Ed.), *Resilience and vulnerability: Adaptation in the context of childhood adversity* (pp. 243–266). New York: Cambridge University Press.

Yates, T. M., & Masten, A. (2004). Fostering the future: Resilience theory and the practice of positive psychology. In P. A. Linley & S. Joseph (Eds.), *Positive Psychology in Practice* (pp. 521–539). Hoboken, NJ: John Wiley & Sons Inc.

Yates, T. M., Tyrell, F. A., & Masten, A. S. (2015). Resilience theory and the practice of positive psychology from individuals to societies. In S. Joseph (Ed.), *Positive Psychology in Practice: Promoting Human Flourishing in Work, Health, Education, and Everyday Life* (2nd ed., pp. 773–78). Hoboken, NJ: John Wiley & Sons, Inc. doi:10.1002/9781118996874.ch44.

Yeager, D. S., & Dweck, C. S. (2012). Mindsets that promote resilience: When students believe that personal characteristics can be developed. *Educational Psychologist*, 47(4), 302–314.

9

AS POSITIVE AS IT GETS

Flow and enjoyment in sport and physical activity

Jay Kimiecik, Robin S. Vealey, Emily Wright, and Deanna Morrison

This chapter explores the positive dynamics of flow and enjoyment within sport and physical activity. Regardless of the varying contexts of physical activity (e.g., walking to class), sport (e.g., playing in a high school basketball game), and exercise (e.g., participating in a yoga class), flow and enjoyment refer to the *positive subjective experience* (Engeser & Schiepe-Tiska, 2012; Jackson & Kimiecik, 2008). Subjective experience is the "bottom line" of existence (Csikszentmihalyi, 1982). If we are interested in understanding and enhancing an individual's sport and physical activity experience, the quality of that experience cannot be ignored. Even if these positive states – flow and enjoyment – are relatively infrequent in a person's life or within sport and physical activity contexts, they can positively impact motivation, performance, and overall well-being (Jackson, 2000; Kimiecik, 2002).

Whether one is participating in sport or physical activity more broadly defined, there is always an accompanying subjective experience with the opportunity for optimal experience. Flow and enjoyment attempt to capture or explain what that positive subjective experience feels like. In this sense, flow and enjoyment certainly fall under the umbrella of positive psychology initially outlined by Seligman and Csikszentmihalyi (2000). Some have suggested that the development of positive psychology was, in fact, "stimulated and inspired by the work on flow" (Engeser & Schiepe-Tiska, 2012, p. 21).

An overview of flow and enjoyment

Beginning with Csikszentmihalyi's (1975) descriptions of flow states in people pursuing a variety of leisure activities (e.g., basketball, chess, rock climbing), the study and application of flow across many settings has steadily grown over the past 40-plus years (Delle Fave & Bassi, 2016; Rheinberg, 2008). Although there are still many conceptual and measurement challenges (see Engeser & Schiepe-Tiska, 2012;

Rheinberg, ibid), the essence of flow has remained relatively the same – a state of full engagement or total absorption in an activity typically accompanied by a harmony of consciousness and balance of perceived challenge/skill (Csikszentmihalyi, 1997).

Dimensions of flow

Several flow characteristics, or dimensions, have been described by Csikszentmihalyi (1990, 1993) and supported in the sport and exercise environment through qualitative and quantitative research (e.g., Jackson, 1995; Jackson & Marsh, 1996). The development of the Flow State Scale (Jackson & Marsh, 1996) and the Dispositional Flow Scale (Jackson, Martin, & Eklund, 2008) are based on nine flow dimensions.

Challenge-skill balance

The challenge-skill balance dimension recognizes the importance of the person's capacity to meet the demands of the activity, and when challenge and skill level are both relatively high and reasonably matched, flow is most likely to occur. If there is an imbalance between skills and challenges, it is highly unlikely that individuals will experience flow. More likely, they will experience anxiety, relaxation, boredom, or apathy. Anxiety occurs when a person perceives the challenges of the situation to be higher than perceived skills; relaxation or boredom results from the skills outweighing the challenges; and apathy occurs when both perceived challenges and skills are balanced but low and are less appealing and engaging than an individual's average experiences. Typically, the quality of an individual's experience is most optimal in flow, least optimal in apathy, and less than optimal in boredom or anxiety.

Merging of action and awareness

Merging of action and awareness suggests that involvement is so deep that it becomes spontaneous or seemingly automatic. Csikszentmihalyi (1990) described how it was because of the sense of seemingly effortless movement that the word "flow" was chosen to describe optimal experience. Individuals are no longer aware that they are separate from their actions. Simply, an individual becomes one with the activity.

Clear goals and feedback

Clear goals and feedback are two flow dimensions frequently discussed concurrently (Csikszentmihalyi, 1990). When in flow, goals are clearly defined by either planning ahead or developed while engaging in the activity. When a person knows and understands the goals for an activity, it is more likely for him/her to become totally immersed or engaged. In addition, a clear goal makes it easier to process feedback, which provides messages that the actor is progressing with the goal. The powerful symbiosis between goals and feedback creates order in consciousness, which is at the core of the flow experience.

Total concentration

According to Csikszentmihalyi (1997, p. 31), "when goals are clear, feedback relevant, and challenges and skills are in balance, attention becomes ordered and fully invested. Because of the total demand on psychic energy, a person in flow is completely focused." It is the complete focus on the task at hand that stands out as the clearest indication of flow. All distractions are kept at a minimum or non-existent, and only a select range of information is allowed into awareness.

Sense of control   — Locus of control

When in flow, a person feels in control of the situation without worrying about losing control. The key to this dimension is the *perception* of control that one feels. An athlete interviewed by Jackson (1992, p. 19) puts it this way: "As strange as it sounds, I don't feel like I am in control of anything at all . . . my body just takes over. On the other hand, though, I feel like I am totally in control of everything."

Loss of self-consciousness

When in flow, there is no room for distractions or worry about how one is perceived by others. There is no self-consciousness; a sense of separateness from the world is overcome, which results in a feeling of "oneness" with the environment. The absence of self-consciousness does not mean that the individual is unaware of her thoughts and bodily movements. Rather, it is a keen awareness that is not threatening. In essence, the self is fully functioning, but not aware of itself doing it.

Time transformation

The perception of time may either speed up or slow down when in flow. In flow, time is distorted by the experience. For example, a distance runner in flow may not even recall what happened during a race and may perceive that it ended more quickly than it actually did. Time transformation is generally the least-mentioned flow dimension in qualitative research (Jackson, 1995), and in psychometric scale work, time transformation has not been found to relate strongly to other flow dimensions (Jackson & Marsh, 1996).

Autotelic experience

Csikszentmihalyi (1990) describes an autotelic experience as the end result of flow, one that is intrinsically rewarding. Statements such as "I was on a high" and "I really had a great experience" illustrate the end product of a flow experience. Importantly, a flow state is such a positive subjective state that the individual desires to perform the activity for its own sake. When an individual has stretched his capacity to the fullest extent, integrates mind and body, and is fully immersed in an activity, the outcome is likely to be autotelic, an activity done for its own sake, because it provides powerful intrinsic rewards.

Enjoyment

Within the flow literature, flow and enjoyment have sometimes been used interchangeably and viewed as two sides of the same optimal experience coin (Jackson, 2000). But within sport and physical activity contexts, enjoyment has also had a life of its own as a *positive affective state* studied for its relevance in explaining exercise motivation across the lifespan as well as youth sport participation (Hagberg, Lindahl, Nyberg, & Hellénius, 2009; McCarthy, Jones, & Clark-Carter, 2008). This two-sided aspect of enjoyment is important to understand when examining its role as a positive subjective experience in physical activity contexts.

Early in Csikszentmihalyi's work (1975, 1990), flow and enjoyment were both viewed as the same subjective, optimal experience state. In fact, in his seminal piece on flow, *Beyond Boredom and Anxiety*, Csikszentmihalyi (1975) titled one of the chapters "A Theoretical Model of Enjoyment." Similar to Csikszentmihalyi's flow, Warner (1987) suggests that enjoyment is experiencing something for its own sake. Around the time that Csikszentmihalyi was formulating and refining his flow theory, other work was emerging in child development, exercise, and sport contexts pertaining to enjoyment (e.g., Kimiecik & Harris, 1996). This research shifted the conceptualization of enjoyment to be a positive affective state (Wankel, 1993) and enjoyment has continued to be most frequently operationalized in this way (McCarthy, 2011; McCarthy et al., 2008; Scanlan & Simons, 1992; Wankel, 1993). Pragmatically, sport and physical activity researchers have measured enjoyment by lumping together a smorgasbord of affective-type concepts such as joy, pleasure, like, fun, pleasant, and happiness and will probably continue to do so (Mullen et al., 2011; Steptoe, de Oliveira, Demakakos, & Zaninotto, 2014).

Positive subjective experience research in sport and physical activity

Together or separate, flow and enjoyment have shed light on the importance of positive subjective experience pertaining to motivation and performance in sport and physical activity. This section presents an overview of some of the common approaches and findings. Although sport and physical activity are discussed in distinct sections, there is certainly overlap and this is somewhat an artificial separation. From here on whenever enjoyment is discussed, the reader should assume that the concept is being presented as a positive affective state, unless otherwise noted.

Elite, recreational, and youth sport

Enjoyment has been found to be a significant factor in building sport commitment, motivation, and performance excellence (Jackson, 1992; Jackson & Roberts, 1992; Scanlan & Simons, 1992). Flow is also very relevant to the lives and experiences of elite athletes (Jackson & Kimiecik, 2008; Swann, Keegan, Piggott, & Crust, 2012), although there is certainly no consensus as to the frequency of these optimal states. For example, Jackson (1992) reported that 81% of elite figure skaters did not experience flow very often, whereas Swann, Keegan, Crust, and Piggott (2016) found that seven of 10 professional golfers interviewed believed they had experienced flow during a round of tournament golf. Interestingly, via semi-structured interviews, these golfers described two different flow-like states, one labeled "letting it happen" and the other described as "making it happen." The process for entering these optimal states was different as well, which demonstrates the complexity of understanding the flow state in sport. In both the Jackson (1992, 1995) and Swann et al. (2016) studies, athletes from multiple sports, skaters, and golfers reported that enjoyment – "enjoying the situation," "enjoying what you are doing," or "you're enjoying it" – was a catalyst for getting into flow.

Within non-elite environments, Stein, Kimiecik, Daniels, and Jackson (1995) found that flow states of recreational basketball players and golfers were significantly related to a one-item measure of enjoyment. Schüler and Brunner (2009) showed in a series of studies on marathon running that flow experienced in training indirectly increased racing performance by enhancing motivation (e.g., "I am looking forward to the next running training."). Could positive affective states, such as enjoyment resulting from flow states, mediate the increased motivation for training runs? A study by Hogan, Catalino, Mata, and Fredrickson (2015) suggests that they could. Relatedly, as qualitative findings from Jackson (1992, 1995) and Swann and colleagues (2016) suggest, enjoyment may also be a precursor or catalyst for the flow experience in competitive sport environments. This possibility pertains to the long-held idea of an autotelic personality or disposition, whereby certain individuals have a social psychological propensity (e.g., openness to experience) for optimal experiences (Nakamura & Csikszentmihalyi, 2009). It could be that a generalized positive affective state (e.g., enjoyment or happiness) could be part of an autotelic personality. A study by Hodge, Lonsdale, and Jackson (2009) supports this idea because elite athletes' positive affect (part of a measure of their sport experience as a whole) was significantly related to their perceptions of dispositional flow.

Sport research examining the role of a generalized tendency to experience positive affective states could look to positive psychology studies in other areas from which to pull in individual difference or dispositional factors (e.g., Bassi, Steca, Monzani, Greco, & Delle Fave, 2014). People who experience frequent positive affective states (i.e., have a happy disposition) are more likely to build enduring personal resources (Fredrickson, 2001), such as openness, playfulness, and creativity, all of which have been associated with flow states. A positive affective state may be helpful for athletes to develop these kinds of meta-skills for flow

(Csikszentmihalyi & Nakamura, 1989).Taking a generalized positive affect approach is especially interesting in that Csikszentmihalyi (1997, p. 33) has written on multiple occasions about the paradox of flow – an optimal experience not generally experienced by most people because "it takes energy to achieve optimal experience, and all too often we are unable, or unwilling, to put out the initial effort." Positive emotionality could be one of those energy sources, which builds flow-like resources leading to more flow experiences and further enjoyment, creating a very powerful cycle of optimal experience.

But this positive emotionality-flow-performance relationship in sport is complex. A study examining emotions, mental effort, and concentration disruption in adult sport performers found that measures of state-related happiness about an hour before competition were not related to athlete attention during competition (Allen, Jones, McCarthy, Sheehan-Mansfield, & Sheffield, 2013). A second study found that high levels of happiness assessed during competition (based on reflection of emotions experienced during a past competition) disrupted attention and concentration (Allen et al., 2013).Thus, although general happiness (akin to enjoyment) may help athletes approach their sport in a positive broaden-and-build way (Fredrickson, 2001), positive emotionality experienced at the wrong time could detract from a positive subjective experience during competition by shifting the mind away from the task at hand.

Enjoyment has also been found to play a role in elite athlete development. In their developmental model of sport participation, Côté, Baker, and Abernethy (2007) suggest that in the development of elite athletes, those who participated in deliberate play when younger had more frequent experiences of enjoyment and immediate psychological rewards, which set the stage for continued participation and skill development as they got older. These researchers define deliberate play as intrinsically motivating, immediately gratifying, and maximizing enjoyment. Importantly, families can play a significant role in the experience of enjoyment by encouraging deliberate play opportunities during the sampling years (Côté, 1999). Without deliberate play, sport can become drudgery, reducing autonomy and enjoyment (Kimiecik, 2016). Studies have also linked young athletes' perceived enjoyment of sport to positive personal development characteristics, such as personal and social skills (MacDonald, Côté, Eys, & Deakin, 2011), and Weiss and Amorose (2008) report on a series of youth sport studies that found enjoyment to play a mediating role between reasons for participation and sport commitment. Enjoyment has also been shown to be a relevant factor in young people's motivation for and participation in health-related physical activity; this topic is discussed in the next section.

Health-related physical activity

Within studies focusing on the motivation for and consequences of physical activity from a health perspective (exercise adherence, disease prevention), flow has been less studied than enjoyment. Within these types of studies, enjoyment has been included as a mediator or moderator of physical activity participation in a variety of settings.

In younger populations, enjoyment has been studied in an attempt to explain why many adolescent physical activity interventions have not resulted in sustainable behavioral change over time (Metcalf, Henley, & Wilkin, 2012). Within school-based interventions, enjoyment has been found to be both a significant mediator and moderator of adolescent physical activity (Dishman et al., 2005; Schneider & Cooper, 2011). Findings from Dishman and colleagues (2005) showed that increased enjoyment resulted in increased physical activity among adolescent girls. Schneider and Cooper (2011) demonstrated that low-active adolescent girls responded differently to an intervention according to baseline levels of enjoyment. Girls with high levels of enjoyment at baseline actually declined in their vigorous physical activity at midpoint of the intervention in contrast to the low-enjoyment girls who increased vigorous physical activity. These differences suggest that the girls' subjective experience of the behavior may be a significant factor in explaining their physical activity behavior.

Interestingly, although flow was not assessed (it rarely is in these contexts), both of these studies designed interventions based on flow-related concepts: novel activities and choice and control over activities selected. Future studies should pursue this relationship among flow-like interventions, enjoyment experiences, and behavior. A study by Fenton, Duda, Appleton, and Barrett (2016) reinforces this idea because children's perceived empowerment of their youth sport environment was positively related to autonomous motivation, enjoyment, and moderate to vigorous physical activity known to impact body mass index.

Enjoyment is also a factor in adult exercise motivation and behavior (Hagberg et al., 2009). In a quality of life study (Steptoe, de Oliveira, Demakakos, & Zaninotto, 2014), older adults who enjoyed life had a decreased risk of impaired function eight years later, and in a leisure-based study, individuals who participated frequently in enjoyable leisure activities, including sports and other forms of physical activity, had enhanced psychological and physical functioning (Pressman et al., 2009). Raedeke (2007) found that exercise enjoyment during fitness classes was related to increases in post-experience feelings of energy and vigor. In intervention studies, Hagberg and colleagues (2009) demonstrated in a group of primary health-care patients who experienced exercise enjoyment mediated frequency of participation, and a tailored print and telephone-based message study with low-active adults found that baseline exercise enjoyment moderated changes in moderate to vigorous physical activity at six months (Williams et al., 2006).

What the above sampling of enjoyment-based studies demonstrates is that positive subjective experience matters before, during, and after exercise experiences. Both enjoyment and flow experiences are part of the exercise motivational process (Jackson & Lee, 2009; Kimiecik, 2002), and yet these positive subjective experiences have typically been left out of traditional exercise prescriptions (Segar & Richardson, 2014). Certainly there is much we don't yet know about positive subjective experience and exercise.

Techniques/interventions for enhancing flow and enjoyment

The importance of enhancing flow and enjoyment in physical activity cannot be understated, because the lack of enjoyment is often the major barrier to physical activity participation (Cox, Smith, & Williams, 2008; Ryan, Frederick, Lepes, Rubio, & Sheldon, 1997). The main reason for playing sports given by children age 5 to 18 years is "to have fun" (Weiss & Amorose, 2008), and "not having fun" is the top reason given by kids for dropping out of youth sport (Sabo & Veliz, 2008). Thus, there is a prominent need for interventions that focus on enhancing flow and enjoyment in physical activity. These interventions can be grouped into social-structural or mental strategy interventions.

Social-structural interventions to enhance flow and enjoyment in physical activity

Flow occurs when individuals experience balance between their skills and the challenges that they perceive in the situation, and when they are "inside the activity" as opposed to looking at it as something that they have to do (merging of action and awareness) (Csikszentmihalyi, 1990). Sport and exercise are often structured as drudgery or overload training with only extrinsic outcomes in mind (typically performance outcomes), which are antithetical to flow. Sport and physical activity directors should create conditions that are challenging and stimulating (not boring), yet not too threatening or difficult. They should include variety and different forms of stimulation to make the movement experience enjoyable.

Multiple studies have supported these ideas for social-structural interventions to enhance enjoyment and flow. Low-active female adolescents increased their activity levels and enjoyment when part of an intervention in which variety of activities was emphasized, participants had choices of activities, they were excused from wearing uniforms, they were not timed or charted in fitness runs and activities, and activities were modified to be more enjoyable for individuals with lower levels of fitness (e.g., half-court versus full-court basketball) (Schneider & Cooper, 2011). A Lunchtime Enjoyment Activity and Play (LEAP) school playground intervention significantly increased the physical activity and enjoyment of 5- to 12-year-old children (Hyndman, Benson, Ullah, & Telford, 2014). Interestingly, the LEAP program provided movable/recycled materials and a large grass field with no fixed purposes or adult direction. Materials included play balls, hoops, ropes, milk crates, bicycle tires, buckets, hay bales, swimming noodles, cardboard boxes, plastic walls and sheets, vacuum/pool hoses, and swimming boards. These materials stimulated active play, with pushing, pulling, lifting, running, dodging, jumping, and the creative construction of playing areas for different types of games. In a study of adult non-exercisers, participants in exercise intervention groups experienced high levels of flow as the result of a variety of activities, including small-sided soccer games, jogging, and strength training (Elbe, Strahler, Krustrup, Wikman, & Stelter, 2010).

Sport training, particularly in the United States and the United Kingdom, focuses on deliberate practice, a highly structured activity with the explicit goal to improve performance (Ericsson, Krampe, & Tesch-Römer, 1993). Deliberate practice is important to develop sport talent, yet the "more is better" philosophy has led to many parents and coaches requiring young athletes to specialize early in one sport. Multidimensionality in terms of participating in multiple activities is related to enjoyment and psychological well-being (Vealey & Chase, 2016). As discussed previously, research shows that many elite athletes spent their formative years engaged in deliberate play, which is informal games that children engage in for enjoyment, but that contribute to skill development (Côté , Erickson, & Abernethy, 2013). Examples of deliberate play are the informal games of street hockey, backyard soccer, family softball, and pickup basketball. Deliberate play is a useful concept for coaches and physical activity directors to consider incorporating within structured sport or fitness training situations. These would include participant-centered, small-sided games and change-of-pace activities that are fun and stimulating. The experience of flow and enjoyment leads people to "fall in love" with physical activity. If we are creative and intentional as physical activity professionals, the innovative ways that we structure physical activity experiences can provide a fertile environment for flow and lead to "falling in love" with the physical sensations of movement.

Mental strategy interventions to enhance flow and enjoyment in physical activity

Various mental skills have been associated with athletes' abilities to experience flow, including imagery (Munroe, Giacobbi, Hall, & Weinberg, 2000), as well as self-talk, activation, emotional control, relaxation, and facilitative anxiety interpretations (Jackson, 1992, 1995; Wiggins & Freeman, 2000).

Imagery

Often called *mental rehearsal* or *visualization*, imagery involves using one's senses to create experiences in the mind (Vealey & Forlenza, 2015). Imagery training enhanced flow in youth swimmers by enhancing their clarity of target goals and inducing feelings of control, confidence, and empowerment (Scurati, Michielon, Longo, & Invernizzi, 2010). Another study with youth swimmers found that imagery training increased their positive affect (emotion) experienced while swimming (McCarthy, 2009). An imagery intervention program with elite golfers found increases in frequency and intensity of flow as a result of the imagery intervention (Nicholls, Polman, & Holt, 2005).

Hypnosis

The similarities between flow and hypnotic states suggest that interventions that utilize hypnosis as a mental training technique may increase personal control of the flow experience (Pates, Oliver, & Maynard, 2001). Multiple studies have examined the effects of hypnosis on flow states in basketball and golf, with results showing the enhancement of flow states post-intervention (Pates, 2014; Pates, Cummings, & Maynard, 2002; Pates et al., 2001; Pates & Maynard, 2000). The authors concluded that flow was accessible via hypnotic techniques, providing a key to increasing personal control over flow states.

Mindfulness

Mindfulness is a non-judgmental focus on the experience of the present moment (Bernier, Thienot, Codron, & Fournier, 2009). By practicing mindfulness, individuals learn to focus not on their negative thoughts and feelings, but on the present moment while accepting the sensations, emotions, and cognitions they are experiencing. Over the past decade, research has shown that there seems to be a relationship between mindfulness and increased flow states as well as the characteristics associated with flow (Gardner & Moore, 2004; Kee & Wang, 2008). More specifically, increased mindfulness seems to be associated with a loss of self-consciousness, a more even balance of challenge and skill in an activity, clear goals, increased concentration, and a merging of action and awareness.

Multiple studies have demonstrated that mindfulness training can lead to an increase in athletes' flow experiences. An eight-week mindfulness training program that used workshop presentations, home meditation, and "mindful spinning sessions" (training on a stationary bicycle using a mindful mental approach) resulted in greater increases in mindfulness and flow for those receiving the intervention compared with the control cyclists (Scott-Hamilton, Schutte, & Brown, 2016). Another six-week mindfulness intervention with university athletes from a variety of sports significantly increased global flow, as well as the "clear goals" and "sense of control" flow dimensions, which are key components of mindfulness (Aherne, Moran, & Lonsdale, 2011). Similar intervention studies have shown enhanced mindfulness and flow in swimmers (Briegel-Jones, Knowles, Eubank, Giannoulatos, & Elliot, 2013), as well as archers and golfers (Kaufman, Glass, & Arnkoff, 2009).

Summary of mental strategy interventions

Clearly, the interventions using imagery, hypnosis, and mindfulness training seem particularly suited to enhance flow and enjoyment because of their emphasis on present-moment focus and relaxed performance. However, many other mental training strategies seem well suited to enhance flow and enjoyment. From the goal literature, planned mental strategies using mastery-oriented and process goals seem important to enhance flow and enjoyment. The development and rehearsal of individually tailored focus plans could enhance the personal meaning that is an important antecedent of positive subjective experiences.

Though this chapter has presented just a brief overview of flow and enjoyment research and interventions conducted in diverse sport and health-related physical activity settings, we hope readers recognize how flow and enjoyment are key concepts for understanding and enhancing the sport and physical activity experience.

Importantly, it is our hope that future applied research incorporates enjoyment and flow as outcomes of interest in intervention studies, moving beyond a preoccupation with performance. We advocate for interventions that consider the meaning of the experience for the participant, which seems an important strategy that has been missing in our quest for sustainable behavioral change over time in physical activity contexts.

References

Aherne, C., Moran, A. P., & Lonsdale, C. (2011). The effects of mindfulness training on athletes' flow: An initial investigation. *Sport Psychologist*, 25, 177–189.

Allen, M. S., Jones, M., McCarthy, P. J., Sheehan-Mansfield, S., & Sheffield, D. (2013). Emotions correlate with perceived mental effort and concentration disruption in adult sport performers. *European Journal of Sport Science*, 13, 697–706.

Bassi, M., Steca, P., Monzani, D., Greco, A., & Delle Fave, A. (2014). Personality and optimal experience in adolescence: Implications for well-being and development. *Journal of Happiness Studies*, 15, 829–843.

Bernier, M., Thienot, E., Codron, R., & Fournier, J. (2009). Mindfulness and acceptance approaches in sport performance. *Journal of Clinical Sports Psychology*, 4, 320–330.

Briegel-Jones, R. M., Knowles, Z., Eubank, M. R., Giannoulatos, K., & Elliot, D. (2013). A preliminary investigation into the effect of yoga practice on mindfulness and flow in elite youth swimmers. *Sport Psychologist*, 27, 349–359.

Côté, J. (1999). The influence of the family in the development of talent in sport. *The Sport Psychologist*, 13, 395–417.

Côté, J., Baker, J., & Abernethy, B. (2007). Practice and play in the development of sport expertise. *Handbook of Sport Psychology*, 3, 184–202.

Côté, J., Erickson, K., & Abernethy, B. (2013). Play and practice during childhood. In J. Côté & R. Lidor (Eds.), *Conditions of Children's Talent Development in Sport* (pp. 9–20). Morgantown, WV: Fitness Information Technology.

Cox, A. E., Smith, A. L., & Williams, L. (2008). Change in physical education motivation and physical activity behavior during middle school. *Journal of Adolescent Health*, 43, 506–513.

Csikszentmihalyi, M. (1975). *Beyond Boredom and Anxiety*. San Francisco, CA: Jossey-Bass.

Csikszentmihalyi, M. (1982). Toward a psychology of optimal experience. In L. Wheeler (Ed.), *Review of Personality and Social Psychology* (pp. 13–36). Beverly Hills: Sage.

Csikszentmihalyi, M. (1990). *Flow: The Psychology of Optimal Performance*. New York: Cambridge University Press.

Csikszentmihalyi, M. (1993). *The Evolving Self: A Psychology for the Third Millennium*. New York: HarperCollins.

Csikszentmihalyi, M. (1997). *Finding Flow: The Psychology of Engagement With Everyday Life*. New York: Basic Books.

Csikszentmihalyi, M., & Nakamura, J. (1989). The dynamics of intrinsic motivation: A study of adolescents. *Research on Motivation in Education*, 3, 45–71.

Delle Fave, A., & Bassi, M. (2016). Flow and psychological selection. In L. Harmat, F. Ørsted Andersen, F. Ullén, J. Wright, & G. Sadlo (Eds.), *Flow Experience* (pp. 3–19). Switzerland: Springer International Publishing.

Dishman, R. K., Motl, R. W., Saunders, R., Felton, G., Ward, D. S., Dowda, M., & Pate, R. R. (2005). Enjoyment mediates effects of a school-based physical-activity intervention. *Medicine and Science in Sports and Exercise*, 37, 478–487.

Elbe, A., Strahler, K., Krustrup, P., Wikman, J., & Stelter, R. (2010). Experiencing flow in different types of physical activity intervention programs: Three randomized studies. *Scandinavian Journal of Medicine and Science in Sports*, 20, 111–117.

Engeser, S., & Schiepe-Tiska, A. (2012). Historical lines and an overview of current research on flow. In S. Engeser (Ed.), *Advances in Flow Research* (pp. 1–22). New York: Springer.

Ericsson, K. A., Krampe, R. T., & Tesch-Römer, C. (1993). The role of deliberate practice in the acquisition of expert performance. *Psychological Review*, 100, 363–406.

Fenton, S. A. M., Duda, J. L., Appleton, P. R., & Barrett, T. G. (2016). Empowering youth sport environments: Implications for daily moderate-to-vigorous physical activity and adiposity. *Journal of Sport and Health Science*, 1–11.doi: 10.1016/j.jshs.2016.03.006.

Fredrickson, B. L. (2001). The role of positive emotions in positive psychology: The broaden-and-build theory of positive emotions. *American Psychologist*, 5, 218–226.

Gardner, F. L., & Moore, Z. E. (2004). A mindfulness-acceptance-commitment-based approach to athletic performance enhancement: Theoretical considerations. *Behavior Therapy*, 35, 707–723.

Hagberg, L. A., Lindahl, B., Nyberg, L., & Hellénius, M. (2009). Importance of enjoyment when promoting physical exercise. *Scandinavian Journal of Medicine & Science in Sports*, 19, 740–747.

Hodge, K., Lonsdale, C., & Jackson, S. A. (2009). Athlete engagement in elite sport: An exploratory investigation of antecedents and consequences. *Sport Psychologist*, 23, 186–202.

Hogan, C. L., Catalino, L. I., Mata, J., & Fredrickson, B. L. (2015). Beyond emotional benefits: Physical activity and sedentary behaviour affect psychosocial resources through emotions. *Psychology & Health*, 30, 354–369.

Hyndman, B. P., Benson, A. C., Ullah, S., & Telford, A. (2014). Evaluating the effects of the Lunchtime Enjoyment Activity and Play (LEAP) school playground intervention on children's quality of life, enjoyment and participation in physical activity. *BMC Public Health*, 14, 1–16.

Jackson, S. A. (1992). Athletes in flow: A qualitative investigation of flow states in elite figure skaters. *Journal of Applied Sport Psychology*, 4, 161–180.

Jackson, S. A. (1995). Factors influencing the occurrence of flow state in elite athletes. *Journal of Applied Sport Psychology*, 7, 138–166.

Jackson, S. A. (2000). Joy, fun, and flow state in sport. In Y. Hanin (Ed.), *Emotions in Sport* (pp. 135–156). Champaign, IL: Human Kinetics.

Jackson, S. A., & Kimiecik, J. C. (2008). The flow perspective of optimal experience in sport and physical activity. In T. S. Horn (Ed.), *Advances in Sport and Exercise Psychology* (3rd ed., pp. 377–399). Champaign, IL: Human Kinetics.

Jackson, S., & Lee, J. (2009). *Active women: factors associated with physical activity involvement in a sample of women across life stages.* Paper presented at the Australia Conference of Science and Medicine in Sport, Brisbane, Australia (October).

Jackson, S. A., & Marsh, H. W. (1996). Development and validation of a scale to measure optimal experience: The Flow State Scale. *Journal of Sport & Exercise Psychology*, 18, 17–35.

Jackson, S. A., Martin, A. J., & Eklund, R. C. (2008). Long and short measures of flow: The construct validity of the FSS-2, DFS-2, and new brief counterparts. *Journal of Sport and Exercise Psychology*, 30(5), 561–587.

Jackson, S. A., & Roberts, G. C. (1992). Positive performance states of athletes: Toward a conceptual understanding of peak performance. *The Sport Psychologist*, 6, 156–171.

Kaufman, K. A., Glass, C. R., & Arnkoff, D. B. (2009). Evaluation of Mindful Sport Performance Enhancement (MSPE): A new approach to promote flow in athletes. *Journal of Clinical Sports Psychology*, 4, 334–356.

Kee, Y., & Wang, C. K. (2008). Relationships between mindfulness, flow dispositions, and mental skills adoption: A cluster analytic approach. *Psychology of Sport and Exercise*, 9, 393–411.

Kimiecik, J. (2002). *The Intrinsic Exerciser: Discovering the Joy of Exercise*. Boston, MA: Houghton Mifflin Harcourt.

Kimiecik, J. (2016). The eudaimonics of health: Exploring the promise of well-being for healthier living. In J. Vitterso (Ed.), *Handbook of Eudaimonic Well-Being* (pp. 349–370). Springer International Publishing.

Kimiecik, J., & Harris, A. (1996). What is enjoyment? A conceptual/definitional analysis with implications for sport and exercise psychology. *Journal of Sport and Exercise*, 18(3), 247–263.

MacDonald, D. J., Côté, J., Eys, M., & Deakin, J. (2011). The role of enjoyment and motivational climate in relation to the personal development of team sport athletes. *Sport Psychologist*, 25, 32–46.

McCarthy, P. J. (2009). Putting imagery to good affect: A case study among youth swimmers. *Sport and Exercise Psychology Review*, 5, 27–38.

McCarthy, P. J. (2011). Positive emotion in sport performance: Current status and future directions. *International Review of Sport and Exercise Psychology*, 4, 50–69.

McCarthy, P. J., Jones, M., & Clark-Carter, D. (2008). Understanding enjoyment in youth sport: A developmental perspective. *Psychology of Sport and Exercise*, 9, 142–156.

Metcalf, B., Henley, W., & Wilkin, T. (2012). Effectiveness of intervention on physical activity of children: Systematic review and meta-analysis of controlled trials with objectively measured outcomes. *British Medical Journal*, 47, 1–11.

Mullen, S. P., Olson, E. A., Phillips, S. M., Szabo, A. N., Wójcicki, T. R., Mailey, E. L., & McAuley, E. (2011). Measuring enjoyment of physical activity in older adults: Invariance of the physical activity enjoyment scale (paces) across groups and time. *International Journal of Behavioral Nutrition and Physical Activity*, 8, 1–9.

Munroe, K. J., Giacobbi, P. R. Jr., Hall, C., & Weinberg, R. (2000). The four Ws of imagery use: Where, when, why, and what. *The Sport Psychologist*, 14, 119–137.

Nakamura, J., & Csikszentmihalyi, M. (2009). Flow theory and research. In C. Snyder & S. Lopez (Eds.), *Handbook of Positive Psychology* (pp. 195–206). Oxford: Oxford University Press.

Nicholls, A. R., Polman, R. C., & Holt, N. L. (2005). The effects of an individualized imagery interventions on flow states and golf performance. *Athletic Insight*, 7, 43–66.

Pates, J. K. (2014). The effects of hypnosis on an elite senior European tour golfer. *Journal of Excellence*, 16, 74–83.

Pates, J. K., Cummings, A., & Maynard, I. W. (2002). The effects of hypnosis on flow states and three-point shooting performance in basketball players. *The Sport Psychologist*, 16, 34–47.

Pates, J. K., & Maynard, I. (2000). Effects of hypnosis on flow states and golf performance. *Perceptual and Motor Skills*, 91, 1057–1075.

Pates, J. K., Oliver, R., & Maynard, I. (2001). The effects of hypnosis on flow states and golf-putting performance. *Journal of Applied Sport Psychology*, 13, 341–354.

Pressman, S. D., Matthews, K. A., Cohen, S., Martire, L. M., Scheier, M., Baum, A., & Schulz, R. (2009). Association of enjoyable leisure activities with psychological and physical well-being. *Psychosomatic Medicine*, 71, 725–732.

Raedeke, T. D. (2007). The relationship between enjoyment and affective responses to exercise. *Journal of Applied Sport Psychology*, 19, 105–115.

Rheinberg, F. (2008). Intrinsic motivation and flow. In J. Heckhausen & H. Heckhausen (Eds.), *Motivation and Action* (pp. 323–348). Cambridge: Cambridge University Press.

Ryan, R. M., Frederick, C. M., Lepes, D., Rubio, N., & Sheldon, K. M. (1997). Intrinsic motivation and exercise adherence. *International Journal of Sport Psychology*, 28, 335–354.

Sabo, D., & Veliz, P. (2008). *Go Out and Play: Youth Sports in America*. East Meadow, NY: Women's Sports Foundation.

Scanlan, T. K., & Simons, J. P. (1992). The construct of sport enjoyment. In G. C. Roberts (Ed.), *Motivation in Sport and Exercise* (pp. 199–215). Champaign, IL: Human Kinetics.

Schneider, M., & Cooper, D. M. (2011). Enjoyment of exercise moderates the impact of a school-based physical activity intervention. *International Journal of Behavioral Nutrition and Physical Activity*, 8, 64–71.

Schüler, J., & Brunner, S. (2009). The rewarding effect of flow experience on performance in a marathon race. *Psychology of Sport and Exercise*, 10, 168–174.

Scott-Hamilton, J., Schutte, N. S., & Brown, R. F. (2016). Effects of a mindfulness intervention on sports-anxiety, pessimism, and flow in competitive cyclists. *Applied Psychology: Health and Well-Being*, 8, 85–103.

Scurati, R., Michielon, G., Longo, S., & Invernizzi, P. L. (2010). Imagery training in young swimmers: Effects on the flow state and on performance. In *XIth International Symposium for Biomechanics & Medicine in Swimming* (Vol. 11, pp. 336–338).

Segar, M. L., & Richardson, C. R. (2014). Prescribing pleasure and meaning: Cultivating walking motivation and maintenance. *American Journal of Preventive Medicine*, 47, 838–841.

Seligman, M. E. P., & Csikszentmihalyi, M. (2000). Positive psychology: An introduction. *American Psychologist*, 55, 5–14.

Stein, G. L., Kimiecik, J. C., Daniels, J., & Jackson, S. A. (1995). Psychological antecedents of flow in recreational sport. *Personality and Social Psychology Bulletin*, 21, 125–135.

Steptoe, A., de Oliveira, C., Demakakos, P., & Zaninotto, P. (2014). Enjoyment of life and declining physical function at older ages: A longitudinal cohort study. *Canadian Medical Association Journal*, 186, 150–156.

Swann, C., Keegan, R. J., Crust, L., & Piggott, D. (2016). Psychological states underlying excellent performance in professional golfers: "Letting it happen" vs. "making it happen." *Psychology of Sport and Exercise*, 23, 101–113.

Swann, C., Keegan, R. J., Piggott, D. J. S., & Crust, L. (2012). A systematic review of the experience, occurrence, and controllability of flow states in elite sports. *Psychology of Sport and Exercise*, 13, 807–819.

Vealey, R. S., & Chase, M. (2016). *Best Practice for Youth Sport*. Champaign, IL: Human Kinetics.

Vealey, R. S., & Forlenza, S. (2015). Understanding and using imagery in sport. In J. M. Williams & V. Krane (Eds.), *Applied Sport Psychology: Personal Growth to Peak Performance* (7th ed., pp. 240–273). Boston, MA: McGraw Hill.

Wankel, L. M. (1993). The importance of enjoyment to adherence and psychological benefits from physical activity. *International Journal of Sport Psychology*, 24, 151–169.

Warner, R. (1987). *Freedom, Enjoyment, and Happiness*. Ithaca, NY: Cornell University Press.

Weiss, M. R., & Amorose, A. J. (2008). Motivational orientations and sport behavior. In T. S. Horn (Ed.), *Advances in Sport Psychology* (3rd ed., pp. 115–155). Champaign, IL: Human Kinetics.

Wiggins, M. S., & Freeman, P. (2000). Anxiety and flow: An examination of anxiety direction and the flow experience. *International Sports Journal*, 4, 78–87.

Williams, D. M., Papandonatos, G. D., Napolitano, M. A., Lewis, B. A., Whiteley, J. A., & Marcus, B. H. (2006). Perceived enjoyment moderates the efficacy of an individually tailored physical activity intervention. *Journal of Sport and Exercise Psychology*, 28, 300–309.

10

GRATITUDE AND ATHLETES' WELL-BEING

Lung Hung Chen

> Make sure you live in the moment and work your butt off every single day, and I hope I inspire people all around the world to just be themselves, be humble, and be grateful for all the blessings in your life. I am truly honored to be your MVP this year.
>
> —Stephen Curry (2015 National Basketball Association Awards)

"Faster – Higher – Stronger" is the Olympic motto, and athletes have long relied on modern sports science technology to achieve this goal. However, some athletes pay a painful price in striving to reach this goal, including suffering through injuries (Heaney, Walker, Green, & Rostron, 2015) and burnout (Goodger, Gorley, Lavallee, & Harwood, 2007). This paradox leads to the following question for the researcher and for practitioners: Can athletes pursue performance excellence without (or with fewer) psychological costs? Informed by research in positive psychology concerning positive subjective experience, individual traits, and institutions (Seligman & Csikzsentmihayli, 2000), I have previously proposed an additional element for the Olympic motto, "psychologically healthier" (Chen, Chang, & Chang, 2015a) to reduce these potential costs. Notably, "psychologically healthier" is functionally equivalent to well-being, which is the focus of positive psychology throughout this chapter.

To achieve the goal of psychological health, researchers must identify the factors that enhance athletes' well-being and that might help athletes achieve peak performance, with less harm as a result. In this chapter, I therefore first introduce the concept of gratitude and argue why this seemingly irrelevant concept is important in sports. Second, I clarify contemporary theory underpinning the relationship between gratitude and athletes' well-being. Third, I present a systematic review of the psychological process and theoretical boundaries of gratitude in general and as it pertains to sport psychology in particular. Fourth, I review certain techniques that aim to enhance the effects of gratitude on well-being. Finally, this chapter closes with recommendations that may advance the scope of research into gratitude in sport psychology.

The necessity of gratitude in sports

Gratitude, the parent of all virtues (McCullough, Kilpatrick, Emmons, & Larson, 2001) and a meta-strategy for achieving happiness (Lyubomirsky, 2008), has been the focus of studies in various scientific and humanities fields since the beginning of the 21st century. Gratitude is "a general tendency[1] to recognize and respond with a thankful emotion to the roles of other people's benevolence in the positive experiences and outcomes that one obtains" (McCullough, Emmons, & Tsang, 2002). Furthermore, Wood, Froh, and Geraghty (2010) expanded the conceptualization of gratitude as a life orientation toward noticing and appreciating the positive in the world (p. 891). These two definitions are slightly different from each other, but they are not contradictory because gratitude contains both cognitive and affective aspects.

McCullough et al. (2001) proposed that gratitude functions as a moral barometer, a moral motivator, and a moral reinforcer. Specifically, the moral barometer function is engaged when individuals assess the help and benefits received from other agents (Bartlett, Condon, Cruz, Baumann, & Desteno, 2012). The moral motivator function, in turn, prompts receivers to act morally to reciprocate (Bartlett & Desteno, 2006) or to "pay it forward" (Chang, Lin, & Chen, 2012). Finally, the moral action function leads the original helping agents to repeat the good deeds for the benefit of the original receivers and to unrelated third parties (Williams & Bartlett, 2015).

When I began my research on gratitude in 2008 (Chen & Kee, 2008), I was challenged several times by journal reviewers. The most common criticism of research in this field often comes in the form of a question: *Does gratitude exist in sports?* Apparently – at least for some – gratitude appears to be an irrelevant concept for athletes; nonetheless, athletes have recognized that gratitude has a role in their lives. For example, Carl Lewis, the Olympic track and field champion, has indicated that showing gratitude to his competitors is a part of his competitive repertoire (Lewis & Marx, 1990). In addition, Stephen Curry openly expressed his gratitude when he became the MVP at the 2015 NBA awards. Whilst at first glance, gratitude may seem to be obscure in sports, these anecdotes suggest that athletes do experience grateful emotions and behave morally according to the script of gratitude.

The second frequently mentioned criticism of gratitude in sports is focused on the *function of gratitude*. For example, an anonymous reviewer once questioned whether it can be shown that gratitude contributes to athletes' performance directly and, as such, whether it was a topic worthy of consideration in sport psychology research. In response, I think it is relevant to note that gratitude has not been empirically found to enhance athletic performance directly; however, our investigations are nonetheless worthwhile because gratitude clearly contributes to the development of athletes' optimal functioning (Chen & Wu, 2014, 2016) such that it may indirectly help athletes achieve better performance. With this in mind, it is not surprising that the reviewer raised this issue because performance enhancement is traditionally the first priority in sport psychology. Although I do not claim that focusing on performance enhancement is inappropriate, I also believe that the importance of athletes' well-being must be integrated into this tradition. Following the example of the positive psychology movement, the aim of sport psychologists must be to seek a balance between the athlete's mind and body, which supports my argument for the need to promote psychological health.

In the following section, I briefly review theories and explanations that underpin the relationship between gratitude and athletes' well-being. In addition, empirical evidence both in general and in the context of sport psychology is presented to enable readers to evaluate the importance of gratitude in sport.

Theoretical underpinning of the relationship between gratitude and well-being

The broaden–and–build theory of positive emotions (Fredrickson, 1998, 2001, 2004a) may be one of the most discussed theories in seeking to elucidate the relationship between gratitude and individual well-being. As opposed to negative emotions that trigger the urge to escape or fight when facing a threat, Fredrickson's theory posits that positive emotions can broaden an individual's momentary thought and action repertoires to build enduring resources to be drawn on in the future. In other words, negative emotions trigger automatic action to prevent people from immediate harm, whereas positive emotions cultivate resources to be used repeatedly in the future. Thus, both positive and negative emotions have their value as evolutionary adaptations.

There are two essential components in the broaden–and–build hypothesis of positive emotions (Fredrickson, 2000, 2013). Fredrickson depicted in detail how different positive emotions may broaden momentary thoughts and actions that then build further resources. For example, *joy* leads to the urge to play (broadening), encompassing not only physical and social play but also artistic play involving invention and just plain fooling around. These unscripted actions cultivate physical strength and skill, which develop into enduring physical resources (building). *Interest* elicits a feeling that seeks to investigate or extend the self to acquire new information and experience (broadening). Those exploratory behaviors gradually increase the knowledge base, which become intellectual resources (building). *Contentment* prompts people to savor their lives and recent successes (broadening), which mindfully broadens individuals' self and world views (building).

Although the focus of my research is on dispositional gratitude, it has been suggested that the grateful individual is inclined to experience grateful moods and emotions (Rosenberg, 1998). Thus, gratitude, like other positive emotions, also broadens and builds. Gratitude is more likely to broaden social capital because people who experience gratitude tend to have flexible worldviews and recognize and interpret the things they have in life as gifts (McCullough et al., 2002), even in negative circumstances (Lambert, Graham, Fincham, & Stillman, 2009). This broadening effect will further help an individual achieve his or her goals (a building process) because an upward spiral of interpersonal connections (Algoe, Gable, & Maisel, 2010) can help individuals accumulate social resources (Fredrickson, 2000). For example, support from coaches, family, and teammates will boost an athlete's self-confidence (Freeman & Rees, 2010), enhancing performance and goal achievement as a result (Rees & Hardy, 2000).

In addition to the broaden-and-build theory of positive emotions, some researchers have proposed specific mechanisms to account for the relationship between gratitude and well-being. For example, grateful people have been found to adopt coping styles such as positive reframing (Lambert et al., 2011) and seeking support (Wood et al., 2008). Gratitude motivates prosocial actions to create *upstream reciprocity*, which is passing on benefit to a person uninvolved in an initial exchange (Nowak & Roch, 2007; Chang et al., 2012). The dynamic processes of giving and receiving develop a range of enduring social resources that contribute to well-being.

Because of space limitations, I cannot conduct a complete review of the theories and mechanisms that underpin gratitude and well-being. However, for those who are interested in the details of alternative mechanisms, I suggest Emmons and Mishra's (2010) influential review. In the following section, I briefly review certain noteworthy empirical studies in the literature to illuminate how and when gratitude enhances individuals' well-being, which will inform later considerations for how it is relevant in sport.

Empirical evidence supports the beneficial effect of gratitude on well-being

Since McCullough et al. (2002) published their influential work on the psychometric properties of the Gratitude Questionnaire (GQ),[2] researchers have had a reliable measurement with which to operationalize gratitude. In the GQ, McCullough et al. (2002) developed and selected six items for assessing gratitude and validated the single-factor structure in a confirmatory factor analysis (Study 1). In terms of convergent and discriminant validity, the GQ was positively related to the gratitude reported by informants and was also associated with spirituality, positive affect, well-being, prosocial traits and behaviors, and the Big Five Personality Traits. The same results were replicated in a large, non-student sample in Study 2. In addition, envy and materialistic attitudes were negatively related to GQ in Study 3. These associations were also maintained after controlling for agreeableness, neuroticism/negative affectivity, and extraversion/positive affectivity in Study 4. Subsequently, the GQ was translated into multiple languages, such as Chinese, Japanese, Spanish, Polish, and Greek. Thus, McCullough et al. (2002) can be regarded as the originators of contemporary scientific research on gratitude.

With a reliable measure, some researchers became interested in the directional relationship between gratitude and well-being. Investigating the directional relationship would allow better interpretation of cross-sectional findings and more accurate speculation regarding how a grateful disposition leads to benefits. For example, Wood et al. (2008) conducted two independent cross-lagged studies, and their data support a direct model in which gratitude leads to the development of social support while reducing stress and depression over time (Study 1). The observed associations were maintained when controlling for the Big Five Personality Traits (Study 2). In addition, model comparisons (stability, reverse, and reciprocal models) found no alternative models that were superior to the direct models. Similar results have also been reported by Zhou and Wu (2015), who found that gratitude may be a stable predictive factor for developing posttraumatic growth in adolescents following the Wenchuan earthquake in China. Conversely, some research has found that the relationship between gratitude and well-being indicators may be reciprocal; for example, Lee, Tong, and Sim (2015) found that over time gratitude predicted relatedness and autonomy but not competence. Furthermore, all three psychological needs also predicted gratitude over time. Supporting this finding indirectly, gratitude and a sense of coherence – the belief that life is manageable, meaningful, and comprehensible – were found to influence one another over time (Lambert et al., 2009).

With respect to sports, I am curious as to how disposition (gratitude) and life experience (athlete burnout) interact with each other based on the correspondent perspective of personality (Caspi, Roberts, & Shiner, 2005). A cross-lagged design with a three-month interval yielded surprising results. Sport devaluation, one of the sub-domains of athlete burnout, led to decreased gratitude over time (Chen & Chang, 2014), as opposed to the findings from the studies previously discussed. We proposed possible reasons for this paradoxical finding; for example, burned-out athletes might tend to detach themselves from sports participation and social interactions, which, in turn, increases the difficulty in exercising gratitude. Second, burned-out athletes have fixed thoughts that might work against the benefit-finding process rooted in gratitude. Finally, there is the possibility that athletes' burnout might be more stable and pervasive than their gratitude tendency, which would make it difficult to relieve their stress. However, those inconsistent results between general psychology and sport psychology suggest that there might be room for researchers to explore possible boundaries such as contexts, population, and the nature of outcomes that may help determine the directional relationship.

The psychological process and theoretical boundaries of gratitude

To uncover the psychological process of gratitude on well-being, certain possible mediators have been examined in previous studies. For example, it was found that grateful individuals have better sleep quality because they tend to have more positive cognitions, such as recently experiencing enjoyable things, and less negative pre-sleep cognitions, such as thinking about the bad things that happen in the world (Wood, Joseph, Lloyd, & Atkins, 2009). In addition, Kleiman, Adams, Kashdan, and Riskind (2013b) used a sample of college students and found that gratitude increases meaning in life and further reduces suicidal ideation. Although I only selectively review a few gratitude studies, this evidence partially supports the notion that gratitude broadens individuals' thoughts to see the positive side of ordinary life, which corresponds to Fredrickson's theory.

In sports, in addition to the intrapersonal process, our research has become interested in how the interpersonal process, that is, athletes interacting with one another, underpins the relationship between gratitude and athletes' well-being. Our research indicated that grateful athletes more easily notice emotional, esteem-related, informational, and tangible support from both coaches and teammates. Experiencing support also contributes to athletes' team and life satisfaction (Chen, 2013). In another study, we adopt a different operationalization of social interaction, team cohesion, which refers to a dynamic process in which individuals subjectively stick to the team, and also to the degree to which team members are united (Carron and Brawley, 2000). Perceived high team cohesion implies that individuals consider themselves to be in a warm, supportive, and psychologically united atmosphere (Chen et al., 2015b). The results indicated that team cohesion partially mediated gratitude and athletes' life satisfaction, which suggests that grateful athletes have high life satisfaction because they feel emotionally connected to their teams. Combined with previous studies in mainstream psychology, the psychological process of gratitude is shown to be a complicated matter involving both intra- and interpersonal pathways that require further investigation.

Another interesting topic involves the boundaries of gratitude: Are there any conditions that facilitate or suppress the effect of gratitude on well-being? For example, Kleiman et al. (2013a) found that both hopelessness and depressive symptoms are less likely to be related to thoughts and suicide intentions when people are grateful. Similarly, it was found that gratitude protects older adults from dwelling on financial strain, thus resulting in fewer depressive symptoms (Krause, 2009). In addition, grateful people have better coping efficacy and higher self-esteem even when facing stressful life events (Li, Zhang, Li, Li, & Ye, 2012). Those studies indicate that gratitude may be an important protector of individuals' well-being. However, gratitude is also (unfortunately) suppressed under certain conditions. For instance, Chen, Chen, and Tsai (2012) indicated that grateful people are less happy when there is ambivalence regarding emotional expression, when there is a tendency to inhibit the desire to express, or when an individual is being expressive but regretting the expressiveness.

With respect to the context of gratitude and sports, my colleagues and I adapted the interactionism perspective (Reynolds et al., 2010; Griffo & Randall Colvin, 2009), which is how dispositional and environmental factors can jointly influence athletes' well-being. In one study, we found that athletes' gratitude and trust in their coach can jointly promote an athlete's self-esteem over time through a broaden-and-build mechanism (Chen & Wu, 2014). When grateful athletes have higher affective trust in their coaches, they are more likely to perceive and obtain more resources from coaches in a supportive relationship and then utilize such resources to achieve personal goals, which helps to increase these athletes' self-esteem. Recently, another study indicated that experiential avoidance, an attempt to escape, avoid, or modify the forms or frequency of uncomfortable experiences, might be reduced over time when grateful athletes perceived that they were autonomously supported by their coach (Chen & Wu, 2016). It was hypothesized that grateful athletes are more likely to embrace negative experiences when they rely on coaches' support without having to worry about evaluative judgment from their coaches. In such a supportive condition, moreover, grateful athletes tend to see themselves as beneficiaries of their coaches and feel esteemed, affirmed, and valued (McCullough et al., 2002), which thus helps them to build on their psychological strengths and to be capable of tolerating negative experiences in their pursuit of excellence.

So far, I have reviewed some noteworthy research that contributes to our knowledge about the directional relationship, mechanisms, and theoretical boundaries of dispositional gratitude on athletes' well-being. Those studies consistently indicate that gratitude is beneficial for athletes. However, some practitioners may be curious regarding one critical question: Can we increase athletes' well-being intentionally by manipulating gratitude, and if so, what, if any, impact might this have on performance? In the following section, I briefly review some techniques that aim to cultivate gratitude.

Cultivating gratitude

Several techniques have been developed to induce gratitude, one of the most well-known being *counting your blessings* (Emmons & McCullough, 2003). Participants were told to count the things for which they are grateful (such as the generosity of friends, God, and wonderful parents) once a week (Study 1) or daily (Study 2). Compared with the other two control conditions (hassles and neutral events or social comparison), people in the gratitude condition reported higher well-being in both studies. Furthermore, these results were replicated with a sample of persons with neuromuscular disease (Study 3), which demonstrated that gratitude can be manipulated through easy self-guided exercises.

In another study, participants were given one week to write and then deliver a letter of gratitude in person to someone who had been particularly kind to them but who had never been properly thanked (Seligman, Steen, Park, & Peterson, 2005); this event was called a *gratitude visit*. Compared with the placebo group, participants in the gratitude visit group increased their happiness, and depressive symptoms were decreased after the intervention; moreover, this effect lasted one month. Notably, however, this effect disappeared after three months. In this regard, we speculate that although it may be easy to exercise gratitude, participants must regularly practice it to benefit from it.

For readers who are interested in understanding the ways in which gratitude is exercised, I strongly recommend the review by Wood et al. (2010). These authors recorded the details of gratitude interventions in the previous literature, such as their duration, how gratitude was manipulated, and what type of control was set up. Moreover, these authors estimated the effect size of gratitude conditions relative to those of the control groups. That information is valuable for setting up a well-controlled gratitude intervention. Unfortunately, I am not aware of any published article that has aimed at manipulating gratitude to increase athletes' well-being, which might be because the traditional focus has been on performance enhancement instead of on well-being. However, following publication of the current book, I believe that this trend might change.

Conclusion and future directions

Although Faster – Higher – Stronger is presented as the golden ideal in sport, some scholars (including me) have attempted to introduce concepts from positive psychology because we believe that optimal performance depends on psychological health as well as physical health. Therefore, my colleagues and I have spent substantial effort investigating the benefits of gratitude in sport. In this chapter, I systematically reviewed the origin of, empirical evidence regarding, psychological processes involved in, and theoretical boundaries of gratitude. Before closing, I propose two possible future directions for those who may be interested in studying gratitude in sport.

The first direction concerns the need for contextualization in future gratitude research and contextualized interpretation of past gratitude research. Most studies in the previous literature assumed that gratitude is a universal phenomenon without contextual particularity. However, people live in specific contexts, experience contextual emotions, and operate with contextual cognition and behavior, which may not be accurately captured by general constructs. Indeed, some researchers have begun to investigate the unique effects of gratitude within specific contexts. For example, Krause, Bruce, Haywar, and Woolever (2014) investigated the effects of gratitude toward God in older adults. These authors slightly modified the operational definition of gratitude to capture the concept in older adults more precisely. Similarly, our team also attempted to refine the concept of gratitude in the context of sport. Unlike general gratitude, which does not identify the targets to whom people are grateful, we specifically defined the explicit targets (e.g., coaches and teammates), and the preliminary results support the incremental validity of explicit gratitude compared with general gratitude (Chen & Chang, 2016, 2017). This direction reminds researchers to consider the specific population and context that they are investigating.

Another direction is to examine the level of gratitude. Recently, Fehr, Fulmer, Awtrey, and Miller (2017) proposed a new theoretical model that suggested that three types of gratitude can be approached from three levels: episodic gratitude at the event level, persistent gratitude at the individual level, and collective gratitude at the organizational level. The first two perspectives were well documented in the literature regarding the state and traits of gratitude. However, the perspective of collective gratitude further embodies the argument that gratitude, as with other positive emotions, transforms organizations and communities (Fredrickson, 2004b). Accordingly, this raises many new questions. For example, does a grateful sports team enjoy better performance than a less grateful sports team? Do grateful sports teams contribute to athletes' well-being? Those questions merit further investigation in the future. In summary, research in gratitude is just beginning, and there are many questions to be answered.

To close this chapter, I quote Robert Frost's famous poem: "Two roads diverged in a wood, and I – I took the one less traveled by, and that has made all the difference" (Frost, 1916). As with Frost's poem, investigating the benefit of gratitude on athletes' well-being is not a well-traveled road, but it is nonetheless a worthy endeavor.

Notes

1 Because of space limitations, I selectively review only dispositional gratitude in the literature. Readers should note that gratitude can also be conceptualized as a rapid emotional reaction and chronic mood status (Rosenberg, 1998). Thus, readers must carefully distinguish the scope of the topic reviewed herein.
2 We are aware that there are other measurements that assess dispositional gratitude; however, only studies that used the GQ-6 were reviewed, because it is the most frequently cited tool.

References

Algoe, S. B., Gable, S. L., & Maisel, N. (2010). It's the little things: Everyday gratitude as a booster shot for romantic relationships. *Personal Relationships*, 17, 217–233.

Bartlett, M.Y., Condon, P., Cruz, J., Baumann, J., & Desteno, D. (2012). Gratitude: Prompting behaviours that build relationships. *Cognition & Emotion*, 26, 2–13.

Bartlett, M.Y., & Desteno, D. (2006). Gratitude and prosocial behavior: Helping when it costs you. *Psychological Science*, 17, 319–325.

Carron, A.V., & Brawley, L. R. (2000). Cohesion: Conceptual and measurement issues. *Small Group Research*, 31, 89–106.

Caspi, A., Roberts, B. W., & Shiner, R. L. (2005). Personality development: Stability and change. *Annual Review of Psychology*, 56, 453–484.

Chang, Y. P., Lin, Y. C., & Chen, L. H. (2012). Pay it forward: Gratitude in social networks. *Journal of Happiness Studies*, 13, 761–781.

Chen, L. H. (2013). Gratitude and adolescent athletes' well-being: The multiple mediating roles of perceived social support from coaches and teammates. *Social Indicators Research*, 114, 273–285.

Chen, L. H., Chang, W. S., & Chang, Y. P. (2015a). When positive psychology encounters sport psychology. *Physical Education Journal*, 48, 123–138.

Chen, L. H., & Chang, Y. P. (2014). Cross-lagged associations between gratitude and adolescent athlete burnout. *Current Psychology*, 33, 460–478.

Chen, L. H., & Chang, Y. P. (2016). Incremental validity of sport domain gratitude on athletes' well-being. *The Journal of Positive Psychology*, 12 (6), 651–659.

Chen, L.H., & Chang, Y.P. (2017). Sport-domain gratitude uniquely accounts for athletes' well-being across two cultures: Incremental validity above the general gratitude. *The Journal of Positive Psychology*, 12(6), 651–659.

Chen, L. H., Chen, M. Y., & Tsai, Y. M. (2012). Does gratitude always work? Ambivalence over emotional expression inhibits the beneficial effect of gratitude on well-being. *International Journal of Psychology*, 47, 381–392.

Chen, L. H., & Kee, Y. H. (2008). Gratitude and adolescent athletes' well-being. *Social Indicators Research*, 89, 361–373.

Chen, L. H., Kee, Y. H., & Chen, M. Y. (2015b). Why grateful adolescent athletes are more satisfied with their life: The mediating role of perceived team cohesion. *Social Indicators Research*, 124, 463–476.

Chen, L. H., & Wu, C. H. (2014). Gratitude enhances change in athletes' self-esteem: The moderating role of trust in coach. *Journal of Applied Sport Psychology*, 26, 349–362.

Chen, L. H., & Wu, C. H. (2016). When does dispositional gratitude help athletes move away from experiential avoidance? The moderating role of perceived coach autonomy support. *Journal of Applied Sport Psychology*, 28, 338–349.

Emmons, R. A., & McCullough, M. E. (2003). Counting blessings versus burdens: An experimental investigation of gratitude and subjective well-being in daily life. *Journal of Personality and Social Psychology*, 84, 377–389.

Emmons, R. A., & Mishra, A. (2010). Why gratitude enhances well-being: What we know, what we need to know. In K. M. Sheldon, T. B. Kashdan, & M. F. Steger (Eds.), *Designing Positive Psychology*. Oxford: Oxford University Press.

Fehr, R., Fulmer, A., Awtrey, E., & Miller, J. (2017). The grateful workplace: A multilevel model of gratitude in organizations. *Academy of Management Review*, 42(2), 361–381.

Fredrickson, B. L. (1998). What good are positive emotions? *Review of General Psychology*, 2, 300–319.

Fredrickson, B. L. (2000). Cultivating positive emotions to optimize health and well-being. *Prevention & Treatment (online journal)*, 3 (1), article 1 (no pagination provided). Retrieved December 5, 2015, from http://content.apa.org/PsycARTICLES/journal/pre/3/1.

Fredrickson, B. L. (2001). The role of positive emotions in positive psychology: The broaden-and-build theory of positive emotions. *American Psychologist*, 56, 218–226.

Fredrickson, B. L. (2004a). The broaden-and-build theory of positive emotions. *Philosophical Transactions of the Royal Society of London Series B-Biological Sciences*, 359, 1367–1377.

Fredrickson, B. L. (2004b). Gratitude, like other positive emotion, broadens and builds. In R. A. Emmons & M. E. McCullough (Eds.), *The Psychology of Gratitude*. New York: Oxford University Press.

Fredrickson, B. L. (2013). Positive emotions broaden and build. In E. A. Plant & P. G. Devine (Eds.), *Advances on Experimental Social Psychology*. Burlington: Academic Press.

Freeman, P., & Rees, T. (2010). Perceived social support from team-mates: Direct and stress-buffering effects on self-confidence. *European Journal of Sport Science*, 10, 59–67.

Frost, R. (1916). *Mountain Interval*. New York: Henry Holt and Company.

Goodger, K., Gorley, T., Lavallee, D., & Harwood, C. (2007). Burnout in sport: A systematic review. *The Sport Psychologist*, 21, 121–157.

Griffo, R., & Randall Colvin, C. (2009). A brief look at interactionism: Past and present. *Journal of Research in Personality*, 43, 243–244.

Heaney, C. A., Walker, N. C., Green, A. J. K., & Rostron, C. L. (2015). Sport psychology education for sport injury rehabilitation professionals: A systematic review. *Physical Therapy in Sport*, 16, 72–79.

Kleiman, E. M., Adams, L. M., Kashdan, T. B., & Riskind, J. H. (2013a). Grateful individuals are not suicidal: Buffering risks associated with hopelessness and depressive symptoms. *Personality and Individual Differences*, 56, 595–599.

Kleiman, E. M., Adams, L. M., Kashdan, T. B., & Riskind, J. H. (2013b). Gratitude and grit indirectly reduce risk of suicidal ideations by enhancing meaning in life: Evidence for a mediated moderation model. *Journal of Research in Personality*, 47, 539–546.

Krause, N. (2009). Religious involvement, gratitude, and change in depressive symptoms over time. *International Journal for the Psychology of Religion*, 19, 155–172.

Krause, N., Bruce, D., Haywar, R. D., & Woolever, C. (2014). Gratitude to god, self-rated health, and depressive symptoms. *Journal for the Scientific Study of Religion*, 53, 341–355.

Lambert, N. M., Fincham, F. D., & Stillman, T. F. (2011). Gratitude and depressive symptoms: The role of positive reframing and positive emotion. *Cognition and Emotion*, 26, 615–633.

Lambert, N. M., Graham, S. M., Fincham, F. D., & Stillman, T. F. (2009). A changed perspective: How gratitude can affect sense of coherence through positive reframing. *The Journal of Positive Psychology*, 4, 461–470.

Lee, L. N., Tong, E. M. W., & Sim, D. (2015). The dual upward spirals of gratitude and basic psychological needs. *Motivation Science*, 1, 87–97.

Lewis, C., & Marx, J. (1990). *Inside Track: My Professional Life in Amateur Track and Field*. New York: Simon & Schuster.

Li, D., Zhang, W., Li, X., Li, N., & Ye, B. (2012). Gratitude and suicidal ideation and suicide attempts among Chinese adolescents: Direct, mediated, and moderated effects. *Journal of Adolescence*, 35, 55–66.

Lyubomirsky, S. (2008). *The How of Happiness: A Scientific Approach to Getting the Life You Want*. New York: Penguin Press.

McCullough, M. E., Emmons, R. A., & Tsang, J. A. (2002). The grateful disposition: A conceptual and empirical topography. *Journal of Personality and Social Psychology*, 82, 112–127.

McCullough, M. E., Kilpatrick, S. D., Emmons, R. A., & Larson, D. B. (2001). Is gratitude a moral affect? *Psychological Bulletin*, 127, 249–266.

Nowak, M. A., & Roch, S. (2007). Upstream reciprocity and the evolution of gratitude. *Proceedings of the Royal Society B-Biological Sciences*, 274, 605–610.

Rees, T., & Hardy, L. (2000). An investigation of the social support experiences of high-level sports performers. *The Sport Psychologist*, 14, 327–347.

Reynolds, K. J., Turner, J. C., Branscombe, N. R., Mavor, K. I., Bizumic, B., & Subašić, E. (2010). Interactionism in personality and social psychology: An integrated approach to understanding the mind and behaviour. *European Journal of Personality*, 24(5), 458–482.

Rosenberg, E. L. (1998). Levels of analysis and the organization of affect. *Review of General Psychology*, 2, 247–270.

Seligman, M. E. P., & Csikzsentmihayli, M. (2000). Positive psychology: An introduction. *American Psychologist*, 55, 5–15.

Seligman, M. E. P., Steen, T. A., Park, N., & Peterson, C. (2005). Positive psychology progress: Empirical validation of interventions. *American Psychologist*, 60, 410–421.

Williams, L. A., & Bartlett, M. Y. (2015). Warm thanks: Gratitude expression facilitates social affiliation in new relationships via perceived warmth. *Emotion*, 15, 1–5.

Wood, A. M., Froh, J. J., & Geraghty, A. W. A. (2010). Gratitude and well-being: A review and theoretical integration. *Clinical Psychology Review*, 30, 890–905. doi:10.1016/j.cpr.2010.03.005.

Wood, A. M., Joseph, S., Lloyd, C, J., & Atkins, S. (2009). Gratitude influences sleep through the mechanism of pre-sleep cognitions. *Journal of Psychosomatic Research*, 66, 43–48.

Wood, A. M., Maltby, J., Gillett, R., Linley, P. A., & Joseph, S. (2008). The role of gratitude in the development of social support, stress, and depression: Two longitudinal studies. *Journal of Research in Personality*, 42, 854–871.

Zhou, X., & Wu, X. (2015). Longitudinal relationships between gratitude, deliberate rumination, and posttraumatic growth in adolescents following the Wenchuan earthquake in China. *Scandinavian Journal of Psychology*, 56, 567–572.

11

POSITIVE PSYCHOLOGY OF RELATIONSHIPS IN SPORT AND PHYSICAL ACTIVITY

*Bridget Grenville-Cleave, Abbe Brady
and Emma Kavanagh*

Introduction

Literature spanning positive psychology (PP), clinical psychology, social psychology and health psychology is replete with findings that highlight the positive psychological, emotional and social benefits of forming and maintaining social relationships (O'Connell, O'Shea, & Gallagher, 2015). Some of the many benefits of connecting with others include both giving and receiving attention, companionship, affection, intimacy and emotional security. Literature also highlights how features of poor relationships such as rejection and conflict can be a source of stress and fear, and the absence of meaningful relationships can lead to isolation and loneliness, which are significantly linked to reduced health and well-being (Jackson-Dwyer, 2014). The risk to health and mortality associated with social isolation and loneliness is comparable with factors such as physical inactivity, obesity and smoking (Holt-Lunstad, Smith, Baker, Harris, & Stephenson, 2015). Individuals who maintain a variety of relationship types, for example, friendships, close family ties, marriage and being a part of social, political and religious groups, are likely to live longer than those who have fewer social ties (Cohen & Janicki-Deverts, 2009).

Notwithstanding some notable exceptions, the psychological study of people in sport and physical activity (PA) has mainly focused its efforts on understanding individual-level aspects and less attention has been allocated to understanding relationships and interpersonal dimensions of people's experience and behaviour. This chapter presents evidence about characteristics of positive relationships and their significance for individual and relational well-being. We briefly outline dominant themes and patterns associated with existing knowledge about relationships in sport and exercise. Drawing upon contemporary findings in PP, some key strategies and interventions are presented to support the development and maintenance of positive and productive interpersonal relations in sport and PA. Finally, we propose several avenues for future enquiry and research so that we may better understand and develop flourishing relationships in sport, exercise and PA settings.

One of the common approaches in research concerning relationships in sport has examined types of relationships and the mechanisms through which they function. For example, the coach-athlete relationship has received a significant amount of attention as one of the most critical dyads encountered by athletes in sport (see Jowett, 2007; Jowett, Paull, Pensgaard, Hoegmo, & Riise, 2005; Sagar & Jowett, 2015). Coach-athlete relationships are considered bi-directional, in that the feelings, thoughts and behaviors of the coach affect, and are affected by, those of the athlete (Rhind & Jowett, 2010). The importance of other social agents such as peer group members or friends is less well understood. Research points to a number of desirable outcomes directly associated with friendship ties, including increased self-esteem, emotional support, introduction to intimacy and assistance in conflict resolution skills (Weiss, Smith, & Theeboom, 1996; Carr, 2009).

Deci and Ryan's Self Determination Theory (SDT, 1985, 2000), recognizes the importance of human connection as a primary source of well-being. SDT posits that socio-contextual factors can influence human motivation by affecting our three basic psychological needs of autonomy, competence and relatedness. Relatedness is defined as caring for and feeling cared for by others and is integral for human growth and development. Similarly, Allen's (2005) social motivation theory is grounded in the energizing nature of striving for social belongingness and demonstrates how individuals seek social environments that support relatedness and avoid those that thwart it. Despite the theoretical significance attributed to relatedness in key theories, compared with competence and autonomy, it receives far less attention in sport and exercise literature.

Competitive situations and training environments may place significant emotional and physical demands on individuals. Research has focused on the assistance we gain from significant relationships through social support (Connaughton, Wadey, Hanton, & Jones, 2008; Rees & Hardy, 2000) and the importance of ties within group settings through examining the forces which act upon group members to maintain team membership through team cohesion (Carron, Colman, Wheeler, & Stevens, 2002). We know that effective relationships in sport and PA rely on mutual trust, support, shared knowledge of goals, co-operation and the ability to communicate (Jowett & Cockerill, 2003; Jowett, 2007) and are considered to have a positive impact on motivation, self- and collective efficacy and team cohesion (e.g. Hampson & Jowett, 2014; Jowett et al., 2012; Jowett & Nezlek, 2012; Jowett & Chaundy, 2004).

There may be occasions or particular contexts in sport and PA when relationships can threaten well-being and cause harm. Our research shows such relationships can serve to reduce the person to feeling isolated and vulnerable, lacking autonomy, disoriented and dislocated from other aspects of their lives, like an expendable commodity or a robot to be programmed (Brady, 2011; Kavanagh & Brady, 2014). The nature of relationships is central to well-being, and Kavanagh and Brady (2014, p. 26) proposed that it is 'only when the athlete is considered as a whole person and their humanness recognized that they are most likely to thrive and flourish within and beyond sport'. Understanding humanizing features of relationships and their relationship with well-being is an area ripe for exploration through PP.

Relationship research in sport and exercise has tended to reflect the structural, functional and instrumental components of relationships and social ties, rather than the personal, experiential and subjective. As a consequence, we know considerably more about topics such as coaching strategies, power and leadership typologies, role and group formation, interpersonal conflict, social contagion and dyadic anxiety than we do about concepts such as dyadic well-being, friendship, socializing, gratitude, caring, kindness, trust, compassion, playfulness, forgiveness, humor and respect. The latter, we would argue, are also important aspects of personally and interpersonally meaningful experiences. As such, we propose that these topics have considerable potential to add to present understanding about how social relationships in sport and exercise may contribute to mental and physical health and well-being. Emerging research suggests that PP activities and interventions can be adopted to increase both the quality of and satisfaction in relationships (O'Connell, O'Shea, & Gallagher, 2015). The next section draws upon developments in PP, sport and exercise psychology and sociology to introduce interventions associated with relational mapping, responding styles, gratitude and forgiveness.

Taking the time to become aware of the relationships we maintain may enable us to reflect upon their significance and importance. In addition, it can help individuals understand where to focus time and attention in relationships in order to work toward personal growth. Raising awareness of relationships can be a valuable activity to direct efforts to maintain the quality and effectiveness of them and seek to limit or prevent conflict arising in the future. Next we describe the stages of a relationship-mapping activity designed to broaden awareness of one's relational context.

Relationship mapping

For this activity, identify and list the key people with whom you maintain relationships (you may wish to break this down into areas, e.g. sport, work, school or college, friends and family).

Rate each relationship 1 through 5 (1 low, 5 high) on:

- frequency of contact;
- current quality of relationship;
- importance of the relationship at this time.

Use the following questions to reflect on these aspects of each relationship: what does this process tell you, and what do you need to do to enhance your relationships?

This activity can be developed further; here we describe four strategies:

1   discuss the map with another person;
2   write a relationship action plan designed to positively influence your relationships;

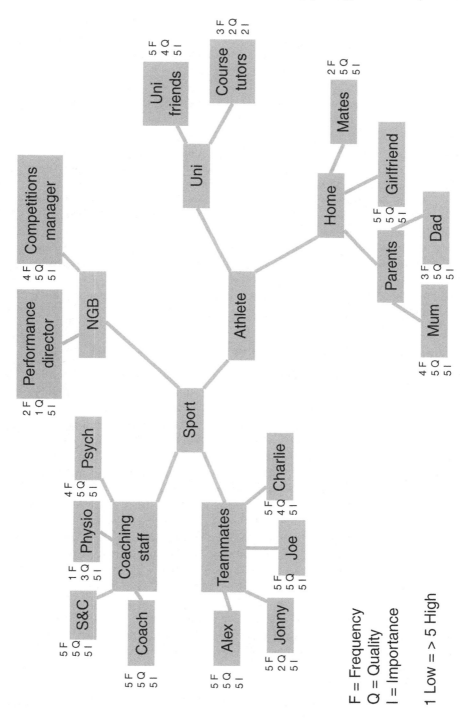

F = Frequency
Q = Quality
I = Importance

1 Low = > 5 High

FIGURE 11.1   Example of a positive relationship map from an elite junior volleyball player

3   consider the character strengths of yourself and the people listed and how these influence your relationships (see Chapter 5 for more information), and also;
4   reflect appreciatively on relationships to highlight the opportunities to give and receive social support (Figure 11.1).

According to Granovetter (1973, 1983), people with whom we have strong ties are more likely to be like us, move in the same social and work circles, and think and behave like us. Over time, this may lead to problems, because new ideas, attitudes and behaviours will only slowly be taken up, if at all. By comparison, our weak ties (i.e. those who live, work and train in different social circles) are more likely to think differently, have access to different information and resources and therefore can introduce us to new ideas and influences. The relative value of strong and weak ties is relevant when we consider our personal relationship maps, and how they have influenced our lives and might do so in the future. How many of the current relationships we identified in the personal relationship map exercise are classic 'strong ties' versus 'weak ties'? How much time do we spend nurturing those strong ties versus the weak ties? How might we deliberately cultivate more weak ties, those that can expose us to new ideas, experiences and opportunities in life and work?

Responding styles and capitalizing

Often the emphasis in relationship research focuses on the value to the relationship of providing social support in difficult times. One of the more remarkable findings in PP with particular relevance for sport and PA concerns research on the personal and interpersonal outcomes of social support in good times through responding to good news. Research led by Shelly Gable and colleagues (Gable, Gonzaga, & Strachman, 2006; Gable & Reis, 2010) shows that when the other responds in an 'active and constructive' manner (rather than in a passive and/or destructive manner), both the discloser and the relationship between the discloser and the responder benefit. Gable et al. (2006, p. 914) found that 'feeling responded to when good things happen plays a vital role in relationship well-being'. Personal benefits include increased positive emotions, subjective well-being, self-esteem and decreased loneliness, and relationship benefits include satisfaction, intimacy, commitment, trust, liking, closeness and stability (Gable & Reis, ibid). Gable et al. (ibid) suggest that capitalizing on good news benefits the discloser and the relationship because it enables the responder to display understanding, validation and caring toward the discloser. The preliminary study by Gable and colleagues (ibid) also suggested that the way people respond to good news (i.e. whether or not they capitalize) predicts relationship break-ups. An example of an active constructive response, and its opposites, is shown in Table 11.1

Given the evidence that capitalization strengthens relationships, it is important to consider how often you convey understanding, caring and validation by enabling others to capitalize on their good news, and how often you encourage them to do the same with their family, friends and teammates. Plenty of opportunities exist to

TABLE 11.1 Active-passive and constructive-destructive responses to good news

Discloser: Child (positive and high energy) '*I scored a goal in hockey today and we won the match!*'

Responder: Parent

Passive Destructive	**Active Destructive**
Parent responds: '*Not now, I'm busy.*' (negative and low energy, ignoring the child, focusing on the self)	Parent responds: '*Only one? I thought you were the top goal scorer! You're going to have to do much better than that if you want to be picked for the next match!*' (positive and high energy, asking questions to help the discloser relive the positive experience)
Passive Constructive	**Active Constructive**
Parent responds: '*That's good.*' (positive, but low energy)	Parent responds: '*Oh wow! That's great news. Well done! I can see that you're over the moon – tell me all about it! What happened?*' (high energy but negative, and focused on reasons why it's not good news)

practice capitalizing on good news in sport and PA, that is, responding in an active and constructive manner. However, as a consequence of the evolutionary negativity bias, and in some settings (e.g. particular elite or professional sports), there may be a situational or cultural bias toward not valuing or showing interpersonal understanding or caring, thus we may need to proactively focus on noticing them.

Gratitude

Though Chapter 10 provides an insight into the importance of gratitude more broadly, it receives attention here because of its significance and relevance to relationships within sport and PA. Here we define gratitude as 'a felt sense of wonder, thankfulness and appreciation for life' (Emmons & Shelton, 2002, p. 460). Recent research has demonstrated that gratitude is an important element of successful and satisfying relationships, and expressing gratitude is associated with relationship formation and relationship maintenance behaviours (Algoe, Haidt, & Gable, 2008; Lambert & Fincham, 2011).

Gratitude functions to nurture social relationships through its encouragement of reciprocal, prosocial behaviour between a benefactor and recipient (Emmons & McCullough, 2003). Therefore, gratitude is considered to strengthen relationships because it can promote forgiveness, increase sympathetic response to distress in others, enhance the adoption of conflict resolution strategies and increase connection to others. As Bartlett and Desteno (2006) note, gratitude may play a pivotal role in building trust by encouraging individuals to adopt behaviours that support working in partnership. In sporting environments, gratitude has been found to support prosocial behavior, which can have a positive impact on team cohesion (Chen, Kee & Chen, 2015) and self-esteem (Chen & Wu, 2014). Gratitude has the potential to influence altruism, which promotes positive relationships and facilitates inclusive and moral behaviours.

Gratitude interventions

The power of expressing gratitude is such that Lyubomirsky (2007) calls it a 'meta-strategy for achieving happiness' (p. 88). Gratitude comes in many forms: savouring what is good in life, thinking about what has gone well, reminiscing on a peak experience, anticipating a positive future event, looking on the bright side of a set-back, 'counting one's blessings' or being grateful when something bad didn't happen. Gratitude can be expressed toward the present, the past or the future. Grateful people are more helpful, forgiving and empathic (Emmons & McCullough, 2003), all qualities which contribute to building strong relationships. There are several evidence-based strategies to develop gratitude, all of which are amenable to sport and PA settings.

Gratitude letters and visits

Seligman, Steen, Park, and Peterson (2005) found that participants who wrote and delivered a thank-you letter to someone who had been kind to them in the past but whom they had never thanked showed a large boost in happiness up to one month afterwards. Dickerhoof (2007) found that simply asking people to write thank-you letters for 15 minutes a week over eight weeks, but not send or deliver them, also increased their happiness. More recent research continues to support the findings (Toepfer, Cichy, & Peters, 2012). Coaches could encourage their athletes and teams to identify all those people who have helped or supported their careers (e.g. the teacher who first spotted their talent, the parent who taxied them to after-school and weekend matches or the university club leader who gave them their first break) and to write thank-you letters, whether or not they are posted. Teri McKeever, the US Women's Olympic Team head swimming coach in 2012, has regularly talked about how she strengthened relationships among her team members by encouraging them to express gratitude openly to others.

Gratitude journals or diaries

The idea of writing down the things that one is grateful for has been around for some time – it is no longer necessary to keep a physical journal, because so many apps and websites exist for this very purpose. Experts suggest spending time regularly, say weekly, to reflect on and keep a record of the people and things you are grateful for (Emmons, ibid; Lyubomirsky, ibid). Not only does this boost well-being in the moment, but it also provides a record of positive moments on which to reflect at a later date. Understanding what other people are grateful for may also offer valuable insights about interpersonal relationships. One such study with elite track and field athletes (n = 15) found that the cohort expression of gratitude related to a number of relationship themes, including: *assistance from others* (the most cited theme, with family/partner and coach the most cited others); *downtime and time with family/partner and friends; support and caring;* and *health of self and others*

(Brady, 2011). As well as significantly enhancing their satisfaction with life, in follow-up interviews 10 of the elite athletes reported that keeping a daily diary of gratitude for two weeks conferred a range of other personal benefits during and months after the intervention, including broadened perspectives about personal experiences, issues and life, changing thinking about gratitude, feeling fortunate, feeling confident and experiencing training benefits. Findings supported Fredrickson's (2001) work regarding the enduring effects of increased well-being, as outcomes experienced by athletes shifted from cognitive-affective benefits during the intervention to cognitive-behavioural outcomes over the following months (ibid).

Forgiveness

Associated with the highly social nature of many experiences in sport and PA, many of our interactions may generate instances of conflict or distress which we may harbour for some time. Examples of such issues may include game-changing decisions or actions of officials, our teammates or our sporting heroes, others' selfishness at the gym and neglect or rude treatment from trainers or coaches. Showing forgiveness in relationships and social interactions has been more frequently studied in the context of clinical, therapeutic and intimate relationship settings than in sport and PA. Recently, forgiveness studies in sport have looked at forgiveness within parasocial interaction (Sanderson & Emmons, 2014) and comparing forgiveness between females playing different sports and non-athlete females (Babadi, Zamanian, & Foroozandeh, 2012), but research outside of the field of PP in applied settings is sparse. So, what is forgiveness and how could practising forgiveness benefit those in sport and PA environments?

Lay and expert conceptions of forgiveness differ somewhat. According to Enright and Coyle (1998) and Freedman (1998), forgiveness is not condoning, excusing, pardoning, forgetting, denying or reconciliation. So what then is forgiveness? In psychology, scholars explain forgiveness in various ways, as follows:

1   Pro-social motivation toward the person who has transgressed against you, such that you do not wish to avoid or harm them, or take revenge (McCullough, 2000; McCullough et al., 1998);
2   A willingness to give up your right to resentment and negative judgement toward the person who has transgressed, whilst fostering compassion, generosity and even love toward them (Enright, Freedman, & Rique, 1998);
3   A transformation in how you think and feel following a transgression, such that whilst you make a realistic assessment of the harm done and acknowledge the transgressor's responsibility for it, you freely choose to 'cancel the debt', giving up the need for revenge, punishment or restitution (Tangney, Fee, Reinsmith, Boone, & Lee, 1999, p. 2);
4   Freeing yourself from the negative attachment to the source of the transgression against you (Thompson et al., 2005).

From the foregoing definitions, it is clear that when you practice forgiveness, it is something you do *for yourself*, not for the benefit of the transgressor. Additionally, early research in forgiveness suggests an evolutionary connection in that practising forgiving behaviour produces positive emotions in onlookers, benefitting the entire group and thereby preserving social order (Enright, 1996; Komorita, Hilty, & Parks, 1991; Kanekar & Merchant, 1982).

It is argued that forgiveness in sport and PA settings merits greater attention than it has received thus far, because evidence from PP suggests that individuals who practice forgiveness are more likely to be physically and mentally healthier, less anxious, angry and depressed, and feel less inferior and inadequate (Lawler et al., 2005; Lawler-Row, Karremans, Scott, Edlis-Matityahou, & Edwards, 2008; McCullough, 2001; McCullough & Witvliet, 2002).

Ways to practice forgiveness

Forgiveness letter

Writing about difficult episodes in our lives helps us process intense negative emotions (Pennebaker, 1997). Writing a forgiveness letter is a common technique in therapeutic settings and, when done in a systematic manner (e.g. answering specific questions about the event and its outcomes, rather than as a stream of consciousness), can enable the writer to make sense of the difficulty without the constant distraction of the negative emotions. Pennebaker (ibid) points out that writing in this way is not easy, and initially may result in the individual feeling worse; however, research suggests that there are long-term health benefits to this kind of intervention (Pennebaker, Kiecolt-Glaser, & Glaser, 1988; Petrie, Booth, & Pennebaker, 1998).

In writing a forgiveness letter, you are asked to describe what happened to you, and the emotions associated with the transgression. You then pledge to forgive the person who harmed you but *you do not send the letter, or discuss the contents with the person you write to*. The letter is for your eyes only. Research suggests that the negative emotion associated with holding a grudge can have a negative health impact (Witvliet, Ludwig, & Laan, 2001). According to Magyar-Moe (2009), 'forgiveness is done to benefit the person who has been wronged in order to reduce his or her level of psychological distress' (p.100).

Benefit-finding activities

An alternative to the forgiveness letter is to focus on the benefits or positive aspects that have resulted from the difficulty. Like many PP interventions, benefit finding may be elicited through various modalities such as thinking, talking and artistic expression as well as writing. Research by King and Miner (2000) suggests that writing about these positive aspects for 20 minutes per day for three days helps people overcome the setback, resulting in higher levels of positive emotion and satisfaction with life. Paying no attention to their spelling, grammar or punctuation, individuals are instructed to write non-stop for 20 minutes about only the positive aspects of the event, considering, for example, how they have grown or otherwise benefitted from the situation.

This chapter has introduced some key themes from PP, and we recommend examining their relational dimensions to gain insight into other qualities and dynamics of relationships that may serve to support rewarding and meaningful interactions in sport and PA contexts. Particular areas that warrant inquiry may include:

- exploring the concepts of caring, gratitude and forgiveness across various sport and PA settings;
- examining the impact and modalities associated with interventions and strategies associated with caring, gratitude and forgiveness in sport and PA settings;
- examining the value of dyadic well-being (and other PP topics such as hope, optimism and gratitude) across different relationship types (e.g. coach-athlete, personal trainer and client, parent-child) and peer-relationships among different stakeholders (e.g. officials, trainers, support staff, athletes, etc.);
- considering how humanizing and dehumanizing relationships affect well-being and flourishing and identifying what may contribute to relationships becoming more humanizing.

References

Algoe, S. B., Haidt, J., & Gable, S. L. (2008). Beyond reciprocity: Gratitude and relationships in everyday life. *Emotion*, 8(3), 425.

Allen, J. B. (2005). Measuring social motivational orientations in sport: An examination of the construct validity of the SMOSS. *International Journal of Sport and Exercise Psychology*, 3(2), 147–161.

Babadi, A., Zamanian, F., & Foroozandeh, E. (2012). Comparing forgiveness between handball and futsal female players. *Annals of Biological Research*, 3(10), 4723–4727.

Bartlett, M.Y., & Desteno, D. (2006). Gratitude and prosocial behavior: Helping when it costs you. *Psychological Science*, 17(4), 319–325.

Brady, A. (2011). *An exploration of subjective well-being in high performance athletes*. Unpublished doctoral dissertation, University of Gloucestershire, Gloucester.

Carr, S. (2009). Adolescent–parent attachment characteristics and quality of youth sport friendship. *Psychology of Sport and Exercise*, 10, 653–661.

Carron, A.V., Colman, M. M., Wheeler, J., & Stevens, D. (2002). Cohesion and performance in sport: A meta-analysis. *Journal of Sport and Exercise Psychology*, 24(2), 168–188.

Chen, L. H., Kee, Y. H., & Chen, M.Y. (2015). Why grateful adolescent athletes are more satisfied with their life: The mediating role of perceived team cohesion. *Social Indicators Research*, 124, 463–476.

Chen, L. H., & Wu, C. H. (2014). Gratitude enhances change in athletes' self-esteem: The moderating role of trust in coach. *Journal of Applied Sport Psychology*, 26, 349–362.

Cohen, S., & Janicki-Deverts, D. (2009). Can we improve our physical health by altering our social networks? *Perspectives on Psychological Science*, 4(4), 375–378.

Connaughton, D., Wadey, R., Hanton, S., & Jones, G. (2008). The development and maintenance of mental toughness: Perceptions of elite performers. *Journal of Sport Sciences*, 26(1), 83–95.

Deci, E. L., & Ryan, R. M. (1985). The general causality orientations scale: Self-determination in personality. *Journal of Research in Personality*, 19, 109–134.

Deci, E. L., & Ryan, R. M. (2000). The "what" and "why" of goal pursuits: Human needs and the self-determination of behavior. *Psychological Inquiry*, 11, 227–268.

Dickerhoof, R. M. (2007). *Expressing Optimism and Gratitude: A Longitudinal Investigation of Cognitive Strategies to Increase Well-Being*. Riverside: University of California.

Emmons, R. A., & McCullough, M. E. (2003). Counting blessings versus burdens: An experimental investigation of gratitude and subjective well-being in daily life. *Journal of Personality and Social Psychology*, 84(2), 377–389.

Emmons, R. A., & Shelton, C. M. (2002). Gratitude and the science of positive psychology. In C. R. Snyder & S. J. Lopez (Eds.), *Handbook of Positive Psychology* (pp. 459–471). New York: Oxford University Press.

Enright, R. D. (1996). Counseling within the forgiveness triad: On forgiving, receiving forgiveness, and self-forgiveness. *Counseling and Values*, 40(2), 107–126.

Enright, R. D., & Coyle, C. T. (1998). Researching the process model of forgiveness within psychological interventions. In E. L. Worthington, Jr. (Ed.) *Dimensions of forgiveness* (pp. 139–161). Philadelphia, PA: Templeton Foundation Press.

Enright, R. D., Freedman, S., & Rique, J. (1998). The psychology of interpersonal forgiveness. In R. D. Enright & J. North (Eds.). *Exploring forgiveness* (pp. 46–63). Madison: University of Wisconsin Press.

Fredrickson, B. L. (2001). The role of positive emotions in positive psychology: The broaden-and-build theory of positive emotions. *American Psychologist*, 56, 218–226.

Freedman, S. (1998). Forgiveness and reconciliation: The importance of understanding how they differ. *Counseling and Values*, 42(3), 200–216.

Gable, S. L., Gonzaga, G. C., & Strachman, A. (2006). Will you be there for me when things go right? Supportive responses to positive event disclosures. *Journal of Personality and Social Psychology*, 91(5), 904–917.

Gable, S. L., & Reis, H. T. (2010). Good news! Capitalizing on positive events in an interpersonal context. *Advances in Experimental Social Psychology*, 42, 195–257.

Granovetter, M. (1973). The strength of weak ties. *American Journal of Sociology*, 78(6), 1360–1380.

Granovetter, M. (1983). The strength of weak ties: A network theory revisited. *Sociological Theory*, 1, 201–233.

Hampson, R., & Jowett, S. (2014). Effects of coach leadership and coach–athlete relationship on collective efficacy. *Scandinavian Journal of Medicine and Science in Sports*, 24(2), 454–460.

Holt-Lunstad, J., Smith, T. B., Baker, M., Harris, T., & Stephenson, D. (2015). Loneliness and social isolation as risk factors for mortality: A meta-analytic review. *Perspectives on Psychological Science*, 10(2), 227–237.

Jackson-Dwyer, D. (2014). *Interpersonal relationships (foundations of psychology)*. Hove, East Sussex: Routledge.

Jowett, S. (2007). Interdependence analysis and the 3 + 1 Cs in the coach–athlete relationship. In S. Jowett & D. Lavellee (Eds.), *Social Psychology in Sport* (pp. 15–27). Champaign, IL: Human Kinetics.

Jowett, S., & Chaundy, V. (2004). An investigation into the impact of coach leadership and coach-athlete relationship on group cohesion. *Group Dynamics: Theory, Research and Practice*, 8, 302–311.

Jowett, S., & Cockerill, I. M. (2003). Olympic medallists' perspective of the athlete–coach relationship. *Psychology of sport and exercise*, 4(4), 313–331.

Jowett, S., & Nezlek, J. (2012). Relationship interdependence and satisfaction with important outcomes in coach – athlete dyads. *Journal of Social and Personal Relationships*, 29, 287–301.

Jowett, S., Paull, G., Pensgaard, A. M., Hoegmo, P. M., & Riise, H. (2005). Coach-athlete relationship. In J. Taylor & G. S. Wilson (Eds.), *Applying Sport Psychology: Four Perspectives* (pp. 153–170). Champaign, IL: Human Kinetics.

Jowett, S., Shanmugan, V., and Caccoulis, S. (2012). Collective efficacy as a mediator of the link between interpersonal relationships and athlete satisfaction in team sports. *International Journal of Sport & Exercise Psychology*, 10, 66–78.

Kanekar, S., & Merchant, S. M. (1982). Aggression, retaliation, and religious affiliation. *The Journal of Social Psychology*, 117(2), 295–296.

Kavanagh, E., & Brady, A. (2014). Humanisation in high performance sport. In C. H. Brackenridge & D. Rhind (Eds.), *Athlete Welfare: International Perspectives* (pp. 22–26). London: Brunel University Press.

King, L. A., & Miner, K. N. (2000). Writing about the perceived benefits of traumatic events: Implications for physical health. *Personality and Social Psychology Bulletin*, 26(2), 220–230.

Komorita, S. S., Hilty, J. A., & Parks, C. D. (1991). Reciprocity and cooperation in social dilemmas. *Journal of Conflict Resolution*, 35(3), 494–518.

Lambert, N. M., & Fincham, F. D. (2011). Expressing gratitude to a partner leads to more relationship maintenance behavior. *Emotion*, 11(1), 52.

Lawler, K. A., Younger, J. W., Piferi, R. L., Jobe, R. L., Edmondson, K. A., & Jones, W. H. (2005). The unique effects of forgiveness on health: An exploration of pathways. *Journal of Behavioral Medicine*, 28(2), 157–167.

Lawler-Row, K. A., Karremans, J. C., Scott, C., Edlis-Matityahou, M., & Edwards, L. (2008). Forgiveness, physiological reactivity and health: The role of anger. *International Journal of Psychophysiology*, 68(1), 51–58.

Lyubomirsky, S. (2007). *The how of happiness*. London: Sphere.

Magyar-Moe, J. L. (2009). *Therapist's guide to positive psychological interventions*. Burlington, MA: Academic Press.

McCullough, M. E. (2000). Forgiveness as human strength: Theory, measurement, and links to well-being. *Journal of Social and Clinical Psychology*, 19(1), 43–55.

McCullough, M. E. (2001). Forgiveness: Who does it and how do they do it? *Current Directions in Psychological Science*, 10(6), 194–197.

McCullough, M. E., Exline, J. J., & Baumeister, R. F. (1998). An annotated bibliography of research on forgiveness and related concepts. In E. L. Worthington, Jr. (Ed.). *Dimensions of forgiveness* (pp.193–317). Radnor, PA: Templeton Foundation Press.

McCullough, M. E., & Witvliet, C. V. (2002). The psychology of forgiveness. *Handbook of Positive Psychology*, 2, 446–455.

O'Connell, B. H., O'Shea, D., & Gallagher, S. (2015). Enhancing social relationships through positive psychology activities: A randomised controlled trial. *The Journal of Positive Psychology*, 11(2), 149–162.

Pennebaker, J. W. (1997). Writing about emotional experiences as a therapeutic process. *Psychological Science*, 8(3), 162–166.

Pennebaker, J. W., Kiecolt-Glaser, J. K., & Glaser, R. (1988). Disclosure of traumas and immune function: Health implications for psychotherapy. *Journal of Consulting and Clinical Psychology*, 56(2), 239.

Peterson, C., & Seligman, M. E. P. (2004). *Character Strengths and Virtues: A Handbook and Classification*. New York: Oxford University Press.

Petrie, K. J., Booth, R. J., & Pennebaker, J. W. (1998). The immunological effects of thought suppression. *Journal of Personality and Social Psychology*, 75(5), 1264.

Rees, T., & Hardy, L. (2000). An investigation of the social support experiences of high-level sports performers. *The Sport Psychologist*, 14, 327–347.

Rhind, D. J. A., & Jowett, S. (2010). Relationship maintenance strategies in the coach-athlete relationship: The development of the COMPASS model. *Journal of Applied Sport Psychology*, 22, 106–121.

Sagar, S., & Jowett, S. (2015). Fear of failure and self-control in the context of the coach-athlete relationship quality. *International Journal of Coaching Science*, 9, 3–21.

Sanderson, J., & Emmons, B. (2014). Extending and withholding forgiveness to Josh Hamilton: Exploring forgiveness within parasocial interaction. *Communication & Sport*, 2(1), 24–47.

Seligman, M. E., Steen, T. A., Park, N., & Peterson, C. (2005). Positive psychology progress: Empirical validation of interventions. *American Psychologist*, 60(5), 410.

Tangney, J., Fee, R., Reinsmith, C., Boone, A. L., & Lee, N. (1999, August). Assessing individual differences in the propensity to forgive. In *Annual meeting of the American Psychological Association*, Boston.

Thompson, L. Y., Snyder, C. R., Hoffman, L., Michael, S. T., Rasmussen, H. N., Billings, L. S., . . . Roberts, D. E. (2005). Dispositional forgiveness of self, others, and situations. *Journal of Personality*, 73(2), 313–360.

Toepfer, S. M., Cichy, K., & Peters, P. (2012). Letters of gratitude: Further evidence for author benefits. *Journal of Happiness Studies*, 13(1), 187–201.

Weiss, M. R., Smith, A. L., & Theeboom, M. (1996). "That's what friends are for": Children's and teenagers' perceptions of peer relationships in the sport domain. *Journal of Sport & Exercise Psychology*, 18, 347–379.

Witvliet, C. V. O., Ludwig, T. E., & Laan, K. L. V. (2001). Granting forgiveness or harboring grudges: Implications for emotion, physiology, and health. *Psychological Science*, 12(2), 117–123.

PART 3

Applying positive psychology in and through sport and physical activity

12

MY FUTURE TODAY

Reflecting on positive psychology in professional football academies

Dan Jolley, Chris McCready, Bridget Grenville-Cleave and Abbe Brady

Introduction

This chapter explores the contribution of positive psychology to the My Future Today (MFT) initiative which was first introduced in English professional football in 2015 to address the need to support holistic development of young professional players. Only recently has empirical research about identity and holistic development in high performance and professional sport emerged. Such research has begun to establish that when the performance culture fully supports holistic development and well-being, the player benefits in the present as well as the future, and this improved player well-being and performance extends benefits to the wider culture and team (Pink, Saunders, & Stynes, 2015).

The chapter first establishes a theoretical harbour through insights about adolescent identity in sport, before providing an account of the contextual origins of the MFT initiative established by Dan, Chris and colleagues. An overview of the player-facing event is provided and Bridget and Abbe show how key concepts and principles in positive psychology are present in the event's activities in the areas of strengths, resilience, engagement in meaningful activities, social support and relationships. The chapter concludes by sharing findings from interim monitoring reports and providing recommendations for future developments.

Athlete identity

Established theory posits that the majority of identity is determined primarily during adolescence (Marcia, 1966) through the choices and commitments one makes regarding certain personal and social traits. This coincides with the period in which elite youth footballers in the UK attend academies with a view to attaining a professional contract. A key theorist, Marcia (2009), argues that a well-developed identity is one where the individual has a sense of their strengths, weaknesses and individual uniqueness. However,

Marcia (ibid) goes on to suggest that identity foreclosure happens when individuals prematurely make a firm commitment to a profession, occupation or ideology without sufficient planning or exploration. In other words, they accept the demands of their adopted role identity (in this case, 'professional footballer') before fully exploring their own personal needs, beliefs and values (Meeus, Iedema, Helsen, & Vollebergh, 1999).

Identity foreclosure in an athletic role is problematic because self-worth and self-esteem may become contingent on sports performance (Gustafsson, Hassmén, Kenttä, & Johansson, 2008) and thus threatened when performance is not as expected or the opportunity to perform is not possible (Brewer, Van Raalte, & Linder, 1993; Verkooijen, Van Hove, & Dik, 2012). Identity foreclosure has also been associated with risk-taking behaviours, maladaptive motivational strategies and athletic burnout through increased pressure to succeed (Brewer et al., 1993; Gustafsson et al., 2008). Not surprisingly, Brewer, Van Raalte, and Linder (1993) suggest that students participating in highly competitive sport have both higher athletic identity and higher identity foreclosure levels than those participating less competitively. Contrary to expectations, recent research suggests that people with foreclosed identities may have relatively high well-being compared with others in different stages of identity development, including achieved identity (Oleś, 2016). It may be that, having made a commitment to a certain identity and self-concept, people with foreclosed identities are not as affected by identity dilemmas, and thus maintain their well-being. Nevertheless, as well as being an issue for established professional players when performance or career success is threatened, we suggest that the consequences of identity foreclosure may also become a problem for the 90% of elite youth footballers who do not continue as professional players. In other words, whilst premature commitment to an identity may promote high well-being in the short term, over the longer term it may result in psychological challenges and adjustment issues for those who leave the profession, particularly if this has not been on their terms or through choice, for example, through injury or deselection.

Dual career development and successful athlete transition

Emerging literature recognises the need to support athletes to develop their whole self to transition successfully both within and out of sport (Friesen & Orlick, 2010; Hickey & Kelly, 2008; Lavallee, 2005; Miller & Kerr, 2002; Pink et al., 2015; Price, Morrison, & Arnold, 2010; Wylleman, Alfermann, & Lavallee, 2004). The athletes most at risk of not transitioning well are those with a less developed sense of self outside of their sport role and who have not engaged in other significant developmental activities during their sport career (Pink et al., ibid; Park, Lavallee, & Tod, 2013; Stambulova, Stephan, & Japhag, 2007). The concept of dual career development has emerged relatively recently and refers to the activities undertaken toward an additional career via education or vocational training whilst still an athlete (Aquilina, 2013). There is growing recognition that developing the whole person through dual career activities and/or other meaningful pursuits also supports player well-being which benefits performance in the present (Price et al., 2010; Pink et al., ibid). The creators of MFT challenged the traditional view that apprentices should be wholly focused on 'Plan

A', i.e. becoming/being a professional footballer with an exclusive focus on enhancing development and performance in the present. Instead MFT recognizes personal development in areas other than football (typically associated with 'Plan B' i.e. preparing to leave football) supports players to flourish and achieve Plan A.

Participation in one of the UK's Premier League football academies, may offer some benefits for youth athletes transitioning through adolescence, for example, helping them cope with uncertainty about who they are and what they stand for by providing the opportunity to identify strongly with and commit wholly to the identity of a professional footballer. However, mindful of the fundamental needs associated with high well-being (autonomy, competence and relatedness – Ryan & Deci, 2000) adopting a particular identity (even one as popular or prized as a Premier League footballer) to the exclusion of everything else, whilst beneficial in the short term may be problematic in the mid or long term.

It is against this backdrop of adolescent and holistic development, sport-related identity and their relationship with well-being and performance that we discuss the one-day My Future Today workshop, which has been delivered to approximately 1,300 elite youth footballers in the UK since 2015. Before we move on to discuss the workshop's content, and its impact on participants, some context is required end sentence at required. Therefore what follows is an outline of the cultural landscape in which it exists, and brief biographies for two of MFT's creators and leaders, Dan Jolley and Chris McCready.

Context of the My Future Today workshop: youth education and apprenticeships in English football

League Football Education (LFE) was incorporated in 2004 and is a partnership between The English Football League (EFL) and The Professional Footballers association (PFA). The primary purpose of LFE is to deliver the Apprenticeship in Sporting Excellence (ASE) programme to the 1,300 or so 16- through 18-year-old apprentices signed to professional clubs in the three EFL Divisions. The government-funded ASE has become the preferred education and development programme for 16- through 18-year-old apprentices across professional football, as well as a number of other sports.

ASE comprises vocational and academic qualifications in subjects allied to performance such as sport science, nutrition and coaching, specifically designed to provide the theoretical and practical knowledge and skills to be a professional footballer. Within the ASE, young footballers spend all their time around football; if they are not playing football, or physically, tactically, technically, mentally preparing to play football, they are in education, which is also fundamentally concerned with performance sport.

LFE is acutely aware, primarily from a moral perspective but also contractually, that the successful progression of apprentices from ASE into employment, education or training is of paramount importance. This is consistent with any education/training provider but its moral relevance is compounded in the elite football environment given the extremely small percentage of trainees that secure long-term professional careers. Furthermore, those who are successful will almost certainly need to seek an alternative career when their footballing one comes to an end: by the age of 21 years, only 10% of apprentice footballers will be employed as professional footballers. Whilst this undoubtedly has serious practical consequences for young ex-footballers in terms of providing the requisite skills, knowledge and behaviours to support themselves outside football, as outlined in the introduction to this chapter, it may also have profound implications in terms of their psychological health, well-being and self-identity.

Wood, Harrison, and Kucharska's (2017) research into professional football and mental health found that for adolescents, 'football may not have been a secure and nurturing environment . . . to develop a sense of self and autonomy' (ibid, p. 6). In support of the aims of My Future Today, Wood et al. (ibid) recommend addressing the personal development of players to increase self-esteem and personal resources to cope with the emotional demands of football and transitions. In a longitudinal study to examine athletic identity and retirement from performance sport, Lally (2007) recommended that supporting the athlete's redefinition of identity long before prospective career termination may offer protection against issues of identity crises during transition from sport. Thus, a need exists to extend the duty of care remit for apprentice players and to be proactive in attempting to support holistic identity development and realise the manifold benefits in both the short term or whilst playing (Plan A) and the longer term or post career (Plan B).

About Dan Jolley

Dan's Football Industries MBA at the University of Liverpool culminated in a research project for the LFE about supporting the exit and progression of young football apprentices completing the ASE programme. Though he'd originally been striving to ensure MFT emotionally engaged apprentices in order that they consider Plan B, hearing about Chris's experiences in a chance meeting, confirmed Dan's belief that dedication to Plan A (being a successful footballer) and considering options for Plan B (being a successful ex-footballer) were not mutually exclusive. Contrary to the received wisdom in the profession, he recognised that for many successful adult footballers the personal development which enabled them to be better players on the pitch (Plan A) also enabled them to be successful ex-footballers when they transitioned out of the profession (Plan B). So Dan set about molding the workshop to enable young footballers to identify the strengths, interests and personal resources that would be useful to them both inside and outside the world of football.

About Chris McCready

Chris is an ex-professional footballer whose career could have completely consumed him had he not made the decision to embark on a university degree whilst still playing. It took him six years; he achieved a first-class Honours and, having now retired from the game, is researching his PhD examining self-identity in professional football at Liverpool John Moore's University. His personal and professional journey in education has been transformational. He is very open about his experience of being an elite footballer not matching up to the public perception, and asks whether retirement needs to feel like a cost. This question has fuelled his post-football career, in which he focuses on encouraging new apprentices to think differently about football, their careers and themselves. A chance meeting at the LFE with Dan Jolley led to the evolution of the MFT workshop as described herein. The idea for this chapter developed after observing MFT events, Abbe and Bridget's recognized the wealth of positive psychology principles present and in discussion with Chris and Dan we decided there was value in communicating this formally.

Elite youth footballer identity and the need for My Future Today

The central aim for MFT is to enable young players to be ready, willing and able to progress, both within and outside of their sport. This was borne from several realisations: firstly, from our collective applied experiences of being 'in' and 'around' the game (i.e. apprentice players and professional clubs) for many years, and secondly, our collective understanding of the research into the identity and personal development of athletes (e.g. Brewer et al., ibid; Horton & Mack, 2000; Marcia, ibid) and, specifically, elite youth footballers. The MFT programme not only addresses concerns about the youth development landscape but also makes the stock of complex, academic research applicable, useful and relevant to the lives of young apprentices.

Our conclusions from both the research and applied world were that little was being done to address the adoption of the 'all or nothing' approaches players had to their careers. Players appeared unwilling to consider themselves to be anything other than a young footballer, naturally assuming this was the only way to achieve success in the game. Being a footballer 24/7 takes precedence over everything else. It is logic in action – more devotion to and immersion in training and playing leads to greater success. If a player has time for other things this means that they are not as interested in or dedicated to football as they could and should be. Therefore, they must hide other interests or be prepared to be seen as a bit different, maybe even trouble. This culture is very persuasive and all-consuming and there is no escape, no time to separate, no time to relax. Players are on trial every day: every game can be likened to an exam in which every player is competing against someone else who is just as talented, and trying to win.

Given that 90% of elite youth footballers are released before the age of 21, this rather singular view of the self, in which the player bases his entire self-worth and identity on being a professional footballer, has been shown to lead to (sometimes severe) transition difficulties (Gouttebarge, Frings-Dresen & Sluiter, 2015; Gouttebarge, Aoki, Verhagen, & Kerkhoffs, 2016; Wood et al., 2017). There are very practical examples of LFE-organised career events at which young players did not engage with future career planning because they were not ready or able to consider themselves as anything other than a footballer. Additionally, there is growing anecdotal evidence of players struggling to adjust, move forward and redefine themselves post-apprenticeship. This is an area ripe for formal research.

It is essential to point out that MFT is not about reducing the dedication or commitment that young footballers have toward the game. The aim is to prompt them to consider how developing themselves as a young person, alongside being a footballer (e.g. through having more and complementary support systems, interests and identities) will be more beneficial to them as players in the short term as well as in the long term.

Having outlined the rationale for the MFT workshop, in the next section we describe some of the activities, their aims and outcomes as well as their evidence base in positive psychology.

Engaging young footballers with My Future Today through drama

One of the key barriers to the effectiveness of the MFT workshop is participant engagement. Having never done anything like this in their academy experience, young apprentices attending the away-day do not know what to expect. How many of us would have known what personal development was at age 16 or 17 years? Coming to the workshop with the mindset of the 24/7 footballer, they are likely to feel that a day away from training is a day wasted. How can a short workshop called 'My Future Today' help them be better footballers?

> My Future Today? How can it be my future today? It can be my future tomorrow but it can't be my future today, can it?

When designing MFT it was imperative to get full participant engagement and interest quickly, and to maintain it throughout the day. To achieve this, MFT uses professional actors to play the part of apprentices in various real-life scenarios – wondering about their future careers, unsure whether they will make the grade and attain a professional contract, and what will happen if they don't.

At times, the scenes played out by the actors are light-hearted, and others are intentionally hard-hitting. Most of the apprentices will not be offered a professional contract. We look at how this might happen, how might they feel about this 'failure' and try to cope, and also what could be the benefits of being a well-rounded young man making his way in a new world. Through the day the young players become more open to the benefits of personal development and how it might support their footballing performance, their personal well-being and potential transition in to football or another career.

MFT activity: the table top

Psychological resilience, referring to the ability to overcome setbacks and persist in the face of adversity, has been a popular topic in therapy, education and business for decades. Positive psychology has provided the research evidence that most people are more or less resilient; indeed Masten (2001) refers to resilience as 'ordinary magic'. Rather than being a particular quality that you are either born with or not, resilience is better thought of as a set of skills to be developed. Positive psychology research suggests that there are several ways to develop greater psychological resilience, for example, experiencing frequent positive affect (Fredrickson, 2002; Fredrickson & Branigan, 2005; Tugade & Fredrickson, 2004), identifying and playing to one's strengths (Linley, 2008; Linley, Nielsen, Wood, Gillett, & Biswas-Diener, 2010; Seligman, Steen, Park, & Peterson, 2005) and learning realistic optimism (Seligman, 2006). This MFT activity encourages participants to consider that they might possess other skills, strengths, attitudes and resources which contribute to their personal resilience, unique personal identity and sense of self.

Players are asked to build a table from newspaper and sellotape; the table which can bear the most weight wins the challenge. This is not a unique activity in development workshops, but the underpinning messaging is powerful. On completing the task we ask participants to consider that they themselves are the tabletop, with one table leg being their identity as a footballer. During the MFT workshop, we encourage players to explore what other resources, qualities and interests they have, and how these might contribute to their resilience and sense of self.

MFT activity: the professionals

A cornerstone of positive psychology is the strengths approach (Peterson & Seligman, 2004). It is worth pointing out that positive psychology differentiates strengths and talents. According to Niemiec (2013, p. 12), 'Character strengths are substantially stable, universal personality traits that manifest through thinking (cognition), feeling (affect), willing (conation or volition), and action (behavior)'. Elite youth footballers will be all too aware that they have footballing talent, but here we refer to character strengths such as forgiveness, curiosity and emotional intelligence. There are several well-known strengths frameworks within positive psychology, and although they have different evidence bases, their principles are similar. The message from positive psychology research is that identifying and appropriately applying one's strengths in context can be beneficial, not just for one's well-being, vitality and concentration but also for performance (Dubreuil, Forest, & Courcy, 2014; Harzer & Ruch, 2014; Linley et al., 2010; Seligman et al., 2005).

'The Professionals' activity does not attempt to identify strengths using any specific positive psychology framework; rather it introduces the idea that we are multidimensional, with different interests, abilities and strengths. The activity highlights how players at the top of the profession are actively engaged in personal development activities, and 'building other legs to their tables'. There are the family men, the Green Party members, the authors, poets, students, activists, community workers, musicians, bloggers and those with a strong faith. It also challenges the received wisdom that giving time and energy to other things prevents you from being successful as a footballer. Apprentices discuss the strengths and abilities these elite athletes have and how they themselves have similar strengths and abilities or might develop them doing things other than football.

MFT activity: time to get personal

Positive psychology research (Diener & Seligman, 2002) suggests that it is only their relationships and active social lives which differentiate the top 10% of the happiest people. In terms of positive psychology principles, this MFT activity continues to build on the ideas discussed in 'The Professionals' by asking participants to consider their relationships with others as well as their interests and skills. What makes these apprentices the individuals they are? Aside from footballing talent, what are their best qualities? What do other people value in them? This activity is central to the MFT workshop since it connects participants directly to their unique contexts, their families, friends and teammates, and starts to develop the idea that relationships are core not just to well-being but also to performance.

MFT activity: how to get where you want to be

During their time at the academy, apprentices will have completed many profile wheels but always focussing on the technical, tactical and physical areas of their game development. Many of them may feel that their lives have been mapped out for them. However, they may have other passions, plans or a sense of purpose unconnected with football which they have not given voice to. Although not specifically designed with the three fundamental needs of autonomy, relatedness and competence (Ryan & Deci, ibid) in mind, completing this profile wheel (Figure 12.1) allows them to take control of their lives, to be responsible for their personal development, their relationships with others and how they develop in other ways outside of the game. Their challenge is to consider the importance of other aspects of their identity apart from that of 'footballer'. This profile wheel asks them to rate themselves in terms of:

- other interests,
- relationships/friendships,
- taking responsibility,
- knowing themselves.

Apprentices also rate themselves against four other key topics of their own choosing and set three specific goals based on their profile wheel, which may relate to areas of strength that they want to maintain or development areas that they want to improve. When given the freedom to choose their own personal development goals, young players can be amazingly creative and thoughtful, as seen in Table 12.1.

It is perhaps pertinent to note how many of the apprentices' goals resonate with eudaimonic components of psychological well-being – in other words, relating to personal growth, meaning and self-realization.

MFT activity: me in 30 seconds

As Biswas-Diener, Kashdan, and Minhas (2011) point out, academic and practitioner focus on strengths has increased significantly in the past decade or so, roughly

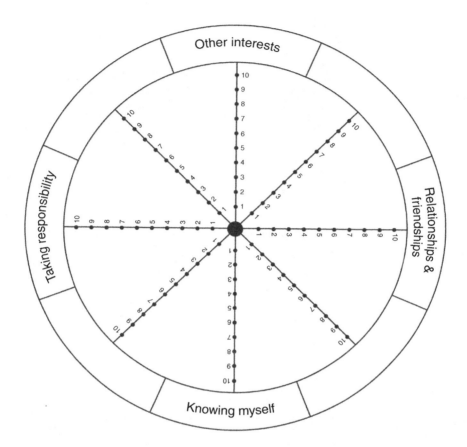

FIGURE 12.1 My Future Today profile wheel

corresponding to the growth in positive psychology. See Chapter 5 to learn more about character strengths. Numerous studies outline the many benefits associated with strengths, from increased resilience (Goodman, Disabato, Kashdan, & Machell, 2016; Martínez-Martí & Ruch, 2017), well-being (Gillham et al., 2011; Govindji & Linley, 2007), performance (Garcea & Linley, 2011) and goal achievement (Linley, Nielsen, Wood, Gillett & Biswas-Diener, 2010) to lower levels of stress (Wood, Linley, Maltby, Kashdan, & Hurling, 2011) and depression (Seligman et al., 2005). As mentioned previously, identifying, owning and applying one's personal strengths (whether through a formal framework such as Values-In-Action or StrengthsFinder™ or informally) using a model such as Aware-Explore-Apply (Niemiec, ibid) is an essential first step toward creating a new personal narrative (Andresen, Oades, & Caputi, 2003). Additionally, it is generally recognised that making a public commitment to clear, self-chosen goals is linked to their achievement (Locke & Latham, 2002).

Using the scenario of introducing themselves to a prospective club manager, the workshop culminates with apprentices voluntarily standing up in front of the group

TABLE 12.1 Football apprentices' personal development goals

Profile domain	Goal
Other Interests	*'Doing other interests at home, away from football, seeing what family/friends do and trying their hobbies. Trying something different'.* (Walsall apprentice) *'I am going to spend more time doing things other than football; I'm going to spend an hour a week on something else'.* (Leyton Orient apprentice) *'Being more productive in spare time – pursue other interests like learning Spanish, writing music, learn the guitar'.* (Newcastle apprentice)
Relationships	*'Play golf with my dad at least twice in the next three months'.* (Newport apprentice)
Time/ relationships	*'Structure my time so I can spend more time with my grandad as he watches every game I play'.* (Port Vale apprentice)
Knowing themselves	*'To know myself better, I will create a diary and fill it in on a daily basis on my feelings and events throughout the day'.* (Carlisle apprentice) *'Put myself in an unfamiliar position where I will have to use my initiative twice in the next month'.* (Southend apprentice)
Friends/ determination	*'Make extra effort to see my friends even if I am very tired and can't be bothered. Try and see two friends at least every two weeks instead of once a month like it is at the moment'.* (Port Vale apprentice)
Progression plan	*'Register my interest in the BDO [a financial services organisation] and the financial advisor school by the end of the season'.* (Swindon apprentice)
Taking responsibility	*'Take responsibility – in a group when set with a challenge, don't wait for others to start, give your own opinion and lead the group'.* (Norwich apprentice)

and, unscripted apart from bullet points in their booklets, talking for 30 seconds about themselves – who they are, their interests outside of football and their goals to move forward in the next three months.

For example:

> I'm a hardworking individual as you know. A very dedicated, innovative thinker. I like to take responsibility for my own actions. I'm a very honest person, very respectful. I like to make sure I make decisions with plenty of time and thought. I've got many interests such as writing poems, reading books, watching movies, singing. I'm trying to learn to play the guitar; I used to play the violin. I own a hostel in Ghana; my family runs that business and I've started putting work into that. I enjoy business studies. In the future what I'd like to do is a bit of voluntary work and project work, working with younger players and people who are homeless and help them out as well.
>
> *(Newcastle apprentice)*

Based on apprentice feedback, this is without doubt the most satisfying moment of the workshop. We are constantly surprised and moved that young footballers can, in one day, gain the insight, courage and confidence to speak in public about their strengths and talents, and what really matters to them. Simply recognising and telling their wider story breaks new ground individually, and may be the beginning of new conversations with teammates at the club. It is especially inspiring that the apprentices who want to develop greater confidence often take this opportunity to start the process by volunteering to speak in front of others.

Understanding the impact of *My Future Today*

As part of the process of determining the impact of MFT with key stakeholders, the LFE team adopted a range of qualitative methods to capture players' impressions of the event and personal outcomes. Data was drawn from apprentice players' written responses during the workshop, follow-up interviews/focus groups with players and individual player review sessions. Overall, findings show players viewed the MFT day as engaging, challenging and constructive. Of particular significance to players was hearing the message that it's okay to have other interests and actually, personal development (PD) outside of football could help them now and during their playing career as well as afterward. Many players referred to the adaptive value of PD and how cultivating a broader identity would help provide choices and confidence to manage challenges both in the present and future.

As a Shrewsbury apprentice noted, PD related to '*growing as a person and becoming more rounded so that you can deal with what life throws at you*'. In thinking more broadly about how a more developed self could contribute to both oneself and to society, Walsall apprentice (1) wrote that PD was about 'Developing myself in terms of who I am and what I offer to myself and the world other than football'.

Players recognised that the MFT workshop was inviting them to think differently about themselves and for some, the impact of the day was dramatic as reflected in the following narrative (shared in a player focus group) when an apprentice describes going home and telling his mother about MFT:

> Yeah, the second I got home, I said to her, 'I've had a great day'. She asked me why, and I said, 'you ask the other lads who might say I didn't like that or I was bored, but I took something away from it, it opened my eyes massively. I'm confident within myself, I sent myself a note, and it's helping me be more confident, and I have already started that trip because at the end I stood up and spoke in front of the group'. She said she was dead proud of me. And, I felt good within myself, you know, like, yeah, this is me as a new person, starting now, and for me, as stupid as it sounds, that one day has changed my life ... but it has, I'll be honest, it opened a lot up to me. It made me think.
>
> *(Port Vale apprentice)*

Next steps for My Future Today

My Future Today provides a starting point for young players to consider their development as a person as well as a footballer, but it is only a one-off, single day event. It is well recognised in off-the-job training that maintaining the commitment is not easy once participants 'return to the day job'. This is a key consideration for moving the program forward and further development ideas in football include:

- an 8- to 10-week community engagement program, based on MFT, to build on the personal development areas identified by apprentice footballers who then work on a project through which to experience personal development;
- a program working with coaches to integrate the MFT principles into the day-to-day training and playing environment;
- piloting the MFT event with similarly aged and high-performance female players and considering whether the different landscape of women's football in the UK might require any tailoring of aims, content and activities, to be as impactful among this population;
- establishing a rigorous multi-method approach to determining impact through the identification of a coherent range of constructs and measurable outcomes.

Given the many powerful testimonies received about MFT, it is essential that we learn more about the many long- and short-term benefits (and possible challenges or issues) associated with holistic identity development and well-being–related PD activities, both for those players remaining in and those leaving professional football.

Finally, with increasing focus on personal development, behaviour and welfare of students of all ages, the innovative perspective and delivery approach of MFT would be valuable in mainstream education in both schools and colleges.

We end with the words of Bradley Thompson, a character in one of the MFT performances, who recognises that he can learn to play the guitar, go and help his dad at his work just to spend some time with him, maybe even learn Spanish, and that this is all within his power to do: 'Because I am Bradley Thompson. The total person in the making!' If every young person who goes through the MFT programme can be half as inspired as Bradley, then they will have started the journey toward a fulfilling life that they are ready, willing and able to achieve.

References

Andresen, R., Oades, L., & Caputi, P. (2003). Experience of recovery from schizophrenia: Towards an empirically validated stage model. *Australian and New Zealand Journal of Psychiatry*, 37, 586–594.

Aquilina, D. (2013). A study of the relationship between elite athletes' educational development and sporting performance. *The International Journal of the History of Sport*, 30(4), 374–392.

Biswas-Diener, R., Kashdan, T. B., & Minhas, G. (2011). A dynamic approach to psychological strength development and intervention. *The Journal of Positive Psychology*, 6(2), 106–118.

Brewer, B. W., Van Raalte, J. L., & Linder, D. E. (1993). Athletic identity: Hercules' muscles or Achilles heel? *International Journal of Sport Psychology*, 24(2), 237–254.

Diener, E., & Seligman, M. E. (2002). Very happy people. *Psychological Science*, 13(1), 81–84.

Dubreuil, P., Forest, J., & Courcy, F. (2014). From strengths use to work performance: The role of harmonious passion, subjective vitality, and concentration. *The Journal of Positive Psychology*, 9(4), 335–349.

Fredrickson, B. L. (2002). Positive emotions. In C. R. Snyder & S. J. Lopez (Eds.), *Handbook of Positive Psychology* (pp. 120–134). Oxford, UK: Oxford University Press.

Fredrickson, B. L., & Branigan, C. (2005). Positive emotions broaden the scope of attention and thought-action repertoires. *Cognition & Emotion*, 19(3), 313–332.

Friesen, A., & Orlick, T. (2010). A qualitative analysis of holistic sport psychology consultants' professional philosophies. *The Sport Psychologist*, 24(2), 227–244.

Garcea, N., & Linley, P. A. (2011). Creating positive change through building positive organizations: Four levels of intervention. In R. Biswas Diener (Ed.), *Positive Psychology as Social Change* (pp. 165–196). Dordrecht: Springer.

Gillham, J., Adams-Deutsch, Z., Werner, J., Reivich, K., Coulter-Heindl, V., Linkins, M., . . . Contero, A. (2011). Character strengths predict subjective well-being during adolescence. *The Journal of Positive Psychology*, 6(1), 31–44.

Goodman, F. R., Disabato, D. J., Kashdan, T. B., & Machell, K. A. (2016). Personality strengths as resilience factors: The importance of lagged analyses and the power of hope. *International Journal of Psychology*, 51, 898.

Gouttebarge, V., Aoki, H., Verhagen, E. A., & Kerkhoffs, G. M. (2016). A 12-Month prospective cohort study of symptoms of common mental disorders among European professional footballers. *Clinical Journal of Sport Medicine* 0:1–6. doi: 10.1097/JSM.0000000000000388.

Gouttebarge, V., Frings-Dresen, M. H. W., & Sluiter, J. K. (2015). Mental and psychosocial health among current and former professional footballers. *Occupational Medicine*, 65(3), 190–196.

Govindji, R., & Linley, P. A. (2007). Strengths use, self-concordance and well-being: Implications for strengths coaching and coaching psychologists. *International Coaching Psychology Review*, 2(2), 143–153.

Gustafsson, H., Hassmén, P., Kenttä, G., & Johansson, M. (2008). A qualitative analysis of burnout in elite Swedish athletes. *Psychology of Sport and Exercise*, 9(6), 800–816.

Harzer, C., & Ruch, W. (2014). The role of character strengths for task performance, job dedication, interpersonal facilitation, and organizational support. *Human Performance*, 27(3), 183–205.

Hickey, C., & Kelly, P. (2008). Preparing to not be a footballer: Higher education and professional sport. *Sport, Education & Society*, 13(4), 477–494.

Horton, R., & Mack, D. (2000). Athletic identity in marathon runners: Functional focus or dysfunctional commitment? *Journal of Sport Behavior*, 23(2), 101.

Kerr, G., & Dacyshyn, A. (2000). The retirement experience of elite female gymnasts. *Journal of Applied Sport Psychology*, 12(55), 115–133.

Lally, P. (2007). Identity and athletic retirement: A prospective study. *Psychology of Sport and Exercise*, 8, 85–99.

Lavallee, D. (2005). The effect of a life development intervention on sports career transition adjustment. *Sport Psychologist*, 19(2), 193–202. Retrieved from http://journals.humankinetics.com/tsp.

Lavallee, D., & Robinson, H. K. (2007). In pursuit of an identity: A qualitative exploration of retirement from women's artistic gymnastics. *Psychology of Sport and Exercise*, 8(1), 119–141.

Linley, A. (2008). *Average to A+: Realising Strengths in Yourself and Others*. Coventry: CAPP Press.

Linley, P. A., Nielsen, K., Wood, A., Gillett, R., & Biswas-Diener, R. (2010). *Using Signature Strengths in Pursuit of Goals: Effects on Goal Progress, Need Satisfaction, and Well-Being, and Implications for Coaching Psychologists.* Retrieved from https://meredithroach.files.wordpress.com/2011/05/strengths-_goals.pdf.

Locke, E. A., & Latham, G. P. (2002). Building a practically useful theory of goal setting and task motivation: A 35-year odyssey. *American Psychologist*, 57(9), 705.

Marcia, J. E. (1966). Development and validation of ego-identity status. *Journal of Personality and Social Psychology*, 5, 551–558.

Marcia, J. E. (2009). Life transitions and stress in the context of psychosocial development. In T. W. Miller (Ed.), *Handbook of Stressful Transitions Across the Lifespan* (pp. 19–34). New York, Springer.

Martínez-Martí, M. L., & Ruch, W. (2017). Character strengths predict resilience over and above positive affect, self-efficacy, optimism, social support, self-esteem, and life satisfaction. *The Journal of Positive Psychology*, 12(2), 110–119.

Masten, A. S. (2001). Ordinary magic: Resilience processes in development. *American Psychologist* 56(3), 227–238. DOI: 10.1037//0003-066X.56.3.227.

Meeus, W., Iedema, J., Helsen, M., & Vollebergh, W. (1999). Patterns of adolescent identity development: Review of literature and longitudinal analysis. *Developmental Review*, 19(4), 419–461.

Miller, P. S., & Kerr, G. A. (2002). Conceptualizing excellence: Past, present, and future. *Journal of Applied Sport Psychology*, 14(3), 140–153.

Niemiec, R. M. (2013). VIA character strengths: Research and practice (the first 10 years). In H. H. Knoop & A. Delle Fave (Eds.), *Well-Being and Cultures: Perspectives on Positive Psychology* (pp. 11–30). New York: Springer.

Oleś, M. (2016). Dimensions of identity and subjective quality of life in adolescents. *Social Indicators Research*, 126(3), 1401–1419.

Park, S., Lavallee, D., & Tod, D. (2013). Athletes' career transition out of sport: A systematic review. *International Review of Sport and Exercise Psychology*, 6(1), 22–53.

Peterson, C., & Seligman, M. E. (2004). *Character Strengths and Virtues: A Handbook and Classification* (Vol. 1). Oxford: Oxford University Press.

Pink, M., Saunders, J., & Stynes, J. (2015). Reconciling the maintenance of on-field success with off-field player development: A case study of a club culture within the Australian Football League. *Psychology of Sport and Exercise*, 21, 98–108.

Price, N., Morrison, N., & Arnold, S. (2010). Life out of the limelight: Understanding the non-sporting pursuits of elite athletes. *The International Journal of Sport and Society*, 1(3), 69e79. Retrieved from http://ijr.cgpublisher.com/product/pub.191/prod.65.

Ryan, R. M., & Deci, E. L. (2000). Self-determination theory and the facilitation of intrinsic motivation, social development, and well-being. *American Psychologist*, 55(1), 68.

Seligman, M. (2003). *Authentic Happiness*. London: Nicholas Brealey Publishing.

Seligman, M. (2006). *Learned Optimism*. New York: Random House.

Seligman, M. (2011). *Flourish: A New Understanding of Happiness and Well-Being and How to Achieve Them*. London: Nicholas Brealey Publishing.

Seligman, M. E. P., Steen, T. A., Park, N., & Peterson, C. (2005). Positive psychology progress: Empirical validation of interventions. *American Psychologist*, 60, 410–421.

Stambulova, N., Alfermann, D., Statler, T., & Cote, J. (2009). ISSP position stand: Career development and transitions of athletes. *International Journal of Sport*, 7(4), 395–412.

Stambulova, N., Stephan, Y., & Japhag, U. (2007). Athletic retirement: A cross-national comparison of elite French and Swedish athletes. *Psychology of Sport & Exercise*, 8(1), 101–118.

Tugade, M. M., & Fredrickson, B. L. (2004). Resilient individuals use positive emotions to bounce back from negative emotional experiences. *Journal of Personality and Social Psychology*, 86(2), 320–333.

Verkooijen, K. T., Van Hove, P., & Dik, G. (2012). Athletic identity and well-being among young talented athletes who live at a Dutch elite sport center. *Journal of Applied Sport Psychology*, 24, 106–113.

Wood, S., Harrison, L., & Kucharska, J. (2017). Male professional footballers' experiences of mental health difficulties and help-seeking. *The Physician and Sportsmedicine*, 45(2), 120–128.

Wood, A. M., Linley, P. A., Maltby, J., Kashdan, T. B., & Hurling, R. (2011). Using personal and psychological strengths leads to increases in well-being over time: A longitudinal study and the development of the strengths use questionnaire. *Personality and Individual Differences*, 50(1), 15–19.

Wylleman, P., Alfermann, D., & Lavallee, D. (2004). Career transitions in sport: European perspectives. *Psychology of Sport and Exercise*, 5(1), 7–20.

13

LIFEMATTERS

Using physical activities and games to enhance the self-concept and well-being of disadvantaged youth

Stephanie J. Hanrahan

Introduction

This chapter focuses on LifeMatters, a program using physical games and psychological skills from sport psychology to benefit disadvantaged youth. In part, the program was developed with Ryan and Deci's (2000) three basic psychological needs in mind: autonomy, competence, and relatedness. When these needs are satisfied, individuals report enhanced self-motivation and mental health, and when these needs are thwarted, individuals report diminished well-being and motivation (Ryan & Deci, 2000). LifeMatters has been run with orphans, teenagers living in poverty, former gang members in Mexico, youth living in the slums of Buenos Aires in Argentina, and with inner-city youth from Cleveland, Ohio. Recently, a train-the-trainer program for LifeMatters was delivered to coaches in Botswana, Africa, followed by some of the coaches running LifeMatters sessions with high school youth. Different dependent variables related to positive psychology have been tested pre- and post-LifeMatters. Quantitative measures indicate significant increases in life satisfaction, global self-worth, happiness, physical appearance self-concept, close friendship self-concept, behavioral conduct self-concept, scholastic competence self-concept, athletic competence self-concept, social acceptance self-concept, resilience, competence, confidence, and connection.

LifeMatters evolved over a period of time. In the early 2000s, in addition to working with elite athletes as a practitioner and holding my academic position at The University of Queensland, I spent one afternoon per week teaching mental skills to students at the Aboriginal Centre for the Performing Arts (ACPA; see Hanrahan, 2004). While working at ACPA I found that using games to teach mental skills was much more effective with this population than traditional lectures or even workshops. One day in 2004 I had presented an introductory lecture on sport psychology at my university, commenting that mental skills were for more than performance enhancement; they also helped to enhance enjoyment of participation as well as increase psychological well-being. That afternoon I worked with a professional men's sporting team, and was rather disgruntled by what I perceived to be a sense of entitlement and minimal motivation to try anything new. When I returned home later that day, there was a newsletter from an orphanage in Mexico. My statement from earlier in the day about the benefits of mental skills beyond performance enhancement combined with my frustration from the afternoon session led me to write a two-page proposal about a mental skills training program that I thought might be of benefit to the orphans. I emailed the proposal to the director of the orphanage. Three months later I received an email saying, "please come." So, I went to the orphanage in January 2015 and ran what eventually evolved into LifeMatters – using many of the games and activities I had trialed at ACPA.

Key challenges

Although LifeMatters was first run at this orphanage in Mexico, it later was applied to teenagers living in poverty and gang members. It is beyond the scope of this chapter to go into depth on the key challenges related to orphanages, poverty, and gang membership. Therefore, what follows is a brief overview of some of the major issues in these contexts.

Orphans tend to be vulnerable to psychological and physical risks. As a result of being orphaned, they tend to feel depressed, sad, and helpless, with an external locus of control (Sengendo & Nambi, 1997). For teenagers with an external locus of control, low self-esteem is associated with higher levels of aggression (Wallace, Barry, Zeigler-Hill, & Green, 2012). With parents no longer in the picture, orphans may benefit from meeting the need for relatedness through other sources. Increasing feelings of competence may help with low self-esteem, and improved autonomy may decrease the strength of an external locus of control.

Adolescents experiencing continuously adverse circumstances, such as poverty, tend to lack perceived control, which, in turn, leads to feelings of helplessness, hopelessness, and diminished willpower (Lefcourt, 1976). These individuals usually have an external locus of control and do not believe they are responsible for what happens in their lives; as a result they do not feel they have the ability to control events or their own behaviors. When people feel hopeless and believe they have only a minimal sense of control, they do not tend to take steps to change their lives. Believing that one is a victim (of life, disease, or self) interferes with the forward motion of therapy or positive change in life (Mosak, 1998). The overall theme of LifeMatters is "control the controllable." Although disadvantaged youth may not be able to control their environment, the factors contributing to poverty, or the economic situations in which they find themselves, they can learn to control their own behaviors, thoughts, and feelings.

For gang members and other youth with identified behavioral issues, a deficit view is common, with many programs focusing on problem reduction or prevention (e.g., trying to avoid or diminish weaknesses to avoid or reduce problem behaviors). An alternative is to focus on positive development – developing the capabilities of the youth so they make positive contributions to their lives and their communities. Brooks-Gunn and Roth (2014) described these two alternatives clearly by indicating many of us are now "thinking about youth as more than problems to be managed but as resources to be cultivated" (p. 1004). Gang members do possess the potential for positive development and have assets that can be used to promote positive development and behavior (Taylor et al., 2004). Instead of focusing on trying to stop unwanted behaviors such as drug use or criminal activity, using a strengths-based approach may result in an increase in desirable behaviors, and by default a decrease in detrimental behaviors.

Key positive psychology concepts related to LifeMatters

Traditionally, research in the area of disadvantaged youth has focused on outcome variables such as deviant behavior, criminal behavior, mental disorders, and health-compromising behavior (e.g., Elliot et al., 1996; Laub & Sampson, 1988). Instead of focusing on negative factors such as depression, recidivism, smoking, illicit drug use, or violence, I chose to investigate if participants in the LifeMatters program showed significant changes in positive concepts of self-concept, life satisfaction, resilience, happiness, and positive youth development. All the instruments used in LifeMatters research had good reliability and validity for the age group and population. Additionally they each had a pre-established version in the appropriate language.

Self-concept

Self-concept is a multifaceted categorization of the information that people have about themselves (Marsh & Shavelson, 1985). These self-perceptions are formed through experiences with and interpretations of the environment, especially evaluations by significant others. General self-concept is stable, but specific facets of self-concept are variable. The more specific the subarea (e.g., soccer self-concept compared with athletic competence self-concept), the more changeable it becomes (Marsh & Shavelson, ibid). Amongst other things, self-concept has been shown to be related to aspirations (Sax et al., 2015), psychological distress (Turner et al., 2015), achievement (Marsh et al., 2015), and recovery (Larson & Sbarra, 2015).

In LifeMatters research, self-concept has been measured using Harter's (1988) Self-Perception Profile for Adolescents (SPPA). In addition to measuring global self-worth, the SPPA measures multiple dimensions of self-concept (e.g., social acceptance, scholastic competence, physical appearance).

Life satisfaction

Most adolescents are satisfied with their overall lives, scoring above the neutral point, yet few report the highest levels of life satisfaction (Huebner & Diener, 2008). Adolescents with high levels of life satisfaction generally show positive functioning across interpersonal, intrapersonal, and school-related domains (Gilman, 2001).

Youth with low levels of life satisfaction tend to experience a lot of difficulties, including issues with aggressive behavior, suicidal thinking, drug and alcohol use, sexual risk taking, physical inactivity, and physical health problems (Huebner & Diener, 2008). The Satisfaction With Life Scale (SWLS; Diener, Emmons, Larsen, & Griffin, 1985) has been the instrument of choice when measuring life satisfaction within the LifeMatters program.

Happiness

An overarching consideration related to happiness is context. People from different cultures vary in how they value factors correlated with happiness such as income and marriage. In addition to values, cultural patterns, social structure, goals, and expectations influence what individuals need, or perceive they need, to be happy (Diener, 2008).

In the LifeMatters research, happiness has been measured using Fordyce's (1988) Happiness Measure. The measure contains two items – a general level of happiness and the percentage of time one feels unhappy, neutral, or happy. Although both items have good stability, construct validity, convergent validity, and discriminative validity, the first item has had stronger correlations with other indices of subjective well-being compared with the second item (Fordyce, ibid). Therefore, LifeMatters research has only used the first item, which asks respondents to designate where they are on a figure of a staircase, with the top step (10) indicating a life that is completely happy and the bottom step (0) indicating an unhappy life. This one-time self-report measure has provided similar results to daily experience sampling and has not led to excessively high estimates of happiness compared with other methods (Diener & Diener, 1996).

Resilience

Resilience has been described as a protective strength and a personal characteristic influencing the ability to recover from adverse experiences (Nygren et al., 2005). In a study of school-aged American youth living in poverty, resilient youth had greater self-regulatory skills (and self-esteem) compared with non-resilient youth, even after controlling for differences in the experiences of negative life events and chronic strain (Buckner, Mezzacappa, & Beardslee, 2003). See Chapter 8 for more information about resilience. In LifeMatters research, resilience has been measured using the Resilience Scale (RS: Wagnild & Young, 1993).

Five Cs of positive youth development

A contemporary framework of positive youth development (Lerner, 2002; Lerner et al., 2005) has been operationalized by the 5 Cs of:

* caring (human values, empathy, a sense of social justice);
* competence (cognitive abilities and healthy behavioral skills);

- confidence (positive self-regard and a sense of self-efficacy);
- character (integrity and moral centeredness);
- connection (positive bonds with people and institutions).

When young people strongly manifest the 5 Cs, they may be said to be thriving, which leads to the emergence of what some people argue is a sixth C – contribution – to self, family, community, and civil society (King et al., 2005). See Chapter 12 for a detailed review of the positive youth development literature as it applies to sport and physical activity. The 5 Cs were measured using the Short Measure of the 5 Cs of Positive Youth Development (PYD-SF; Geldhof et al., 2011, 2014).

Effective program structure

Now that the main outcome variables investigated in the LifeMatters program have been introduced, I turn to spending a little time describing two concepts that underpin LifeMatters: the characteristics of effective programs in the area of youth development and the benefits of physically active games.

Characteristics of effective youth development programs

Youth development programs need to provide youth with support, empowerment, boundaries and expectations, and constructive use of time (Edwards, Mumford, & Serra-Roldan, 2007) and so LifeMatters sought to embrace these qualities. When considering the context for effective youth sport programs in terms of fostering psychosocial development, Petitpas, Cornelius, Van Raalte, and Jones (2005) suggested five guidelines:

- Programs should encourage participants to develop a sense of initiative. Within the LifeMatters program there are many opportunities for participants to make decisions, come up with solutions, and determine their own goals.
- Programs should allow participants to find valued roles within the group. LifeMatters involves numerous small-group activities, with participants encouraged to trial a variety of roles.
- Programs should be voluntary with clear rules, requiring concerted effort over time. In the majority of cases, attendance at LifeMatters has been voluntary, but in some locations the program has been incorporated into pre-existing programs (e.g., schools, residential summer programs) where participants have been expected by others to attend. Even when attendance has been required though, participation in various activities within the program has been voluntary. There are multiple challenges and tasks throughout the program that do require concerted effort over time.
- Programs should be psychologically safe, with participants willing to take risks and learn from their mistakes. The games within LifeMatters are intentionally ordered in such a way as to slowly build up the amount of trust, communication,

and problem-solving required, thereby creating a psychologically safe environment. The sequence of games involves four levels – icebreakers, deinhibitizers/ energizers, trust and empathy games, and initiative activities (see Hanrahan, 2013).

• Programs should be challenging. LifeMatters incorporates both physical and mental challenges.

Benefits of physically active games

Sports and games provide children with the opportunity to become sensitive to others' needs and values, manage emotions, and handle dominance and exclusion (Henley, Schweizer, de Gara, & Vetta, 2007). Through games youth can learn self-control and to express emotions in acceptable ways. Games also encourage youth to learn new problem-solving skills and enhance peer relationships (Henley et al., ibid). In a systematic review of the effects of game-centered approaches to teaching, Miller (2015) found that the use of games is associated with increased interest/ enjoyment and effort/importance with the task, as well as increased perceived competence.

The effectiveness of games is enhanced if they involve physical activity. Physical activity on its own is related to life satisfaction in adolescents (Valois, Zullig, Huebner, & Drane, 2004). Witman (1987) found that adventure-based/active recreation programs were better than social recreation programs for improving attitudes and actions regarding cooperation and trust. Therefore, LifeMatters incorporates physically active games as a main component of the program.

Overview of the LifeMatters program

The previous section outlined factors that create an effective program structure that were taken into account during the development of LifeMatters. It began as an un-named 15-session program (Hanrahan, 2005), but has been refined into ten 90-minute sessions. An outline of the specific activities within the 10-session program can be found in Hanrahan (2012). Each of the 10 sessions contains games, discussions/activities, a handout, a thought for the day, and a take-away task. The specific psychological skills covered within the program are activation control, goal-setting, attention and concentration, imagery, self-talk, and self-confidence. The games within the program are designed to be fun; teach skills such as trust, communication, and problem-solving; and provide opportunities to explore some of the psychological skills in action. Detailed descriptions of some of the games can be found in Hanrahan (2013).

Autonomy is encouraged by providing participants with choices (e.g., color of folder, games to be played), self-direction (e.g., goal-setting activities), and peer responsibility (e.g., reviewing program content in the last session). Icebreakers, group problem-solving, trust exercises, and regular discussions/reflections with others promote relatedness. Competence is developed through skill acquisition, opportunities to demonstrate skills, and non-exclusionary games (i.e., no winners/losers).

Results of LifeMatters interventions

The original implementation of the un-named 15-session program was with a group of 14 girls and a group of 20 boys aged 15 to 20 years at an orphanage in Cuernavaca, Mexico (Hanrahan, 2005). Average attendance was 8.82 sessions out of 15 (range 1 to 13). Even with less than optimal attendance, they showed significant increases in life satisfaction and self-worth. Although there was no control group, the pre/post results for the four individuals who only attended one or two sessions showed that their life satisfaction was virtually unchanged, and their self-worth deteriorated over the time of the program. One indication of what they learned in the program comes from when they were asked to list things in their lives they could and could not control. At the beginning of the program the participants struggled to think of anything that they could control ("My temper, maybe, sometimes"), but could easily list factors they could not control (e.g., what they ate, when they ate, sharing a room with more than 30 others, what time to wake up/ go to bed). Near the end of the program they were again asked to list factors they could control, and everyone listed at least 20 things they felt they could control (e.g., my thoughts, how I react to others, whether or not I pay attention, my level of activation). Long-term results were also evident. For example, one of the attendees who the orphanage director had pushed to attend the program because of "behavior problems" ended up getting a university scholarship to study psychology – a result she attributed to having attended the life skills program.

Two years later the 10-session version of LifeMatters was trialed with teenagers living in poverty in San Jose del Cabo and Cabo San Lucas (Los Cabos), Mexico. The only skill cut from the original 15-session program was time management (primarily because in these populations finding enough time to do particular tasks was rarely an issue). Some highlights from this intervention were a young girl too shy to speak out loud in the first session loudly explaining to an adult the different types of attention, and another girl commenting that because of the program she now felt that she had control over the future for her life and would not end up pregnant as a teenager. The effects of the LifeMatters program were noticed beyond the immediate term of the intervention, indicating that the positive effects may accrue over the longer term. For example, three years after the program was run in Los Cabos, a new scholarship scheme became available to support youth to undertake higher education or training for particular trades. Approximately 50% of the initial scholarship recipients were from the 40 youth who had completed the LifeMatters program.

The LifeMatters program was then run in Buenos Aires, Argentina (see Hanrahan, 2011 for a description of the cultural issues encountered). Three groups attended the program across seven weeks, with one or two sessions held each week. Two groups (one all girls and one co-ed) were run in the villas (slums) of Buenos Aires. The third group ran in a poor town on the outskirts of Buenos Aires. For these programs many games had to be modified or deleted because of issues such as dangerous neighborhoods, child care responsibilities, limited space, heat, and dogs. The frustration of real-life research was experienced when post-test data could not be collected because of political demonstrations in the city that affected public transportation and the mechanical breakdown of a beat-up van that had been used for transport to the villas. Nevertheless, qualitative data indicated games, imagery, and goals were appreciated, with the most valued components of the program being learning how to develop confidence and the idea of controlling the controllable.

LifeMatters returned to Mexico in 2011, this time in Monterrey. The program was run with boys and girls separately at a group home (the first five sessions for each group were run at the group home; the youth were bused to a university [Tecnológico de Monterrey] for the final five sessions). Quantitative results showed significant increases in happiness, life satisfaction, self-concept, and control of good events. Psychology students from Tecnológico de Monterrey assisted in running the program. Several of those students went on to run the program with other groups of youth (e.g., through their church). An additional program took place in Monterrey with former gang members and drug users (Hanrahan & Francke, 2015). Aged 15 to 29, these participants showed significant increases in happiness, life satisfaction, global self-concept, and many specific types of self-concept (i.e., physical appearance, close friendship, behavioral conduct, scholastic competence, athletic competence, and social acceptance). The mean attendance of 7.9 out of 10 sessions suggested the participants were getting something out of the voluntary program.

In 2013 a two-week program was run in English for the first time with high school students from a low-income community as part of the National Youth Sport Program at Case Western Reserve University in Cleveland, Ohio. From pretest to posttest the students showed significant increases in resilience.

In 2015 the LifeMatters program was run with a new cohort of minority youth from the same community. Because of scheduling constraints, only eight of the 10 LifeMatters sessions were included, omitting the content that focuses on developing self-confidence. With a measure of the 5 Cs of positive youth development, there was a significant increase in character. Confidence did not increase, suggesting that positive results related to confidence seen elsewhere were not just due to youth having participated in a program involving group work and games. The content of the program appears to influence the results.

The same measure of the 5 Cs of positive youth development was used in Botswana in 2015. Coaches (mostly males) completed a train-the-trainer version of the program in one of three cities. Aged 24 to 62, the coaches had been coaching for two to 29 years, with the most popular sports being football (i.e., soccer), softball, and athletics (i.e., track and field). The train-the-trainer program was run in an intensive format over three or four days. In two of the three cities, many of the coaches who had completed the train-the-trainer program got together in groups of three, and then ran 75% of the LifeMatters program over a weekend with 186 students ages 12 to 20. Roughly half of the students missed out on the imagery component of the program, with the remainder missing out on the attention/ concentration component. They all received the self-confidence section that the 2015 Ohio cohort missed. The Botswana students showed significant increases in confidence and competence. It should be noted that the pretest scores for these students on character and connection were already quite high, so a ceiling effect may have come into play. Results from the train-the-trainer program suggest that it is not only beneficial for youth, but also coaches showed significant increases in competence, confidence, and connection (Hanrahan & Tshube, 2016). Coaches' comments reflect the impact of the program on them as well as on young participants:

- "It taught me that you don't just need to be physically fit to win; your mental readiness is also important."
- "Every time I coach, I will reflect and implement all the techniques and strategies learnt."
- "[The skills learned in LifeMatters] help make a better me."

Also in 2015, the LifeMatters program was run with ninth-graders at a school in the poorest community near Monterrey, Mexico. For the first time data were also collected from a control group containing other ninth-graders who did not participate in the program. For the intervention group there were significant increases in conduct self-concept, school self-concept, and belonging. For the control group there was a significant increase in school self-concept, but a significant decrease in friendship self-concept. The LifeMatters program was also delivered to six males who were not attending school or working. Nine months after the intervention I was informed that of those six, two were working every day at a carpenter shop and one was studying to become an English teacher.

Recommendations for practice and future research

When administering life skills programs such as LifeMatters, it is important to take into account the culture and circumstances of the situation. Aside from the obvious cultural difference of language (i.e., Spanish versus English), minor modifications have been made to the LifeMatters program for different cultures. For example, one of the icebreaker activities in the first session involves people coming up with their three favorite Cs – color, cuisine, and cartoon character. I was told that it was not culturally appropriate to ask the men in Botswana (i.e., male coaches) to talk about cartoon characters, so this C was changed to "car." Changes have also been made to the process of some sessions depending on the literacy levels of participants. For example, instead of having participants write down their goals, they might instead draw pictures of their goals.

From a research perspective, it would be ideal to run randomized controlled trials. In many of the groups where the program has been run in the past, it had not been feasible to obtain a control group let alone randomly assign people to either the intervention or the control. One of the challenges of doing real-world research is that often there is no control group. To make the research credible, other strategies such as having multiple baselines or using participants who drop out early may provide a comparative data set. Even without a control group the narratives captured during the program offer testimony to the importance and effectiveness of the LifeMatters program. Structured follow-up data would also help determine whether the positive changes that have been observed from before the program to after the program remain long term. It could also be helpful to understand the relative importance of the games – whether similar positive results would be found if LifeMatters was run without the games.

References

Brooks-Gunn, J., & Roth, J. (2014). Invited commentary: Promotion and prevention in youth development: Two sides of the same coin? *Journal of Youth and Adolescence*, 43, 1004–1007. doi:10:1007/s10964-014-0122-y.

Buckner, J. C., Mezzacappa, E., & Beardslee, W. R. (2003). Characteristics of resilient youths living in poverty: The role of self-regulatory processes. *Development and Psychopathology*, 15, 139–162.

Diener, E. (2008). Myths in the science of happiness, and directions for future research. In M. Eid & R. J. Larsen (Eds.), *The Science of Subjective Well-Being* (pp. 493–514). New York: Guilford Press.

Diener, E., & Diener, C. (1996). Most people are happy. *Psychological Science*, 7, 181–185.

Diener, E., Emmons, R., & Larsen, R. J., & Griffin, S. (1985). The satisfaction with life scale. *Journal of Personality Assessment*, 49, 71–75.

Edwards, O. W., Mumford, V. E., & Serra-Roldan, R. (2007). A positive youth development model for students considered at-risk. *School Psychology International*, 28, 29–45.

Elliot, D. S., Wilson, W. J., Huizanga, D., Sampson, R. J., Elliott, A., & Ranking, B. (1996). The effects of neighborhood disadvantage on adolescent development. *Journal of Research in Crime and Delinquency*, 33, 389–426.

Fordyce, M. W. (1988). A review of research on the happiness measure: A sixty second index of happiness and mental health. *Social Indicators Research*, 20, 355–382.

Geldhof, G. J., Bowers, E. P., Boyd, M. J., Mueller, M. K., Napolitano, C. M., Schmid, K. L., Lerner, J.V., & Lerner, R. M. (2011). *The creation and validation of short and very short measure of PYD*. Research Report for the Thrive Foundation for Youth.

Geldhof, G. J., Bowers, E. P., Boyd, M. J., Mueller, M. K., Napolitano, C. M., Schmid, K. L., Lerner, J.V., & Lerner, R. M. (2014). Creation of short and very short measures of the five Cs of positive youth development. *Journal of Research on Adolescence*, 24, 163–176. doi:10.1111/jora.12039.

Gilman, R. (2001). The relationship between life satisfaction, social interest, and frequency of extracurricular activities among adolescent students. *Journal of Youth and Adolescence*, 30, 749–767.

Hanrahan, S. J. (2004). Sport psychology and indigenous performing artists. *The Sport Psychologist*, 18(1), 60–74.

Hanrahan, S. J. (2005). Using psychological skill training from sport psychology to enhance the life satisfaction of adolescent Mexican orphans. *Athletic Insight*, 7(3). Retrieved from www.athleticinsight.com.

Hanrahan, S. J. (2011). Working in the villas of Buenos Aires: Cultural considerations. *Journal of Clinical Sport Psychology*, 5, 361–371.

Hanrahan, S. J. (2012). Developing adolescents' self-worth and life satisfaction through physically active games: Interventions with orphans and teenagers living in poverty. In R. J. Schinke & S. J. Hanrahan (Eds.), *Sport for Development, Peace, and Social Justice* (pp. 135–148). Morgantown, WV: Fitness Information Technology.

Hanrahan, S. J. (2013). Using games to enhance life satisfaction and self-worth of orphans, teenagers living in poverty, and ex-gang members in Latin America. In R. J. Schinke & R. Lidor (Eds.), *Case Studies in Sport Development: Contemporary Stories Promoting Health, Peace, and Social Justice* (pp. 89–101). Morgantown, WV: Fitness Information Technology.

Hanrahan, S. J., & Francke, L. (2015). Improving life satisfaction, self-concept, and happiness of former gang members using games and psychological skills training. *Journal of Sport for Development, 3*(4), 41–47.

Hanrahan, S. J., & Tshube, T. (2016). Training the trainers in Botswana: The LifeMatters program tailored to community youth coaches. In G. Cremades & L. Tashman (Eds.), *Global Practices and Training in Applied Sport, Exercise, and Performance Psychology: A Case Study Approach* (pp. 154–162). London: Routledge.

Harter, S. (1988). *Manual for the Self-Perception Profile for Children.* Denver, CO: University of Denver.

Henley, R., Schweizer, I., de Gara, F., & Vetta, S. (2007). How psychosocial sport & play program help youth manage adversity: A review of what we know & what we should research. *International Journal of Psychosocial Rehabilitation, 12*(1), 51–58.

Huebner, E. S., & Diener, C. (2008). Research on life satisfaction of children and youth. In M. Eid & R. J. Larsen (Eds.), *The Science of Subjective Well-Being* (pp. 371–392). New York: Guilford Press.

King, P. E., Schultz, W., Mueller, R. A., Dowling, E. M., Osborn, P., Dickerson, E., & Lerner, R. M. (2005). Positive youth development: Is there a nomological network of concepts used in the adolescent development literature? *Applied Developmental Science, 9*(4), 216–228. doi:10.1207/s1532480xads0904_4.

Larson, G. M., & Sbarra, D. A. (2015). Participating in research on romantic breakups promotes emotional recovery via changes in self-concept clarity. *Social Psychological and Personality Science, 6*, 399–406. doi:10.1177/1948550614563085.

Laub, J. H., & Sampson, R. J. (1988). Unraveling families and delinquency: A reanalysis of the Gluecks' data. *Criminology, 26*, 355–380.

Lefcourt, H. M. (1976). *Locus of Control: Current Trends in Theory and Research.* Hillsdale, NJ: Lawrence Erlbaum.

Lerner, R. M. (2002). *Concepts and Theories of Human Development.* Hillsdale, NJ: Lawrence Erlbaum.

Lerner, R. M., Lerner, J. V., Almerigi, J., Theokas, C., Phelps, E., Gestsdottir, S., . . . von Eye, A. (2005). Positive youth development, participation in community youth development programs, and community contributions of fifth grade adolescents. Findings from the first wave of the 4-H study of positive youth development. *Journal of Early Adolescence, 25*(1), 17–71.

Marsh, H. W., Abduljabbar, A. S., Parker, P. D., Morin, A. J. S., Abdelfattah, F., Nagengast, B., . . . Abu-Hilal, M. M. (2015). The internal/external frame of reference model of self-concept and achievement relations: Age-cohort and cross-cultural differences. *American Educational Research Journal, 52*, 168–202. doi:10.3102/0002831214549453.

Marsh, H. W., & Shavelson, R. (1985). Self-concept: Its multifaceted, hierarchical structure. *Educational Psychologist, 20*(3), 107–123.

Miller, A. (2015). Games centered approaches in teaching children & adolescents: Systematic review of associated student outcomes. *Journal of Teaching in Physical Education, 34*, 36–58. doi:http://dx.doi.org/10.1123/jtpe.2013-0155.

Mosak, H. H. (1998). Interrupting a depression: The pushbutton technique. In J. Carlson & S. Slavik (Eds.), *Techniques in Adlerian Psychology* (pp. 267–272). London: Routledge.

Nygren, B., Alex, L., Jonsen, E., Gustafson, Y., Norberg, A., & Lundman, B. (2005). Resilience, sense of coherence, purpose in life and self-transcendence in relation to perceived physical and mental health among the oldest old. *Aging & Mental Health*, 9, 354–362. doi:10.1080/1360500114415.

Petitpas, A. J., Cornelius, A. E., Van Raalte, J. L., & Jones, T. (2005). A framework for planning youth sport programs that foster psychosocial development. *The Sport Psychologist*, 19, 63–80.

Ryan, R. M., & Deci, E. L. (2000). Self-determination theory and the facilitation of intrinsic motivation, social development, and well-being. *American Psychologist*, 55, 68–78. doi:http://dx.doi.org/10.1037/0003-066X.55.1.68.

Sax, L. J., Kanny, M. A., Riggers-Piehl, R. A., Whang, H., & Paulson, L. N. (2015). "But I'm not good at math": The changing salience of mathematical self-concept in shaping women's and men's STEM aspirations. *Research in Higher Education*, 56, 813–842. doi:10.1007/s11162-015-9375-x.

Sengendo, J. & Nambi, J. (1997). The psychological effect of orphanhood: A study of orphans in Raika district. *Health Transition Review*, 7(Suppl.), 105–124.

Taylor, C. S., Lerner, M., von Eye, A., Bobek, L., Balsano, A. B., Dowling, E. M., & Anderson, P. M. (2004). Internal and external developmental assets among African American male gang members. *Journal of Adolescent Research*, 19, 303–322.

Turner, H. A., Shattuck, A., Finkelhor, D., & Hamby, S. (2015). Effects of poly-victimization on adolescent social support self-concept, and psychological distress. *Journal of Interpersonal Violence*. 32(5), 755–780. doi:10.1177/088626051558376.

Valois, R. F., Zullig, K. J., Huebner, E. S., & Drane, J. W. (2004). Physical activity behaviors and perceived life satisfaction among public high school adolescents. *The Journal of School Health*, 74(2), 59–65.

Wagnild, G. M., & Young, H. M. (1993). Development and psychometric evaluation of the Resilience Scale. *Journal of Nursing Measurement*, 1, 165–178.

Wallace, M. T., Barry, C. T., Zeigler-Hill, V., & Green, B. A. (2012). Locus of control as a contributing factor in the relation between self-perception and adolescent aggression. *Aggressive Behavior*, 38, 213–221. doi:10.1002/ab.21419.

Witman, J. P. (1987). The efficacy of adventure programming in the development of cooperation and trust with adolescents in treatment. *Physician & Sports Medicine*, 15, 22–29.

14

POSITIVE PSYCHOLOGY AND PHYSICAL EDUCATION IN SCHOOLS

Graham Mallen and Bridget Grenville-Cleave

Introduction

Although the current focus on children's mental health and well-being in the UK is very welcome, the issues have existed for many years. Williams and Kerfoot (2005) argued that child and adolescent mental health care appeared on the political agenda in the UK in the early 1990s. By 2007, UNICEF report card 7 (2007) highlighted that the UK was 21st out of 21 developed countries for child well-being. Nearly a decade on, some progress has been made, with UNICEF report card 13 (2016) ranking the UK 14th out of 35.

UNICEF report card 7 (2007) argued that it is the changing ecology of childhood which affects children's quality of life. Claveirole and Gaughan (2011) suggest that nurturing children and young people's well-being is not prioritised over more traditional measures of progress such as economic stability. The Office for National Statistics' (ONS) *Insights into Children's Mental Health and Well-Being Report* (Beardsmore, 2015) outlines that relevant ecological issues for children and young people's well-being and resilience include bullying, parental relationships, body image, social media and school. Schools are often the focus of policy and interventions designed to address these social and ecological issues. However, they are under increasing pressure to focus their energies on achieving better academic grades in core subjects such as math, science and English. As a King's College report commissioned by the National Union of Teachers (NUT) stated, 'Life in the data cage is impacting on students and teachers alike' (*A curriculum for all?*, 2016). Findings revealed how teachers are concerned that they cannot devote appropriate time to students' learning and that reforms entrench an exam culture which undermines students' mental health and well-being. Of particular concern was the report's finding that the 'curriculum is becoming narrower and less inclusive and that the experience of students is increasingly shaped by the data-driven demands of accountability. Creativity and independence of thought was being sacrificed across the curriculum' (2016, para 6). In the UK the introduction of 'Progress 8' is seen as a new approach to assessing students' and schools' achievements. Instead of looking solely at final grades, Progress 8 measures the year-on-year progress made by pupils from age 11.

Allocated practical physical education (PE) time has decreased in recent years (Carroll, 2003). Carrington (2016) explains that three-quarters of UK children spend less time outdoors than prison inmates. In UNESCO's 2014 Worldwide Survey of School Physical Education (Hardman, Murphy, Routen, & Tones, 2014), some head teachers considered PE less important than traditional academic subjects and many schools did not offer the recommended amount of PE, with the global weekly average in primary schools being 103 minutes and secondary 100 minutes, with significant regional and national variations. Children's physical activity levels are also impacted by the finding that outdoor free play, which is critical to developing competence and confidence, may be declining because of restrictions imposed by adults (Singer, Singer, D'Agostino, & DeLong, 2009). Physical movement enhances children's capacity to learn (Jensen, 1998), supporting a more holistic approach to education. When delivered well, PE plays an important role in developing the whole child (Shimon, 2011), supporting children's development mentally, emotionally, morally and socially as well as physically.

The purpose of this chapter is to highlight Graham Mallen's experience, as a PE teacher, in one UK secondary school (Manor School Sports College, Northamptonshire) over the course of a two-year period during which a well-being program was implemented through PE as well as the wider school. He describes how the opportunity arose with support from the Youth Sport Trust and how he progressively learned about and implemented the ideas and activities from positive psychology (PP), which have been transformative for both students and staff.

The Youth Sport Trust (YST) is a UK charity whose remit is to improve the quality of PE and school sport. It aims to promote physical activity in those under the age of 25, based on the three principles of leadership, achievement and well-being. In 2015, YST developed the PE2020 Active Healthy Minds Program, running a pilot in Northamptonshire schools with the aim of improving the physical, social and emotional well-being of young people aged 11 to 18. Based in Northamptonshire, Mallen's school took part in the pilot, devising its own PE2020 pilot program for pupils in Years 7 and 8.

The importance of PE, physical activity and sport for physical and mental well-being

Kirk, MacDonald, and O'Sullivan (2006) highlight that PE can potentially teach young people the importance of being physically active for current and future health. Existing research shows how children's engagement in physical activity positively supports their physical health by maintaining desirable functioning in areas such as bone health, blood pressure, weight management and flexibility (Bailey,

2006). Developing movement skills and physical literacy early in childhood are likely to facilitate ongoing engagement in physical activity, with the potential benefit of maintaining health and involvement in physical activity through adolescence and into adulthood (ibid).

In a recent meta-analysis of 75 studies examining children's physical activity and mental health, Ahn and Fedewa (2011) concluded that though there were varying effects according to methodological and participant characteristics, 'on average physical activity led to improved mental health outcomes for all children' (p. 385). In particular, an increased level of physical activity was effective in reducing the children's emotional disturbance, distress, anxiety and depression (ibid).

Recent research shows that fitness in children and young people is associated with increased cognitive function and academic performance (Geertsen et al., 2016; Tomporowski, Davis, Miller, & Naglieri, 2008). In their review of research examining the relationship between physical activity and educational attainment, Bailey et al. (2009) concluded that whilst many educational benefits are claimed for physical education and school sport (PESS), rather than being a straightforward or guaranteed outcome, such benefits were likely to be dependent on many contextual and pedagogical factors.

The UK Government Office for Science recommends physical activity as one of five evidence-based ways to well-being, promoting it across the whole population (Foresight, 2007), yet arguably the importance of physical education is being undermined within contemporary educational reforms which emphasise academic targets.

Positive education

Within the school setting, one area of positive psychology (PP) which has had considerable impact is positive education. Seligman, Ernst, Gillham, Reivich, and Linkins (2009) define positive education as 'education for traditional skills and for happiness' (p. 293). What this means, in short, is teaching children and young people about happiness, either directly and/or indirectly, using the evidence from the science of PP. Seligman et al. (ibid) argue that well-being should be taught in schools for three reasons:

1   as an antidote to depression;
2   as a way of increasing children and young people's happiness;
3   as a tool to enable better learning and creative thinking.

Positive education has also been defined as an 'umbrella term used to describe empirically validated interventions and programmes from positive psychology' (White & Murray, 2015, p. 14). White (2016) recognises three types of positive education programs in schools, including using empirically validated well-being interventions, whole-school proactive mental health programs (e.g. Bounce Back!; McGrath & Noble, 2011), and philosophy-based lessons which focus on character, virtues and values.

However, it would be a mistake to assume that the positive emphasis of a positive education program means that it is easy to introduce and implement. Both Shute and Slee (2016) and White (2016) highlight numerous applied and theoretical hurdles, some of which are outlined as follows:

1   Well-being is not a core curriculum subject. Often, happiness and well-being are viewed as a distraction from traditional subjects such as English, science and math, rather than as a means to support better learning and creative thinking. There is evidence, however, that higher well-being is linked to higher academic attainment (Briner & Dewberry, 2007).
2   Unqualified providers. White (2016) warns that some providers of positive education programs are untrained and have no qualifications. Such mavericks may make unrealistic claims for the outcomes of a positive education program. However, at the moment there is no recognised or certified qualification in positive education, nor requirement from the PP community to undergo practical training, assessment, supervision or Continuing Professional Development (CPD).
3   Schools are complex organisations although the increasing focus on education as a transaction rather than a process diminishes and underestimates the relevance and importance of this. Schools have many stakeholders (e.g. pupils, teachers, managers, leaders, parents, governors, local community, school inspectors, etc.), which makes implementation both more challenging and time consuming. Whereas businesses and large organisations are often used to managing complex change initiatives, setting aside a budget and even employing qualified managers specifically for this purpose, UK schools may not have access to such funds, skills and expertise.
4   Prevention of problems is prioritised over promotion of well-being. It is logical, and therefore unsurprising, that schools focus more resources on fixing problems than they do on teaching happiness. For example, by law all UK state schools must have a behavior policy which outlines the steps taken to address bullying. However, very few schools outline how they teach pupils to make and keep friends, develop empathy, caring and compassion, overcome conflict or disagreement and other life skills which are essential to developing helpful and harmonious social relationships.

Interestingly, availability of funding is not necessarily a straightforward hurdle to implementation. It is true that some of the popular programs can be very expensive, and would therefore be out of the reach of many UK state schools, especially given the 2017 changes to the education funding formula which has created budget shortfalls for many schools. The funding hurdle is more likely to be indirect, that is, linked to the availability of staff to take on additional responsibilities to plan and organise a well-being program whilst delivering their usual curriculum topics, staff training, succession planning and the ability to make such a program sustainable in the school over the longer term.

On top of all of the foregoing, serious consideration must also be given to the issue of the well-being of the staff themselves. Evidence from Briner and Dewberry (ibid) highlights the link between staff well-being, pupil well-being and pupil attainment, suggesting that pupil attainment is not only connected to pupil well-being (which supports Lyubomirsky, King, and Diener's [2005] findings that happiness is both the cause and the consequence of success) but also that pupil well-being is linked to staff well-being. It is concerning, therefore, that the volume and pace of educational reform is such that teachers' well-being is being undermined (Grenville-Cleave & Boniwell, 2012).

Other important issues which must be considered in positive education specifically as well as within PP generally include culture and context (Flores & Obasi, 2003; Pedrotti, 2014; Worth & Smith, in press) and how they impact well-being as well as its teaching and learning. According to White (2016, p. 4), '(t)oo many well-being programs are imposed without the care taken to consider existing values within communities before they are integrated'.

Repositioning the purpose of PE in school

At Manor School Sports College in Northamptonshire, leaders and PE staff worked together to ensure that their PE2020 well-being program would meet the specific needs of students. Initially a program targeting approximately 300 year 7 and 8 students (aged 11 − 13) was piloted. Staff considered how PE lessons could be adapted to improve the psychological well-being of students at the same time as delivering PE skills. One consideration was the amount of actual practical time allocated in PE lessons to 'physical activity' rather than 'teacher talk', an issue highlighted in OFSTED's *Beyond 2012 − outstanding physical education for all* report (OFSTED, 2013). This report identified that in PE lessons, teachers often talked for too long and that students, therefore, had less time for strenuous activity and practising skills. It was decided that instead of the traditional approach to PE whereby the teacher focused explicitly on traditional PE-skill lesson objectives, such as accuracy, speed and stamina, they would use an approach called 'My Personal Best' (My PB).

My PB was created as part of a 12-month Department for Education (DfE)– funded pilot working with secondary schools to teach students life skills such as collaboration, empathy, self-motivation and resilience. This approach reduces teacher talk time at the start of the lesson, and increases the time students have to take part in a physical activity at the same time as enabling them to develop My PB life skills. Thus, students may be given a leadership opportunity in the PE lesson, for example, being responsible for team tactics during a hockey lesson and deciding which are the most effective tactics to apply. Students may discuss with each other their 'strengths portfolio' and how each player could use their strengths to influence the game. If one student lacks confidence about his or her ability, another may focus on helping that student apply a growth mindset (Dweck, 2006; see also Chapter 8). If a student becomes over-emotional, his or her peers can help that student to become calmer.

In September 2015, staff from outside the PE department and students were introduced to the PE2020 plans, which would require them to see PE from a different perspective, one built around developing well-being, character and life skills, rather than the traditional focus on specific PE skills and sporting achievement.

How positive psychology, character education and philosophy underpin PE

Seligman (2003) postulates that there are three pathways to happiness: the Pleasant Life, the Good Life and the Meaningful Life. The Good Life is more closely connected to hedonic well-being and achieving happiness through experiencing positive emotions by, for example, savouring and appreciating life's pleasures. The Good Life and the Meaningful Life are pathways more closely connected to eudaimonic well-being, achieving happiness through using one's character strengths for personal development and in the service of others, and fulfilment of leading a purposeful existence. Peterson and Seligman's (2004) Values-in-Action (VIA) classification of character strengths and virtues, a major contribution to PP which underpins many school well-being programs, including PE2020, is a measure of 'good character' based on findings from various philosophical and religious texts, as well as literature from across the world. To date, hundreds of research studies have been carried out using the VIA strengths framework, linking the identification and appropriate use of character strengths with numerous positive outcomes, including increased happiness, resilience, optimism and performance, and lower depression, stress and anxiety (Clifton & Anderson, 2002; Peterson & Seligman, 2004; Seligman, Steen, Park, & Peterson, 2005). For a more in-depth discussion of character strengths as they apply in sport and physical activity, see Chapter 5.

Understanding 'good character' can be approached by different routes as reflected by the way some programs draw their inspiration and activities from philosophical perspectives on the positive qualities of people, whereas others are underpinned by psychology. The PE2020 program not only draws on the character education and life skills approach of YST's My PB, but also a philosophical approach to good character promoted by the University of Birmingham's Jubilee Centre for Character and Virtues. The positive attributes promoted by the Centre's program include courage, justice (fairness), honesty, compassion, self-discipline, gratitude and humility/modesty. Readers who are familiar with Peterson and Seligman's (2004) work will readily recognise these amongst the 24 VIA character strengths. Interestingly, research by Park, Peterson, and Seligman (2004) has suggested that the VIA strengths of hope/optimism, zest, gratitude, love and curiosity are most robustly correlated with life satisfaction, whereas the strengths of humility/modesty, appreciation of beauty, creativity, judgement and love of learning are only weakly associated with life satisfaction. As well as facilitating well-being, the Jubilee Centre's approach to character education is about 'helping students grasp what is ethically important in situations and to act for the right reasons, such that they become more autonomous and reflective' (Jubilee Centre, n.d., p. 2).

Therefore, there is considerable value in exploring the interplay between the philosophical and psychological dimensions of good character, especially when doing the right thing may not necessarily lead to feeling good in the moment, or in the longer term. Similarly, acting to feel good in the moment may compromise doing the right thing. Being honest, fair or courageous, for example, may be far harder to achieve and may delay or even deny individual well-being.

PE and sport are often attributed with character development precisely because they provide challenges which transcend personal, interpersonal, physical, technical, social, aesthetic and moral domains of experience. Thus, in a PE setting there are many opportunities for teachers to invite children and young people to recognise character strengths in action explicitly and consider the benefits and dilemmas that using and developing one's strengths may elicit.

The following sections outline two activities developed and used by Graham Mallen in the PE2020 program.

Activity: selfie interval training

Interval training is a core activity in school PE lessons, consisting of alternating periods of high-intensity exercise with low-intensity rest or relaxation. Traditional interval training might involve sprinting 50m round the school football pitch, walking or jogging for another 50m before sprinting the next 50m, and so on. Research suggests that interval training results in increased fitness in less time compared with 'steady-state' endurance exercise (Gibala et al., 2006). However, it is also more mentally demanding. In this selfie interval training activity, students work in pairs and are given a series of selfies they must take around the sports field, for example, in front of certain school signs, trees/plants or on particular spots of the school playing field. Each time they take a photo they must return to the PE teacher to get it signed off. The first pair to get all their photos signed off wins. There are certain rules to add a little complexity to the challenge, for example, 'photo-bombed' selfies are void and cannot count toward the final number. Not only does selfie interval training allow the students to use their much-loved cell phones, but also it builds their intrinsic motivation (Ryan & Deci, 2000) by giving them autonomy in deciding the order of the photos, building relatedness in that they are working closely with others, and competence through developing their physical fitness, decision-making skills and strategic thinking. Finally we should not overlook the fact that selfie interval training is a lot more enjoyable for students than the traditional version, thus building hedonic well-being.

Activity: M&Ms Secret PE challenge

In this activity, students each select one M&Ms candy from a bag. The colour they choose corresponds with a particular challenge to be completed during the PE lesson.

Examples used in the M&Ms Secret PE challenge activity include:

- Red: Give two to three peers some feedback on their performance and how they could improve a particular skill.
- Orange: Make two to three positive comments to peers.
- Yellow: Set up two to three shooting opportunities.
- Blue: Create a tactic and share it with teammates.
- Brown: Think of a behavior that your role model might demonstrate in a lesson and model it.
- Green: Take an impossible shot!

These are just two examples of activities in PE; both lend themselves to supporting greater student autonomy, relatedness, competence and creativity through giving students opportunities to develop further challenges for themselves and other students. These challenges are not only relevant PE tasks but also take into account a number of key PP principles, for example:

- overcoming the negativity bias and deliberately cultivating a more appreciative perspective (Sheldon & King, 2001) by specifically noticing positive behaviours or strengths-spotting in others;
- cultivating a sense of autonomy (Ryan & Deci, 2000) by allowing students a choice of challenges;
- bringing greater fun, enjoyment and engagement into lessons by allocating the challenges using creative approaches (Fredrickson, 1998; Morrison, 2008; Starko, 2013);
- building self-efficacy through modeling the effective behaviour of others (Bandura, 2016);
- developing a growth mindset and greater psychological resilience by pushing oneself to take small risks and learning from the experience of operating outside one's comfort zone (Dweck, ibid).

Evaluation of the PE2020 program

The PE2020 program was incorporated into a wider positive education program within the school, which was evaluated using the EPOCH (engagement, perseverance, optimism, connectedness and happiness) measure of adolescent mental well-being (Kern, Benson, Steinberg, & Steinberg, 2016). Thus, it is not possible to evaluate the effectiveness of PE2020 separately. The EPOCH evaluation showed that by the end of the school year (July 2016), 83% of year 7 and 8 students had shown an improvement in their well-being scores. Additionally, the school's SIMS (Student Information Management System), used to measure students' achievement and behaviour, also showed significant improvement compared with the average ratings of years 7 and 8 in previous years, suggesting that the PE2020 program was beneficial.

Recommendations

Manor School's PE teachers believe that the PE2020 pilot program has not only increased students' enjoyment of and engagement with PE lessons, but it has also raised their well-being and added to, rather than detracted from, developing traditional PE abilities and skills. Research into PE and well-being (e.g. Mutrie & Faulkner, 2004) has encouraged PE teachers in this school to experiment with other evidence-based approaches, for example, focusing on how engaging with PE can foster positive emotions. The school is currently trialling a 'fun semester' of sports, which gives students more choice of physical activities, and more time for actual physical activity rather than 'teacher talk', and makes having fun experiences the center of each lesson, whilst still developing PE abilities and life skills. Readers will recognise that Barbara Fredrickson's broaden-and-build theory of positive emotions (1998, 2004) is central to this decision to focus on fun, as is the 'P' for positive emotions of Seligman's (2011) PERMA theory of well-being (see Chapter 2).

The PE2020 program has had the added benefit of giving PE a 'whole school' priority; PE is not only about developing the individual's or team's sports skills but also good character and life skills such as greater resilience, leadership and self-discipline. As such, PE deserves greater recognition on the school curriculum, and should be valued on a par with traditional academic subjects. The evidence from PP research as well as YST's PE2020 evaluation is that active engagement with and enthusiasm for PE in school is linked to wider academic, work and life success and should not be seen as a distraction from the core curriculum. With this in mind, we recommend qualitative and quantitative research from varied stakeholders on the impact of engaging in PE on wider and longer-term well-being of students, as well as measuring academic achievement and post-school transitions alongside this.

References

Ahn, S., & Fedewa, A. L. (2011). A meta-analysis of the relationship between children's physical activity and mental health. *Journal of Pediatric Psychology*, 36(4), 385–397.

Bailey, R. (2006). Physical education and sport in schools: A review of benefits and outcomes. *Journal of School Health*, 76, (8), 397–401.

Bailey, R., Armour, K., Kirk, D., Jess, M., Pickup, I., Sandford, R., & BERA Physical Education and Sport Pedagogy Special Interest Group. (2009). The educational benefits claimed for physical education and school sport: An academic review. *Research Papers in Education*, 24(1), 1–27.

Bandura, A. (2016). The power of observational learning through social modeling. In R. J. Sternberg, S. T. Fiske, & D. J. Foss (Eds.), *Scientists Making a Difference: One Hundred Eminent Behavioral and Brain Scientists Talk About Their Most Important Contributions* (pp. 235–239). New York: Cambridge University Press.

Beardsmore, R. (2015). *ONS insights into children's mental health and well-being report.* UK Office for National Statistics.

Briner, R., & Dewberry, C. (2007). *Staff Well-Being Is Key to School Success.* London, UK: Worklife Support Ltd.

Carrington, D. (2016, March 25). Three-quarters of UK children spend less time outdoors than prison inmates – survey. *The Guardian.* Retrieved from www.theguardian.com/environment/2016/mar/25/all.

Carroll, B. (2003). *Assessment in Physical Education: A Teacher's Guide to the Issues*. London: Routledge.

Claveirole, A., & Gaughan, M. (Eds.), (2011). *Understanding Children and Young People's Mental Health*. Chichester: John Wiley & Sons.

Clifton, D. O., & Anderson, E. (2002). *StrengthsQuest: Discover and Develop Your Strengths in Academics, Career, and Beyond*. New York: Gallup Press.

Dweck, C. (2006). *Mindset: The New Psychology of Success*. New York: Random House.

Flores, L. Y., & Obasi, E. M. (2003). Positive psychological assessment in an increasingly diverse world. In S. J. Lopez & C. R. Snyder (Eds.), *Positive Psychological Assessment: A Handbook of Models and Measures* (pp. 41–54). Washington, DC: APA.

Foresight. (2007). *Tackling obesities: Future choices – summary of key messages*. UK Government Office of Science. Retrieved January 16, 2017, from www.gov.uk/government/uploads/system/uploads/attachment_data/file/287943/07-1469x-tackling-obesities-future-choices-summary.pdf.

Fredrickson, B. L. (1998). What good are positive emotions? *Review of General Psychology*, 2(3), 300–319.

Fredrickson, B. L. (2004). The broaden-and-build theory of positive emotions. *Philosophical Transactions: Royal Society of London Series B Biological Sciences*, 359(1449), 1367–1378.

Fredrickson, B. L., & Branigan, C. (2005). Positive emotions broaden the scope of attention and thought-action repertoires. *Cognition & Emotion*, 19(3), 313–332.

Geertsen, S. S., Thomas, R., Larsen, M. N., Dahn, I. M., Andersen, J. N., Krause-Jensen, M., et al. (2016). Motor skills and exercise capacity are associated with objective measures of cognitive functions and academic performance in preadolescent children. *PLoS ONE*, 11(8), e0161960. doi:10.1371/journal. pone.016196.

Gibala, M. J., Little, J. P., Van Essen, M., Wilkin, G. P., Burgomaster, K. A., Safdar, A., Raha, S., & Tarnopolsky, M. A. (2006). Short-term sprint interval *versus* traditional endurance training: Similar initial adaptations in human skeletal muscle and exercise performance. *The Journal of Physiology*, 575, 901–911.

Grenville-Cleave, B., & Boniwell, I. (2012). Surviving or thriving? Do teachers have lower perceived control and well-being than other professions? *Management in Education*, 26(1), 3–5.

Hardman, K., Murphy, C., Routen, A. C., & Tones, S. (2014). *UNESCO-NWSPEA, World-Wide Survey of School Physical Education, Final Report*. Paris: UNESCO. ISBN: 978-92-3-100048-5.

Jensen, E. (1998). *Teaching With the Brain in Mind*. Alexandria, VA: ASCD.

Jubilee Centre, University of Birmingham. (n.d.). *A Framework for Character Education in Schools*. Birmingham, UK: University of Birmingham.

Kern, M. L., Benson, L., Steinberg, E. A., & Steinberg, L. (2016). The EPOCH measure of adolescent well-being. *Psychological Assessment*, 28(5), 586.

Kirk, D., MacDonald, D., & O'Sullivan, M. (Eds.). (2006). *Handbook of Physical Education*. London: Sage.

Lyubomirsky, S., King, L. A., & Diener, E. (2005). The benefits of frequent positive affect: Does happiness lead to success? *Psychological Bulletin*, 131, 803–855.

McGrath, H., & Noble, T. (2011). *Bounce Back! A Wellbeing and Resilience Program* (2nd ed.). Melbourne: Pearson.

Morrison, M. K. (2008). *Using Humor to Maximize Learning: The Links Between Positive Emotions and Education*. Plymouth, UK: R&L Education.

Mutrie, N., & Faulkner, G. (2004). Physical activity: Positive psychology in motion. In P. A. Linley & S. Joseph (Eds.), *Positive Psychology in Practice* (pp. 146–164). Hoboken, NJ: Wiley & Sons.

NUT King's College. (2016). A curriculum for all? *The Effects of Recent Key Stage 4 Curriculum, Assessment and Accountability Reforms on English Secondary Education*. London, UK: National Union of Teachers.

OFSTED. (2013). *Beyond 2012 – outstanding physical education for all*. Retrieved from www.gov.uk/government/publications/beyond-2012-outstanding-physical-education-for-all

Park, N., Peterson, C., & Seligman, M. E. (2004). Strengths of character and well-being. *Journal of Social and Clinical Psychology*, 23(5), 603–619.

Pedrotti, J. T. (2014). Taking culture into account with positive psychological interventions. In A. C. Parks & S. M. Schueller (Eds.), *The Wiley-Blackwell Handbook of Positive Psychological Interventions*. Chichester, West Sussex: John Wiley & Sons.

Peterson, C., & Seligman, M. E. (2004). *Character Strengths and Virtues: A Handbook and Classification* (Vol. 1). Oxford: Oxford University Press.

Ryan, R. M., & Deci, E. L. (2000). Self-determination theory and the facilitation of intrinsic motivation, social development, and well-being. *American Psychologist*, 55(1), 68.

Seligman, M. E. (2003). *Authentic Happiness*. London: Nicholas Brealey Publishing.

Seligman, M. E. (2011). *Flourish: A New Understanding of Happiness and Well-Being*. London: Nicholas Brealey Publishing.

Seligman, M. E., Ernst, R. M., Gillham, J., Reivich, K., & Linkins, M. (2009). Positive education: Positive psychology and classroom interventions. *Oxford Review of Education*, 35(3), 293–311.

Seligman, M. E., Steen, T. A., Park, N., & Peterson, C. (2005). Positive psychology progress: Empirical validation of interventions. *American Psychologist*, 60(5), 410–421.

Sheldon, K. M., & King, L. (2001). Why positive psychology is necessary. *American Psychologist*, 56(3), 216.

Shimon, J. M. (Ed.). (2011). *Introduction to Teaching Physical Education: Principles and Strategies*. Champaign, IL: Human Kinetics.

Shute, R. H., & Slee, P. T. (Eds.). (2016). *Mental Health and Wellbeing Through Schools: The Way Forward*. Abingdon: Routledge.

Singer, D. G., Singer, J. L., D'Agostino, H., & DeLong, R. (2009). Children's pastimes and play in sixteen nations. Is free-play declining? *American Journal of Play*, 1(3), 283–312.

Starko, A. J. (2013). *Creativity in the Classroom: Schools of Curious Delight*. Routledge.

Tomporowski, P. D., Davis, C. L., Miller, P. H., & Naglieri, J. A. (2008). Exercise and children's intelligence, cognition, and academic achievement. *Educational Psychology Review*, 20(2), 111–131. doi:10.1007/ s10648-007-9057-0; PMID: 19777141.

UNICEF. (2007). *Child Poverty in Perspective: An Overview of Child Well-Being in Rich Countries, Innocenti Report Card 7*. Florence: UNICEF Office of Research.

UNICEF Office of Research. (2016). Fairness for children: A league table of inequality in child well-being in rich countries, *Innocenti Report Card 13*. Florence: UNICEF Office of Research.

White, M. A. (2016). Why won't it stick? Positive psychology and positive education. *Psychology of Well-Being*, 6(2), 1–16.

White, M. A., & Murray, A. S. (2015). Building a positive institution. In M. A. White & A. S. Murray (Eds.), *Evidence-Based Approaches in Positive Education* (pp. 1–26). Dordrecht: Springer.

Williams, R., & Kerfoot, M. (2005). *Child and Adolescent Mental Health Services: Strategy, Planning, Delivery, and Evaluation*. Oxford: Oxford University Press.

Worth, P., & Smith, M. (in press). Critical positive psychology: A creative convergence of two disciplines. In N. Brown, T. Lomas, & P. Worth (Eds.), *The Routledge Handbook of Critical Positive Psychology*. Abingdon: Routledge.

15

POSITIVE PEDAGOGY FOR SPORTS COACHING

The influence of positive psychology

Richard L. Light

Introduction

One of the aims of this book is to explore the benefits that positive psychology offers sport and physical activity. This chapter focuses on sports coaching and the innovative concept of positive pedagogy (PPed) for sports coaching (Light, 2017). This is a concept I have been developing in practice and theorizing over the past five years (Light, 2014a, 2014b; Light & Harvey, 2015) but which originates in my early attempts to inform coaching individual sports with a constructivist perspective on learning (e.g. Light & Wallian, 2008). PPed for sports coaching draws on Antonovsky's (1979) work on the origins of health and well-being and positive psychology to extend the positive experiences and learning that game-based approaches (GBA) can generate in team sports to sport more broadly. In particular, it aligns with Seligman's (2012) PERMA model that allows it to emphasize meaning, achievement and relationships as well as positive emotions and engagement that seem to get more attention in the literature on positive psychology.

PPed modifies the core pedagogical features I have identified for the Game Sense approach to coaching team sports, as a GBA that is widely used in sports coaching (Jones, 2015; Light, 2013), to enable their application to coaching beyond team sports. GBAs focus on the game as a whole to contextualize learning and enhance the transfer of improvement in practice to the game on the field (Jones, 2015). They focus on empowering the athlete as an active learner in contrast to traditional approaches that break the game up into discrete parts, such as technique, that are drilled out of the context of the game. PPed is underpinned by constructivist perspectives on learning and draws on the work of medical sociologist Anton Antonovsky and positive psychology to emphasize the positive nature of experience and learning. Recently I have focused more on the PERMA model (Seligman, 2012) to provide a framework for promoting positive experience and learning and also well-being, which is developing as a stronger focus for the approach (Light, 2017).

The PPed approach redresses the need in the sport psychology, physical education and sports coaching literatures for more attention to be paid to enjoyment, excitement, friendship and meaning in sport that is highlighted in the introduction to this book. Like positive education, it draws on positive psychology but to less of an extent, with the primary focus being on pedagogy and developing performance.

I am not a psychologist but the multi-disciplinary approach I take in my research on coaching and learning in sport draws significantly on the psychology and sport psychology literatures. This chapter provides an example of the influence that positive psychology is having in fields beyond psychology.

The development of positive pedagogy

The physical education and sports coaching literatures have seen sustained interest over the past two decades by researchers and practitioners in GBAs as an alternative to a traditional 'skill–drill' approach that reduces the complexity of team sports to a number of fundamental skills or techniques. As Bunker and Thorpe noted in the presentation of their Teaching Games for Understanding (TGfU), traditional approaches improve skill but do not lead to better game play while also taking the enjoyment and interaction out of team sports (Bunker & Thorpe, 1982; Light, 2013). GBAs have been shown to be effective in improving performance, increasing motivation, enhancing interpersonal relationships, boosting confidence, promoting positive experiences of learning and contributing toward well-being (Light, 2013). Despite these positive outcomes and the ongoing development of a range of GBAs, the application of their pedagogical features beyond team sports has been limited (Light, Curry, & Mooney, 2014); I have been working on this aspect with colleagues over the past eight years (Light & Wallian, 2008; Light, 2014a; Light & Harvey, 2015). PPed extends the pedagogical features of GBAs such as Game Sense (Light, 2013) beyond team games to individual sports while drawing on Antonovsky's work and positive psychology to promote positive learning experiences and outcomes (Light & Harvey, 2015).

While GBAs focus on improving performance, their athlete-centered and inquiry-based pedagogy fosters positive experiences of learning and a range of positive social, moral and personal development as a type of 'secondary' and typically implicit learning (Dyson, 2005; Sheppard & Mandigo, 2009). However, as Harvey, Kirk, and O'Donovan (2014) contend, rather than being automatically 'caught', this learning must be 'taught'. It must be an intended outcome of coaching and teaching.

Beginning with a brief outline of PPed's three core features, this chapter moves on to focus on how I have integrated positive psychology into the development of PPed for sports coaching and physical education.

Positive Pedagogy as a holistic approach

PPed sits upon the philosophical principle of holism (Light, 2017) and the idea that complex phenomena can only be explained and understood as a whole. In epistemology, holism contrasts with reductionism and the view that complex systems can be explained through reducing them to their component parts. This holistic approach is assisted by drawing on monist, Eastern philosophical traditions to circumnavigate some of the tensions arising from Western, mind-body dualism as has been explained by others (see, Varela, Thompson, & Rosch, 1991). Positive psychology also draws on elements of Eastern philosophical traditions such as its appropriation of the Buddhist concept of *mindfulness* that Cohen (2010) describes as the 'psychologicalisation' of Buddhism with the concept of flow resonating with an Eastern, holistic world view.

In Buddhism the concept of mindfulness refers to a state of awareness of the individual's being and doing (Cohen, 2010) that has some relevance to putting PPed into practice (Light, 2014b, 2017) though more in the vein of its original Buddhist meaning than as a coping mechanism. Csikszentmihayli's (1991) concept of *flow* resonates with Eastern philosophical traditions, and concepts such as the Japanese concept of *mushin* (Light, 2014b) have informed the holistic principles of PPed by emphasizing the inseparability of mind from body, from spirit (Light, 2014b).

PPed offers an understanding of athlete experience in competition and practice that mimics competition intensity and contrasts with reductionist and dualistic approaches to coaching that emphasize drilling technique out of the context of the game – in the case of team sports. It also generates positive emotions such as enjoyment or delight (Kretchmar, 2005), engagement in learning, the building of relationships and a sense of belonging (Light, 2008, 2016; Chen & Light, 2006), meaning, and opportunities for individual and collective achievement to align with the PERMA model of well-being. Positive pedagogy emphasizes what the learner *can* do and how s/he can draw on existing individual and social resources to meet learning challenges through reflection and dialogue.

Core features of positive pedagogy

The positive pedagogy framework has three core features that require the coach to: (1) design and manage experience of engagement with the physical learning environment, (2) ask questions in preference to telling athletes what to do, and (3) adopt an inquiry-based approach. My use of engagement in this chapter refers to learning that involves the curiosity, interest, and the intellectual, emotional and physical commitment needed to maximize learning and the links between non-cognitive factors such as motivation, interest, determination and perseverance and conscious cognition (Newmann, 1992).

Designing and managing the learning environment/ experience

The focus on the whole game in GBA such as Game Sense is evident in PPed for individual sports as a whole-person approach that involves all the senses and other dimensions of experience such as 'feel' in swimming (Light, 2014a). Typically, learning experiences aimed at achieving specific outcomes are encouraged by placing physical constraints on the athlete such as performing butterfly with one arm in swimming to focus attention on the kick or running with the hands held behind the back to focus on the use of the arms (Light, 2017, 2014b). As similar as it may seem, this is different to Constraints-Led Theory (CLT) because of the different aims of the constraint, with CLT developed from motor-learning theory and sitting upon empiricist epistemology and PPed informed by constructivist epistemology. In PPed the aim of imposing a restraint (seen in CLT as a physical constraint) is not to produce a predetermined movement or movement pattern but, instead, to create problems to be solved by the athlete through processes of non-conscious thinking or adaptation (doing) and conscious thinking promoted through questioning and interaction. In individual sports that are typically skill-intensive, this involves discovery learning (Bruner, 1961) in which the athlete discovers the most efficient way to perform a skill or technique through problem-solving. When using PPed for coaching individual sports, constraints are used to highlight or create a problem that is to be solved through interaction and active learning that would normally involve formulating, testing and evaluating solutions. Although the end result could well look the same as it would when using a constraints-led approach, the learning process is different, with PPed also acknowledging the importance of learning how to learn.

When a coach introduces a new group or an individual athlete to the indirect coaching methods of PPed, they should begin with a more 'traditional' approach that the athletes are accustomed to and gradually move toward more empowering methods (Light, 2017). As athletes adapt to the approach, they can take on more autonomy, ownership and responsibility for participating in the design, modification and evaluation of learning activities. This leads to increasing empowerment through a growing understanding of the activity and of how to learn. As players/athletes adapt and become more prepared to engage in purposeful social interaction, they rely less upon the coach and begin to take more responsibility for their own learning, which is a positive developmental experience. This typically involves a coach-athlete relationship that is more equitable in the repositioning of the coach from a director of learning to a facilitator of it and the empowerment of the athlete.

Ask questions to generate dialogue and thinking

There is a range of challenges that coaches and teachers typically have to meet when taking up athlete-centered, inquiry-based approaches such as PPed and GBA. These include designing and managing practice games and moving from being a director of learning to a facilitator, but the literature on GBA consistently identifies coach and teacher questioning as the most challenging aspect of adopting these athlete-centered approaches (Harvey & Light, 2015). Questioning is one of the central mechanisms employed for promoting learning in PPed and GBA, but it typically presents challenges for coaches and teachers (Forrest, 2014; Harvey & Light, 2015; Roberts, 2011; Wright & Forrest, 2007). In PPed, questions vary between situations and sports, but are not posed to get answers. They are asked to promote thinking, reflection and dialogue and/or to assist in the discovery of effective technique although it takes time for coaches to become skillful enough with questioning to achieve these aims. Where possible, questions should stimulate a range of possible answers or solutions rather than leading athletes to predetermined answers. Of course, this can vary when coaching a skill or skill-intensive individual sport because of the focus on understanding established principles of movement or technique efficiency and the smaller range of response options available when compared with the greater complexity of game play in team sports (Light & Harvey, 2015). There may also be times when there is a predetermined 'answer' or most effective technique that the athlete is encouraged to discover.

Although questions asked in PPed can be designed to help athletes discover predetermined knowledge, it requires coaches to have a disposition toward promoting divergent thinking, creativity and a sense of curiosity. When a solution developed by an athlete does not work, the PPed coach would usually ask him/her to reflect upon why it did not work and how it could be modified to work, or decide it cannot work and to seek a different solution. This could be in a small group or in a one-on-one situation between coach and athlete. It is 'solution-focused', which allows it to provide a positive experience by focusing athlete attention on the goals of the activity and what they can do to achieve these goals (Clarke & Dembowski, 2006; Grant, 2011). Here the athlete solves problems by drawing on the available resources (including social) with discussions focused on solutions to keep the athlete(s) engaged in the task (Grant, 2011).

An inquiry-based approach to athlete learning

PPed adopts an inquiry-based approach in which productive interaction is of central importance for learning. This helps athletes improve while developing confidence in their ability to become independent learners and problem-solvers and so remain motivated to participate in the activity for the longer term (Renshaw, Oldham, & Bawden, 2012). The productive social interaction involved in this process can also lead to athletes understanding each other in humanistic ways. It can encourage empathy, compassion, meaningful relationships, a sense of connection and care for one another. In PPed, coaches build an environment in which athletes feel secure. This involves coaches making it clear that mistakes provide opportunities for learning (Renshaw et al., ibid) and can be seen as positive learning experiences with the provision of opportunities for adequate reflection and analysis.

Enhancing positive experience

The three core features of PPed encourage positive learning experiences that are enhanced by drawing on Antonovsky's Salutogenic Theory and Sense of Coherence (SoC) model (1979, 1987) and positive psychology, with a growing focus on the PERMA model as a guide for providing positive experiences of learning (Seligman, 2012).

Salutogenic Theory (ST)

In PPed, I use the three features of Antonovsky's SoC model to help make athlete learning positive by making practice comprehensible, manageable and meaningful (Light & Harvey, 2015). Antonovsky's ST and SoC model (1979, 1987) focus on the socially constructed resources that facilitate attaining and maintaining good health and are used in PPed to provide conditions in practice that both enhance learning and contribute to the athlete's well-being. Antonovsky's focus on experience offers coaches a way of working with a holistic focus on the affective and social dimensions of sport that are emphasized in athlete-centered approaches (Kidman & Lombardo, 2010; Light, 2013) instead of taking a purely cognitive approach. Antonovsky suggests that good health and well-being emerge from the individual feeling that life has a) comprehensibility, b) manageability, and c) meaningfulness. In PPed, these concepts are used to create conditions that promote positive experiences of learning that I briefly describe here:

Comprehensibility is developed through experience and refers to the extent to which things make sense for the individual by being ordered and consistent. For learning to be *comprehensible* in sport, it should help athletes to know not only *how* to do something, but also *when, where* and *why*. It should also foster deep understanding of the concepts or 'big ideas' (Fosnot, 1996) that underpin learning and performance in sport (Light, 2017). Comprehensive understanding in sport involves not only rational, conscious and articulated knowing, but also a practical understanding or 'sense' of the game or activity (Bourdieu, 1986) developed through experience and engagement in the unfolding of knowledge.

Manageability is the extent to which an individual feels s/he can manage stress and challenge by having the resources at hand to do so. In PPed, this includes the resources available from interaction within groups and teams and/or the whole team in dialogue and the 'debate of ideas' (Gréhaigne, Richard, & Griffin, 2005). For sports coaching, the athlete should feel that the challenges of learning are manageable and can be met by drawing on individual resources (e.g. skill, physical capacity, knowledge and/or social resources such as social interaction with peers and the teacher/coach) that are emphasized in PPed.

Meaningfulness refers to how much the individual feels that life makes sense and its challenges are worthy of commitment. There is a useful overlap here with Seligman's (2012) PERMA model. When activities engage athletes affectively and socially as well as physically and intellectually, they are more likely to be meaningful for them. For example, when a swim coach adopts PPed, s/he might ask the swimmer to reflect upon the feel of his/her stroke and discuss it with a training partner who provides an external, objective perspective that can be drawn on along with the swimmer's subjective perspective. In this example, learning emerges from interaction between the two athletes and the sharing of two different perspectives. This should involve them linking the technical detail to one of the core concepts of reducing resistance or increasing propulsion. This not only promotes physical, affective, intellectual and physical engagement in learning but also gives meaning to practice through deep understanding of *why* a technique is performed as it is. It empowers the swimmer to work through problems and challenges as they arise (Light, 2014a).

The PERMA model

Positive psychology's focus on the positive aspects of life complements the positive experiences encouraged by the athlete-centered, inquiry-based pedagogy of PPed and the three elements of Antonovsky's (1979, 1987) SoC model. My understanding of positive psychology is that it sets out to redress a preoccupation of psychology with pathologies and repairing the 'worst aspects' of life by discovering and promoting its positive qualities (Seligman & Csikszentmihalyi, 2000). Positive psychology focuses on encouraging well-being by focusing on what is good about life and what the individual can do to make life better. It aims to promote satisfaction in the past, happiness and the experience of *flow* in the present and hope and optimism in the future (Jackson & Csikszentmihalyi, 1999). All these features of positive psychology align with the aims of PPed, but it is the PERMA model (Seligman, 2012) that frames the intent of PPed to promote positive experiences and learning.

PPed does not have a specific focus on developing well-being or happiness but does aim to foster positive 'secondary' learning that can contribute toward well-being. With importance placed on meaning, relationships, achievement and sense-making in PPed, it aligns well with all five elements of Seligman's (2012) PERMA (positive emotions, engagement, relations, meaning and achievement) model as a guide for promoting well-being. This association with PERMA is becoming more apparent in my research and thinking on the implementation of PPed. Many aspects of the PERMA model influence the ongoing development of PPed, with this emerging as an inviting area for further inquiry (Light, 2017). The five elements of the PERMA model are particularly useful for coaches (and teachers) who are interested in the promotion of well-being as a major aim, such as those working in schools and youth sport.

Discussion

Positive pedagogy maintains a focus on the improvement of performance at any level of competition and aims to foster an enjoyment of learning and confidence in the athlete's ability to learn (Light, 2017), without which performance achievements would be diminished. This can also include what can be considered to be the secondary learning of many of the same positive characteristics that receive attention in positive psychology such as compassion, empathy, resilience, self-confidence, creativity, coping ability, health, resilience and positive well-being. It would also include the moral, ethical and social learning arising from the pedagogy used. Although the nature of the athlete-centered pedagogy used in PPed inherently encourages these characteristics, coaches can draw on the orientation of positive psychology to enhance this.

For the athlete, having a comprehensive understanding of what s/he is doing and why s/he is doing it can make the practice session, and the season, meaningful and manageable. Being appropriately challenged in ways that produce experiences of flow or *mushin* during the activity of the session and feeling that s/he has what it takes to manage the challenge in practice is likely to generate optimal learning and to make the experience, and outcomes, meaningful and enjoyable. In PPed, I draw on positive psychology to make learning positive but also to assist in realizing the positive social learning and social skills that participation in sport is commonly assumed to deliver but which merely playing sport will not necessarily produce (see, e.g. De Martelaer, De Bouw, & Struyven, 2012).

The development of well-being, happiness and positive experiences of practice are important issues for coaches to consider for athletes at any age and any level of performance but are typically of more concern for youth sports coaches and physical education teachers. This is because positive states such as delight and joy and satisfaction arising from achievement and a sense of competence make such valuable contributions toward children's and young people's experiences of playing sport (Kretchmar, 2005; Kirk, 2005; Light, Curry, & Mooney, 2014).

PPed emphasizes the holistic, social nature of learning, and the role that experience, the body and its senses play in athlete learning. It encourages the development of the social skills involved in engaging in purposeful dialogue, a willingness and ability to negotiate and compromise and the understanding of democratic processes involved in making and enacting decision-making while making learning enjoyable.

At a subjective level, positive psychology's attention to feeling good and experiencing states such as joy, happiness and well-being makes a valuable contribution toward promoting positive experiences of practice for athletes that enhance learning and improvements in performance. The personal qualities identified in positive psychology as being needed to lead a 'good life', such as human strengths and being future minded, are also evident in PPed. These human strengths and the work of Antonovsky and his SoC are recognized in the development of the new Australian Health and Physical Education curriculum. The curriculum is future oriented, with the strength-based focus being one of its five propositions (Macdonald, 2013) and the salutogenic approach used to understand associated issues, and to secure curriculum implementation (McCuaig, Queenerstedt, & Macdonald, 2013). The strengths-based approach takes a positive route to help students deal with adversity by being 'future focused' and drawing on the strengths they bring with them to adapt to the challenges they face.

The focus of positive psychology at the community level influences PPed by encouraging thinking about creating positive collectives such as the team and the club and how the promotion of learning positive lessons through sports could and should flow on to them. It also builds humanistic relationships between coach and athlete and between pairs, or small groups, of athletes in individual sports (Light, 2017). The emphasis here on developing characteristics such as tolerance and social responsibility in individuals is of prime importance when coaching children and young people. As educational philosopher John Dewey (1938) argues, education should provide students with experiences in the short term that are immediately valuable for the individual but which also enable them to contribute to society in the long term.

Learning to learn and the positive inclinations toward learning that PPed aims to generate, and some of the social learning that can accompany it, are more likely to transfer into life off the court or sports field than improved sport technique and fitness. The way in which it can develop a positive inclination toward learning, and the contribution it can make toward well-being, would clearly be beneficial for children and young people participating in sport. It would be of benefit for improving performance at any level and could make a contribution toward helping elite-level, professional athletes meet the challenges of developing post-playing careers and enhance their well-being.

Along with other innovative developments in coaching over the past few decades, PPed challenges the reductionist and objectivist nature of traditional approaches to sports coaching that have dominated for so long. The contemporary GBAs such as Game Sense that PPed builds on are beginning to influence coaching practice across all levels of sport and a wide range of cultural and institutional contexts. This is promising for PPed, but the key to its development and ability to influence coaching practice probably lies in having coaches and organisations buy into the philosophical and psychological stances and perspectives of humanism and holism that underpin it. I would also suggest that exploring the ways in which the PERMA model could guide coaches and teachers to make learning more positive and to contribute more effectively to well-being is well worthy of consideration.

References

Antonovsky, A. (1979). *Health, Stress, and Coping*. San Francisco, CA: Jossey-Bass.

Antonovsky, A. (1987). *Unraveling the Mystery of Health*. San Francisco, CA: Jossey Bass.

Bourdieu, P. (1986). *Distinction*. London: Routledge and Kegan Paul.

Bruner, J. S. (1961). The act of discovery. *Harvard Educational Review*, 31(1), 21–32.

Bunker, D., & Thorpe, R. (1982). A model for teaching games in secondary school. *Bulletin of Physical Education*, 10, 9–16.

Chen, Q., & Light, R. (2006). 'I thought I'd hate cricket but I love it!' Year six students' responses to Game Sense pedagogy. *Change: Transformations in Education*, 9(1), 49–58.

Clarke, J., & Dembowski, S. (2006). The art of asking great questions. *The International Journal of Mentoring and Coaching*, [Online] 4(2), 1–6. Retrieved February 11, 2015, from www.solutionsurfers.com/pdf/TheArtOfAskingGreatQs.pdf.

Cohen, E. (2010). From the Bodhi tree to the analyst's couch then into the MRI scanner: The psychologisation of Buddhism. *Annual Review of Critical Psychology*, 8, 97–119.

Csikszentmihalyi, M. (1991). *Flow: The psychology of optimal experience*. Harper Collins.

De Martelaer, K., De Bouw, J., & Struyven, K. (2012). Youth sport ethics: Teaching pro-social behaviour. In S. Harvey & R. Light (Eds.), *Ethics in Youth Sport: Policy and Pedagogical Applications* (pp. 55–73). London: Routledge.

Dewey, J. (1938). *Experience and Education*. Indianapolis, IN: Kappa Delta Di.

Dyson, B. (2005). Integrating cooperative learning and tactical games models: Focusing on social interactions and decision-making. In L. L. Griffin & J. I. Butler (Eds.), *Teaching Games for Understanding: Theory, Research, and Practice* (pp. 149–168). Champaign, IL: Human Kinetics.

Forrest, G. (2014). Questions and answers: Understanding the connection between questioning and knowledge in game-centred approaches. In R. Light., J. Quay, S. Harvey, & A. Mooney (Eds.), *Contemporary Developments in Games Teaching* (pp. 167–177). London: Routledge.

Fosnot, C. T. (1996). Constructivism: A psychological theory of learning. In C. T. Fosnot (Ed.), *Constructivism: Theory, Perspectives and Practice* (pp. 103–119). New York: Teachers College, Columbia University.

Grant, A. M. (2011). The solution-focused inventory: A tripartite taxonomy for teaching, measuring and conceptualising solution focused approaches to coaching. *The Coach Psychologist*, 7(2), 98–105.

Gréhaigne, J-F., Richard, J-F., & Griffin, L. L. (2005). *Teaching and Learning Team Sports and Games*. London: Routledge.

Harvey, S., Kirk, D., & O'Donovan, T. M. (2014). Sport education as a pedagogical application for ethical development in physical education and youth sport. *Sport, Education and Society*, 19(1), 41–62.

Harvey, S., & Light, R. L. (2015). Questioning for learning in games-based approaches to teaching and coaching. *Asia Pacific Journal of Health, Sport and Physical Education*, 6(2), 175–190.

Jackson, S. A., & Czikszentmihalyi, M. (1999). *Flow in Sports*. Champaign, IL: Human Kinetics.

Jones, E. (2015). Transferring skill from practice to the match in rugby through game sense. *Healthy + Active Magazine*, 22(2/3), 56–58.

Kidman, L., & Lombardo, B. J. (Eds.). (2010). *Athlete-Centred Coaching: Developing Decision Makers*. Worcester: IPC Print Resources.

Kirk, D. (2005). Physical education, youth sport and lifelong participation: The importance of early learning experiences. *European Physical Education Review*, 11(3), 239–255.

Kretchmar, S. (2005). Understanding and the delights of human activity. In L. Griffin & J. Butler (Eds.), *Teaching Games for Understanding: Theory Research and Practice* (pp. 199–212). Champaign, IL: Human Kinetics.

Light, R. L. (2008). *Sport in the Lives of Young Australians*. Sydney: Sydney University Press.

Light, R. L. (2013). *Game Sense: Pedagogy for Performance, Participation and Enjoyment*. London: Routledge.

Light, R. L. (2014a). Positive Pedagogy for physical education and sport: Game Sense as an example. In R. L. Light, J. Quay, S. Harvey, & A. Mooney (Eds.), *Contemporary Developments in Games Teaching* (pp. 29–42). London and New York: Routledge.

Light, R. L. (2014b). Learner-centred pedagogy for swim coaching: A complex learning theory informed approach. *Asia-Pacific Journal of Health, Sport and Physical Education*, 5(2), 167–180.

Light, R. L. (2016). *Children, Young People and Sport: Studies in Experience and Meaning*. Newcastle: Cambridge Scholars Press.

Light, R. L. (2017). *Positive Pedagogy for Sport Coaching: Athlete-centred Coaching for Individual Sports*. London and New York: Routledge.

Light, R. L., Curry, C., & Mooney, A. (2014). Game Sense as a model for delivering quality teaching in physical education. *Asia-Pacific Journal of Health, Sport and Physical Education*, 5(1), 67–81.

Light, R. L., & Harvey, S. (2015). Positive pedagogy for sport coaching. Published ahead of print (March 4, 2015). *Sport, Education and Society*. Retrieved from www.tandfonline.com/doi/full/10.1080/13573322.2015.1015977#abstract.

Light, R., & Wallian, N. (2008). A constructivist approach to teaching swimming. *Quest*, 60(3), 387–404.

Macdonald, D. (2013). The new Australian health and physical education curriculum: A case of/for gradualism in curriculum reform? *Asia-Pacific Journal of Health, Sport and Physical Education*, 4(2), 95–108.

McCuaig, L. Queenerstedt, M., & Macdonald, D. (2013). A salutogenic, strengths-based approach as a theory to guide HPE curriculum change. *Asia-Pacific Journal of Health, Sport and Physical Education*, 4(2), 109–125.

Newmann, F. (1992). *Student Engagement and Achievement in American Secondary Schools*. New York: Teachers College Press.

Renshaw, I., Oldham, A. R., & Bawden, M. (2012). Non-linear pedagogy underpins intrinsic motivation in sports coaching. *The Open Sports Sciences Journal*, 5, 1–12.

Roberts, S. J. (2011). Teaching games for understanding: The difficulties and challenges experienced by participation cricket coaches. *Physical Education and Sport Pedagogy*, 16(1), 33–48.

Seligman, M. E. P. (2012). *Flourish: A Visionary New Understanding of Happiness and Wellbeing*. Sydney: Random House.

Seligman, M. E. P., & Csikszentmihalyi, M. (2000). Positive psychology: An introduction. *American Psychologist*, 55(1), 5–14.

Sheppard, J., & Mandigo, J. (2009). PlaySport: Teaching life skills for understanding through games. In T. Hopper, J. L. Butler, & B. Storey (Eds.), *TgfU . . . Simply Good Pedagogy: Understanding a Complex Challenge* (pp. 73–86). Toronto: HPE Canada.

Varela, F. J., Thompson, E., & Rosch, E. (1991). *The Embodied Mind: Cognitive Science and Human Experience*. Cambridge, MA: MIT Press.

Wright, J., & Forrest, G. (2007). A social semiotic analysis of knowledge construction and games centred approaches to teaching. *Physical Education and Sport Pedagogy*, 12(3), 273–287.

16

PERFORMANCE LIFESTYLE IN OLYMPIC AND PARALYMPIC SPORT

Where positive psychology informs practice

Arabella Ashfield, Joanna Harrison and Samuel Giles

Introduction

This chapter presents an insight into the contribution of positive psychology to the practice of Performance Lifestyle, a support service in high-performance sport. The chapter sets out the first known account of Performance Lifestyle (PL) and aspects of empirical literature which inform the discipline and practice. PL is rarely communicated beyond a high-performance sport environment, and receives comparatively little academic attention, so understanding exactly what it is and how it works can be difficult to grasp. The first half of this chapter describes what PL is, why it is valuable, what its guiding principles are and how it has evolved. The second half explores its connections with positive psychology, in particular, passion, perspective, athlete-specific well-being, the holistic view of living well as an athlete – termed *athlete flourishing* – and the impact on health, narratives in sport and positive retirement. The chapter is infused with real-world examples drawn from our experiences and those of our colleagues working in the field within the UK.

Performance Lifestyle: what it is and why it is valuable

PL is a nuanced and complex discipline that has grown extensively since its inception a little over a decade ago. Put simply, PL practitioners support athletes and sports to create environments and ways of living where an athlete's sporting and non-sporting lives work together and complement each other for the benefit of the individual long-term as well as their current sporting performance. PL sits alongside sport science and sport medicine disciplines as a service to support performance; however, there is also a moral and ethical rationale for the discipline, bound by the responsibility of the Great Britain (GB) high-performance sporting system toward the people it asks the most of – the athletes themselves. The active pursuit of medals by sports has meant increasingly high demands on performers, too often leading to negative consequences for athletes' mental health and effective transition through and out of sport. Thus, there is a duty of care to athletes and their wider holistic development.

Within high-performance sport in the UK, Olympic and Paralympic sports and the athletes selected onto GB world class programs are supported by UK Sport, receiving state funding and national lottery money to compete and train as full-time athletes. With this unique opportunity comes significant challenges. Relocating to the training venue without family and friends and prioritising training and sporting commitments can lead to the exclusive investment in the athletic role. Education can be balanced with being a full-time athlete but it can also be compromised. As athletes progress, other life areas and interests can be sidelined, and a strong athletic identity can be forged which has been found to exacerbate the difficulties experienced by retiring athletes (Erpič, Wylleman, & Zupančič, 2004). Once retired, a former athlete's job prospects and ability to lead a very different life after being an elite performer for the majority of their years can present very different challenges for which they can be unprepared without appropriate support.

Support from a PL practitioner exists at a variety of transition points in an athletic career to ensure the holistic and balanced development of an athlete. Practitioner work varies to reflect the needs and demands of the particular sport(s) and athletes. Key areas include: managing transitions, career development, education, supporting well-being and personal and professional development. Underpinned by coaching and mentoring techniques using an athlete-led approach, PL provides support and development in a holistic manner during the athlete's career and beyond. The essence of PL practice can perhaps be best described by the eight delivery principles:

- proactively engaging athletes in future life-planning and career development, with emphasis on early intervention and continued personal and professional development throughout their time on the World Class Programme (WCP);
- encouraging and facilitating dual career aspirations with effective management of the balance between sporting and non-sporting commitments, to protect performance potential;
- promoting the importance and impact of athletes creating and developing broader identities and interests beyond their sport to maintain personal well-being;
- providing support and education around finding and managing the optimal personal balance for conflicting demands (e.g. from education, employment, family, financial, etc.) to protect performance potential;
- supporting athletes from a lifestyle perspective as they transition on to, through and from the WCP;
- providing proactive exit support for athletes leaving the WCP for up to six months after funding cessation;
- providing a safe, impartial and where appropriate confidential space to support athletes – signposting and referring onward where necessary to safeguard the well-being of the athlete;

• working in partnership with all athlete and high-performance stakeholders to support and encourage a culture that delivers performance and responsibly cares for its people.

The evolution and diversification of PL

The discipline of PL originated from the Athlete Career and Education (ACE) programme licensed from the Australian Institute of Sport. It developed into a reactive service, providing support directly to an athlete, and very often proceeded with little or no interaction with the sport or the coach. Today, core funding from UK Sport for PL has enabled practitioners to work as part of embedded multidisciplinary support teams. Collaborative approaches with nutritionists, strength and conditioning coaches, sport psychologists and sports coaches allow for integrated strategies to get the best from the athlete. Contextual differences of sports results in subtle distinctions in focus of activities and delivery by practitioners. For example, PL advisors may assess and flag support requirements for potential athlete recruits who have been selected through a talent identification process. Equally a PL advisor may deliver a programme of activities aimed at improving independent living skills in a group of athletes relocating to a new training base. See Figure 16.1 for three further basic examples.

Helping an athlete create better structure to their lives	Helping an athlete begin to plan for life after sport	Supporting an athlete around choosing a sports agent
• Improved use of time to be able to prepare and cook food, meaning nutrition support is maximised • Greater use of time to come prepared and rested for strength and conditioning sessions	• Planning for what the future could look like can allow an athlete to address anxiety about the future and subsequently focus on related sport psychology areas which need addressing in performance • From the coach's perspective, an athlete who is involved in other activities could be retained on programme for longer rather than retiring, as well as gaining skills that are also useful for performance	• Increased sporting success can lead to a rise in media attention and commercial offers – a PL advisor can help to select an agent to help manage these demands, meaning the athlete can focus on performance • Dealing with social media and aligning the personal values of the athlete with commercial opportunities is an important aspect of personal development for the athlete

FIGURE 16.1 Examples of three common goals and strategies for support encountered by Performance Lifestyle

Supporting athletes during career-related transitions

Athletes face a number of transitions during their athletic career, and a primary focus of the PL practitioner is to facilitate the effective passage through each. The adapted model by Wylleman and Lavalle (2003) in Figure 16.2 shows how the demographics of athletes in four world class programme sports span different age ranges; thus, the stages of athletic development have been elongated. The psychosocial development has also been extended because practitioners increasingly see the continued involvement of parents in the athlete's career into their mid-twenties. In terms of the support given, a practitioner in gymnastics is likely to work with young athletes needing to progress through compulsory secondary education whilst in the athletic development phase and entering the world class programme. In rowing, entrants may be over age 18 and in higher education; therefore, a practitioner may identify a need to support athletes in their thirties in the discontinuation phase by exploring career options after post-graduate education.

A specific support point emerging in both boxing and cycling is where athletes may be in their early to mid-twenties when they first experience success. This prompts a need for support to manage their media profile and finances because of an increase in UK Sport funding as a result of successful performances and an increase in sponsorship income. However, at this stage few cyclists and very few boxers are involved in higher education and few athletes of primary education age tend to be on world class programmes. These examples highlight the need for carefully tailored PL support.

The impact of Performance Lifestyle support

PL is in its infancy as a discipline, and the evidence base for its efficacy is limited at present. This means that PL often draws upon the testimony of athletes, coaches and practitioners to demonstrate impact. For example, Danny Kerry, women's head coach with GB Hockey, explains, 'I have witnessed first-hand the benefits of athletes developing skills, acquiring learning or gaining perspective and insight from other environments. Without question, these activities not only benefit the individual, but also the results can have a direct impact on performance. Behind this work has been Emma Mitchell, our GB Hockey PL practitioner'. Former GB women's track endurance cyclist Ciara Horne explained, 'Arabella Ashfield was my PL advisor whilst at British Cycling and helped me a tremendous amount in ensuring I maintained my physiotherapy CPD whilst ensuring my training was at the heart of the focus for the Olympic Games'. Finally, Dr Katie Ludlam, performance psychologist for GB Boxing, explains, 'By working closely with Rich Smith [PL advisor for GB Boxing] we are aligned in the messages we are reinforcing to athletes. This applies to the design and delivery of the education programme and promoting values and influencing culture. At an individual level, together we ensure that the boxers' life outside of the sport is complementary to the demands of being an elite athlete'.

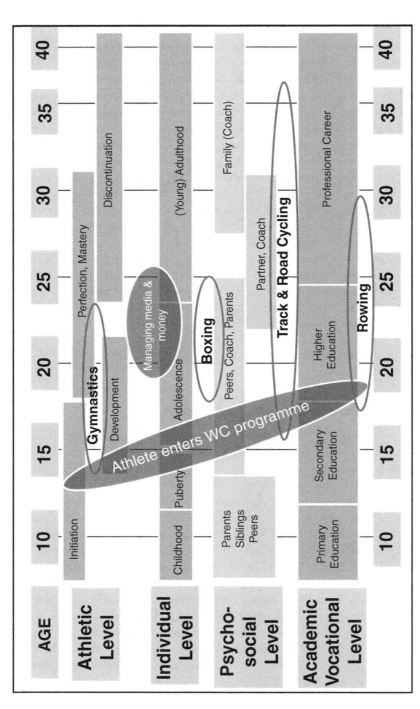

FIGURE 16.2 Schematic representation of high-performance athlete transitions across athletic, individual, psychosocial and academic/vocational domains

Source: Adapted from Wylleman and Lavallee (2003)

Having established the background to PL, and its direct and indirect benefits and impact for the athlete and the sport, the chapter now examines a series of topics within positive psychology which strongly resonate with the work of PL, which may be ripe for future research.

Passion

Passion to pursue one's sporting activity can take a disproportionate space in an elite athlete's identity, causing conflict with other life areas. Consequently, the athlete may fail to maintain their school or university commitments; for the PL advisor, this presents a challenge when the need for alternative activities in the athlete's life is necessary. Similarly, an injured athlete may fail to adhere to a rehabilitation programme, which presents problems for the medical team. Furthermore, an athlete's reluctance to rest prevents desired physiological adaptations, thus causing problems for the sport science and coaching staff.

High-performance sport can unwittingly encourage this obsessive passion (Chichekian & Vallerand, see Chapter 4). For example, the introduction of UK Sport funding directly to the athlete in 2000 ensures that athletes can train full time and *do not* have to balance training alongside other pursuits. This precludes the benefits that would arise from a dual career, such as greater perspective and intellectual stimulation (Aquilina, 2013). Undoubtedly to achieve outstanding performance an athlete has to focus on their performance, and their diet, sleep patterns and physical health are monitored closely by the sport science team. Hence, environments can be created in which the sole focus is to improve performance, with little regard for anything else. Athletes with harmonious passion, however, are adaptive, show flexibility and perspective in situations and are able to prioritise where to focus their energy (Chichekian & Vallerand, *ibid*). Performance directors, coaches and sport science practitioners, therefore, may wish to reflect on some of the benefits and pitfalls of working with athletes displaying obsessive or harmonious passion. Attention to detail in both sports science and coaching produces world-class performance, but we are starting to recognise that having a one-dimensional rather than a well-rounded athlete may be detrimental to performance.

Perspective

The compartmentalisation of life and intense scrutiny of performance can result in the athlete losing perspective and being unable to see the wider picture. Anecdotally, practitioners see the consequences of this loss of perspective in a lack of understanding of normal life roles and responsibilities, an evolving sense of entitlement and higher demands on coaches and support staff. However, PL practitioners argue that by allowing athletes to 'come up for air' from the performance domain by being involved in alternative pursuits, perspective can be regained. Experiencing alternative viewpoints through volunteering or short work placements can help realign perspective and can help build a multidimensional identity which is perceived as helpful for coping with stressful situations (Lundqvist & Sandin, 2014). Arguably, participation in alternative activities may provide another realm through which positive experiences may occur. As the broaden-and-build theory of positive emotions suggests, frequent positive emotions could broaden the athlete's thought action repertoires and help develop additional resources (Fredrickson, 2001) (see Chapter 2 for a more detailed description of this theory). For example, the emotion of joy creates the urge to play, thus encouraging people to explore and be creative. Then, by taking on new information or approaching a problem in an alternative way, intellectual resources may be developed. Athletes who are able to think creatively may be more able to contribute to ideas such as recovery protocols or race strategies in the training and competing environment.

Athlete well-being

The topic of well-being has seen extensive growth in research and increased relevance in applied practice from both ethical and performance perspectives. To remain medal competitive, elite athletes must thrive in a culture of high expectation and constant striving for achievement where the pursuit of excellence in high-performance sport is the norm. Without doubt there are challenges and experiences of adversity in the life of an athlete; however, the need for focus and physical dominance can impair well-being if a degree of balance does not feature. The ability to manage ordinary life responsibilities, adopt value-driven behaviours, regulate autonomy, maintain functional relationships and utilise strategies to respond positively during setbacks become critical for an athlete's progression on world class programmes (Lundqvist & Sandin, 2014).

Although previous studies in sport have adopted either a hedonic (i.e. centred on affective experience) or eudaimonic (i.e. focused on optimal human functioning) viewpoint (cf. Lundqvist, 2011), practitioners should consider a holistic approach, as both emotional and psychological functioning are fundamental to overall well-being (Huta & Ryan, 2010; Ryan & Deci, 2001). In practice, athlete well-being could be considered to centre on a state of balance that is shaped through the ability to manage life events and sport-specific challenges (Dodge, Daly, Huyton, & Sanders, 2012). Specifically, psychosocial factors such as perceived social support, athlete identity, organizational stressors, physical and mental vitality and personality characteristics are key contributors that influence a perceived state of well-being (Lundqvist, 2011; Lundqvist & Raglin, 2015; Theberge, 2008). For example, social support has been associated with enhanced levels of well-being in athletes (e.g. increased positive affect and life satisfaction) and could be conveyed through supportive coaching behaviours which facilitate decision-making and build trust through the use of non-controlling feedback. In addition, personality and coping characteristics such as conscientiousness, self-esteem, perfectionism and coping styles are important predictors of well- and ill-being states (Hill, Huelsman,&

Araujo, 2010; Smith et al., 2015). Hence, there is a need to develop appropriate psychological resources (e.g. resilience, emotion regulation strategies, optimistic explanatory styles and increased psychological flexibility) that will enable athletes to navigate – or even thrive on – the numerous demands and stressors that accompany sport at elite level.

Para-athlete well-being

Although similarities exist in the factors which influence the well-being of Olympic and Paralympic athletes, a number of well-being needs and strengths are particularly significant in the para-sport context (cf . Macdougall, O'Halloran, Sherry, & Shields, 2016), for instance, reduced self-acceptance (i.e. a core component of psychological ill-being) and factors related to the training environment such as stigmatisation of physical impairment, large age span of athletes and issues related to the professionalisation of para-sport (Macdougall, et al., ibid; Macdougall, O'Halloran, Shields, & Sherry, 2015). Furthermore, transitioning out of sport can be challenging; thus, supporting para-athletes when they leave sport requires an in-depth understanding of the retirement context. For example, 'declassification' or being 'unclassifiable' might be a reason for retirement that only para-athletes have to manage. Findings from Project PRISM (Para-Athlete Retirement: Insights, Support and Management) have highlighted that these transitions could prove difficult or even traumatic as athletes perceived their 'disabled identity' to be undermined in addition to losing their athletic identity (Bundon, 2016).

The impact of positive emotions and living a flourishing life

Considerable emotional highs and lows exist in elite sport, and it is demanding mentally and physically, requiring significant effort, energy and commitment from athletes (Conzelmann & Nagel, 2003; Lundqvist, 2011; Wilding, Hunter-Thomas, & Thomas, 2012). Yet these demands are not confined to the performance domain but extend through the way the athletes live their lives. Anecdotally it is known that a psychologically well-functioning and flourishing athlete often trains and competes better than a languishing athlete. However, through positive psychology we now know that experiencing positive emotions can have physical benefits. In addition, eudaimonic well-being has been associated with lower proinflammatory cytokines (a form of protein which promotes systemic inflammation) (Ryff, Singer, & Love, 2004); this *may* be beneficial to rehabilitating athletes. Furthermore, higher rates of eudaimonic well-being are linked to lower levels of daily salivary cortisol (stress hormone), which can affect whole-muscle size (Crewther, Cook, Cardinale, Weatherby, & Lowe, 2011), suggesting implications for athletes aiming to achieve hypertrophy.

Until recently it was not known what a flourishing life looked like for an athlete. Equally little qualitative research has captured nuances of the felt experience, meaning of and interaction between aspects of an athletic life well lived. Athlete flourishing is now known to comprise feelings of determination and challenge, confidence in their ability and themselves, and being eager, happy, excited and content, whilst enjoying being an athlete, and notably these characteristics were associated with periods of successful performance (Ashfield, McKenna, & Backhouse, 2012). Research by Ashfield et al. (2012) found that areas perceived by athletes as important to flourishing included family and friends, having a social life, relationship with the coach and having the correct environment; all had to be fulfilled to their own unique optimal level. Thus, flourishing is not only personal and holistic but also impacted by different environments, lifestyle and relationships. Athletes also report a desire to be worry free, which coaches may view as justifying the need for exclusive investment in sport and, rather than working with the athlete to manage challenges, some coaches prefer to remove all distractions completely. Equipped with this knowledge of athlete flourishing, PL advisors can support athletes in creating and managing the optimal environment to support performance and the athlete's well-being.

Narratives in sport

As relational beings, humans story their lives to create meaning, exchange ideas and learn about themselves and others (Smith & Sparkes, 2009). The process of storytelling also helps form one's understanding of past and current identity (Pasupathi, 2001), and this is no different for the athlete. When a PL advisor works with athletes to create balance in their lives, understand what their future could look like and what employment aspirations they have, it is common to hear a variety of narrative types. The 'performance narrative' (Douglas & Carless, 2006) where the resounding theme is 'sport is life and life is sport' (Dacyshyn, 1999, p. 217) can be heard when an athlete is anxious about the future outside of sport. Elite sport can foster a strong athletic identity (Carless & Douglas, 2009) for some individuals, who describe sacrifice, challenge and overcoming pain to succeed. These types of stories are often promoted by the popular press. When supporting an athlete with their social media interaction and presenting themselves as a role model, it is often important to challenge the stereotyping so that an athlete can differentiate between their public image and brand, and who they really are as people.

Many athletes will resonate with the 'discovery narrative' (Douglas & Carless, ibid) – this orientates around how the 'job' of an athlete and the person are not permanently intertwined and are not one and the same. The 'relational narrative' of how involvement in sport is focused on the importance of another person or interaction with others also features (Douglas & Carless, ibid), but these narrative types are not fixed. Athletes have a variety of stories to tell and emotions to convey, and some will resist the dominant narrative and create their own story which challenges stereotypes (Carless & Douglas, 2013). Regardless of whether an athlete connects with a specific narrative type, stories can help athletes understand their experiences of sport and the process of writing to understand emotions and past experiences (Niederhoffer & Pennebaker, 2002) can also be useful, as described in the forthcoming case study. By understanding the individuality of these stories as well as employing effective questioning and appropriate challenge (Rogers, 2008) in coaching conversations, PL practitioners are able to support and co-construct present and future narratives for an optimal and flourishing life.

Positive retirements

When an athlete decides to retire, it is necessary to find meaning and purpose in alternative pursuits. For some, moving away from sport is, as described by Coakley (1983), a process of re-birth, whilst others experience distress and a profound loss of identity (Kerr & Dacyshyn, 2000). There is a need for athletes to reorient their lives and find new goals and competencies appropriate to their new careers or life responsibilities, having gone from being extraordinary in their sport to a member of the mundane world (Stephan, Bilard, Ninot, & Delignieres, 2003; Sparkes, 1998). PL ideally aims to prevent an extremely challenging retirement by encouraging a broader identity as well as preparing for life after sport through pursuing alternative activities. Yet, supporting an athlete to navigate the emotional transition can be challenging, requiring highly versatile practitioners who adapt their approach once an athlete has left the World Class Programme.

Character strengths for retirement

Introducing the area of character strengths (Peterson & Seligman, 2004) when working with a retiring athlete can be a useful tool to add into the career-coaching techniques used by PL practitioners. Exploring what strengths a future career may need to harness, as well as understanding one's values, are key to making the right choices and subsequently living a fulfilling and meaningful life. People are often not comfortable with talking about their strengths (Gordon & Gucciardi, 2011), but understanding one's self through character strengths is one method of establishing what work environments, systems and types of work would be of interest. Lavallee and Coffee (2016) have recently identified that former athletes in general exhibit higher levels of initiative and confidence to take on broader workplace roles than non-athletes. Equally, athletes in the study were reported by their supervisors as having superior job performance compared with matched control participants. Therefore, helping athletes make the connection between their character strengths and what they have gained from their sporting experiences can be important for career choices and to articulate during interviews.

Case Study 'Reflecting positively on a sporting career' – Applying positive psychology

To conclude this chapter is a real-life example of the application of positive psychology in PL practice. Specific details have been anonymised, a fictitious name used and permission granted by the athlete.

Background

The athlete Ashley had undertaken some career and emotional preparation and was content with the decision to retire after not being re-selected. However, the PL advisor had recognised there were few opportunities to celebrate career successes because Ashley's achievements were not the Olympic or Paralympic successes which impart fame. In consultation with the sport psychologist and athlete, the PL practitioner set out to create an opportunity for Ashley to reflect on performances, emotions and events experienced during her sports career and for these to be more broadly acknowledged. Through the act of writing the aim was for her to make better sense of her 20-year career, acknowledge her achievements and enhance her well-being, thus creating a lasting positive narrative rather than focus on selection failure.

What took place

Ashley wrote a 600-word reflective article about her career and the move to a coaching role. The PL practitioner worked with the athlete to think specifically about her experiences, and the sport psychologist supported by asking reflective questions such as:

- What did you learn?
- What was enjoyable?
- What personal qualities were developed during your career?

This article was published on the sport's website as an additional step toward Ashley feeling comfortable talking about her successes.

The impact of the work

After publication Ashley was asked about the process, specifically how it made her feel and what she got from it. She experienced a range of emotions when writing, including sadness that her career was coming to a close, frustration at not achieving some results and excitement for the future working within the sport she loved. More generally she expressed how the article prompted 1) reflections on her entire career, 2) celebrating her successes, 3) feeling at peace with her achievements and 4) gaining a sense of closure – allowing her to move on and look forward.

Understanding of the work

This activity was based upon literature which found that expressive writing and guided reflective practice can improve well-being, coping with emotional upheavals and self-awareness (Hudson & Day, 2012; Neil, Cropley, Wilson, & Faull, 2013; Pennebaker, 2016). Furthermore, reflexivity is clearly fostered through the writing (c.f. Kaufman, 2013), and similar approaches exploring values and strengths are common practice in coaching psychology and positive psychology coaching (Linley et al., 2010). Yet most importantly, the impact of this work is evidenced by the athlete's positive reaction to the process at the time and now, several years later: Ashley still feels it was beneficial and has since contributed to her coaching philosophy through sharing her knowledge with the athletes.

Chapter summary and thoughts on future research

This chapter has set out how PL is a complex and all-encompassing role which requires significant skill and adaptability from the practitioner in the fast-paced sector of high-performance sport. The swift evolution of the discipline now means practitioners are part of the multidisciplinary sport science and medicine team working to support the athlete as a person as well as to help them maximise their potential. Athletes will continue to face the challenge of managing their various commitments, making suitable lifestyle choices and transitioning to a new world after athletic retirement. Therefore, the discipline will continue to develop by drawing upon ideas, reflecting on examples and learning from positive psychology literature.

The greatest value for PL can now come from research in several distinct areas. First, there is a need for research which allows us to understand and overcome the barriers to having conversations about personal development earlier in an athlete's career. It is possible obsessive passion plays a role in this reluctance to engage with developmental activities not directly related to an individual's athletic role. Though many athletes relish being able to devote their time to performance, the result of not pursuing any other development makes the post–sport transition experience and transfer to the employment market very challenging. Second, the intense and demanding nature of elite sport will not abate; therefore, understanding well-being within stressful environments where there are high expectations will equip practitioners with knowledge about how to better support athletes and help them develop improved skills to manage a varied lifestyle. By exploring these two areas it will be possible to build upon current understanding and practice to target resources and adopt approaches which will support the duty of care responsibility owed to athletes as well as enhance their performance.

References

Aquilina, D. (2013). A study of the relationship between elite athletes' educational development and sporting performance. *The International Journal of the History of Sport*, 30(4), 374–392.

Ashfield, A., McKenna, J., & Backhouse, S. (2012). The athlete's experience of flourishing. *Qualitative Methods in Psychology Bulletin*, 14(2), Special Issue, 4–13.

Bundon, A. (Ed.). (2016). Para-athlete retirement: Insights, support, management. *Research Report. Prepared for the English Institute of Sport (Performance Lifestyle Division)*, The Peter Harrison Centre for Disability Sport, Loughborough University, Loughborough, February.

Carless, D., & Douglas, K. (2009). 'We haven't got a seat on the bus for you' or 'all the seats are mine': Narratives and career transition in professional golf. *Qualitative Research in Sport & Exercise*, 1(1), 51–66.

Carless, D., & Douglas, K. (2013). Living, resisting, and playing the part of athlete: Narrative tensions in elite sport. *Psychology of Sport and Exercise*, 14, 701–708.

Coakley, J. J. (1983). Leaving competitive sport: Retirement or rebirth? *Quest*, 35(1), 1–11.

Conzelmann, A., & Nagel, S. (2003). Professional careers of the German Olympic athletes. *International Review for the Sociology of Sport*, 38(3), 259–280.

Crewther, T. B., Cook, C., Cardinale, M., Weatherby, R. P., & Lowe, T. (2011). Two emerging concepts for elite athletes: The short-term effects of testosterone and cortisol on the neuromuscular system and the dose-response training role of these endogenous hormones. *Sports Medicine*, 41(2), 103–123.

Dacyshyn, A. (1999). When the balance is gone. In J. Coakley & P. Donnelly (Eds.), *Inside Sports* (pp. 214–222). London: Routledge.

Dodge, R., Daly, A. P., Huyton, J., & Sanders, L. D. (2012). The challenge of defining wellbeing. *International Journal of Wellbeing*, 2, 222–235.

Douglas, K., & Carless, D. (2006). Performance, discovery, and relational narratives among women professional tournament golfers. *Women in Sport and Physical Activity Journal*, 15(2), 14–27.

Erpič, C. S., Wylleman, P., & Zupančič, M. (2004). The effect of athletic and non-athletic factors on the sports career termination process. *Psychology of Sport and Exercise*, 5(1), 45–59.

Fredrickson, B. L. (2001). The role of positive emotions in positive psychology: The broaden-and-build theory of positive emotions. *American Psychologist*, 56(3), 218–226.

Gordon, S., & Gucciardi, D. F. (2011). A strengths-based approach to coaching mental toughness. *Journal of Sport Psychology in Action*, 2(3) 143–155.

Hill, R. W., Huelsman, T. J., & Araujo, G. (2010). Perfectionistic concerns suppress associations between perfectionistic strivings and positive life outcomes. *Personality and Individual Differences*, 48, 584–589.

Hudson, J., & Day, M. C. (2012). Athletes' experiences of expressive writing about sport stressors. *Psychology of Sport & Exercise*, 13, 798–806.

Huta, V., & Ryan, R. M. (2010). Pursuing pleasure or virtue: The differential and overlapping well-being benefits of hedonic and eudaimonic motives. *Journal of Happiness Studies*, 11, 735–762.

Kaufman, P. (2013). Scribo ergo cogito: Reflexivity through writing. *Teaching Sociology*, 41(1), 70–81.

Kerr, G., & Dacyshyn, A. (2000). The retirement experiences of elite, female gymnasts. *Journal of Applied Sport Psychology*, 12(2), 115–133.

Lavallee, D., & Coffee, P. (Eds.). (2016). *Game changers: Elite athletes as a model for employability potential*. Research Report for Dame Kelly Holmes Trust, London.

Linley, P. A., Nielsen, K. M., Gillett, R., & Biswas-Diener, R. (2010). Using signature strengths in pursuit of goals: Effects on goal progress, need satisfaction, and well-being, and implications for coaching psychologist. *International Coaching Psychology Review*, 5(1), 6–15.

Lundqvist, C. (2011). Well-being in competitive sports – The feel-good factor? A review of conceptual considerations of well-being. *International Review of Sport and Exercise Psychology*, 4, 109–127.

Lundqvist, C., & Raglin, J. S. (2015). The relationship of basic need satisfaction, motivational climate and personality to well-being and stress patterns among elite athletes: An explorative study. *Motivation and Emotion*, 39, 237–246.

Lundqvist, C., & Sandin, F. (2014). Well-being in elite sport: Dimensions of hedonic and eudaimonic well-being among elite orienteers. *The Sport Psychologist*, 28, 245–254.

Macdougall, H., O'Halloran, P., Sherry, E., & Shields, N. (2016). Needs and strengths of Australian Para-athletes: Identifying their subjective psychological, social, and physical health and well-being. *Sport Psychologist*, 30, 1–12.

Macdougall, H., O'Halloran, P., Shields, N., & Sherry, E. (2015). Comparing the well-being of Para and Olympic sport athletes: A systematic review. *Adapted Physical Activity Quarterly*, 32, 256–276.

Neil, R., Cropley, B., Wilson, K., & Faull, A. (2013). Exploring the value of reflective practice interventions within applied sport psychology: Case studies with an individual athlete and a team. *Sport & Exercise Psychology Review*, 9(2), 42–56.

Niederhoffer, K. G., & Pennebaker, J. W. (2002). Sharing one's story: On the benefits of writing or talking about emotional experience. In C. R. Snyder, & S. J., Lopez, (Eds.), *Handbook of Positive Psychology* (pp. 573–583). New York: Oxford University Press.

Pasupathi, M. (2001). The social construction of the personal past and its implications for adult development. *Psychological Bulletin*, 127(5), 651–672.

Pennebaker, J. (2016). Expressive writing. In R. J. Sternberg, S. T. Fiske, & D. J. Foss. (Eds.), *Scientists Making a Difference* (pp. 462–465). New York: Cambridge University Press.

Peterson, C., & Seligman, M. E. P. (2004). *Character Strengths and Virtues: A Handbook and Classification*. Washington, DC: American Psychological Association Oxford University Press.

Rogers, J. (2008). *Coaching Skills, a Handbook*. Maidenhead: Open University Press, McGraw Hill.

Ryan, R. M., & Deci, E. L. (2001). On happiness and human potentials: A review of research on hedonic and eudaimonic well-being. *Annual Review of Psychology*, 52, 141–166.

Ryff, C. D., Singer, B., & Love, G. D. (2004). Positive health: Connecting well-being with biology. *Philosophical Transactions of the Royal Society Biological Sciences*, 359, 1383–1394.

Smith, B., Hanrahan, S., Anderson, R., & Abbott, L. (2015). Predicting homesickness in residential athletes. *Journal of Clinical Sport Psychology*, 9, 138–155.

Smith, B. & Sparkes, A. C. (2009). Narrative inquiry in sport and exercise psychology: What can it mean, and why might we do it? *Psychology of Sport and Exercise*, 10(1), 1–11.

Sparkes, A. C. (1998). Athletic Identity: An Achilles' heel to the survival of self. *Qualitative Health Research*, 8(5), 644–664.

Stephan, Y., Bilard, J., Ninot, G., & Delignieres, D. (2003). Repercussions of transition out of elite sport on subjective well-being: A one-year study. *Journal of Applied Sport Psychology*, 15, 354–371.

Theberge, N. (2008). "Just a normal bad part of what I do": Elite athletes' accounts of the relationship between health and sport. *Sociology of Sport Journal*, 25, 206–222.

Wilding, A. J., Hunter-Thomas, L., & Thomas, R. (2012). Sacrifice: The lonely Olympic road. *Reflective Practice: International and Multidisciplinary Perspectives*, 13(3), 439–453.

Wylleman, P., & Lavallee, D. (2003). A developmental perspective on transitions faced by athletes. In M. Weiss (Ed.), *Developmental Sport Psychology* (pp. 503–524). Morgantown, WV: Fitness Information Technology.

17

EMBRACING POSITIVE PSYCHOLOGY IDEAS AND INTERVENTIONS WITHIN SPORT AND EXERCISE PSYCHOLOGY CONSULTANCY

Paul McCarthy

Introduction

The story of sport and exercise psychology over the past century presents itself in many chapters. These chapters resemble its parent discipline – psychology – though one could argue that sport and exercise psychology wields a varied ancestry, with forebears in physical education, sport sciences and psychology (e.g., Triplett, 1898), among others. This heritage offered diversity to the field though without a definitive home; sport and exercise psychology follows other fields (e.g., positive psychology) to lead its own. Such pragmatism served researchers and practitioners well, yet one cannot tell the story of sport and exercise psychology candidly without its own voice revealing its experiences, contributions and challenges.

Embracing positive psychology ideas and interventions within sport and exercise psychology consultancy seems sensible when we examine the goals of each field. The positive psychology movement studies "the conditions and processes that contribute to the flourishing or optimal functioning of people, groups, and institutions" (Gable & Haidt, 2005, p. 104) while those involved in sport and exercise psychology hold similar values with a common denominator: optimal functioning. For example, sport and exercise psychology textbooks present this idea of optimal functioning among the traditional interventions of goal setting, self-talk, mental imagery and relaxation. These interventions intend to improve the psychological well-being and performance of the individual. Other points of overlap and divide shall follow.

I organised this chapter to capture how we understand positive psychological interventions in sport and exercise settings. Sport and exercise psychology and positive psychology resemble sets of rail tracks built in parallel and crossing over. Though these tracks often lead people in different directions, their common goal remains to improve the lives of those who use them. I open this chapter by understanding the self and others as well as the need for positive change in our lives. Next I explore positive psychological interventions in sport and exercise psychology before examining how I embrace positive psychology ideas and interventions in private practice.

About me

I am a chartered sport and exercise psychologist with the British Psychological Society and a practitioner psychologist with the Health and Care Professions Council. My therapeutic style grew within the scaffolds of a humanistic perspective and matured on the foundations of person-centred therapy. I embroider my work (research and lecturing) and my life with positive psychological interventions. Many years ago I sketched a path toward self-compassion, gratitude, persistence, humility and curiosity. And because "there is nothing so practical as a good theory" (Lewin, 1951, p. 169), I walk the path to work and home again.

Championing the self and others

Involvement in sport and exercise offers an opportunity to peer inward to know oneself. It is an opportunity to choose optimism over pessimism; to recognise one's gains rather than one's losses; to rise each time you fall. And perhaps sport in particular does inherently offer such rewards though they remain clouded by performance and winning (Brady & Maynard, 2010). The athlete who trained all year to compete in her national championships crosses the line in fifth place, receives no medal, little praise and a related assumption that she has failed. Yet few recognise the gains made to achieve fifth place. In her commitment to training, discipline in diet and deserting other pursuits in the hunt for objective success, she finds a reason to train and loses the reasons for training. The precepts from positive psychological interventions ask us to see the picture in front of us with different eyes. Sport and exercise appear as visual and cognitive illusions – some of us see a positive and optimistic sketch while others see a negative and pessimistic one or somewhere in between. But as meaning-making machines we can choose to see ourselves as chessboards (Hayes, Strosahl, & Wilson, 1999) filled with possibilities.

Positive psychology represents the science of positive aspects of human life, including happiness, optimism and flourishing. Whilst important to sport and exercise, positive experiences, attributes and behaviours such as positive emotion, flow, hope, optimism and flourishing relationships are (except for flow) only just emerging within the research landscape. This broad perspective on human flourishing ought to be maintained lest we fall into the trap of seeking only one goal (e.g., to be happy). To explain, from Aristotle to the Dalai Lama, a singular, resonating precept suggests that the purpose of life is to be happy.

This suggestion appears reasonable but it does fall foul to the mistake of monism, in which one reduces all human motives to just one. This parsimonious view might unreasonably lessen the variables to so few that we lose its richness (Gernert, 2007; Seligman, 2011b).

Happiness, its pursuit and scope, might unduly persuade readers that positive psychology offers little depth – its critics arguing that it is nothing more than happiology (Joseph, 2015). But positive psychology offers depth and a counterargument to the notion of happiology because it developed beyond joy and pleasure toward meaning and purpose. The conduits with humanistic psychology revealed themselves over the past decade, and the pioneers of humanistic psychology such as Maslow (1968) and Rogers (1963) had the same goals in mind – as had philosophers such as Aristotle epochs before them.

But what good is it to be happy? Happy people are likely to be successful and accomplished across several life domains (Lyubormirsky, King, & Diener, 2005). In Lyubormirsky et al.'s view, success not only leads to happiness but happiness also stimulates success. In a broader sense, positive affect relates to characteristics such as confidence, optimism, self-efficacy, prosocial behaviour, effective coping strategies and sociability activity. Together, these attributes involve the person, other people and the environment interacting to fulfil precise goals. Sport and exercise settings integrate the person, other people and the environment to meet subjective (e.g., improve one's physical fitness) and objective (e.g., win a championship) goals. This rich texture is the foundation on which we erect positive change in our lives.

A need for positive change

One's tendency toward positivity, hope, optimism/pessimism and resilience augur success in everyday life and in sport and exercise settings. Critically, we can develop these characteristics through informal and formally derived strategies to support growth and well-being. Positive psychological interventions are a new wave of intervening to enhance and fulfil people's lives. Indeed our mental health and primary and secondary prevention are critical aspects of our research and professional practice. Evidence-based interventions and non-evidence-based interventions are vital to people involved and those considering participating in sport and exercise. Some evidence-based interventions from the positive psychology movement relate to gratitude visits, finding three good things in one's life, random acts of kindness, active-constructive responding, identifying signature strengths, savouring, best possible self, positive reminiscence and exercise. Certain untested interventions involve giving time, writing a life summary and worry reduction. Positive change is also part of counselling and coaching therapy, which applies to sport, education and business (Seligman, 2011a). Many of these positive psychological interventions occur organically in sport and exercise settings especially through interaction with coaches, teams and exercise groups (e.g., giving time, identifying signature strengths and best possible self).

Challenges we experience in life overflow in sport and exercise contexts. Whereas optimists label their problems as local and temporary, pessimists label their problems as lasting and inescapable. But people, in general, present an optimistic bias in their thoughts and actions. They overestimate their prospects for professional achievement; they miscalculate their lifespan and expect to be healthier than the average person and more successful than their peers. They hugely underestimate their likelihood of divorce, cancer and unemployment (Sharot, 2011). Given the plentiful challenges inherent in sport and exercise contexts and the meritocracy in exercise and (some) sports, one needs an optimistic outlook. Resilience lies at the heart of much human striving because it captures persisting in the face of challenges and bouncing back from adversity (Seligman, 2011a).

Several factors contribute to one's resilience such as close relationships, effective problem-solving, empathy, faith, flexibility, impulse control, optimism, self-efficacy, sense of meaning and spirituality (Masten & Reed, 2002). What appears most sustaining about resilience lies not in the fact that it is one's ability but rather that many aspects of it are teachable. If components of resilience are teachable, then we can all benefit. Recently, Fletcher and Sarkar (2016) presented an evidence-based approach to develop psychological resilience for sustained success. They outlined and explained the construct with a training programme and how to implement it. These developments in a sporting context propose that although sport engenders resilience in some people, others can learn from and harness their experiences. To imagine success in the future, for example, one needs a system that amenably reconstructs novel scenarios, sifts through old memories (e.g., peak performances in a national competition) and binds them with something new (e.g., a future peak performance at the Olympics) to create scenes that have not happened yet. Brain-imaging studies show that the same brain structures that are activated when we recollect our past are called upon when we think about the future (Addis, Wong, & Schacter, 2007). Our optimistic brain tends toward optimistic potentialities (Sharot, 2011). Sport performers, in their quest for a psychological advantage over opponents, lean on imagery to achieve these benefits (Morris, Watt, & Spittle, 2005). Interventions such as imagery have a long history in sport and exercise settings, illustrating the constructive interventions that already exist in sport and exercise psychology.

Positive psychological interventions in sport and exercise psychology

With most of our training as sport and exercise psychologists emerging from academic institutions, it seems reasonable to expect that science-based tools forge the strongest influence on our professional practice. Positive psychological interventions (PPIs; Parks & Schueller, 2014) efficaciously increase happiness and decrease depressive symptoms, but most of these studies emerge from lab settings. Although these studies maximise experimental control, applying these interventions in the real world means learning about how to best disseminate such interventions among the caprices of everyday life. We are taking this step in sport and exercise contexts. One could argue that this step has been taken many years ago through the self-help process where people self-administer psychology to succeed in sport and exercise settings by reading books and watching videos. Regrettably, we know little about the value of these activities in sport and exercise settings; however, compelling evidence does exist among other therapeutic approaches in general. For example, cognitive behavioural therapy (CBT)-based self-help books for reducing depressive symptoms can produce a long-lasting improvement for depression (Gregory, Schwer Canning, Lee, & Wise, 2004).

Sport and exercise psychologists tend to work with those who choose to work with them. This voluntary starting point encourages choice and volition on the part of the client. Yet it would be folly to assume that PPIs work well for all. Although research supports how well PPIs work for some individuals, they do not work for others (Sergeant & Mongrain, 2011). In sport and exercise settings, this person-activity fit ought to account for the person (e.g., personality type), environment (e.g., amateur, professional) and task (e.g., on-court or off-court) to realise its potential. The formulation, administration and evaluation of each intervention will bring us closer to a better understanding of the efficacy and effectiveness of these positive psychological interventions.

Although book-based interventions present dedicated skills and guidance for integrating these skills into one's life, web-based interventions can offer these advantages and even more facilities and support. Seligman, Steen, Park, and Peterson (2005) presented one of the earliest accounts of web-based PPIs in which they examined the efficacy of individual happiness activities via an online intervention. This intervention, and others since 2005 (e.g., Schueller & Parks, 2012), are user-driven. Participants receive instructions and follow them in their daily lives. A level of customisation and flexibility in delivery and feedback seems necessary for continued involvement and adherence. Cobb and Poirier (2014) reported that users participating in the website fared better than an information-only control group on measures of overall well-being such as emotional health, work satisfaction, physical health and general life evaluation.

Recently Lane et al. (2016) developed 12 brief psychological interventions for online delivery in conjunction with BBC Lab UK. The researchers delivered interventions to 44,742 participants using video recordings and captured data using self-report measures. The participants competed in a concentration task against an individually matched computer opponent. The researchers used imagery, self-talk and if-then planning with each skill directed toward one of four different conditions: outcome goal, process goal, instruction or arousal-control, creating 12 different intervention participation groups and a thirteenth group as a control. Performance improved following practice with incremental effects for imagery-outcome, imagery-process, self-talk outcome and self-talk process over the control group. The results of the study suggest that online interventions for teaching psychological skills have utility. Also, brief interventions can effectively increase motivation, arousal, effort and pleasant emotions.

The Lane et al. (2016) study presents at least two principles to other researchers in the field. It holds a conceptual base in scientific literature and aims to demonstrate efficacy through controlled research trials acknowledging the challenges of real-world research. This study begins to show that brief psychological interventions delivered online can be exported to real-world practice. The marriage of technology (e.g., Fitbit) with guidelines for one's psychological health and well-being (e.g., goal setting to manage stress) could present convincing evidence to the user to show how exercise changes one's mood or improves one's sleep pattern.

Positive psychological interventions tend to encourage change from the "shoulders up", but the evidence from the physical activity and mental health literature endorses a holistic appreciation of psychological well-being (especially connecting with others and behaving/noticing differently). Academic textbooks by Carless and Douglas (2010) and Clow and Edmunds (2013) illustrate not only substantial growth in the study of physical activity and mental health but also its reception in sport, education and the community (Faulkner, Hefferon, & Mutrie, 2015). The accumulated research literature argues that physical activity helps to (a) prevent mental health problems, (b) serve as a treatment for existing mental illnesses, (c) improve one's quality of life and (d) promote psychological well-being. Physical activity, therefore, serves in prevention and treatment: preventing poor mental health and treating existing mental health challenges; however, one needs to participate in physical activity for these mental and physical health benefits to ensue.

Many people seek to "feel better now". Exercise helps people to feel better now and in the long run (pardon the pun). This flush of positive emotions from engaging in physical activity forms a central pillar for one to flourish (Seligman, 2011b). Meta-analytic support illustrates how physical activity meets one's need to "feel good" through acute (Reed & Ones, 2006) and regular (Reed & Buck, 2009) aerobic physical activity. When we peer beyond these results to the mechanisms to explain the benefits for one's mental health from physical activity, we find several possible answers ranging from biochemical changes (Dishman & O'Connor, 2009) to physiological changes and psychological changes (Hefferon & Mutrie, 2012). Hefferon and Mutrie (2012) argued that physical activity may foster the six main elements of Ryff and Singer's (1996, 2006) model of psychological well-being: enhancing self-acceptance, offering autonomy, gaining environmental mastery, fostering positive relationships, giving new purpose in life and overall personal growth.

In summary, by taking part in sport, exercise and physical activity, we engage in positive psychological interventions (directly and indirectly) as we navigate toward optimal functioning. The challenge remains, however, for sport and exercise psychologists to document through published research how exactly sport, exercise and physical activity achieves these goals and how these mechanisms work. Now, I show some positive psychological interventions undertaken in sport and exercise settings.

Changing thoughts and feelings, simply

If we accept the argument that our feelings are associated with specific behaviours (e.g., feeling sad and withdrawing from social interaction or feeling happy and seeking social interaction), would it be possible to change how one feels and by extension change our behavior in the short and long term? Perhaps the nuances of our daily lives (e.g., listening to music, securing a contract) serendipitously influence our mood. Mood states are cumulative, long-term emotional states that are usually positive (e.g., happy) or negative (e.g., sad), though not exclusively (Robinson, Grillon, & Sahakian, 2012). Mood states influence our psychological and emotional well-being and specifically, cognitive functions such as our memory and our ability to plan (Mitchell & Phillips, 2007). Cumulatively, our mood and its effect on cognitive and emotional processes contribute to our overall clinical profile of mood disorders such as anxiety disorders and major depression. But what happens to our mood when we are exposed to music, film or recall from our own lives? These three procedures are used experimentally to induce emotion. Experimenters have successfully manipulated mood among participants using music, reading emotionally charged sentences (Velten mood induction) and recalling situations in their own lives in which they experienced a specific emotion (self-referential mood induction).

Robinson et al. (2012) have shown that such procedures reliably alter self-report measures of mood state corresponding to condition (e.g., positive, negative and neutral). Our simplest of actions can create the mood we seek. Even simply recalling those things in our lives for which we are grateful (i.e., gratitude) affects our mood profoundly. Chen and Kee (2008) explored gratitude and adolescent athletes' well-being using two cross-sectional studies. Study 1 examined the relationship between dispositional gratitude and well-being, with Study 2 researching the relationship between sport-domain gratitude and well-being. In Study 1, dispositional gratitude positively predicted team satisfaction and life satisfaction and negatively predicted athlete burnout. In Study 2, sport-domain gratitude positively predicted team satisfaction and negatively predicted athlete burnout. These initial findings suggest that gratitude and adolescent athletes' well-being are related. More recently, Chen and Wu (2014) examined whether gratitude enhances change in athletes' self-esteem. Athletes completed measures of gratitude, affective trust (i.e., confidence placed in another based on care and concern received) in the coach and self-esteem six months apart. Athletes with higher levels of gratitude increased their self-esteem over time when they had higher affective trust in their coaches.

Positive psychology in private practice

The bridge between positive psychological interventions and interventions commonly associated with sport and exercise psychology offers a useful starting point. Any study of a sport and exercise psychology textbook would convince most readers that interventions in sport psychology emerge from the traditional workhorses in the sport psychology canon: goal setting, self-talk, mental imagery and relaxation. The intervention (e.g., goal setting), therefore, rather than the client or psychologist, brings about noticeable change; however, this insouciance to thoroughly examine the professional practice landscape and evidence-based practice encourages "more of the same". My central argument here remains to capture the intervention and mode of intervention: what and how. "What" is the client bringing to the psychologist (e.g., thoughts, feelings, behaviours, and experiences), and "how" are we working together and making sense of what is happening between us? The practitioner plays a crucial role in the intervention process. Most psychologists work with a conceptual plan to make sense of this process. Such a plan helps us to understand our clients, what has been happening and what needs to happen next for the client to arrive at a fulfilling conclusion (Culley & Bond, 2011). In the next section, I present the "what" and "how" of positive psychological interventions in private practice.

Where to begin with a client?

Sport and exercise psychologists researching and practising in sport and exercise settings follow many personal and professional goals. This blend of goals varies according to the people and the sociocultural environments where they work. In practice, sport and exercise psychologists hold specific values and assumptions. These principles guide and inform our practice. For example, by telling my clients what to do, my actions reflect a belief that clients cannot choose for themselves and rely on experts for direction (Culley & Bond, 2011). Now, one recognises through one's actions which beliefs one holds. The athletes choosing to work with me as a psychologist present various issues. Yet, when I ask them how I can help, they expect that I provide schemes for coping or managing their issue(s). This endemic firmness resonates with most self-help books that seek to understand the issue presented and strategise to ease the distress. I hold various assumptions or guiding values but if I were not aware of them, they would not be open to challenge and change from my work with clients.

What do I believe in private practice?

Positive psychology embodies the science of positive aspects of human life such as happiness, well-being and flourishing (Boniwell, 2008). These principles of positive psychology run throughout my practice yet are tempered too. I hold various assumptions that guide and inform my practice. They are the pillars I recognise amidst the muddle of professional practice. For instance, I assume that people create their own meaning; they have the capacity for change; they have a wish to realise their potential; and they deserve respect and understanding as people. These principles guide and inform my practice, and I embody these principles in my actions and how I work.

Though the confines of this chapter preclude an extensive examination of positive psychological interventions, I am drawn to a place for self-compassion. Images from television of professional sport swamp us in power displays, prominence and dominance – to the victor go the spoils. The notion of compassion has its place yet the persuasive "win at all cost" attitude spares precious time for compassion. Self-compassion, "a basic kindness with a deep awareness of suffering of oneself and others" (Gilbert, 2009, p. xiii), seems an odd notion to encourage among athletes. But when we examine the engine of self-compassion, we unveil several benefits such as an increase in optimism, social connectedness and resilience against depression and anxiety. Personal and professional faults scar the sporting landscape. Yet realising and accepting one's faults are a precondition for compassionate care. In an odd way, the sport psychologist also benefits from an awareness of self-compassion. In psychotherapy, self-critical therapists with limited self-compassion are also critical of patients and show poorer patient outcomes (Henry, Schacht, & Strupp, 1990).

On helping Graeme

I arranged to meet a client, Graeme, at a café near his training facility. I bought a coffee and sat in the café waiting for Graeme. When he arrived he shook my hand, asked if he could get me another coffee and if I wanted something to eat. He seemed as polite and genuine as everyone said. He began to speak about himself and his golf. He spoke harshly about his golf game yet compassionately about himself. He rarely "let me in" to the conversation so I encouraged him to take his time and stay with some of the points he raised. For example, he explained "I'm my own worst enemy in golf" and felt "there must be another way to play the game". Then he sprung to other points about his coaching, practice and travel. The disjointed story betrayed his turbulent thoughts. Golf on tour had become a runaway train passing through familiar stations, but he was unable to alight. I felt an uneasiness listening to Graeme, as if I were bounced into his world and caught in the storm. I tried earnestly to draw myself back to make sense of Graeme's story without the interview appearing stilted and contrived. I leant heavily on restating, paraphrasing and summarising to stay with Graeme's frame of reference lest my culture, values and personal issues draw an external frame of reference for the interview. In other words, my need for order and structure often seeps out, tapping the client on the shoulder: "By the way, here's how you should live your life".

Graeme: I feel I should have done better by now. Players I played against and beat at amateur level are doing better than me now. They've risen and not missed a step.

Me: You're comparing your achievements as a professional with other professionals and concluding you're behind.

Graeme: Yes. They've won tournaments and got more money in the bank. But it's not like I haven't been successful – I'm doing well for myself (sounding downbeat).

Me: You sound sad. You seem to be saying, "I've achieved but it's just not good enough".

Graeme: Everyone knows I should have done better by now. Still, you see where I've come from, my background and how I got to this point – not easy, you know?

Me: You're annoyed because you've had to get here the hard way, and others have had it easy.

Graeme: Of course, I am. I was stacking shelves three years ago. I didn't get any support. Hard graft has got me here, not like some others.

Me: You resent the help others were given ahead of you.

Paraphrasing helped to bring Graeme to express his feelings. I followed Graeme's story to communicate my understanding rather than fall into the argument. I felt I needed to match the depth of feeling expressed by the client and preserve congruence rather than feigning understanding.

Graeme: I'm used to people telling me what to do – my swing coach, my putting coach, my strength and conditioning coach. But you're telling me to make my own choices. How does that work?

Me: I have my beliefs and basic assumptions that I follow in my work. One of my basic assumptions is that people are capable of making their own choices. They don't need an expert to guide them all the time. Another of my assumptions is that people are capable of change. Given the right supportive environment, people can realise the changes they wish to make without ridicule or rejection. I also believe that people work harder to achieve the goals they value rather than ones set for them. We're trying to find those goals. These are my assumptions – they are open to challenge and change.

Graeme: I see where you are coming from now. My girlfriend calls it "choosing from the menu". When we sit in a restaurant choosing from the menu there are no right or wrong options – it's just what works for you – a compassionate way of looking after yourself.

Me: Self-compassion.

Graeme: You know that's funny – self-compassion. And it also shows that I'm not always ready to hear what people say, especially on the golf course. You see, an older Tour player said to me a few times recently, "Try to be a little kinder to yourself on the golf course". I thought it was odd because I didn't understand how you win or get better by being nice to yourself; but I think I do now – I'm pretty good with other people – I handle them gently, so why not me?

Graeme's need for success overwhelmed him on the golf course. One mistake often unlocked a cascade of further mistakes when his round tumbled into free fall. These moments seemed unstoppable and degraded his tee shots because he bore little confidence in where the ball might land. Our interview stumbled upon self-compassion, and Graeme recognised it plainly. He also recognised that kindness and humanity are vital when he fails or feels inadequate. Self-compassion became a significant theme of our work together.

In summary, positive psychology interventions (i.e., treatments or intentional activities) aim to nurture positive feelings, behaviors and cognitions. The intervention through which Graeme's awareness emerged was open dialogue, in a face-to-face meeting with a foundation of unconditional positive regard, close attending and paraphrasing to facilitate interpretation. We worked together to cultivate these positive feelings, behaviors and cognitions. Graeme also began to use his signature strengths (e.g., compassion) in a new way with himself as well as with others (Seligman et al., 2005). He replayed positive experiences and self-monitored instances of happiness and well-being (all of which raise happiness and lower depression) (Fava, Rafanelli, Cazzaro, Conti, & Grandi, 1998). Not only was positive psychology running through the intervention but also through our relationship in our work together.

Conclusion

Sport and exercise psychology travels in the same direction as positive psychology. Not only do we value well-being and performance, but also we teach sensible ways to engage in sport and exercise (Turner, 2014; Turner, Slater, & Barker, 2014). Grit, character and achievement pervade sport; those in sport recognise the virtues of self-control and self-discipline. Those in sport and exercise search for good things, and inspire themselves and others. We unveil the virtues of sport and exercise slowly because we appreciate the drawbacks (e.g., injuries, concussion, emotional disturbances, cheating and drug and alcohol abuse). Yet the benefits outweigh the costs. What we in sport and exercise settings have forgotten to do is to distil what sport and exercise encourages us to do: to seek happiness, flow, hope and optimism; to develop positive traits and a positive self to cope with change; and to build positive relationships, bringing these strengths to bear within our challenges.

References

Addis, D. R., Wong, A. T., & Schacter, D. L. (2007). Remembering the past and imagining the future: Common and distant neural substrates during event construction and elaboration. *Neuropsychologia*, 45(7), 1363–1377. doi:10.1016/j.neuropsychologia.2006.10.016.

Boniwell, I. (2008). *Positive Psychology in a Nutshell* (2nd ed.). London: PWBC.

Brady, A., & Maynard, I. (2010). At an elite level the role of a sport psychologist is entirely about performance enhancement. *Sport & Exercise Psychology Review*, 6(1), 59–66.

Carless, D., & Douglas, K. (2010). *Sport and Physical Activity for Mental Health*. Oxford: Wiley-Blackwell.

Chen, L. H., & Kee, Y. H. (2008). Gratitude and adolescent athletes' well-being. *Social Indicators Research*, 89(2), 361–373.

Chen, L. H., & Wu, C. (2014). Gratitude enhances change in athletes' self-esteem: The moderating role of trust in coach. *Journal of Applied Sport Psychology*, 26(3), 349–362.

Clow, A., & Edmunds, S. (Eds.). (2013). *Physical Activity and Mental Health*. Champaign, IL: Human Kinetics.

Cobb, N. K., & Poirier, J. (2014). Effectiveness of a multimodal online well-being intervention: A randomized controlled trial. *American Journal of Preventive Medicine*, 46, 41–48.

Culley, S., & Bond, T. (2011). *Integrative Counselling Skills in Action* (3rd ed.). London: Sage.

Dishman, R. K., & O'Connor, P. J. (2009). Lessons in exercise neurobiology: The case of endorphins. *Mental Health and Physical Activity*, 2(1), 4–9.

Faulkner, G., Hefferon, K., & Mutrie, N. (2015). Putting positive psychology into motion through physical activity. In S. Joseph (Ed.), *Positive Psychology in Practice: Promoting Human Flourishing in Work, Health, Education, and Everyday Life* (2nd ed.). Hoboken, NJ: John Wiley & Sons, Inc. doi:10.1002/9781118996874.ch12.

Fava, G. A., Rafanelli, C., Cazzaro, M., Conti, S., & Grandi, S. (1998). Well-being therapy: A novel psychotherapeutic model for residual symptoms of affective disorders. *Psychological Medicine*, 28, 475–480.

Fletcher, D., & Sarkar, M. (2016). Mental fortitude training: An evidence-based approach to developing psychological resilience for sustained success. *Journal of Sport Psychology in Action*, 7(3), 135–157.

Gable, S. L., & Haidt, J. (2005). What (and why) is positive psychology? *Review of General Psychology*, 9, 103–110.

Gernert, D. (2007). Ockham's razor and its improper use. *Journal of Scientific Exploration*, 21, 135–140.

Gilbert, P. (2009). *The Compassionate Mind*. London: Constable & Robinson Ltd.

Gregory, R. J., Schwer Canning, S., Lee, T. W., & Wise, J. C. (2004). Cognitive bibliotherapy for depression: A meta-analysis. *Professional Psychology: Research and Practice*, 35, 275–280.

Hayes, S. C., Strosahl, K. D., & Wilson, K. G. (1999). *Acceptance and Commitment Therapy: An Experiential Approach to Behaviour Change*. New York: Guilford Press.

Hefferon, K., & Mutrie, N. (2012). Physical activity as a "stellar" positive psychology intervention. In E. Acevedo (Ed.), *Oxford Handbook of Exercise Psychology* (pp. 117–128). Oxford: Oxford University Press.

Henry, W. P., Schacht, T. E., & Strupp, H. H. (1990). Patient and therapist introject, interpersonal process, and differential psychotherapy outcome. *Journal of Consulting and Clinical Psychology*, 58(6), 768.

Joseph, S. (2015). Applied positive psychology 10 years on. In S. Joseph (Ed.), *Positive Psychology in Practice: Promoting Human Flourishing in Work, Health, Education and Everyday Life* (2nd ed.). Hoboken, NJ: John Wiley & Sons.

Lane, A. M., Totterdell, P., MacDonald, I., Devonport, T. J., Friesen, A. P., Beedie, C. J., Stanley, D., & Nevill, A. (2016). Brief online training enhances competitive performance: Findings of the BBC Lab UK psychological skills intervention study. *Frontiers in Psychology*, Retrieved from http://journal.frontiersin.org/article/10.3389/fpsyg.2016.00413/full [Accessed 10.02.17].

Lewin, K. (1951). *Field Theory in Social Science: Selected Theoretical Papers*. New York: Harper & Row.

Lyubormirsky, S., King, L., & Diener, E. (2005). The benefits of frequent positive affect: Does happiness lead to success? *Psychological Bulletin*, 131(6), 803–855. doi:10.1037/0033-2909.131.6.803.

Lyubormirsky, S., King, L., & Diener, E. (2005). The benefits of frequent positive affect: Does happiness lead to success? *Psychological Bulletin*, 131(6), 803–855. doi:10.1037/0033-2909.131.6.803.

Maslow, A. H. (1968). *Toward a Psychology of Being* (2nd ed.). New York: Van Nostrand Reinhold.

Masten, A. S., & Reed, M. G. J. (2002). Resilience in development. In C. R. Snyder & S. J. Lopez (Eds.), *Handbook of Positive Psychology* (pp. 74–88). New York: Oxford University Press.

Mitchell, R. L., & Phillips, L. H. (2007). The psychological, neurochemical and functional neuroanatomical mediators of the effects of positive and negative mood on executive functions. *Neuropsychologia*, 45(4), 617–629.

Morris, T., Watt, A. P., & Spittle, M. (2005). *Imagery in Sport*. Champaign, IL: Human Kinetics.

Parks, A. C., & Schueller, S. M. (2014). *The Wiley-Blackwell Handbook of Positive Psychological Interventions*. Oxford: Wiley-Blackwell.

Reed, J., & Buck, S. (2009). The effect of regular aerobic exercise on positive-activated affect: A meta-analysis. *Psychology of Sport and Exercise*, 10(6), 581–594.

Reed, J., & Ones, D. S. (2006). The effect of acute aerobic exercise on positive activated affect: A meta-analysis. *Psychology of Sport and Exercise*, 7(5), 477–514.

Robinson, O. J., Grillon, C., & Sahakian, B. J. (2012). The mood induction task: A standardized, computerized laboratory procedure for altering mood state in humans. *Protocol Exchange*, Retrieved from www.nature.com/protocolexchange/protocols/2336, [Accessed 10.02.17].

Rogers, C. R. (1963). The concept of the fully functioning person. *Psychotherapy: Theory, Research and Practice*, 1, 17–26.

Ryff, C. D., & Singer, B. H. (1996). Psychological well-being: Meaning, measurement, and implications for psychotherapy research. *Psychotherapy and Psychosomatics*, 65, 14–23.

Ryff, C. D., & Singer, B. H. (2006). Best news yet for the six-factor model of psychological wellbeing. *Social Science Research*, 35, 1103–1119.

Schueller, S. M., & Parks, A. C. (2012). Disseminating self-help: Positive psychology exercises in an open online trial. *Journal of Medical Internet Research*, 14, e63.

Seligman, M. (2011a). *What You Can Change . . . and What You Can't*. London, UK: Nicholas Brealey Publishing.

Seligman, M. (2011b). *Flourish*. London, UK: Nicholas Brealey Publishing.

Seligman, M. E. P., Steen, T. A., Park, N., & Peterson, C. (2005). Positive psychology progress: Empirical validation of interventions. *American Psychologist*, 60, 410–421.

Sergeant, S., & Mongrain, M. (2011). Are positive psychology exercises helpful for people with depressive personality styles? *Journal of Positive Psychology*, 6(4), 260–272.

Sharot, T. (2011). *The Optimism Bias*. New York: Pantheon Books.

Triplett, N. (1898). The dynamogenic factors in pacemaking and competition. *American Journal of Psychology*, 9, 507–533.

Turner, M. J. (2014). Smarter thinking in sport. *The Psychologist*, 27(8), 596–599.

Turner, M. J., Slater, M. J., & Barker, J. B. (2014). Not the end of the world: The effects of rational emotive behavior therapy on the irrational beliefs of elite academy athletes. *Journal of Applied Sport Psychology*, 26(2), 144–156.

18

COACHING THE COACHES

Appreciative reflection and appreciative inquiry in the development of sport coaches

Liam McCarthy and Abbe Brady

Introduction

Sports coaching is a complex and dynamic endeavour occuring in an ever changing open-system (Jones, 2006; Piggott , 2015a). North (2017) captures the manifold
nature of coaching in his definition, 'sport coaching has depth, is embedded, complex and contextual, is goal-orientated, resource dependent, involves/engages with
reasoning, reflecting, strategizing and produces outcomes'. When the complexity
of coaching is recognised, the value of supporting coach learning through challenge setting and reflective practice (RP) is particularly salient. RP is particularly
important for coaches' development when we recognise that effective coaching is
'a never ending process of learning, discovery, and self-transformation' (Denison &
Avner, 2011, p. 224).

Whilst the importance of RP for learning and development has been acknowledged (Bolton, 2014; Schön, 1983) and it is now embedded in many formal coaching qualifications (Cropley, Miles, & Peel, 2012; Knowles, Borrie, & Telfer, 2005;
Nelson & Cushion, 2006), issues abound about how best to respectfully introduce
and support quality RP without it becoming overly academic, depersonalised,
prescriptive and/or process driven. Paradoxically perhaps, those of us who are
involved in supporting RP among coaches need to recognise the deeply personal
nature of authentic RP and thus guard against being too wed to set ideas about
'how to do RP', as sometimes prescribed. A case in point may be that we assume
RP is something to be stimulated by a problem situation, an error or a weakness
within our practice as coaches. Though understandable from an evolutionary perspective (since we are primed to attend to problems first), to routinely or exclusively use RP to identify or resolve only our 'deficits' may lead us to ignore the
rich opportunity to learn from and further develop aspects of our own (or others')
effective practice or 'assets'. Just as problem situations are stimuli for reflection,

so too can reflection be stimulated from situations in which we are effective or successful.

Appreciative Inquiry (AI, Cooperrider & Srivasta, 1987) is a specific change methodology based on identifying strengths and assets and considering what went well. Though barely present within the sports coaching literature, we propose that it has much to offer coach development. This chapter presents ideas and activities informed by AI to illustrate how adopting an appreciative approach in reflective practice can provide new insights, meaningful outcomes and motivation for coach learning and development. Examples are drawn from a range of coach development contexts including early-career, highly experienced and high-performance coaches.

Coaching practice and roadmaps

When coaching is the territory we seek to understand, any model of coaching can be viewed as a map, that is, one version of particular aspects of the territory. In this sense, research can be viewed as a process of map-making, though we should recognise that research can never exhaust practice, that is, the map can never fully capture the reality of the territory because it is always a simplified representation. At best, research provides glimpses of practice (territory) generated from the inquirer's chosen gaze. As North (2017) argues, 'No outside knowledge base or distant organisation or stakeholder, can account for the uniqueness of the contextual conditions in the coaching moment'. In field settings such as the sports-coaching arena, too many variables are at play to even contemplate seeking the type of protocol or control we may exhibit in a laboratory.

Although all of this sounds very daunting, we should welcome this exploration of complexity. Acting as roadmaps for the vast and unforgiving sports-coaching terrain, models and frameworks can support coaches in sense-making to inform better, more appropriate decisions by guiding planning and practice. Coaches (and coach developers) should use these with caution acknowledging that since models and frameworks are simplified representations of coaching, they are not to be taken literally.

The role of the coach (and coach developer)

It should be said at this stage that we need to remain aware of the impermanence of professional knowledge and be careful about how we privilege the content of today's coach development programs. With this in mind, as coach developers we must show intellectual humility through being appreciative of other ways and others' experiences of knowing, how knowledge is co-constructed (and sometimes co-constrained), and the broader perspective about who sets the agenda for coach development at the occupational and personal levels. Only when we realise all knowledge is fallible, temporary and partial (Popper, 1963) can we begin to appreciate the strengths and also the inevitable limitations of any framework or method in coach learning and development (including the ideas at the heart of this chapter).

In sport, a level of expectation exists that 'the coach knows', and this results in distorted conceptions of teaching and learning which infiltrate much of the culture and 'layered ecology' of sports coaching (North, 2016). When the coach is seen as the problem solver as opposed to a problem setter (though the coach could be both), coaches may unwittingly seek out ready-made solutions from coach education, and thus the problem perpetuates, as both coach, athletes and others expect the coach to have the answer. Therefore, it is suggested that a shared, developmental and humble approach to growth and development is required to support coaches to recognise the complexity of practice and that appreciative reflection may offer helpful alternative insights.

Emotions and reflection

Emotions influence our thinking, our decisions and our ways of relating (Isen, 2001; Dixon, Lee, & Ghaye, 2013) and as such, they can have considerable implications for various personal and interpersonal processes associated with coach learning and development. Though the immediate effects of negative emotions are linked with human survival, positive emotions also have evolutionary and developmental significance (Fredrickson, 2001). Positive emotions encourage environmental engagement, play and exploration through which knowledge and skills are acquired, and these physical, intellectual, social and psychological resources facilitate adaptive responses in challenging or uncertain situations.

Negative emotions (e.g. fear, anxiety, anger) elicit a narrowing or tunnel vision impact on cognition associated with a flight or fight response; this contrasts with the broadened attentional capacity elicited by positive emotion (e.g. joy, gratitude, awe) which leads to greater cognitive flexibility and creativity. Contemporary research shows that across many situations positive affect enhances memory, problem-solving, decision-making, creativity, flexible and efficient cognitive activity and, in terms of interpersonal behaviour, it promotes helping, generosity and interpersonal understanding (Isen, 2001; Fredrickson, 1998, 2001).

As well as influencing our learning experience, affective states, patterned thinking and relating responses can be contagious. Dixon et al. (2013) note that 'in coach education' understanding emotional contagion is important for two reasons. Firstly, it may contribute to explaining why some coaching/coach development activities are more/less effective, and secondly, it underpins the importance of adopting a positive stance in reflection. Thus, there is an opportunity for coach developers and coaches to consider the implications of emotions and their impact on cognitive efficiency, reflection, relating and learning as well as the potential for ripple effects in their own and others' developmental experiences. Based on what we know about the impact of positive emotions on thinking, adopting an appreciative stance to reflection may be a fruitful strategy.

Reflective practice and sports coaching

Much has been said in the literature (Huntley et al., 2014) over the past 30 years to emphasise the importance of RP as a mechanism for sense-making (if done well).

Many outcomes are attributed to RP, including acceptance of and confidence with the essential complexity of professional life; reflexive critique of the workplace and of one's self (e.g. values, assumptions, decision-making processes); identification of learning needs; development of observation and communication abilities; and emotional awareness and respect for others' feelings (Bolton, 2014). Further, RP is now seen as central to many National Governing Bodies' (NGB) coach education programs, Higher Education (HE) programs of study and other discreet professional development opportunities that exist within sports coaching. Though much has been written about the importance *of* RP, less has been said to help coaches or coach developers *with* RP (Piggott, 2015b).

In relation to coach education and assessment, Dixon et al. (2013) raise a concern about the tendency of RP to be a rationalistic performance review process which focuses on problems and which can neglect the emotional, relational or other human dimensions of experience. It is argued that a deficit/problem-based reflective process is questioned as simplistic because it assumes that 'by fixing and getting rid of performance problems, weaknesses and undesirable aspects of practice, individuals, teams and squads . . . will get better' (ibid, p. 589). In this chapter we propose using a more expansive and appreciative view of reflection which encourages curiosity and creativity so that we may better understand our achievements, successes and strengths.

Emergent literatures in positive psychology (PP) and AI describe how a 'strengths-based' perspective can identify and make explicit highly effective practice (Ghaye & Lee, 2016). Appreciating the 'best of what is' can be a powerful tool in creating behavior change and generating a commitment to 'what might be'. An appreciative approach provides new insights to success and presents itself as a more uplifting alternative to what may be perceived as 'fire-fighting' problems and attending only to deficits in practice.

Appreciative inquiry (AI) and sports coaching

As a methodology AI is based on understanding what contributes to success. Whilst most often used to introduce and implement change, AI can be adapted and used for other purposes such as to identify good practice, to gain alternative insights and for building morale. Contemporary applications of AI typically use a four-stage (4Ds) collective discovery process to 1) identify the best of what is (Discover), 2) develop a vision of what might be (Dream), 3) engage in shared discussion to decide on what should be (Design) and 4) engage in collective experimentation to reveal what can be (Deliver *or Destiny*), (Bushe, 2011; Cooperrider & Whitney, 2001; Pill, 2015).

Five guiding principles inform AI, and these have particular resonance for how we may embrace a more appreciative approach to reflection in coach development and coaching (adapted from Enright, Hill, Sandford, & Gard, 2014, p. 917):

1   Reality is socially constructed through language.
2   Change begins from the moment a question is asked.

3   Our choice of what we study determines what we discover.
4   Our image of the future shapes the present.
5   Positive questioning leads to positive change.

The principles of AI invite us to recognise we all have a potent capacity to direct our own (and others') discovery, and our choices and approaches to reflection will shape the things we will find. It may be helpful to consider how we presently communicate this potency and the possibilities of it among the coaches with whom we work. The AI principles also encourage us to notice and give credence to positive aspects of practice and the power of language, narrative and questioning for eliciting meaning and initiating change in coach development. We may wish to consider how we attend to our own use of language, narratives and questioning and for what (whose) purposes. Importantly, how, if at all, do we support coaches to recognise that focusing on their strengths and factors associated with success is also appropriate and tangible?

Enright et al. (2014) used AI to consider how change is managed and to generate new thinking based on eliciting some of the otherwise hidden stories of success in physical education. They found the value of AI was centred on open and flexible collaborative conversations which empower the participants to be the 'authors of change and the source of new directions' for inquiry (p. 912). Bertram, Culver, and Gilbert (2016) described how through the 4D cycle the principles of AI could facilitate coach learning by developing a more appreciative framework for coaching communities of practice. Dixon et al. (2013) described how as part of his preparation for Rugby World Cup success, Clive Woodward, then the England Head Coach, adopted an AI approach to understand what led to success because that was what he wanted to achieve.

Pill (2015) developed valuable insight about coaches' experiences of engaging in Game Sense (GS), though he noted achieving the fourth stage of 'deliver', that is, sustaining the change, was potentially unrealistic for the coaches because GS was not always going to be the most suitable pedagogical strategy. This raises the point about how we might usefully and flexibly engage with AI. Whilst usually presented as a four-stage process, value can be gained through using fewer stages as evident in Pill's study and through engaging with the principles of AI in other ways, as we illustrate in the next section.

Examples from practice

It is the aim of this chapter to provide context-rich examples, not with the intention of providing any 'best practice' or 'clean treatments', but to demonstrate what might be possible when our attention is shifted to new ideas. Appreciative RP and AI have been used to some extent in a variety of settings, with varying success. In line with the philosophy of the chapter, there are no silver bullets nor would any external body wish to direct you (the practitioner) in any singular direction without any knowledge of the multifarious contextual characteristics of the coaching situation.

However, these examples serve to platform ideas which have received less attention in the popular literature; you may or may not wish to consider them as 'useful'. Following, we share four contrasting examples drawn from our own experiences of using appreciative reflection and AI principles in coaching and coach development:

1 A sport non-governmental organization (NGO) seeking to operationalise an AI approach to coach development
2 A high-performance football coach working with university-level female footballers using several PP techniques to elicit appreciative reflection through technology
3 Research examining the impact of appreciative reflection among undergraduate sports-coaching students associated with envisioning their best future self as a coach
4 Highly experienced Level 4 (UK Coaching Certificate) coaches in a formal coach education event using an appreciative approach to explore a character strengths resource and its potential use in their own sports-coaching context

In recent years British Triathlon has sought to reimagine their coach development strategy to embody a more developmental, personally relevant and humble approach. Using AI techniques, appreciating the best of 'what is' and dreaming of 'what might be', the NGO reimagined coach development as a 'coach-first' endeavour. Coach developers were tasked with working with coaches at a personal level, to understand 'why' particular decisions were made and explore what other decisions 'could have been made', recognising that different 'things' work for different coaches, in different circumstances (Pawson, 2013). With this as an underpinning philosophy, coach developers made a shift from understanding coaches against a checklist of competencies (first and foremost), to understanding coaches for who they are, where they operate and why they might take particular courses of action (and not others). The recognition that coaches enter the coaching pathway with differing motivations, pre-existing (and deeply held) knowledge and experiences and with different needs, affords the coach developer an opportunity to take a more humanistic approach to development. The impact has been incredibly powerful.

Tony Jolly, lead coach developer, British Triathlon, noted:

A recent example saw a female coach experimenting with her coaching approach, adopting 'being an invisible coach' as her coaching strategy. The objective was about getting the athletes to communicate in a group riding situation. She did this by passing a message to individual athletes and getting them to control and manage the rest of the group. Her view being, if it was about the athletes' learning about communicating in a group, it made sense they did all the communicating. She realised that the thinking and planning beforehand therefore was the most important aspect, and when she was coaching it became easier to see important aspects developing and interject at important moments. She was clear afterwards that without the 'permission to fail' she had got from an educator she would have stuck to an 'old school' delivery approach.

Although powerful at the organisational and coach-developer layers of the sports coaching ecosystem, it is important to consider what this looks like and the potential for impact at the layer of coach and player. An appreciative approach to reflection was taken with a university women's football performance squad in 2016/17, during a British Universities and Colleges Sport (BUCS) Premier division, season-long campaign. Using web 2.0 technologies (Hudl, Agile Sports Technologies) the coach engaged players in an appreciative video feedback and review process using Google Forms (Google), ensuring this could be carried out remotely, when each individual player felt most comfortable. As a tool for RP and AI, Hudl allows players to rewatch, comment upon and make sense of performance (both their own and their teammates). Moving beyond performance analysis, Hudl affords coaches and players an opportunity to co-construct a positive narrative around practice.

Before the fixture, players were asked to complete a short paragraph in answer to the following questions:

- 'Expectations of myself tomorrow are . . .' (thoughts, behaviours/actions, what I think will happen in the game, how I expect to react, what strategies I'll use, what I hope to achieve)
- 'Expectations of the team tomorrow are . . .' (how will we play, will we achieve success, what does success look like)

The intention here was twofold: for players to envisage the best future for themselves and the team, and for the players to set expectations against which they could reflect post-game. Following the fixture, players were asked to complete questions linked to the GROW process (Whitmore, 2009):

- Goal(s) – What did you set out to achieve?
- Reality – What actually happened (tell me your story of the game)?
- Opportunities – Where the reality fell short of our goals (i.e. where we didn't do what we hoped to do), what opportunities have we got to put that right (i.e. what do we need to work on)?
- Will – "I will . . ." (What commitment will you make ahead of the next fixture?)

Outcomes of this process included players demonstrating a greater level of understanding (self, others and performance), feeling appreciated (valued for what they are doing) and seeing progression (unambiguous evidence of progress each week).

A study using the first two stages of AI (i.e. 'discover' and 'dream') involved undergraduate sports coaches (n=60) who engaged in a coach-development activity over two weeks requiring them to think about and envision their best future self (BFS) as a coach (Brady & Hughes, 2013). As well as enhancing the student-coaches' subjective well-being, thematic analysis of their written accounts highlighted how in articulating their 'dream' a successful coaching career comprised working in a *desired context, cultivating developmentally valuable qualities* and *positively influencing participant outcomes*. Consistent with contemporary theory about the longer-term effect of positive emotions, beyond the short-term elevation of subjective well-being, these coaches retained a motivating vision of an achievable future, which they reported aided them in thinking about and making decisions about purposeful developmental activities toward realising that desired career (dream).

An example of engaging with the discover stage of AI occurred during a formal coach education event as part of the UKCC Level 4 qualification (the highest recognised vocational coaching award in the UK). The aim of the hour-long unstructured session was to foster meaningful curiosity and creativity through an appreciative group discussion about character strengths. Seven highly experienced rowing and equestrian coaches were provided with strengths resource cards covering 24 character strengths from the Values-In-Action (VIA) strengths of Peterson and Seligman (2004) (see Workmad.co.uk for resource). None of the coaches had prior formal experience of the topic or the resource. Each card described a single character strength and using Linley's (2008) idea of the 'golden mean', the card stated how the strength might appear when used optimally, and also how it might appear when underplayed or overplayed. To kick-start the session the coach developer framed the session as a peer group discussion and posed the single question, 'In what ways might these strengths cards be of benefit to you?' The coach developer then became an observer and noted the following sequence of events: Coaches shared which strengths were most personally significant and discussed how they recognised particular strengths in others too, both in their coaching and personal lives (at times generating much humour). The notion of under- or overplaying a strength was considered particularly helpful and thought-provoking for noticing or not noticing how a particular strength may become too dominant, and whether and how strengths could be dialled up or down. Discussion moved on to considering a problem they (or other coaches) might encounter, in that reliance on just a few 'super' strengths might increase the risk of limiting one's behavioural repertoire. Coaches identified several ways that they could make use of the character strengths cards back in their respective coaching environments, including having their colleagues do exactly the same open activity; using it as a team-building activity; - a peer-review activity to identify one another's top strengths; and as a fun challenge to choose or have a strength chosen for you that you would have to use over a particular period.

Thinking about and using diverse strengths was viewed by coaches as quite liberating because it provided fresh and constructive ways of thinking about themselves (and others) and it seemed to suggest that strengths were amenable to change. Had the coach developer more formally led the session or frequently intervened, though some similar insights may have emerged in the moment, the experience may well have generated less enduring curiosity, personal meaning or appreciative reflection among the coaches. Coaches in the session were very experienced and had good rapport, and the learning climate was open and supportive, all of which were considered central to the highly personal and generative nature of this 'discovery' session.

A common thread throughout the chapter has been a call to action for policy architects, system builders and coach developers to present coach education and coach development as a more humanistic, positive and empowering experience. Coach educators and those charged with the development of coaches are encouraged to embrace an appreciative approach to explore practice with coaches, rather than prescribe strategies *for* practice, upfront. In doing so, RP will likely be an integral part of the process by identifying 'the best of what is', as a platform for enhancing practice further. We propose that new territories may be discovered when RP is framed appreciatively. Although the size of step-change will be different in each and every organisational or interpersonal scenario, some tentative solutions as to how this might be achieved are provided:

- Recognise and embrace sports coaching as a complex and contextual practice, which by its very nature, is challenging.
- Develop an environment where curiosity is valued, and an 'inquiry over advocacy' approach is demonstrated (e.g. What if? What could be? How can I help?).
- Acknowledge the impact of positive emotion on learning through broadening thought-action repertoires and building personal resources.
- Adopt an appreciative stance to reflection and learning, supporting coaches to notice the 'best of what is' and 'what might be' and recognise strengths through best past, present or future selves.
- Approach coach learning and the exploration of a range of coaching strategies with a level of humility and appreciation that what works with one coach under particular conditions will not necessarily work with another.
- Model an appreciative approach in our own reflection and learning.

Establishing an evidence base about participants' experiences and outcomes associated with adopting an appreciative stance is essential. We suggest that future research is also needed to generate insight about how acknowledging the role of positive emotion and appreciative reflection in coach learning and development may inform the practices of coach developers and coaches. Context-rich case studies would be particularly helpful for illuminating what an appreciative stance to coach development does, or could, look like in a variety of settings.

Although many of these ideas, committed to paper, appear appealing, ensuring such an approach manifests in practice is a challenge. A long history and tradition of education, preceding coach education, locates the educator as the knower of knowledge and the learner as passive recipient (often mirrored in coach and athlete relationships). This level of expectancy which still infiltrates coaching and coach education today may present challenges when experimenting with approaches such as those detailed in this chapter.

References

Bertram, R., Culver, D., & Gilbert, W. (2016). Using Appreciative Inquiry to create high-impact coach learning: Insights from a decade of applied research. *AI Practitioner*, 18(2), 59–65.

Bolton, G. (2014). *Reflective Practice: Writing and Professional Development*. London: Sage Publications.

Brady, A., & Hughes, S. (2013). *Exploring the impact of a best future-self intervention on the well-being of early career sport coaches: The mediating role of mindset*. Presentation at 3rd Biennial Meeting of the British Psychological Society's Division of Sport and Exercise Psychology, Manchester. December.

Bushe, G. R. (2011). Appreciative inquiry: Theory and critique. In: Boje, D., Burnes, B., and Hassard, J. (Eds.), *The Routledge Companion to Organizational Change*, (pp. 87–103). London: Routledge.

Cooperrider, D. L., & Srivastva, S. (1987). Appreciative inquiry in organizational life. *Research in Organizational Change and Development*, 1, 129–169.

Cooperrider, D. L., & Whitney, D. (2001). A positive revolution in change: Appreciative inquiry. *Public Administration and Public Policy*, 87, 611–630.

Cropley, B., Miles, A., & Peel, J. (2012). *Reflective Practice: Value, Issues, and Developments Within Sports Coaching*. Sports Coach UK Original Research. Leeds: SCUK.

Denison, J., & Avner, Z. (2011). Positive coaching: Ethical practices for athlete development. *Quest*, 63, 209–227.

Dixon, M., Lee, S., & Ghaye, T. (2013). Reflective practices for better sports coaches and coach education: Shifting from a pedagogy of scarcity to abundance in the run up to Rio 2016. *Reflective Practice*, 14(5), 585–599.

Enright, E., Hill, J., Sandford, R., & Gard, M. (2014). Looking beyond what's broken: Towards an appreciative research agenda for physical education and sport pedagogy. *Sport, Education and Society*, 19(7), 912–926.

Fredrickson, B. L. (1998). What good are positive emotions? *Review of General Psychology*, 2(3), 300–319.

Fredrickson, B. L. (2001). The role of positive emotions in positive psychology: the broaden-and-build theory of positive emotions. *American Psychologist*, 56(3), 218–226.

Fuller, A., Unwin, L., Felstead, A., Jewson, N., & Kakavelakis, K. (2007). Creating and using knowledge: An analysis of the differentiated nature of workplace learning environments, 33(5), 743–759.

Galvin, K., & Todres, L. (2007). The creativity of 'Unspecialization:' A contemplative direction for integrative scholarly Practice. *Phenomenology & Practice*, 1(1), 31–46.

Ghaye, T., & Lee, S. (2016). Bettering sport through appreciative lenses and practices. *AI Practitioner*, 18(2), 4–7.

Hill, P. C., & Sandage, S. J. (2016). The promising but challenging case of humility as a positive psychology virtue. *Journal of Moral Education*, 45(2), 132–146.

Huntley, E., Cropley, B., Gilbourne, D., Sparkes, A., & Knowles, Z. (2014). Reflecting back and forwards: An evaluation of peer-reviewed reflective practice research in sport. *Reflective Practice*, 15(6), 863–876.

Isen, A. M. (2001). An influence of positive affect on decision making in complex situations: Theoretical issues with practical implications. *Journal of Consumer Psychology*, 11(2), 75–85.

Jones, R. (2006). How can educational concepts inform sports coaching? In: Jones, R. (Eds.), *The Sports Coach as Educator: Reconceptualising Sports Coaching* (pp. 3–13). London: Routledge.

Knowles, Z., Borrie, A., & Telfer, H. (2005). Towards the reflective sports coach: Issues of context, education and application. *Ergonomics*, 48(11–14): 1711–1720.

Linley, A. (2008). *Average to A+: Realising Strengths in Yourself and Others*. Coventry: CAPP Press.

Nelson, L. J., & Cushion, C. J. (2006). Reflection in coach education: The case of the national governing body coaching certificate. *The Sport Psychologist*, 20(174), 174–183.

North, J. (2016). Benchmarking sport coach education and development: Using programme theories to examine and evolve current practice In W. Allison, A. Abraham, & A. Cale (Eds.), *Advances in Coach Education and Development* (pp. 17–29). London: Routledge.

North, J. (2017). *Sport Coaching Research and Practice: Ontology, Interdisciplinarity and Critical Realism.* London: Routledge.

Pawson, R. (2013). *The science of evaluation: A realist manifesto.* London: Sage Publications.

Peterson, C., & Seligman, M. E. P. (2004). *Character Strengths and Virtues: A Handbook and Classification.* Washington, DC: APA Press.

Piggott, D. (2015a). The Open Society and coach education: A philosophical agenda for policy reform and future sociological research. *Physical Education and Sport Pedagogy*, 20(3), 283–298.

Piggott, D. (2015b). An(other) conceptual model for coach learning. In *International Coaching Conference*, 9–10 September 2015, Manchester, Unpublished.

Pill, S. (2015). Using Appreciative Inquiry to explore Australian football coaches' experience with game sense coaching. *Sport, Education and Society*, 20(6), 799–818.

Popper, K. (1963). *Conjectures and Refutations: The Growth of Scientific Knowledge.* London: Routledge.

Schön, D. (1983). *The reflective practitioner: How professionals think in action.* London: Temple Smith.

Whitmore, J. (2009). *Coaching for performance: The principles and practices of coaching and leadership (people skills for professionals)* (4th ed.). London: Nicholas Brealey Publishing.

19

POSITIVE PSYCHOLOGY COACHING FOR SPORTS LEADERS

John M. Yeager and Kathryn H. Britton

Background

By working with an executive coach whose practice is informed by positive psychology, a sports leader can achieve greater clarity of purpose, greater capacity to lead others toward that purpose, and greater ability to manage self and others in the face of the complex challenges of modern sports.

What is coaching?

Within this chapter, the unmodified word *coaching* is used for executive or life coaching, not for athletic coaching. Coaches work with clients to help them understand and make progress toward important goals. In words taken from the International Coach Federation website, clients gain "fresh perspectives on personal challenges, enhanced decision-making skills, greater interpersonal effectiveness, and increased confidence" (International Coach Federation, n.d.).

Coaches are not teachers or consultants, but collaboration partners helping clients make sense of their own experiences. They listen closely both to what is said and what is not said, reflect back their perceptions to help clients understand themselves more clearly, ask questions that often elicit new ways to think about situations, help clients brainstorm next steps to move toward goals, and serve as accountability partners.

As Grant (2012) explains, a wide range of positive coaching outcomes are possible. He defines the four-quadrant well-being and engagement framework (WBEF), with well-being (high/low) as one dimension and engagement (high/low) as the other. Engagement refers to vigorous dedication to work. With the help of a positive psychology coach, leaders can increase the number of participants in their organizations that are high in both engagement and well-being. According to Grant, "Individuals in this area would be highly involved with and absorbed in their work, have a well-developed sense of work-related meaning and purpose and enjoy positive relations with work colleagues. In an organisational or workplace coaching context, this area may well represent the ideal (or target) state" (2012, p. 7).

What is positive psychology coaching?

According to Biswas-Diener and Dean, "positive psychology offers an answer to the call for an increased role of research in coaching" (2007, p. 5). Positive psychology coaches listen for strengths and assets that a client may not be aware of, reflect back what is going right, ask questions that elicit images of better futures, and help clients define action steps supported by well-being theories.

Theoretical underpinnings of positive psychology coaching (Passmore & Oades, 2014) include focusing on strengths, the broaden-and-build theory of positive emotions, self-determination theory, and the well-being theory defined by Martin Seligman (2011) and summarized by the acronym PERMA: that human well-being is based on positive emotions, engagement, positive relationships, meaning, and accomplishments.

Many aspects of positive psychology underlie coaching practices. In this chapter, we have selected four that make a difference to leaders of organizations: leading with a strong strategic narrative, building trust, enhancing psychological capital, and focusing on strengths.

Who are leaders in sports?

Sports leaders are the policy makers in a national governing body, general managers at the professional level, athletic directors in universities and secondary schools, or volunteer administrators at the local level. They are responsible for balancing the conflicting demands that affect the sport, managing challenges such as those described in the next section.

Every sports organization is a system that has its own unwritten rules and complex relationships. Webs of behavior determine how well the system works. Talking specific situations over with coaches can help sports leaders juggle conflicting requirements, establish priorities, treat people as individuals rather than machines, and deal effectively with conflicts.

To illustrate the topics in this chapter, John interviewed two leaders of national governing bodies: Scott Hallenbeck, the Chief Executive Officer (CEO) of USA Football, the organization that governs youth and amateur football and Steve Stenersen, the President and CEO of US Lacrosse. He also interviewed Brian Wylie, Athletic Director at Endicott College in Beverly, Massachusetts. We also draw on John's experiences collaborating with the high school athletic department at the Culver Academies in Indiana.

First we outline some of the key challenges faced by sports leaders. Then we explore ways that positive psychology coaching can help sports leaders bring the collective talents of their organizations together to meet the challenges.

Challenges

First let us explore some of the challenges that sports leaders face.

The Red Queen effect

In the sports world, nothing stands still. In 1954, Roger Bannister broke the impossible four-minute-mile barrier by six tenths of a second. Less than six weeks later, John Landy beat the new record by more than a second. Bannister's accomplishment not only cracked the mile time, but it also changed the belief system about human ability. In sport after sport, athletes are extending the boundaries of human performance. This is exciting for spectators, but it creates a Red Queen effect for athletes, the sense that they have to run as hard as they can to stay in one place. Leaders have the challenge of helping athletes and trainers face this reality with zest rather than discouragement, forestalling the temptation to resort to illegal steroids or other unhealthy ways to gain advantages.

The complexity of sports organizations: zero- and non-zero sum games

On the playing field, competitive sports appear to be zero-sum games with mutually exclusive goal attainment: for one participant to win, another must lose. Often the difference between winning and losing is very narrow. Reflecting on one-goal games, Dom Starsia, former University of Virginia's Men's Lacrosse coach, said, "What is the difference in play between the two teams? . . . those individual battles, deflecting a pass, making a save, etc., and one final shot determines the outcome" (Yeager, 2006). Starsia observed that the emotional response of winning can be miles apart from the response to losing.

At the same time, sports are non-zero sum endeavors (Wright, 2000) with complex collaboration both within organizations and between them to reach common goals such as entertaining and inspiring spectators. A team plays best against competitors with similar levels of skill where outcomes are uncertain. Actions that lead to safer practices and greater sportsmanship benefit both the winner and the loser of a particular match. The manager of Arsenal, a top-tier English football team, Arsène Wenger challenges his team to play a brand of football that is based on producing a "beautiful" style of play. According to Miller (2015), "It's his faith – his belief that there's a code of rightness other than success . . . that virtue, magic, and beauty might be more important than the trophy case."

Similarly, the production of a particular match relies on complex collaboration within and between the members of the participating organizations.

A game observed by spectators is the tip of the iceberg of the complex human endeavor of modern sports. For just a few of the activities that happen before a game begins, the venue has to be reserved and properly prepared, marketing and ticket sales are needed to fill the stands, and travel has to be arranged for away games. Sports leaders also manage product endorsements, team sponsorships, and postgame media contacts.

Safety challenges

With bigger, stronger, and faster athletes, there is an increasing occurrence of serious sports-related injuries, particularly brain injuries. For example, American football is not just a contact sport; it is a collision sport. Many sports have dangers of serious injuries that can affect the ongoing physical well-being of athletes and even the willingness of future athletes to participate in the sport.

Financial motivations that challenge sports cultures

Winning maintains spectator interest and loyalty, which stimulate attendance and revenue. Pope and Pope (2009) claim that a winning season brings college programs both significant revenue and substantially more applications for admission. Villanova University, winner of the National Collegiate Athletic Association (NCAA) Division 1 basketball championship in 2016, also reached the NCAA basketball tournament final round in 2009. That year, the university received free publicity valued at $6 million (Snyder, 2016).

If not controlled effectively by sports leadership, over-focus on winning can threaten the underlying culture of a sport. Stenersen (interview May 10, 2016) sums up the threats to the lacrosse culture: "The sport's growth has created a legitimate market that more and more people are trying to leverage into personal gain. A growing number of college recruiting services, private club programs, camps and tournaments, the sometimes 'false' promise of college scholarships a result of playing the game, along with a healthy dose of parental pride, have served as fuel for the growing trends we see in all youth sports today – sport specialization, poor sportsmanship, dishonesty, aggressive parental behavior, lapses in integrity and, ultimately, a negative sports experience for millions of young athletes."

Management challenges

A sports organization, whether it is a non-profit governance body or a sports program at a university or a professional sports team, has all the management challenges of any business, including managing people with different personalities, viewpoints, and motivations. As in any other business, sports leaders can reach greater clarity of thought by talking through their management challenges with coaches. Acting on positive psychology concepts can help them build environments that support high levels of employee engagement and motivation.

A sample of positive psychology ideas relevant to sports leaders

In the face of the challenges described in the previous section, there are many theories and practices in positive psychology that are relevant to sports leaders. Many are addressed elsewhere in this book. We focus on four ideas in this chapter: the importance of a clear inspiring purpose shared across the organization, actions that build trust and collaboration, management of psychological capital, and strengths-based leadership.

Because coaching involves helping clients find their own answers to important questions, each topic includes a number of questions that a coach might ask to help clients reflect on what would work for them.

Making shared meaning

In their study of employee engagement, MacLeod and Clarke (2009) pointed out that leaders contribute to employee engagement by providing a strong strategic narrative so that all members of the organization can draw a direct line of sight from their own jobs to a shared purpose. Coaches can help sports leaders by asking questions that lead to a strategic narrative that is compelling, that contributes to the experience of meaning at work (the M of PERMA), and that people can remember, retell, and use to make decisions as they go about their daily jobs.

Coaching questions might help the client preserve what is already good:

- What do you want to hold on to?
- What gives you the most satisfaction about the program as it is today?

Other questions help clients imagine positive images of the future. The Anticipatory Principle of Appreciative Inquiry tells us that positive images lead to positive action (Orem, Binkert, & Clancy, 2007, p. 130).

- What do you want more of?
- What opportunities exist in the present moment?
- What is exciting to you about the situations you face today?
- What do you picture you and your team contributing to the world?

We asked the sports leaders that we interviewed about their strategic narratives, the words they use to convey the broad meaning shared across their organizations. Often this is related to the primary challenge faced by the organization. Here are some of their answers.

Shared meaning at USA Football

How does USA Football get the various stakeholders, including the nearly 10,000 youth football organizations around the United States, on board with new practices to protect players from sports injuries? Considering this challenge, Hallenbeck stated, "We have to evolve, we have to change, we have to frankly get smarter and better and safer if we are going to see the next generation of football survive" (interview May 4, 2016). He draws a picture of a possible future: "If we do our jobs well in terms of developing the right standards and best practices, and resources, and tools and ensure that those are providing a safer environment and wherever possible communicate the values that the participants are getting in a coaching environment, in a playing environment, . . . that in and of itself will help inspire participation."

Shared meaning at US Lacrosse

How does US Lacrosse counteract the threats to lacrosse culture that have emerged from rapid growth in the sport? First, Stenersen reminds his people of the way lacrosse culture is summarized in *Tewaarthon*, the Akwesasne Mohawk nation's history of lacrosse: "Our grandfathers told us that when lacrosse was a pure game and was played for the enjoyment of the Great Spirit, everyone was important, no matter how big or how small, or how strong or how weak" (North American Indian Travelling College, 1978). According to Stenersen (interview May 10, 2016), "We are a national non-profit collaborative that is focused on surrounding ourselves with the best minds in the sport to really drive decisions and initiatives that are focused on providing a quality lacrosse experience for every player."

Building trust

Sports leaders often understand that trust is the foundation for effective cooperation in an organization. But they do not always know how to build and support trust.

Mishra and Mishra's ROCC model of trust (2008) suggests leaders can build trust by increasing reliability, openness, competence, and/or compassion. This model breaks down a complex abstraction into four simpler ideas that are easier to act upon.

Coaches can ask questions that help clients figure out actions that can contribute to greater trust. For example, here are questions they might ask about reliability:

- Can people count on you and one another to follow through, or at least explain why not if it's not possible?
- What could be done to make it easier for people to rely on one another?

Lencioni (2013) makes a strong argument that being open about one's own vulnerabilities is crucial for establishing trust. Here are questions that explore behaviors around openness:

- Do people share the information that others need to do their jobs?
- When you are worried or upset, do you share enough that people know why you are responding in a particular way?

Competence questions include:

- Is what people deliver good enough so that others can focus on their own work without having to worry about what others will deliver?

- What could be done to increase the confidence that people have in other people's work?

Finally, compassion means that people see one another as human beings managing multiple demands. Questions related to compassion include:

- How do you deal with efforts that do not succeed?
- What happens if life outside the sport interferes with performance?
- When people are experiencing special needs, does the organization support them?

 Lencioni (2002) claims that trust leads to four other essential components of high-functioning teams: healthy conflict so that people can speak honestly about shortcomings and other realities, commitment, accountability, and focus on results.

Compassion at US Lacrosse

Stenersen (interview May 10, 2016) models the need for openness and compassion. "...We are a work in progress and we always will be. We are going to be imperfect. We don't have all the resources we need, we are going to make mistakes, but we are going to learn from them and we are going to do our best to be a better organization as a result. It is amazing how most people respond positively to that."

Accountability and trust at Endicott College

Wylie (interview May 5, 2016) felt that some of his people were making excuses when things did not go well, which was influencing both the staff and the student-athletes. In response, he reminded them of the three guiding principles for the Endicott community expressed in his words as follows:

1 Hold yourself ACCOUNTABLE ... no excuses. "It was my fault, and I will take care of it!" Everything that happens or fails to happen is the responsibility of the leader or coach!
2 Encourage POSITIVE confrontation with a colleague – go directly to the source! Don't hide behind email. Don't avoid subjects ... encourage dialogue by framing the conversation correctly. Do this immediately.
3 Look to constantly do things a little bit better. Distinguish yourself and the department with your passion and sense of belief by doing your responsibilities better than anyone else.

The first and third principles enhance the shared sense of competence and reliability. The second principle enhances openness and compassion in daily interactions.

To live by the guiding principles, Wylie (interview May 5, 2016) facilitated a rigorous exercise with his coaching staff to set four core standards for the athletic program. By doing this, he gave his staff a voice. MacLeod and Clarke (2009, p. 75)

Core Standards of Leadership
Committed – "Totally invest yourself socially, athletically, and academically to your team, department, and Endicott."
Coaching Points

- ✓ Own it
- ✓ Buy in
- ✓ Engaged
- ✓ Accountable
- ✓ No excuses

Character – "Be the best version of yourself to consistently do the right thing and own it when you don't."
Coaching Points

- ✓ Look in the mirror
- ✓ Surround yourself with good people and evaluate
- ✓ Respect
- ✓ Trust

Effective **Communicator** – "Make honesty, active listening, and follow-through the highest priority when communicating and be open to new ideas."
Coaching Points

- ✓ No grey areas/clear expectations
- ✓ Turn negative into positive (know pulse of team)
- ✓ Face-to-face (in-person)

Confident – "Show mental and physical toughness and believe in yourself even in the face of adversity."
Coaching Points

- ✓ Resilient
- ✓ Willingness to make mistakes

FIGURE 19.1 Core standards of leadership defined by the Endicott Athletic Department

observe that employee engagement is enhanced by ". . . an effective and empowered employee voice – employees' views are sought out; they are listened to and see that their opinions count and make a difference. . . . A strong sense of listening and of responsiveness permeates the organization. . ."

Wylie tries to imbue the four core standards shown in Figure 19.1 – committed, character, effective communicator, and confident – in "what we do each and every day in our staff meetings and our daily dialogue and our conversations and our emails. . . . We talk about trust among the coaches and we talk about being transparent, as well as demanding the student-athletes to communicate effectively." As a result the feedback that Wylie has received from the student-athletes has been extremely positive.

Building psychological capital

Studying behavior in organizations, Luthans, Youssef, and Avolio (2007) identified four human qualities that are measurable, can be enhanced through effort, and have demonstrated positive impacts on organizational performance. An organization with these characteristics has *psychological capital (PsyCap)*. They have identified four PsyCap qualities: optimism, hope, self-efficacy, and resilience.

By asking questions, coaches can help sports leadership recognize the PsyCap already present in their organizations and take action to enhance it.

Optimism means holding a realistic and flexible outlook that supports taking positive action. Questions related to optimism include:

- What can you do to help the people in your organization get more benefit out of things that go right and less harm out of things that go wrong?
- How can you help them interpret events in ways that prepare them for the next challenge?

Hope Theory suggests that hopeful people have clear goals, a sense that they are able to move toward those goals, and multiple pathways in case any pathway gets blocked (Snyder et al., 2005). A question related to hope might be:

- When one pathway to a particular goal is blocked, what can you do to open up new pathways for yourself and for the people in your organization?

Self-efficacy, often thought of as confidence, involves a belief that one is capable of effective action. Bandura (1994) describes four processes that help people build self-efficacy: personal mastery experiences, vicarious mastery experiences where they observe others meeting goals, social persuasion, and better interpretations of physical responses to challenge. Questions related to self-efficacy might be:

- What actions can you take to give your people mastery experiences?
- How can you increase the collective belief that the people in your organization can achieve ambitious goals together?
- How can you help your people find strong role models for vicarious mastery?

Resilience involves building the capability to face adversity effectively (Caza & Milton, 2012). Questions related to resilience include:

- What coping strategies have you formed to deal with things that go wrong?
- What steps can you take to help the members of your organization reach positive outcomes in response to negative stressors that are bound to emerge?
- How can you help your people develop protective factors that will help them face whatever happens?

PsyCap at USA Football

Making the shift to greater safety on the football playing field is no easy task. USA Football's *Heads Up* tackling program requires players literally to keep their heads up when they tackle a teammate in practice or opponent in a game. This huge departure from common practice reduces helmet-to-helmet contact commonly associated with concussions. But getting the idea out was difficult. Football coaches generally teach the way they learned without any requirements for continuing education or certification, so there were no established conduits to convey this new practice.

The entire *Heads Up* program leadership team was despondent because they were not effectively convincing state and coaches associations to support the new practices. Hallenbeck encouraged multiple departments, including legal, sales, marketing, and product development, to work together. That helped them recognize their own shortcomings and external barriers to success. Together they came up with new pathways toward their mission of safer football. They shared coping strategies.

Hallenbeck's executive philosophy focuses on clear responsibilities so that employees are empowered and accountable, with the authority to do their jobs, which enhances self-efficacy and group efficacy. Through Hallenbeck's leadership, the organization drew on hope, optimism, and resilience to reposition the *Heads Up* program as a gold standard safety program at least at the youth level. The first year they had about five high school state associations that gave endorsements without making active commitments. By persisting, they have persuaded 26 states and many athletic coaching associations to push school systems to adopt the *Heads Up* program.

Strengths-based leadership

Rath and Conchie (2008, p. 2) claim that "when leaders focus on and invest in their employees' strengths, the odds of each person being engaged goes up eightfold . . . this increase in engagement translates into substantial gains for the organization's bottom line and each employee's well-being." Positive psychology coaches can help sports leaders become more aware of their own particular strengths, more perceptive of the strengths of others, and better able to create complementary mixes of strengths on organizational teams.

Some coaching questions help sports leaders understand their own strengths, both singly and in combination:

- What are your strengths? How do you know?
- How do your various strengths work with each other?
- What is the one strength in your toolbox that you can call upon whenever you need to deal with a conflict?
- How do your strengths help you communicate your needs to others?

When people know their own strengths, they are better observers of strengths in others and are more attentive to spotting what is good instead of trying to find fault. They may also see ways that their strengths work well or conflict with the strengths of the people around them.

- How do your strengths match up with, complement, and/or conflict with the strengths of others around you?

Once people can spot, manage, articulate, and relate their strengths to others, the next step is to spread the ability (Yeager, Fisher, & Shearon, 2011):

- How can you help the people around you learn more about using strengths?

US Football as a mix of strengths

Hallenbeck grew concerned when he saw that silos of excellence were being created that featured strong skill sets, but did not always communicate well with one another. He has worked very hard to evolve a culture that is interdependent while focusing on individual and collective strengths. Hallenbeck claims that "we have to understand . . . that our success depends on marketing's ability to actually help sales sell, football development's ability to develop really good products and resources so that when marketing and sales are functioning that they can be at their best. We each have to respect each other's area of responsibility and operate as a team but also do the best possible work we can do within our own area of responsibility" (interview May 4, 2016).

Using a strengths-based approach at the Culver Academies

At the Culver Academies, some of the athletic coaches were placing too much focus on the needs of their own specific programs while neglecting the needs of the entire athletic department. This was very frustrating for the athletic director and their peer coaches.

John walked the lead athletic coaches and athletic director through the process of discovering the best in one another before they started important conversations about trust, open communication, and collaborative relationships.

Some people exaggerate their own strengths, while others understate them. Sharing observations helps people calibrate their own self-images and become more understanding of the abilities and contributions of others. John used the 360° Feedback Gallery technique (Yeager et al., 2011, p. 308), which involves getting members of a group to name the strengths they see in one another and to tell stories about times they have seen these strengths in action. Positive psychology coaches could suggest this technique to sports leaders when they need to prepare a group to work together on difficult challenges.

Organizational integrity at US Lacrosse and USA Football

We conclude the discussion of strengths with the example of one of the 24 *Values in Action* character strengths that is important at the organizational level as well as the individual level: integrity, defined by Peterson and Seligman (2004, pp. 249–250) as "a character trait in which people are true to themselves, accurately representing – privately and publicly – their internal states, intentions, and commitments." People with integrity take responsibility for their actions. MacLeod and Clarke (2009) define organizational integrity as having minimal distance between stated values and actual behavior. They claim that integrity is one of the four primary enablers of employee engagement, thus positively affecting performance.

Organizational integrity is highly affected by how clearly leaders define the strategic narrative of the organization. If all members of the organization can remember and use the narrative in day-to-day decision-making, there is a better chance that behavior stays lined up with stated values.

Although there is healthy debate among passionate people at US Lacrosse about everything from how to prioritize different goals and what tactics to use to pursue them, Stenersen (interview May 10, 2016) says all staff members easily tie what they do back to the strategic narrative: enhancing the quality of experience of every player.

Similarly, the central organizing principle for USA Football is to foster a safer environment and attract participants by making the value of the sport clear. Everybody from marketing to product development to front office can continually calibrate their actions with the organization's purpose.

Conclusion

We call on sports leaders to expand their leadership capacity by paying focused attention to positive organizational practices such as defining a compelling shared meaning, building trust, managing strengths, and building psychological capital. We call on coaches to help leaders adapt these practices to their specific situations. Finally we call on researchers to explore the resulting impact on the bottom line: how much do these practices affect the ability of sports leaders to meet their missions?

References

Bandura, A. (1994). Self-efficacy. In V. S. Ramachaudran (Ed.), *Encyclopedia of Human Behavior* (pp. 71–81). New York: Academic Press.

Biswas-Diener, R., & Dean, B. (2007). *Positive Psychology Coaching: Putting the Science of Happiness to Work for Your Clients*. Hoboken, NJ: John Wiley & Sons.

Caza, B. B., & Milton, L. P. (2012). Resilience at work: Building capability in the face of adversity. In: K. S. Cameron & G. M. Spreitzer (Eds.), *The Oxford Handbook of Positive Organizational Scholarship* (pp. 895–908). Oxford: Oxford University Press.

Grant, A. M. (2012). ROI is a poor measure of coaching success: Towards a more holistic approach using a well-being and engagement framework. *Coaching: An International Journal of Theory, Research and Practice*, 5(2), 74–85.

International Coach Federation (n.d.). *Benefits of using a coach.* [Online] Retrieved May 23, 2016, from http://tinyurl.com/CoachingBenefits.

Lencioni, P. (2002). *The Five Dysfunctions of a Team: A Leadership Fable.* San Francisco, CA: Jossey Bass.

Lencioni, P. (2013). *Five dysfunctions of a team: Talk at the HTB leadership conference.* [Online] Retrieved from www.youtube.com/watch?v=inftqUOLFaM.

Luthans, F., Youssef, C. M., & Avolio, B. J. (2007). *Psychological Capital: Developing the Human Competitive Edge.* Oxford: Oxford University Press.

MacLeod, D., & Clarke, N. (2009). *Engaging for success: Enhancing success through employee engagement.* [Online] Retrieved May 23, 2016, from http://dera.ioe.ac.uk/1810/1/file52215.pdf.

Miller, C. (2015, April 21). Arsene Wenger: The martyr of Islington. *Eight by Eight.* Retrieved from http://8by8mag.com/wenger/.

Mishra, A., & Mishra, K. (2008). *Trust Is Everything: Become the Leader Others Will Follow.* Total Trust Coaching & Consulting.

North American Indian Travelling College. (1978). *Tewaarathon (Lacrosse) Akwesasne's Story of Our National Game.* Hogansburg, NY: North American Indian Travelling College.

Orem, S. L., Binkert, J., & Clancy, A. L. (2007). *Appreciative Coaching: A Positive Process for Change.* San Francisco, CA: Jossey-Bass.

Passmore, J., & Oades, L. G. (2014). Positive psychology coaching: A model for coaching practice. *The Coaching Psychologist,* 10(2), 68–70.

Peterson, C., & Seligman, M. E. P. (2004). *Character Strengths and Virtues: A Handbook and Classification.* Oxford: Oxford University Press.

Pope, D. G., & Pope, J. C. (2009). The impact of college sports success on the quantity and quality of student applications. *Southern Economic Journal,* 75(3), 750–780.

Rath, T., & Conchie, B. (2008). *Strengths Based Leadership: Great Leaders, Teams, and Why People Follow.* New York: Gallup Press.

Seligman, M. E. P. (2011). *Flourish: A Visionary New Understanding of Happiness and Well-Being.* New York: Free Press.

Snyder, C. R., Rand, K. L., & Sigmon, D. R. (2005). Hope theory: A member of the positive psychology family. In C. R. Snyder & S. J. Lopez (Eds.), *Handbook of Positive Psychology* (pp. 257–276). Oxford: Oxford University Press.

Snyder, S. (2016). Villanova proving a winner on and off the court. *Philadelphia Inquirer,* April 1.

Wright, R. (2000). *Non-Zero.* New York: Vintage Books.

Yeager, J. (2006). *Our Game: The Character and Culture of Lacrosse.* Port Chester, NY: Dude Publishing.

Yeager, J., Fisher, S., & Shearon, D. (2011). *Smart Strengths: Building Character, Resilience and Relationships in Youth.* New York: Kravis Publishing.

PART 4

Embracing positive psychology in sport and exercise: reflections and considerations

20

EMBRACING POSITIVE PSYCHOLOGY

Implications for practitioners and researchers

Abbe Brady and Bridget Grenville-Cleave

This chapter seeks to bring together the main ideas and recommendations from the preceding chapters. It is organised in three parts. The chapter opens by sharing some of the key messages and insights from positive psychology and its application to sport and physical activity. The chapter then considers challenges and implications for practitioners, and concludes by making recommendations for future research.

Language

What has become obvious to us the editors, and we hope to you the readers, is that regardless of the topic covered, positive psychology (PP) has succeeded in introducing a relatively new conceptual language to sport practitioners. Scott Bradley and Piers Worth (Chapter 5) urge us to explore the evolution and application of individual character strengths, which is a prime example of embracing the call to engage in new topics and terms; other chapters have similar calls to action. Powerful and life-affirming topics, such as gratitude, passion, optimism and positive emotions, are not commonplace in sport and exercise psychology. Learning a new language, be that of strengths, well-being or optimism, for example, opens up new vistas for exploration, discovery and personal development.

Although there are overlaps, of course, you may not necessarily agree with Paul McCarthy's starting point that sport and exercise psychology (SEP) already *is* positive psychology. Fundamentally, the definition of optimal human functioning is key – how do we reconcile our understanding of 'high performance' and 'well-being' in sport – are they one and the same, and how does health fit in? What is clear is that there remains much to do in SEP if we are to begin to develop an evidence base and understand how to harness the consequences of well-being as evident in other sub-disciplines and domains of practice.

Well-being and performance: Not mutually exclusive

Individual chapter authors have each made a compelling case for the benefits of applying PP in various sport and exercise settings. It would appear that the win-at-all-costs culture associated with many elite sports, and even with some amateur clubs and school teams, is not necessarily a golden ticket to high performance that logic might infer. Far from being just post-performance states, positive emotions and well-being are likely to be critical precursors to progressive and sustainable long-term achievement. Practitioners who work with children and youth will be especially mindful of the ideas in Chapters 8, 9 and 12 about resilience, enjoyment and holistic identity development, and that achievement and success in sport do not guarantee long-term self-esteem, happiness and well-being. We suggest that we should strive to put well-being first, based on evidence that well-being is associated with other valued outcomes such as more effective transitions within and outside sport, empowering coach behaviors, stronger athlete/coach and team relationships, psychological resilience as well as behaviors leading to optimal functioning and high performance. Hopefully you have encountered many new ideas and have been inspired to try out some of the activities and interventions for yourself, with your own participants or teams, and you have ideas about how to tailor activities to best fit the participants in your context. Graham Mallen and Bridget Grenville-Cleave's chapter on secondary school physical education provides an example of how practitioners can successfully develop their own evidence-based PP approach within sport and physical activity, with the result in this case that children's lives are directly changed for the better. It is inspiring to discover that this process also enabled Graham himself to reconnect with his reasons for joining the teaching profession. Can there be any stronger recommendation than that?

Recognising holistic and physical dimensions of well-being

Across a range of sport and exercise settings, greater awareness of well-being and PP topics will be helpful for gaining a more holistic account of experience and informing the development of more appropriate environments and practices. Although we have not majored in this book on the physical aspects of well-being (we refer readers to Hefferon's 2013 text for this purpose), many authors make clear that adding a PP dimension to our sport and exercise practice enables us to see the athlete in a holistic or systemic way. In their research with Parasport athletes, Mac-Dougall et al. (2016) emphasized the need to recognise a physical component to well-being which supports the need to recognise well-being as a multidimensional phenomenon in sport and physical activity settings. Illustrating the need to recognise participants' humanness and wholeness beyond their athletic role, Lundqvist and Sandin (2014) found crossover effects in well-being (and ill-being) between sport and other realms of life when elite orienteers identified how their global well-being had a protective effect on their sport-specific health and well-being. In Chapter 12, Dan Jolley and Chris McCready make a strong case for the importance to performance on and off the pitch of seeing young apprentice footballers (and enabling them to see themselves) as more well-rounded individuals, with other interests, strengths and passions aside from football. Through recognition of the value of holistic development for elite athlete flourishing, in Chapter 16, Arabella Ashfield, Joanna Harrison and Samuel Giles identify some of the ways in which PP informs and supports the practice of Performance Lifestyle support.

Future challenges and implications for practitioners in understanding and applying PP to sport and physical activity

Examine existing cultural beliefs about well-being and performance relationships

The emergence of PP and findings about the consequences and correlates of well-being have implications for a range of practitioners in sport and physical activity across varied contexts. Much could be gained by understanding the experiences, causes and consequences of well-being and other PP topics. In achievement contexts, understanding existing ideas and attitudes about relationships among optimal functioning, well-being and other PP constructs in particular contexts is essential before attempting to introduce PP. Such investigations may illuminate a range of distinct sub-cultural beliefs (e.g. Lundqvist & Sandin, 2014; MacDougall et al., 2016). For example, particular elite or professional sports settings may hold beliefs about well-being that serve to enhance and/or undermine participant or practitioner flourishing with consequences for ongoing well-being, health and performance success (e.g. Pink et al., 2015; Theberge, 2008), and awareness of these cultural beliefs is likely to have considerable implications for how one might consider introducing ideas from PP.

Understand how well-being and positive emotions may provide valuable insights into existing practices in sport and physical activity

Sport and exercise psychologists, coaches, trainers, strength and conditioning coaches, and sport medics may wish to consider that positive and negative emotions serve to illuminate different pathway processes, and as such both may offer unique insights when used to monitor and inform practices such as: training load and recovery from training, managing the impact of lifestyle, travel or major competitive events as well as understanding affective responses to injury, rehabilitation protocols and return to sport strategies. To develop greater insight about the antecedents and consequences of positive affect and other domains of well-being in applied and research work, students, academics and sport and exercise psychologists are encouraged to empirically examine the broaden-and-build theory of positive emotions (Fredrickson, 2001) and existing theories in sport that include positive emotion such as Individual Zones of Optimal Functioning (Hanin, 1997) and the Theory of Challenge and Threat States in Athletes (Jones, Meijen, McCarthy, & Sheffield, 2009). Coaches, leaders and trainers are encouraged to consider how their staff, teams and clients may experience the broadening and building effects of positive emotions which, in addition to eliciting motivation, may also generate many adaptive personal resources (e.g. such as widened thought repertoires, creativity, problem-solving and resilience) central to learning and thriving.

A key recommendation is the monitoring of positive (as well as negative) emotions and other psychological indices of well-being during training and recovery, and rehabilitation and return to sport periods to provide rich and more nuanced affective profiles. Personalizing various interventions in recognition that people are not equally expressive or sensitive to affective change will be an important aspect of effective intervention designs. For example, specific loading and tapering protocols may be individualised in the light of more balanced and potentially sensitive emotional profiles. Combining both biological correlates and psychological indicators of well-being and ill-being in research would provide valuable holistic insight.

Consultancy considerations

In our roles as lecturers, coach/trainers, consultants and practitioners, we, the editors, have met many people in the past decade or so who, inspired by what they have read about PP, wish to undertake research and/or become practitioners. They wish to apply the science of PP in their own life and homes, as well as in their sport and physical activity settings, to enable others to thrive and be at their best, whatever that might be. The following is a distillation of what we have found most useful in practical situations, and what we have learnt works best based on discussions with the practitioner-authors in this book and elsewhere. For experienced practitioners, most will be self-evident, but if you are relatively new to applying PP, we urge you to read on.

Given that PP stands or falls on its scientific credentials, we emphasize the importance of keeping up to date with academic studies whether they support or criticize PP. It is often difficult to convey the nuances of applications in a few words, or alternatively, it is easy to summarise research findings such that a different, more certain position is presented. Therefore, at all times keep an open, critical and questioning mind and be aware of the 'overselling' (Ferguson, 2015, p. 1) that takes place. As has been pointed out very clearly by Brown, Lomas, and Eiroa-Orosa (in press) and Ferguson (ibid), academics in many universities are under pressure to publish, particularly where data support their a priori hypotheses. Despite the rigor associated with the peer review process, publication bias is an ongoing issue, and the psychological sciences in particular have an aversion to publishing null results (Brown et al., in press). Therefore, we would advise all readers to bear this context in mind as you carefully examine both sides of the story.

For a brief review of some of the most frequent criticisms of PP, refer back to Chapter 1. In the meantime, we suggest you start with comprehensive critiques from writers such as Lazarus (2003), Fineman (2006), Hackman (2009), and Miller (2008) and continue forward to the most recent, for example, Brown et al. (in press). At all times we would suggest remaining open to new knowledge and continuing to ask questions; sometimes even the critics disagree with one another. Making the effort to stay well informed in this way will also help you devise practical, evidence-based strategies and approaches for your target audience.

Recommendations for advancing research associated with PP in sport and physical activity

Conceptual considerations

Across the chapters and in some of the studies shared, a number of themes and recommendations emerge associated with advancing PP research in sport and physical activity. Here we outline some that seem to us to be the priorities for accelerating these developments. Because PP is relatively young, there is considerable cross-fertilization in the application of PP across disciplines and domains and so conducting PP research in sport and physical activity has the potential not only to glean new insights but also to feed this knowledge upstream and broaden the scope and foci of positive psychology per se. Identifying existing and emerging PP topics that have particular resonance for gaining new insights in sport and physical activity is an exciting prospect, particularly if it contributes to a better understanding of the ways in which involvement in sport and physical activity contributes to well-being. Another reason for researchers and practitioners to explore PP applications in sport and physical activity is because they have the potential to provide a more holistic and humanistic insight to people's experiences of optimal functioning.

Methodological recommendations

In its short tenure PP's achievements have been significant, as reflected in the scale and impact we see through the number of publications, research initiatives, and large-scale and high-profile intervention programs. The majority of research in PP has been characterised by experimental or large-scale quantitative methodologies seeking to generalise findings. Lyubomirsky et al. (2005) endorse this when they recommend that, to examine the causal effects of positive emotions on behaviours leading to success, research adopts rigorous experimental and longitudinal research designs. Stephanie Hanrahan (Chapter 13) highlights the challenges of field-based real-world interventions and research, and the need to undertake randomised controlled trial (RCT) studies to understand the importance of games in the LifeMatters program. Whilst this type of research is undoubtedly important, there is also a need for practitioners to be ever-mindful of context (see the next paragraph). We square this circle, at least in part, by calling for more qualitative and mixed methodologies in PP research in sport and exercise, recognising the messiness and complexity of being human and to better understand human experience (rather than cause-effect) within these settings (Brady & Shambrook, 2003; Lundqvist, 2011). The potential for rich insight with many practical implications is exemplified by the findings emerging from early research in this area (e.g. Lundqvist & Sandin, 2014; MacDougall et al., 2016).

There is a need to develop context-specific measures of well-being because, as Lundqvist and Sandin (2014) and MacDougall et al. (2015) have demonstrated, context is crucial in appreciating how well-being is experienced and interpreted. In pursuing greater awareness of well-being-performance relationships, and recognising that positive emotions are an important indicator of well-being and optimal functioning, we echo calls for research to use a spectrum of positively and negatively valenced emotions to capture a more accurate account of how emotions relate to performance (Lundqvist & Kentta, 2010; McCarthy, 2011). Similarly, we recommend that researchers use two or more indicators of well-being to help us gain a better understanding of when, how and why particular dimensions of well-being seem most valuable. Liam McCarthy and Abbe Brady call for context-rich case studies to generate insight and an evidence base about the role of positive emotions and appreciative reflection in coach learning and development and coach developer practices.

Positive psychology interventions: Contextualisation and person-fit approach

The importance of understanding positive psychology interventions (PPIs) within the specific context of sport and physical activity is a constant thread running throughout the book from the first chapter to the last. Lung Hung Chen (Chapter 10) talks about the need to research the effects of athlete gratitude toward coaches and teammates specifically, as opposed to more general expressions of gratitude that would be found in interventions such as the classic 'Three Good Things' exercise (Seligman, Steen, Park, & Peterson, 2005). In Chapter 5, Scott Bradley and Piers Worth refer to the need to research the language of strengths in order to facilitate personal strengths-spotting as well as spotting strengths in other people, perhaps teammates and coaches, or even competitors. Which strengths assessments are most appropriate for sport and physical activity settings? What contextual influences help or hinder strengths development in athletes? John Yeager and Kathryn Britton (Chapter 19) highlight the value of PP in supporting leaders in sport and physical activity to establish thriving cultures and organisations. Carolina Lundqvist and Henrik Gustafsson in Chapter 6 call for research into the ways that hopeful and optimistic coaches are perceived by their athletes. Paul McCarthy stresses the need for us to better understand person-activity fit in sport and physical activity settings: to account for the person (e.g., personality type), the environment (e.g., amateur, professional) and the task (e.g., on-court or off-court). As PP researchers and practitioners, it is not sufficient to know what makes a difference; we also need to understand how, why and for whom it makes a difference. For example, we need to study the way interventions are formulated, administered and evaluated in sport and physical activity settings to better understand their effectiveness. In Chapter 7, Hanna Kampman and Tim Lomas call for research to examine the differences between Langer's and Kabat-Zinn's approaches to mindfulness within sport and physical exercise settings. When physical activity is the intervention, we need to understand by what mechanisms the activity enhances or thwarts well-being and/or optimal functioning.

Collective and individual effects

We need to study collective effects as well as individual benefits. For example, how does the collective gratitude or resilience of, for example, a football team or walking group, affect the group and performance of that team as well as that of individual players? How can teams benefit from understanding their collective strengths (and potentially the gaps) as well as their individual strengths? Responding to the call to action by Huppert et al. (2017), we may ask how can sport and PA contribute to universal well-being? We cannot simply assume that the whole is the sum of the parts; it could be that the whole is greater (or possibly smaller). If so, how? When? And why? Tanya Chichekian and Bob Vallerand (Chapter 4) ask how teachers and coaches inspire passion in their students and athletes. What environment is needed for this transmission from teacher/coach to student/athlete and for the latter to cultivate their own passion? Does passion for sport prevent students disengaging from and dropping out of school? Emma Kavanagh and we, the editors (Chapter 11), recommend examining how the PP constructs of caring, gratitude and forgiveness can provide new insights which may serve to support rewarding and meaningful interactions in different sport and physical activity contexts. Potential also exists to examine how interventions may impact dyadic experiences of well-being among various professional and peer relationships.

Sustainability

At this stage in the life-cycle of applying PP within sport and exercise settings, we simply do not have sufficient evidence to say that the benefits of short-term PP interventions are sustainable over the longer term. Their durability needs to be tested and evaluated. Carolina Lundqvist and Henrik Gustafsson (Chapter 6) ask how we can develop interventions which increase hope and optimism over the longer term. Stephanie Hanrahan (Chapter 13) calls for research to test the long-term benefits of the LifeMatters program with disadvantaged youth. In Chapter 8 Rudy Alleyne and Abbe Brady review how a growth mindset supports adaptive behaviors and resilience, and call for research to examine the impact on athletes and exercisers of their coaches' and trainers' mindsets and beliefs about resilience. Dan Jolley and Chris McCready (Chapter 12) highlight the need to research the long- and short-term benefits, as well as the possible challenges or issues, associated with holistic identity development both for footballers remaining in and those leaving the profession. How do ex-players succeed and flourish post-apprenticeship and post-retirement?

Given that this is the first text of its kind to apply PP to sport and physical activity, we encourage sport and exercise psychologists and other practitioners to take notice of contemporary findings about the generative nature of many PP topics for optimal functioning and performance. Using innovative and rigorous qualitative and mixed-methods research, there is much scope to examine many topics such as those in this book (and others) in sport and physical activity contexts. Research is also crucial for understanding when, how and for whom applications of PP and PPIs are particularly meaningful and effective. We hope that practitioners will embrace the potential of PP with open minds, and we propose that engagement with PP has the potential to enrich the landscape of sport and exercise psychology.

Positive psychology offers practitioners a new vocabulary with which to access and further understand people's experiences of sport and physical activity. Used well, this vocabulary has the capacity to illuminate many hitherto unconsidered aspects of experience which, because of their importance in life and for well-being generally, can provide valuable alternative insights to understanding how and when sport and physical activity is most likely to contribute to our well-being, and when and how our well-being is most likely to support optimal functioning and thriving in sport and physical activity.

References

Brady, A., & Shambrook, C. (2003). Towards an understanding of elite athlete quality of life: A phenomenological study. *Journal of Sports Sciences*, 21, 341–342.

Brown, N. J. L., Lomas, T., & Eiroa-Orosa, F. J. (in press). *The Routledge International Handbook of Critical Positive Psychology*. New York: Routledge.

Ferguson, C. J. (2015). "Everybody knows psychology is not a real science": Public perceptions of psychology and how we can improve our relationship with policymakers, the scientific community, and the general public. *American Psychologist*, 70(6), 527.

Fineman, S. (2006). On being positive: Concerns and counterpoints. *Academy of Management Review*, 31, 270–291.

Fredrickson, B. L. (2001). The role of positive emotions in positive psychology: The broaden-and-build theory of positive emotions. *American Psychologist*, 56(3), 218–226.

Hackman, J. R. (2009). The perils of positivity. *Journal of Organizational Behavior*, 30, 209–319.

Hanin, Y. L. (1997). Emotions and athletic performance: Individual zones of optimal functioning model. *European Yearbook of Sport Psychology*, 1, 29–72.

Hefferon, K. (2013). *Positive Psychology and the Body: The Somatopsychic Side to Flourishing.* London: McGraw-Hill Education.

Huppert, F., Roffey S. King, V., Grenville Cleave, B., & deVries, M. (2017). How Can Positive Psychology Contribute to Universal Well-Being? An Invitation to Conversation and Action. Culture & Global Issues Panel session at 5th World Congress on Positive Psychology, Montreal, Canada, July.

Jones, M., Meijen, C., McCarthy, P. J., & Sheffield, D. (2009). A theory of challenge and threat states in athletes. *International Review of Sport and Exercise Psychology*, 2(2), 161–180.

Lazarus, R. (2003). Does the positive psychology movement have legs? *Psychological Inquiry*, 14, 93–109.

Lundqvist, C. (2011). Well-being in competitive sports—The feel-good factor? A review of conceptual considerations of well-being. *International Review of Sport and Exercise Psychology*, 4(2), 109–127.

Lundqvist, C. & Kentta, G. (2010). Positive emotions are not simply the absence of the negative ones: Development and validation of the emotional recovery questionnaire (EmRecQ). *The Sport Psychologist,* 24, 468–488.

Lundqvist, C., & Sandin, F. (2014). Well-being in elite sport: Dimensions of hedonic and eudaimonic well-being among elite orienteers. *The Sport Psychologist*, 28(3), 245-254.

Lyubomirsky, S., King, L., & Diener, E. (2005). The benefits of frequent positive affect: Does happiness lead to success? *Psychological Bulletin,* 131(6), 803–855.

MacDougall, H., O'Halloran, P., Shields, N., & Sherry, E. (2015). Comparing the well-being of Para and Olympic sport athletes: A systematic review. *Adapted Physical Activity Quarterly*, 32(3), 256–276.

MacDougall, H., O'Halloran, P., Sherry, E., & Shields, N. (2016). Needs and Strengths of Australian Para-Athletes: Identifying Their Subjective Psychological, Social, and Physical Health and Well-Being. *The Sport Psychologist*, 30(1), 1-12.

McCarthy, P. J. (2011). Positive emotion in sport performance: Current status and future directions. *International Review of Sport and Exercise Psychology*, (4)1, 50–69.

Miller, M. (2008). A critique of positive psychology- or "the new science of happiness". *Journal of Philosophy in Education, 42*, 591–608.

Norem, J. K., & Chang, E. C. (2002). The positive psychology of negative thinking. *Journal of Clinical Psychology*, 58(9), 993–1001.

Pink, M., Saunders, J., & Stynes, J. (2015). Reconciling the maintenance of on-field success with off-field player development: A case study of a club culture within the Australian Football League. *Psychology of Sport and Exercise*, 21, 98–108.

Seligman, M. E. P., Steen, T., Park, N., & Peterson, C. (2005). Positive psychology progress: Empirical validation of interventions. *American Psychologist*, 60(5), 410-421.

Theberge, N. (2008). "Just a normal bad part of what I do": Elite athletes accounts of the relationship between health and sport. *Sociology of Sport Journal*, 25, 206–222.

INDEX

Made in the USA
Las Vegas, NV
28 March 2021